Beckford's Fonthill

The Rise of a Romantic Icon

Beckford's Fonthill

The Rise of a Romantic Icon

ROBERT J. GEMMETT

MICHAEL RUSSELL

© Robert J. Gemmett 2003

The right of Robert J. Gemmett to be identified
as the author of this work has been asserted by him
in accordance with the Copyright, Designs
and Patents Act, 1988

First published in Great Britain 2003
by Michael Russell (Publishing) Ltd
Wilby Hall, Wilby, Norwich NR16 2JP

Typeset in Sabon by Waveney Typesetters
Wymondham, Norfolk
Printed and bound in Great Britain
by Biddles Ltd, Guildford and King's Lynn

TO KENDRA
FOR HER GENEROUS SPIRIT

Contents

CONTENTS

CONTENTS

CONTENTS

List of Illustrations

Acknowledgements

I am indebted, first of all, to Professor William Fleming, prominent scholar of Western culture and author of *Arts and Ideas*, who, in the early Sixties when I was conducting research on Keats, suggested that Beckford might be an absorbing subject of investigation. I decided to look into it, and thus began the journey that led to my extended exploration of the life and works of one of the most fascinating figures of the English Romantic movement. I would also like to thank my colleague Dr Peter Marchant, whose comments about Fonthill a few years ago served as the springboard for writing this book.

I am also indebted to the Department of Western Mss., Bodleian Library, University of Oxford, where the Beckford Papers are located, for permission to quote and reproduce unpublished material from this collection – with special thanks to T. D. Rogers, Deputy Keeper, for his assistance. The Beckford Collection of the Beinecke Library at Yale University also provided invaluable information which aided this study, as did the Britton Collection in the Library of the Wiltshire Archaeological and Natural History Society, Devizes, England.

The completion of this book was facilitated by a number of individuals. During my third visit to the Fonthill estate, the Hon. Alastair Morrison (now Lord Margadale) generously took me on a guided tour of the various grottoes, the hermitage, boathouse and landing in the Old Park area which I appreciated and found helpful. Special thanks also to his parents, the late Lord Margadale and his wife, for extending their hospitality during my stay in the nearby Beckford Arms. Thanks to Michael Coote, who braved the mud roads of the Fonthill estate in March in his lumbering vehicle to show me the Abbey, now looking even more forlorn and solitary than it did at the time of my earlier visit in 1976.

I also wish to acknowledge and express appreciation to the following individuals who made special contributions: to Joan Sussler and Anna Malicka of the Lewis Walpole Library, Yale University, for facilitating my examination of their Fonthill files; to Jon Millington, editor of the *Beckford Journal*, and Professor Jonathan Alexander, New York University, for answering my queries about extant Fonthill drawings; to Robert Gilliam, SUNY Brockport librarian, for hunting down numerous early nineteenth century books and periodicals; to James Dusen, SUNY Brockport, for his fine work in the preparation of the illustrations; and to the following curators who supplied me with important information about Fonthill paintings and drawings in their collections: Mark Wisbey, Bolton Museum and Art Gallery, Charles Nugent, The Whitworth Art Gallery, Ian Warrell, Tate Britain, Mara Meikle, the Art Gallery of Ontario, Jenny Ramkalawon, British Museum, Department of Prints and Drawings, Scott Wilcox, Yale Center for British Art, Moira Thunder, Victoria and Albert Museum, Jane Standen, the Salisbury Museum, and Danielle Blanchette, Musée des Beaux-Arts de Montréal.

A special note of thanks to my publisher, Michael Russell, for his willingness to take on another Beckford project as a follow up to the *The Consummate Collector*, my edition of the Beckford-Clarke correspondence, which he handsomely produced and published in 2000.

For financial assistance in support of necessary trips to England which enabled me to visit Fonthill and Oxford University, I am very grateful to the Scholarship Incentive Program at SUNY Brockport and to the United University Professions of the State of New York

To my children, Steve, Scott, David and Kerry, for all of their contributions, witting and unwitting, and for tolerating their father's unusual antiquarian interests throughout the years, I am very grateful. Finally, it is only fitting that I dedicate this book to my wife, Kendra. She was there when it all started with my early research on Beckford and Fonthill – reading my handwriting on yellow pads, typing deep into the night before the age of the computer, making her usual astute editorial suggestions and being supportive in a myriad of ways since 1964.

When Fleming first mentioned Beckford to me, I knew very little about him. The one thing that did come to mind, however, was the image of Fonthill Abbey which I had remembered from an engraving I had seen – it was a brooding architectural presence sitting in a commanding position overlooking the downs of Wiltshire, its tall tower reaching heavenward. I felt that it had a compelling quality and that it seemed emblematic of a period of time that had already captured my imagination. I decided to pursue the matter. Little did I know then where it would lead me.

> Thy firmness makes my circle just,
> And makes me end, where I begun.
> JOHN DONNE

Preface

Taking on the task of publishing a new book on William Beckford's Fonthill, I follow in the footsteps of H. A. N. Brockman whose fine work, *The Caliph of Fonthill* (1956), constituted the first full-length study of the work that Beckford considered to be his greatest artistic achievement. Brockman's book was a source of inspiration not only because of the insights he brought to the subject as an architect but because he left open some tantalizing avenues to pursue. It was the goal of writing this book to follow these unexplored trails and thereby extend what he had started.

My study of Fonthill actually began in the mid-Sixties in preparation for the completion of a doctoral dissertation, 'William Beckford and the Picturesque: A Study of Fonthill', which was submitted for a degree at Syracuse University in 1967. While this dissertation laid the groundwork, this new study has benefited from continuing research on the subject since then and from the array of scholars who have tilled the fields of Beckfordiana over the last thirty years. I am particularly indebted to Boyd Alexander's edition of Beckford letters, *Life at Fonthill 1807–1822* (1957), and to his book *England's Wealthiest Son* (1962). In these two volumes, Alexander, who was custodian of the Beckford Papers at the time, made previously unpublished material available that spurred further study of Beckford and his works. More recently, I was aided by John Wilton-Ely's efforts to trace the stages of the Abbey's development in a series of published essays and by Clive Wainwright's chapter on the Fonthill art collection in his impressive work *The Romantic Interior* (1989). Of course, having access to the wealth of documents among the Beckford Papers, now housed in the Bodleian Library at Oxford, was essential to this present telling of the Fonthill story. Important also were the collections relating to Fonthill at the Beinecke Library at Yale as well as smaller archival holdings in museums and libraries in England. Research for this book also included an extensive investigation of the newspapers and journals from 1796, the year that marked the beginning of Fonthill, to Beckford's death in 1844, to uncover published news accounts, letters, original essays and other information about Fonthill that reflect the impact it had during the nineteenth century. While it builds upon previous scholarly work on Fonthill, this new study adds information and perspectives that have not been made available in previously published work on the subject and which help to explain how Fonthill has achieved today the status of an indelible icon of the Romantic period in England.

William Beckford's prominence, immense wealth, and inaccessibility created an interest in him and in the Fonthill Abbey estate that reached extraordinary proportions during the time he lived there, developing into 'Fonthill fever' when the newspapers of the day announced in 1822 that the Abbey, its contents, and the surrounding property would be sold. For the first time in its history, Fonthill became accessible to the public and a visit to the estate became a major social event. Thousands of people responded to the announcement and in their eagerness to see Fonthill eventually clogged all roads that led to the estate. Numerous artists were among the visitors, anxious to paint the Abbey in its setting, along with the interior rooms and their contents. Before long, engravings of their work began to appear in books and periodicals that served to stimulate the public appetite for even more access to Fonthill. During the two public openings in 1822 and 1823, prominent authors published original essays, verse, and descriptive accounts about the Abbey, the artistic treasures it held, and the surrounding grounds in major magazines and newspapers throughout England. These written works and engraved 'views' now provide a historical record of the popularity of Fonthill in its day and the extent of its artistic achievement.

Utilizing all of these materials, this study provides an extended account in ten chapters of the origin, design and development of Fonthill. It assesses Fonthill within the context of the aesthetics of the picturesque and sublime as defined by such eighteenth-century theorists as William Gilpin, Uvedale Price and Edmund Burke and attempts to make a case for appreciating Fonthill as an artistic totality that included an imposing Gothic residence, an impressive collection of art works and a dramatic landscape garden. Central to the rise of Fonthill as an enduring work of art were the two public sales in 1822 and 1823. This book examines the public impact of these sales, the reaction of the press, the behind-the-scene negotiations that led to the sale of Fonthill itself, and the controversies that erupted during the auction of its contents. It discusses in detail some of the most important appraisals of Fonthill that appeared in the press, particularly original works by John Britton, John Rutter, William Hazlitt, Peter Patmore, William Garbett, and J. C. Loudon. It concludes with an examination of the critical assessment of Fonthill in the twentieth century.

The Appendices bring together for the first time a selection of the essays, poems, and personal accounts that appeared during Beckford's lifetime. These are not readily accessible and are of considerable value in enabling the student to estimate Beckford's artistic achievement. Included among them are hitherto unrecorded or unattributed work on Fonthill by John Britton, Charles Knight, Thomas F. Dibdin, Abbé Denis Macquin, William Garbett, Isaac Reed and Alaric Watts. Of particular importance are the numerous views of the Abbey in its setting and the interior views of the rooms within the Abbey by such artists as John Martin, Thomas Higham, Charles Wild, George Cattermole, and J. M. W. Turner. Since Fonthill was primarily a visual experience, their works appear within this book as essential iconographic documents. The book concludes with an extensive Fonthill bibliography devoted to Beckford manuscript collections and other primary sources relevant to a study of Fonthill, books, guidebooks, auction catalogues, a census of sketches, drawings and paintings of the Abbey currently held in private and public collections, an extended list of articles published on Fonthill from 1797 to the present day and a list of secondary source material that was helpful in this study.

I

The Origin of Fonthill

William Beckford's Fonthill Abbey stands today as an enduring icon for a period of history when aesthetic experience in the arts was shifting towards an emphasis on self-revelation, sensory appeal, and emotional values (fig. 1). *Vathek*, Beckford's oriental fantasy which preceded the creation of Fonthill by ten years, had already revealed the Romantic sensibilities that represented a significant break from the restrictions of classicism. This distinctive literary work broke new ground as a *tour de force* of imagination with the creation of the Beckfordian persona in the form of a caliph who was allowed to relish unorthodox behaviour and indulge in a world of sensory opulence. It placed Beckford among the 'Devil's party', as Blake would characterize it, as a pioneer writer who exposed the undermind of a repressed European society in an amoral world of Romantic aestheticism, celebrated later by such writers as Keats, Byron, and Poe. The Fonthill Abbey estate, considered as an artistic totality that included an imposing Gothic residence, an impressive collection of works of art and sumptuously bound books and a dramatic landscape setting, was a kindred creation to *Vathek*, a piece cut from the same artistic fabric and also inextricably associated with the creator's complex personal life. Both works were constructs of imagination in the new mode of artistic expression that cultivated self-dramatization and a taste for sensational effects; both were in accord with the newly formulated aesthetics of the picturesque and the sublime that fused sensory appeal with emotional transport. But it was Fonthill, despite the influence of *Vathek* in the literary world, that Beckford felt was the 'great work of his life' in which he displayed his taste and knowledge more conspicuously than in 'anything he had ever done besides'.[1]

The background for Fonthill and the factors that led to its creation can be traced in Beckford's early life. The wealth that made such an extravagant scheme possible came from his father, the owner of Jamaican sugar estates and a figure of public prominence as Lord

Mayor of London, whom Beckford greatly admired. His untimely death in 1770 left the nine-year-old Beckford exposed to other shaping influences. His mother, Maria Beckford, tended to be autocratic, fiercely possessive of her son's affection and ambitious for him to follow in his father's footsteps as a prominent public figure. She instilled in him a Calvinistic sense of fate and sin which pervaded so much of what he later wrote and which cultivated a taste for religious art that ultimately manifested itself most dramatically in the artistic design of Fonthill Abbey as a monastic residence. She was a contributing factor in another way by turning his attention to a study of his own ancestry, which increased his self-centredness and bred in him a vanity of birth that led to the celebration of his lineage as a central motif for Fonthill and its interior decoration.

The preoccupation with his own solitariness that developed in Beckford as a young man might have been mitigated by sending him away to school, but Mrs Beckford refused to allow it, educating him instead at home, where he was constantly subjected to the pressures of a family council composed of dowager aunts and people removed from his generation. It was a stifling atmosphere that made him lonely and secretive, and prone to extended periods of exaggerated introspection. Before long, he began to show signs of growing rebelliousness. The dull civilities of polite society bored him, dampened his spirits, and sometimes stirred in him a sense of outrage:

> Delivered up to a Sword, Bag and pretty Cloathes, I am obliged to go dangling about to assemblies of sweet, dear, prim, tulipy variegated Creatures, oppressed with powder and pomatum, and tired with the lisping nonsense I hear all around me…. At home I am infested with a species which, like mathematical points, have neither *parts* nor magnitude – Alas, fat Bulls of Basan encompass me around. – Tubs upon two legs, crammed with Stupidity, amble about me. Some of them mere trivets and Footstools, supple, pliant, and complaisant.[2]

His private education was rigidly classical in character and in accord with the expectations for gentlemen of the day. The regimen of discipline required was at odds with his artistic temperament. Beckford was precociously intelligent, but he was also intensely emotional and wilful by nature – a mercurial personality who sought other gardens of delight. These he soon found in the more volatile imaginative literature of the day, particularly the *Arabian Nights* and its imitations. This became evident as early as the age of eleven when he made his first-known book purchase, a five-volume set of Pétis de la Croix's *Mille et un Jour, Contes Persians* (1711–13).[3] Here was food for daydream, an outlet to escape the heavy demands at home. Once aware of the depth of this unclassical interest, the family took steps to curb it. On one occasion, the guardian tutor, the Revd John Lettice, forced the boy to burn a 'splendid heap of oriental drawings', but the repressive effort failed partly because of another tutor, Alexander Cozens, who consistently encouraged the young Beckford's exotic tastes and escapist longings. A widely travelled watercolourist, he stimulated the boy's lively imagination with extravagant stories from his own past. Beckford also enjoyed sharing with Cozens his readings of Ariosto, Milton, Dante, Spencer and the melancholy Gray, all of whom had fired his imagination and cultivated his taste for dramatic representation.

Cozens also taught him much of what he knew about the graphic arts in the 1770s, the depth of which would become apparent in Beckford's first published work, *Biographical Memoirs of Extraordinary Painters,* which he wrote when he was seventeen. Under Cozens's tutorship, Beckford developed his pictorial sense of the natural landscape and a highly picturesque literary style. Almost from the date of his relationship with Cozens, Beckford was in the habit of making observations about the world around him as if he were examining a painting in one of the galleries in his father's house. The young writer's letters to the watercolourist, especially those from Switzerland in 1777 and 1778, where Beckford spent some time as part of his private education, provide evidence of his ability to describe Alpine scenery from the perspective of a painter. As he wrote from Thun:

> The Mountain from whose summit I wrote my last letter, is my chief comfort, and I resort to it once every Fortnight. It consists of two huge masses of Rock, separated by a chasm, the one called the Great, the other the Little Salève. No sooner do I reach the Summit than I leap off my Horse and spring into a Valley concealed as it were in the Bosom of the Mountain. There, two stupendous Rocks present an uninterrupted Range of Cliffs for about a quarter of a Mile, and the Vale between is formed by a smooth Lawn nicely fitted by the hand of Nature into every crevice. The opening at the farther end discovers a plain, at the

foot of the precipice, quite even for the space of 15 Leagues and level all the way with the Lake, that together with a chain of Azure Mountains terminates the vast Horizon.... I think I behold you charmed with hearing nothing but the trickling of a small Rill that oozes out of the Rock, quite an Hermit's Spring.... Then the fresh Underwood that extends on the right of the Dell under the lofty Cliffs would please you beyond expression; so green, so flourishing and mellowed by the gleams of the setting Sun.[4]

Or, as he wrote the following year from Aix en Savoy on another excursion:

After crossing a cultivated Plain I heard the roar of some considerable Torrent, and, approaching nearer and nearer to the woodlands from whence the Sound proceeded, was startled at the sight of a deep cleft dividing another wide extended valley – probably rent by some dreadful Earthquake. A Stream rushes turbulently from the distant Hills and fills this rocky Channel along which it hurries with a loud bellowing.

The Slender withered Trees which hang over it on one side and the tall Mountain Ash which springs from the Cliffs on the other have a fine effect, nor is the dark colour of the rocks opposed to the Silver brightness of the Stream less pleasing. I leaned a long while on the barrier of a Bridge which crosses the Precipice and gazed on the dark Gulph, on the foaming waters and the Lights reflected from the variegated Sky with great delight and wished you was with me to enjoy them. A few miles on we came to the Bridge of Cope consisting of one bold Arch, thrown over the same torrent we had crossed before and soon after passing thro' *Rumilly* traversed a beautiful plain bounded on every side by Mountains as varied as a picturesque Eye could desire and above whose Summits rise the distant Glaciers in all their majesty.[5]

Reading these letters, it is apparent that Beckford was making a studied effort to reconstruct a natural landscape in prose by incorporating the elements needed to fill and frame a picture, similar to the efforts of many of his contemporaries who were using a convex mirror called a 'Claude glass' to study a landscape scene. The letters also provide evidence of Beckford's growing interest in the aesthetics of the picturesque that laid the groundwork for the creation of Fonthill.

While it may seem improbable that Beckford at the early age of seventeen was contemplating anything remotely connected with Fonthill, a remarkably prophetic essay-letter, which he wrote to Cozens in 1777, recapitulates a dream they shared of creating a solipsistic retreat that would allow them to indulge their 'romantic inclinations' in an English countryside separated from the world. This retreat, as Boyd Alexander first noted, suggests Fonthill in a rudimentary form:

> Yes the time will arrive when we may abstract ourselves at least One hundred Days from the World, and in retirement give way to our romantic inclinations. There we will sit on the banks of the river which flows by my native walls and looking up amongst the Shrubs which surround them fancy ourselves on Hesperian ground. There we will execute those plans you have imagined and realize in some measure the dreams of our Fancy. We will obey no other Sovereign than Nature and follow no other guide than pure simplicity.[6]

It is also interesting to note that a central element in this plan, as Beckford described it, is a tower constructed on a hill:

> Sometimes, when our minds are exalted by the sublime reveries of philosophy we will ascend a lofty Hill which till lately was a Mountain in my eyes. There I hope to erect a Tower dedicated to meditation on whose summit we will take our station and survey the vast range of countries beneath... . At midnight when the planets roll brightest, and universal stillness prevails we will recline on stately couches placed on the roof of our Tower and our eyes shall wander amongst the stars [p. 27].

So important was Beckford's relationship with Cozens that it is believed he kept Cozens's letters in a bedside table to the end of his life. 'All your Letters', he wrote to the artist, 'were deposited in a Drawer lined with blue, the colour of the Aether.'[7]

Unfortunately, these letters to Beckford have never been found and may have been destroyed after Beckford's death. They would have given a fuller picture of the thoughts the two shared regarding this plan for a romantic retreat. They would have helped to clarify, for example, a tantalizing reference to a scheme that Cozens had laid out in a letter in November 1777, involving a romantic garden that could have been a stimulus to the writing of the prophetic essay. 'Reserve with care your

System of sentimental Gardening,' Beckford wrote, 'the time may come perhaps when we shall execute it.'[8]

The similarities to the future Fonthill in the essay to Cozens do not end with the construction of a tower in pursuit of seclusion. Beckford also managed to weave his taste for things medieval into the fabric of his fantasy by providing a description of the sumptuous interior of the building as decorated with armorial bearings, religious images, and priceless objects; he even forecast the inclusion of a baronial hall, noting that the

> painted windows of a Hall high above in the Tower will gleam with the light of many tapers and summon us to our evening's repast. We shall ascend the hundred steps which lead to the spacious Hall wainscoted with Cedar, whose arched roof will be strangely sculptured with gothic devices. The pavement is ruddy marble and the seats are painted with achievements, the tall windows are crowded with gorgeous Figures coloured in antient times. Here are Knights, and Sovereigns clad in rich mosaic, Saints, distinguished by their glories and divers quaint forms unintelligible to modern Ages. Above the great window and below the others, is a broad and ample Gallery inclosed with gilt Lattices and supported by thin wasted pillars fretted with scrupulous dexterity. The Doors of old oak are large and folded; in the huge Chimney, useless in this Season, will be placed grotesque vases of antique china filled with Tube roses and on the Gallery you will find stout coffers of Cedar whose laborious carving[s] will amuse you for some moments. Open them and you will discover, robes of state, rich chalices and censers, glistening apparel, coral rosaries and uncouth Trinkets, the treasure of the imaginary Lady of the Tower [p. 31].

At this very early stage of his life Beckford was also exhibiting a strongly romantic characteristic in the way his imaginings tended toward concrete realization. His tendency to particularize bears a resemblance to Blake whose quest for 'strong and better lineaments' gave his own art a distinctive quality. But the character of Beckford's imaginings suggest an even stronger relationship with Keats, since he tended to transport himself imaginatively in order to indulge his senses more fully. In the dream-state developed in this essay, for example, Beckford inevitably paused to savour the pleasing appeal of the baronial hall as Keats did later in the 'The Eve of St Agnes': 'We shall gaze at the Objects in our sight, admire the rich imagery of the plate, the tapers flaming with the wind and diffusing so grand a lustre about the Hall and all its barbarous magnificence' (p. 32). Turning to the landscape setting for his imaginary tower, he continued: 'Every object will convey to us some agreeable sensation, the richness of the Herbage which we tread, the bleating of the sheep that graze it, the contentment and innocent hilarity of those that tend them and the vivacity of the Birds that flying from bough to bough and warbling upon every spray, seem to revel with the rest of nature in the beams of the morning Sun...' (p. 34). Finally, in the midst of this landscape of imagination stood one of the most important ingredients of his later creation – the ruined monastery, a germinal element in the Fonthill plan: 'The shadows cast by the declining Sun on the meads beneath and the reflection of a ruined Monastery in the water at this hour when the Merit of every little circumstance is enhanced, are exquisitely agreeable. A rising ground on the other side covered with inclosures, whose hedges are filled with Broom in blossom and a little Glen shaded with Underwood where the stream loses itself and gurgles unseen terminate the prospect character-ized by a calmness and serenity that will sooth[e] our minds' (p. 37). More than twenty years would pass before the young Beckford's pre-occupation with sensory appeal, love of unspoiled nature and the aesthetic qualities of the religious experience would be realized in another, more dramatic artistic form, but it is evident that the ground-work was laid for it at this early stage of his life.

The impact of Cozens on Beckford is also evident in two additional writings of this period: *The Long Story* (published as *The Vision* in 1930) and *Dreams, Waking Thoughts and Incidents*, both of which were addressed to the artist. 'Your approbation,' he wrote to Cozens, 'is the approbation of a Multitude. It is all I desire and all I seek for in venturing to commit to writing the inspirations of my Fancy, those pleasing Dreams in which perhaps consist the happiest moments of the Life of WILLIAM BECKFORD.'[9] *The Long Story* seems to be an extension of the prophetic essay-letter to Cozens, carrying forward some of the same romantic subject matter of dream fantasy expressive of the search for prelapsarian innocence and voluptuous seclusion. It is an initiation story that plays out Beckford's own desire at this time for self-determination, which he finds in the interior world of imagi-nation. At one point in the story the narrator seeks refuge with the beautiful Nouronihar in a sequestered cave, which turns out to be an extravagant apartment carved in rock of yellow jasper and lit by a myriad of crystal lamps which engulf the room in a continuous glow of evening light:

> The pavement was intirely covered with mats of the nicest work-manship, on which some skilful artist had imitated fruits and flowers with so much success that at first sight they could not be distinguished from bunches of real ones... . A pile of aromatic wood, neatly cleft, was placed by the side of a cheerful fire, fed with the same fuel and three large baskets heaped with cocoa nuts and all the variety of fruits the valleys produced stood on the other side. The fountain I heard in the dark trickled from a nook in the interior grot and was received in a cavity on the brink of which were placed a variety of clear crystal vases, some empty, others filled with cinnamon and wild roses in full bloom.[10]

As the storm rages in the valley outside, these two delicate beings enjoy the 'perfect security' of their cell. The story, in short, constitutes the Beckfordian dream of separation from the kinds of responsibilities that were being imposed upon him in terms of a scheduled political future. He sought, instead, self-realization in the realm of aesthetics – the self-indulgent world of the artist as monarch. Beckford desired to 'immure' himself, a word that he and Cozens shared frequently together, which expressed his own solipsistic longing for seclusion and private happiness and which would ultimately lead him to his own palace of art at Fonthill.

Dreams, Waking Thoughts and Incidents demonstrates Cozens's influence in other significant ways. In this early work, Beckford appears to be purposely appealing to the reader's eye as we have seen in his early letters from Switzerland.[11] By now, however, his writing style is more developed and displays an even stronger alliance with picturesque aesthetics. Page after page of the book demonstrates an eye eager for colour, lights and shades, surface textures, distant lines, perspectives and picture-like views. 'Beyond, in the centre of this strik-ing theatre,' he wrote from Bonn, 'rises a romantic assemblage of distant mountains, crowned with ruins of castles, whose turrets, but faintly seen, were just such as you have created to compleat a prospect' (p. 83). His picturesque orientation also explains why he reveals in *Dreams* his partiality for seeing objects in the 'dubious visionary light' of dusk, and why in the fashion of the picturesque theorists he is consistently drawn to the paintable qualities of rough, rugged surfaces and irregular lines. Nor is it a coincidence that his own descriptions are frequently linked to the works of famous painters, so that irregular hills, clumps of cypress and pastoral cottages become the ingredients for a scene that 'Zuccarelli loved to paint', or rocks and grottoes 'half lost in thickets from which rise craggy pinnacles crowned by mouldering towers' constitute 'just such scenery as Polemburg and Peter de Laer introduce in their paintings'. Aside from its psychological interest, *Dreams, Waking Thoughts and Incidents* remains one of the best illustrations of 'literary picturesque' that was produced in the declining years of the eighteenth century with its heavy emphasis on visual imagery and pictorial composition.

While Cozens was an important influence, Beckford's European travels promoted his artistic interests even further in support of the development that led to Fonthill, particularly his visit to the Grande Chartreuse. Having read the life of St Bruno, the founding father of this Carthusian monastery, and inspired by Thomas Gray's poem on the subject, Beckford made an excursion to this remote site in 1778. Once there, he admitted to its profound effect on him: 'It is more wonderfully wild than I can describe, or even you can imagine. It has possessed me to such a degree, that I can at present neither think, speak, nor write upon any other subject.'[12] The details of Bruno's life obviously struck a responsive chord in Beckford. Bruno was a man of noble descent and of great wealth. Known for his remarkable qualities of mind and being always 'poetical, singular, and visionary', he became disenchanted with the world and the 'charms of society', thereafter seeking retirement from it in claustral life. In short, Bruno's biography mirrored many of Beckford's own longings and feelings about himself. Beckford's owner-ship of Witham Abbey, a sister monastery in ruins on one of his prop-erties in England, promoted an immediate bond with the resident monks who urged him to preserve Witham: 'The Secretary, almost with tears in his eyes, beseeched me to revere these consecrated edifices, and to preserve their remains for the sake of St. Hugo, their canonized Prior. I replied greatly to his satisfaction; and then declaimed so much in favour of Saint Bruno, and the holy prior of Whitham, that the good fathers grew exceedingly delighted with the conversation, and made me promise to remain some days with them' (pp. 269–70).

The Grande Chartreuse appears to have captured Beckford's

imagination partly because it represented a realization of his dream of protective security away from the vicissitudes of the world. But there was also a strong aesthetic attraction. The Grande Chartreuse symbolized the fusion of religion and art in its visual appeal and evocation of feelings of awe that Beckford would re-create at Fonthill. As he examined the interior of the monastery, he was deeply affected by its ambience as he passed from the chapel with its 'two altars with lamps burning before them, on each side of a lofty portal' to the 'grand coved hall, adorned with historical paintings of St. Bruno's life and the portraits of all the Generals of the order'. It was a setting he would not forget. 'I could, in some moments,' he wrote, 'fancy myself capable of plunging into the horrors of a desart, and foregoing all the vanities and delights of the world, to secure my memory so sublime a consecration' (p. 271). The internal scenic effects also had an enormous appeal to him during a service: 'The illumination of so many tapers, striking on the shrines, censers, and pillars of polished jasper, sustaining the canopy of the altar produced a wonderful effect; and, as the rest of the chapel was visible only by the faint external light admitted from above, the splendor and dignity of the altar was inconceivable... the sparkling of several lamps of chased silver, that hung from the roofs, and the gleaming of nine huge tapers... began to be visible, just as I left the chapel' (pp. 272–3).

Besides the monastery itself, the remote and sublime setting in which it was located presented another unforgettable experience. At one point, as he explored the external grounds, the approach of storm clouds and their modifying effect on the surrounding landscape provided an ecstatic moment that had such a potent effect on him that he re-created it in prose:

... Escaping from the courts and cloisters of the monastery, all hushed in stillness, [I] ascended a green knoll, which several antient pines marked with their fantastic shadows: there, leaning against one of their trunks, I lifted up my eyes to the awful barrier of surrounding mountains, discovered by the trembling silver light of the moon, shooting directly on the woods which fringed their acclivities. The lawns, the vast woods, the steep descents, the precipices, the torrents, lay all extended beneath, softened by a pale blueish haze, that alleviated, in some measure, the stern prospect of the rocky promontories above, wrapped in dark shadows. The sky was of the deepest azure; innumerable stars were distinguished with unusual clearness from this elevation, many of which twinkled behind the fir-trees edging the promontories. White, grey, and darkish clouds came marching towards the moon, that shone full against a range of cliffs, which lift themselves far above the others. The hoarse murmur of the torrent, throwing itself from the distant wildernesses into the gloomy vales, was mingled with the blast that blew from the mountains.

It increased. The forests began to wave, black clouds rose from the north, and, as they fleeted along, approached the moon, whose light they shortly extinguished. A moment of darkness succeeded: the gust was chill and melancholy; it swept along the desart, and then subsiding, the vapours began to pass away, and the moon returned: the grandeur of the scene was renewed, and its imposing solemnity was increased by her presence. Inspiration was in every wind: I followed some impulse, which drove me to the summit of the mountains before me; and there, casting a look on the whole extent of wild woods and romantic precipices, thought of the days of St. Bruno: I eagerly contemplated every rock, that formerly might have met his eyes; drank of the spring which tradition says he was wont to drink of; and ran to every withered pine, whose appearance bespoke a remote antiquity, and beneath which, perhaps, the Saint had reposed himself, when worn with vigils, or possessed with the sacred spirit of his institutions. It was midnight: the convent bell tolled; for the most solemn hour of prayer was arrived. I cannot, nor would I, attempt to unfold to you, in prose, half the strange things, of which I thought; and which, I seemed to see, during this wild excursion. [pp. 278–9]

Beckford left after a few days, but the total experience of the Grande Chartreuse, the vision of a secluded monastery set in Alpine scenery, was forever imprinted on his mind, providing substance to the dream he had shared with Cozens. It was one of those 'spots of time', as Wordsworth would later describe the indelible personal experience. Even in the latter years of his life he underscored its importance to him: 'There never was a finer field for poetry – a more striking scene. I have a vivid recollection of its grand solitudes.'[13]

While travelling in the years that followed, Beckford's artistic interests and ideas began to mature. His grand tour of Europe, of which

Dreams, Waking Thoughts and Incidents is a record, is a case in point. There are times in this work when Beckford combines pictorial accent with a poetic sensibility linking him in another vital way to the full-blown Romanticism that was emerging in Europe and in his own country. If Beckford had the facility for portraying with accuracy the genuine aspect of things, he also began to merge the exterior world with the interior landscape of the self. There are times in *Dreams* when he does not stop with a mere literal transcription of objective reality, but goes beyond to render the mood and feeling associated with it. There is a sense, as Richard Garnett once pointed out, in which some of Beckford's pictures become 'equally objective and subjective... brilliantly clear in outline... yet steeped in the rich hues of his own peculiar feeling'.[14] Beckford's sunsets, in particular, partake of this combination of pictorial and emotional values. Whether the closing scenes of day are described in terms of a final blush of crimson in a darkening sky, or as the last sunbeams purpling the sails of ships at rest in the harbour, or as a glow lingering on the verge of a landscape, which slowly fades into a variety of warm hues and then into a deeper, more melancholy blue – these scenes, with their emphasis on colour, take their meaning from the feeling observer, the self actively blended with the scene.

This shift from topographical description to the landscape of sensibility can also be seen in the paintings that John Robert Cozens, the son of Alexander, made for him on his second Grand Tour in 1782. Beckford commissioned these works as a pictorial record of this journey. Recent research has shown that their importance as a group of paintings lies in the extent to which they reflected Beckford's own personal taste, since he exercised considerable control over the subjects selected and the style of the finished works.[15] The evidence indicates that the end result was a collaborative effort between the patron and the artist involving ultimately a series of ninety-four watercolours. Cozens, in other words, modified his own style to illustrate Beckford's response to a visual experience, resulting in an unusual extension of *ut pictura poesis*. The reconciliation of Beckford's descriptions and the medium of paint called for extraordinary empathy and produced an advancement in Cozens's work that may have had an impact on the evolution of English landscape art. Cozens employed colour enrichment and sometimes storm scenes to capture Beckford's emotional responses and growing taste for sublime effects, as in the case of a painting entitled *Between Brixen and Bolzano: Storm* or the dramatically realized *Storm over Padua* with its depiction of lightning over the city of St Anthony, Beckford's chosen patron saint. It is evident that the placid landscape of Claude Lorrain was no longer sufficient; Beckford's growing interest in dramatic effect required a more intense transaction, one which elicited pleasurable emotions of awe in the face of nature in a state of turbulence. Beckford's explanation was that 'a thunder-storm gave character to the landscape',[16] revealing his interest in emotional impact and his shift toward the agenda of Romanticism.

That the formulation of the aesthetics of the picturesque and the sublime deepened during this period in Beckford's mind is also apparent in his interest in Giovanni Piranesi, particularly in the artist's architectural fantasies displayed in the *Carceri d'invenzione* (*Imaginary Prisons*). Beckford's fascination with Piranesi may have started with his father who collected the dramatic prints of this artist and to whom Piranesi dedicated two *Vasi, candelabri* prints. When Beckford visited Venice and encountered the Bridge of Sighs, it was Piranesi who came immediately to his mind, as he explained in *Dreams, Waking Thoughts and Incidents*:

> I left the courts; and, stepping into my bark, was rowed down a canal, over which the lofty vaults of the palace cast a tremendous shade. Beneath these fatal waters, the dungeons I have been speaking of, are situated. There, the wretches lie marking the sound of the oars, and counting the free passage of every gondola. Above, a marble bridge, of bold, majestic architecture, joins the highest part of the prisons to the secret galleries of the palace; from whence criminals are conducted over the arch, to a cruel and mysterious death. I shuddered whilst passing below, and believe it is not without cause, this structure is named PONTE DEI SOSPIRI. Horrors and dismal prospects haunted my fancy upon my return. I could not dine in peace, so strongly was my imagination affected; but, snatching my pencil, I drew chasms and subterraneous hollows, the domain of fear and torture, with chains, rocks, wheels, and dreadful engines, in the style of Piranesi [pp. 123–4].

On another occasion, as he approached the town of Bonn and was struck by a set of irregular mountains that bounded his view, he imagined that he was transported to their summits and there, he wrote: 'I shot swiftly from rock to rock, and built castles, in the style of Piranesi, upon most of their pinnacles. The magnificence and variety of my aerial towers, hindered my thinking the way long' (p. 83).

Piranesi, who first published the *Carceri* in 1745, defied the artistic conventions of the time by giving full play to his imagination in creating scenes of gigantic architectural proportions and spatial complexity that dwarfed the human figures within a landscape of the mind. Highly original in their display of structural forms that overwhelm and control the viewer, these innovative architectural scenes derive their reality from the realm of dreams and nightmare. The confinement of prison is not simply visually realized but presented so dramatically that it is experienced as both physical and psychic imprisonment. The enormous masonry forms resist penetration and contribute to the heavy weight of the experience; the dominance of curvilinear arches symbolizes the state of oppressive entrapment; and the series of stairs presented at various levels add to the spectator's deep sense of claustrophobia by leading nowhere. Significantly, the second edition, published in the early 1760s, Piranesi made even darker in tone with the addition of shadows, wheels, pulleys, winches and other instruments of torture, modifications that prefigured the development of the Gothic novel. Here Beckford could experience the sublime in another form besides the Grande Chartreuse and the melancholy works of Thomas Gray. Piranesi's art represented the new aesthetics of pleasing terror that Edmund Burke defined in *The Origin of Our Ideas of the Sublime and the Beautiful* in 1756, particularly in the emphasis on obscurity, vastness, and magnificence, which the theorist identified as constituent elements of the sublime. The appeal of Piranesi's art had to do with the way it fostered a freer expression of imagination by rendering explicit the images of fear and the aesthetic power of darkness. It was art freed from the shackles of the conventional tenets of artistic taste in the eighteenth century, which would naturally appeal to Beckford's own proto-Romantic imagination. Moreover, behind Piranesi's theatrical display was also a psychological dimension that must have had a catalytic effect on Beckford's own introspective art. The subterranean passages and web-like complexities of Piranesi's architectural dreams are revelatory of the repressed self finding expression in the world of dream while simultaneously recording the nature of the forces working against that freedom.

The influence of Piranesi's potent architectural imagery on Beckford can also be seen in a description of a Christmas party held at Fonthill in

December 1781, following the first European tour. For the occasion, Beckford hired Philippe Jacques de Loutherbourg, the famed scene designer and master of lighting effects, to create a *mise en scène* that would bathe the rooms in a 'necromantic light' producing a mysterious and other-worldly effect. One of the rooms in the mansion was called the Egyptian Room which Beckford described in terms remarkably similar to Piranesi's prison scenes:

> The solid Egyptian Hall looked as if hewn out of a living rock – the line of apartments and apparently endless passages extending from it on either side were all vaulted – an interminable stair case, which when you looked down it – appeared as deep as the well in the pyramid – and when you looked up – was lost in vapour, led to suites of stately apartments... the mystic look, the vastness, the intricacy of this vaulted labyrinth occasioned so bewildering an effect that it became impossible for any one to define – at the moment – where he stood, where he had been, or to whither he was wandering – such was the confusion – the perplexity so many illuminated storys of infinitely varied apartments gave rise to. It was, in short, the realization of romance in its most extravagant intensity. No wonder such scenery inspired the description of the Halls of Eblis.[17]

What happened shortly after this unusual Christmas gathering has been told many times: Beckford left Fonthill for his London residence; and sometime in January 1782, with the visions of the festival still swirling in his head, he composed his masterwork, *Vathek*. In this tale, Beckford's dissident imagination frequently found expression in strange architectural structures of no known human order that one might experience in a dream. At the very beginning of the story, Beckford tells us that the Caliph Vathek constructed an immense tower of fifteen hundred stairs where 'he cast his eyes below, and beheld men not larger than pismires; mountains, than shells; and cities, than beehives.'[18] The perspective here is Piranesian, with the created effect of spatial immensity designed to promote a sense of awe and power. Piranesi's visual idiom seems even more obvious near the end of the story, when Vathek visits the vast ruins of Istakhar with his mistress Nouronihar:

> A death-like stillness reigned over the mountain and through the air. The moon dilated on a vast platform, the shades of the lofty

columns which reached from the terrace almost to the clouds. The gloomy watch-towers, whose number could not be counted, were covered by no roof; and their capitals, of an architecture unknown in the records of the earth, served as an asylum for the birds of night... . On the right rose the watch-towers, ranged before the ruins of an immense palace, whose walls were embossed with various figures. In front stood forth the colossal forms of four creatures, composed of the leopard and the griffin, and though but of stone, inspired emotions of terror... . [As they proceeded into the Palace of Eblis] the Caliph and Nouronihar beheld each other with amazement, at finding themselves in a place, which though roofed with a vaulted ceiling, was so spacious and lofty, that, at first, they took it for an immeasurable plain. But their eyes, at length, growing familiar to the grandeur of the surrounding objects, they extended their view to those at distance; and discovered rows of columns and arcades, which gradually diminished, till they terminated in a point radiant as the sun [pp. 107, 109].

There are many threads of influence in the creative tapestry of *Vathek*, but Piranesi's surrealistic vision reinforced the distinctive visual quality of Beckford's literary vocabulary, and was a powerful stimulus to Beckford's own architectural visualizations that would ultimately find expression in the creation of Fonthill.

Beckford's visit to Portugal in 1794 also played an important role in shaping the interest that led to Fonthill. At that time he saw the Gothic monasteries of Alcobaça and Batalha, an experience that led over forty years later to the publication of his *Recollections of an Excursion to the Monasteries of Alcobaça and Batalha*. The first monastery he saw was Alcobaça. 'The first sight of this regal monastery is very imposing,' he wrote, 'and the picturesque, well-wooded and well-watered village, out of the quiet bosom of which it appears to rise, relieves the mind from a sense of oppression the huge domineering bulk of the conventual buildings inspire.'[19] Once inside the building, he found it gloomy and somewhat austere, but he was affected by the soft light that relieved the darkness 'where the perpetual lamps burning before the high altar diffused a light most solemn and religious' (II, 273). The quality of subdued light became a sustained interest throughout his lifetime and a dominant element in the interior designs at Fonthill and in Lansdown Tower in Bath. It was the light of repose and the 'true light of devotion', as he explained in his later years to Cyrus Redding. 'It is an excitement in itself to solemn thoughts and prayer – the dim religious light of the sanctuary.' He also believed that it was the interior light most characteristic of the older Gothic cathedrals, observing that the 'Bath abbey-church is of the later Gothic — too light for such an effect'. [20]

Here Beckford accented the religious associations of subdued light, but as a young man he was strongly drawn to the aesthetic qualities of the interior lighting effects of cathedrals he visited during his travels. Although he never embraced Roman Catholicism, he felt that it devoted more attention than Protestantism to the aesthetics of the interior world of the cathedral. Comparing the two religions, he once told an artist friend, 'The one is the opera and the other the dress rehearsal.' His fascination with the Roman Church was always more secular than religious despite attempts on the part of some of his contemporaries to link him to it. In response to an accusation in the *Sunday Times* that he had 'apostatised to the Catholic religion' while in Portugal, he wrote: 'I plead guilty of almost unbounded extravagance, but not of having apostatised in Portugal, or any where else. I never took the trouble. At Lisbon I warmly admired the picturesque pomp of its patriarchal Church & felt its sublime music at my heart's core, but between a *professor* & an *amateur* there exists an essential difference. I never belonged to the former *description God knows*.' [21] It was simply good theatre; the pageantry of religion that he indulged as art. Anglicanism was too austere and coldly intellectual to appeal to Beckford's artistic temperament, as he once made clear: 'Gracious God! the Roman Catholic religion is filled with fine stage effects, glittering crosses, censers, mitres, crosiers, dresses, candles, pictures, banners, processions, perfumes, dolls, and music from the deep tones of the organ to the delightful squeakings of the pope's eunuchs.' [22]

Besides the lighting effects at Alcobaça, the apartment where he stayed had walls that were naked, but 'the ceiling was gilt and painted, the floor spread with Persian carpets of the finest texture, and the tables in rich velvet petticoats, decked with superb ewers and basins of chased silver, and towels bordered with point-lace of a curious antique pattern' (II, 275). Elsewhere there were gilded ornaments, effigies of kings, a full-size portrait of St Thomas à Becket, a glistening sacristy, carvings in rock crystal, and golden reliquaries, all of which were to have their place in the antiquarian and religious motifs of Fonthill.

Proceeding to Batalha, Beckford was led to comment again on the picturesque quality of the Gothic architecture, noting 'the great church, with its rich cluster of abbatial buildings, buttresses, and pinnacles, and fretted spires, towering in all their pride, and marking the ground with deep shadows that appeared interminable' (II, 289). After passing through a sculptured gateway, he was confronted by the grand western façade of the church with a portal fifty feet in height, an awe-inspiring sight that may well have inspired the western entrance to Fonthill Abbey that was fifteen feet shorter but equally impressive. 'As soon as we drew near,' he wrote, 'the valves of a huge oaken door were thrown open, and we entered the nave, which reminded me of Winchester in form of arches and mouldings, and of Amiens in loftiness' (II, 297). A dominant scenic effect – and an influence on Beckford's plans for the interior of Fonthill – was once again the ambience of subdued light to accent a sumptuous interior scene, utilizing stained glass, drapery and candle-light to achieve a heightened emotional response. He had observed this play of light and colour before at the Grande Chartreuse. The trans-mutation of light in the nave of the cathedral at Batalha into rich golden hues seemed to have had a profound impact on his imagination as well:

No tapestry, however rich – no painting, however vivid, could equal the gorgeousness of tint, the splendour of the golden and ruby light which streamed forth from the long series of stained windows: it played flickering about in all directions, on pavement and on roof, casting over every object myriads of glowing mellow shadows ever in undulating motion, like the reflection of branches swayed to and fro by the breeze. We all partook of these gorgeous tints – the white monastic garments of my conductors seemed as it were embroidered with the brightest flowers of paradise, and our whole procession kept advancing invested with celestial colours [II, 297–8].

Batalha provided a further inspiration. After attending the cathedral service, he visited the mausoleum where he saw the effigies of John I and Philippa on their tombs in the middle of the chapel, along with their children. (Philippa was the granddaughter of Edward III, to whom Beckford would dedicate a wing of Fonthill.) This very likely inspired him to consider incorporating his own tomb in the early plans of the Fonthill design. He was also deeply impressed by the armorial bearings that displayed historical associations with English nobility, which became another constituent element of Fonthill:

I withdrew from the contemplation of these tombs with reluctance, every object in the chapel which contains them being so pure in taste, so harmonious in colour; every armorial device, every mottoed lambel, so tersely and correctly sculptured, associated also so closely with historical and English recollections – the garter, the leopards, the fleur-de-lis, 'from haughty Gallia torn'; the Plantagenet cast of the whole chamber conveyed home to my bosom a feeling so interesting, so congenial, that I could hardly persuade myself to move away, though my reverend conductors began to show evident signs of impatience [II, 299].

Batalha, in short, captured Beckford's imagination to such an extent that the first design of Fonthill as a residence was based on the monastery, and when that plan was rejected for another, he maintained the connection by incorporating three great stained glass windows in the Octagon Hall that were copied from windows at Batalha.

One other formative influence that fuelled Beckford's architectural ideas was the house he leased in Sintra, Monserrate (fig. 2), after he left the monasteries of Alcobaça and Batalha. It was owned by a London merchant by the name of Gerard Devisme who built it in 1789, and it is still considered to be the earliest example of Gothic revival architecture in Portugal. Beckford was attracted to the place because of its elevation, which afforded expansive views of the countryside surrounding it. He once described it as 'a beautiful Claude-like place, surrounded by a most enchanting country'.[23] But its medieval architectural style also had a strong appeal to him: it was flanked on two sides by twin towers, with a principal entrance that led to an octagonal room which gave onto extended internal vistas down the wings radiating from it, a principal feature that Beckford would incorporate at Fonthill. While in residence there, Beckford made his own improvements in the house and the gardens. He liked the place well enough to acquire it when Devisme died in 1798.[24] This was the site that inspired Byron to pen some reflections of Beckford when he saw the house and gardens in a neglected state in 1809:

> There thou too, Vathek! England's wealthiest son,
> Once form'd thy Paradise, as not aware
> When wanton Wealth her mightiest deeds hath done,
> Meek Peace voluptuous lures was ever wont to shun.

Here didst thou dwell, here schemes of pleasure plan,
Beneath yon mountain's ever beauteous brow:
But now, as if a thing unblest by Man,
Thy fairy dwelling is as lone as Thou!

Here giant weeds a passage scarce allow
To Halls deserted, portals gaping wide:
Fresh lessons to the thinking bosom, how
Vain are the pleasaunces on earth supplied;
Swept into wrecks anon by Time's ungentle tide!

Sir Francis Cook acquired the estate in 1856, and with the aid of an English architect orientalized the exterior in a Moorish design. The interior, however, remained unchanged and still retains the character of Beckford's occupancy.[25]

While Beckford's early visual training and travel experiences helped to forge his artistic interests, there were other critical events in his personal life, to which Byron alluded in the above lines, that led to the decision to devote himself to his vision of Fonthill. It was during his tour of England in 1779 that he met and developed almost instantly a 'strange wayward passion' for William Courtenay, the effeminate eleven-year-old son of Lord Courtenay of Powderham Castle. Initially, the relationship appeared to be innocent enough, falling more in the category of adoration fantasy. In the end, however, it would be a fateful moment in Beckford's life that would ultimately lead to his social ostracism in England and affect the way he led the rest of his life. 'I grew sensible,' Beckford wrote, 'there was a pleasure in loving something besides oneself and felt there would be more luxury in dying for him than living for the rest of the Universe.'[26] Following the initial contact, Beckford experienced constant anxiety in his efforts to keep in touch with the 'little C.'; he was also frequently agitated by the efforts of his family to dissolve what they felt was an unhealthy relationship.

While the relationship with Courtenay has been subject to varying interpretations, there can be little doubt about its profound emotional impact. It marked an awakening of latent homosexual feelings of which Beckford became fully aware a year later, when on his Grand Tour he became involved in the decadence of Venetian high society, largely through the help of the adventuress Contessa d'Orsini-Rosenberg and her lover Count Benincasa; and, before long, he was drawn into a homosexual entanglement with a young member of the aristocratic

Cornaro family which left him in a feverish state of mind. Years later he attempted to explain the relationship in discreet terms as a 'passion of the mind – resembling those generous attachments we venerate in ancient history, and holy writ. What David felt towards the brother of his heart, the son of Saul.'[27] But the immediate impact on him was traumatic; and, for the rest of the tour, he was haunted by one object: 'One image alone possesses me and pursues me in a terrible way. In vain do I throw myself into Society – this image forever starts up before me. In vain do I try to come up to the great expectations formed of me – my words are cut short and I am halted in mid-career. This unique object is all I hope for – and I am dead to everything else.'[28]

By the time he reached Naples in November, he had worked himself into such a state that he could no longer contain his feelings and unloaded all his emotional freight upon the shoulders of a new friend and confidante, Lady Hamilton, the first wife of Sir William Hamilton, the English ambassador to the Court of Naples. Beckford stayed with the Hamiltons for a month during which time Catherine Hamilton acted as a positive influence; and, disapproving completely of his Venetian affair, she made him aware of the dangers he might be led into if he continued it. On his return trip to the 'pestilential air' of Venice, she pleaded with him to 'resist nobly a Sentiment that in your soul you cannot approve, and which if indulged must end in your misery and in the destruction of a Mother that dotes on you'.[29] In Venice at the end of December he wrote assurances that he would not yield to the 'insinuating whisper of a soft but criminal delight',[30] and she answered with a letter imploring him to continue the resistance: 'Every day you will find the struggle less – the important struggle! What is it for? No less than *honor*, *reputation* and all that an honest and noble Soul holds most dear, while Infamy, eternal infamy (my soul freezes while I write the word) attends the giving way to the soft alluring of a criminal passion.'[31] Beckford surmounted the temptation, because by 10 January 1781 he had abandoned his 'Venetian state' and with it the 'fatal connection'.

There followed another complication in his life at this time, involving an intense relationship with the unhappily married Louisa Pitt-Rivers, wife of Beckford's cousin, Peter. She was another confidante with whom he could share his deepest feelings and anxieties. In reality, however, the relationship was lopsided. Louisa was desperately in love with Beckford, which he encouraged but never to the extent that would involve an equivalent commitment. Still, the liaison between the wealthy heir of Fonthill and his cousin's wife became the source of considerable rumours among the social set that added to the alarm of the dowagers at Fonthill and increased concern about Beckford's behavioural patterns.

If the culmination of the emotional experiences with Courtenay, Cornaro and Louisa did not wear him thin mentally, the prospect of entering public life did. As he neared majority in 1781, he began to exhibit increasing signs of psychological stress over the thought of embarking on a political career as his mother had expected. He was also faced with a major financial threat from Chancery proceedings involving a bastard brother which he would have to address before his twenty-first birthday, or risk losing control of some profitable sugar estates in Jamaica.

> I am fated, it seems [he wrote to Lady Hamilton], to return to a country where sober, sullen realities must put ['my happy fantastic imaginations'] all to flight – where I have no friend like you to sustain my spirits and receive my ideas except Mr. Cozens.... Not an animal comprehends me. At this disastrous moment, too, when every individual is abandoned to terrors and anxieties, which way can I turn myself? Public affairs I dare not plunge into. My health is far too wavering. Whilst I write my hand trembles like that of a paralytic Chinese. Strange colours swim before my eyes and sounds keep ringing in my ears for which I can hardly account.[32]

Increasingly, Beckford turned to writing as an escape from the sullen realities he knew he would have to face. In fact, the period following his twenty-first birthday on 29 September 1781 marked a particularly fertile literary phase of his life, despite the psychological strain. Never again would he write at such a productive pace. While *Vathek* was composed in a great rush in January 1782, he did spend a portion of the spring refining it. In the same year he began writing a long Eastern narrative called the *Histoire de Darianoc, jeune homme du pays de Gou-Gou*, concluded *Dreams, Waking Thoughts and Incidents* for the press, and wrote to Samuel Henley that additional 'Arabian Tales' were springing up like mushrooms all over the downs of Fonthill. Before the winter season ended, he had embarked on the *Episodes of Vathek*.

When he attempted to place 500 quarto copies of *Dreams, Waking Thoughts and Incidents* on the market in March 1783, Mrs Beckford and several members of the family moved in, forced him to order their withdrawal and confiscated most of the copies. To publish a book which began with the words, 'Shall I tell you my dreams? – To give an account of my time, is doing, I assure you, but little better. Never did there exist a more ideal being', seemed to run counter to the *gravitas* expected of a future member of the House of Commons. The suppression of an important literary work, however, was not enough to satisfy Mrs Beckford; she took even sterner action to ensure her son's entrance into the political world by arranging his marriage to Lady Margaret Gordon, the daughter of the fourth Earl of Aboyne. On 5 May 1783 the couple recited their vows under the mother's watchful eye.

Beckford's marriage was a triumph for the family; and it seemed for a time that he was ready to settle down to the practical affairs of life. He even wrote to his family friend Lord Chancellor Thurlow in the following spring that he was inclined to sit in Parliament; and, before the year was over, he had obtained the seat for Wells in Somerset. But the romance with politics was short-lived. He had no taste for sitting through the tedious proceedings of the House and sought freedom from these responsibilities by means of a peerage with the title of 'Lord Beckford of Fonthill'. He tried to obtain it through Thurlow and might have been successful had it not been for the scandal that erupted after a visit to Powderham Castle, Devon, where William Courtenay lived. Following his stay there with Lady Margaret in 1784, a series of stories began to circulate about a sexual liaison between Beckford and Courtenay which spread to the London newspapers by the end of November. One of the most damning reports appeared in the *Morning Herald*: 'The rumour concerning a *Grammatical mistake of Mr. B* – and the *Hon. Mr. C*–, in regard to the genders, we hope for the honour of Nature originates in *Calumny*! For, however depraved the being must be, who can propagate such reports without foundation, we must wish such a being exists, in preference to characters, who, regardless of Divine, Natural and Human Law, sink themselves below the lowest class of brutes in the most *preposterous* rites.'[33]

The instigator was Lord Loughborough, husband of William's aunt, Charlotte Courtenay, and a man who harboured a personal dislike for Beckford. Loughborough considered Thurlow his major political rival and was jealous of Beckford's potential for a peerage with the Lord Chancellor's support. Destroying Beckford would be a way of undermining his political enemy as well.

While the charges were never substantiated, they effectively eliminated the sought-after barony and marked Beckford as a paederast for
the rest of his life. Throughout the furore of these reports, Beckford
protested his innocence. He solemnly declared to both friends and relatives that the sordid tales were groundless, but he never publicly refuted
the charges. The result was a shadow of suspicion that persisted in the
mind of the public. From time to time, the subject would emerge in the
press, reminding the readers of Beckford's 'depravity,' as in the case of a
piece that appeared in *The Monthly Visitor* in October 1797:

> When the character of an individual has been publicly understood
> as degraded to the foulest practices of the most foul and unnatural
> *times*, it is not sufficient to assign such a belief to the efforts of
> 'detraction,' 'malice,' 'ignorance,' and 'ingratitude'; it is necessary
> to prove, that individuals have been slanderous and ungrateful –
> that a nation has been ignorant and malicious. By a sophism
> which our laws permit – TRUTH IS A LIBEL; and we dare not
> explain to the public, the wretched enormities of certain men.[34]

With the Powderham event unanswered, Beckford became a marked
figure in British society. It began the process of marginalization that has
prevented him from being taken seriously even to the present day.

As the word of the 'Courtenay affair' spread throughout England,
Beckford plunged into a despair which soon gave way to bitterness.
Reaching a breaking point, he finally decided, at the suggestion of his
wife, to return to the 'tranquil pure atmosphere' of Vevy on the shores
of Lake Geneva where he had found solace before. He was there less
than a year, however, when he suffered another serious setback: the
death of Lady Margaret on 26 May 1786, after she had given birth to
their second daughter. For Beckford it was a severe shock, the abrupt
loss of someone he had grown to love and respect. She had been one of
the few individuals who stood by him during this very dark period of
his life. To make matters worse, when the news of her death reached
England, a few newspapers claimed that it was due directly to his brutal
treatment of her. It was an unwarranted and gratuitous attack that
caused a wound that would never heal. As he wrote to a friend years
later:

> You was in Turkey or in Lubberland when the storm raged against
> me, and when I was stabbed to the heart by the loss of Lady

Margaret. And what was the balm poured into my wounds – a set
of paragraphs accusing me of having occasioned her death by ill
usage. Allowances were to be made for former attacks but none
for this; and I will own to you that the recollection of this black
stroke fills me with such horror and indignation that I sigh for the
pestilential breath of an African serpent to destroy every English-
man who comes in my way.[35]

Beckford, at twenty-six, discovered that his life lay about him in
ruins. He could not show his face in society without fear of criticism.
His beloved wife, the one faithful friend during the harrowing experience of 1784, was now gone. He had two daughters but no male heir.
His barony had been lost; his mother's political dreams for him had
been shattered. A major literary work had been suppressed. Mocked by
those who did not know him, shunned by some of his friends and relatives, he spent the next ten years of his life, from 1786 to 1796, on the
Continent in virtual exile from England. It was during these years that
Fonthill began to play a significant role in his life. Chastened by self-
examination while abroad and sobered by the grim realities of his early
manhood, he began to think that he might make Fonthill his home.
Often during his travels, his thoughts would return to his birthplace. 'I
have been haunted all night with rural ideas of England,' he recorded in
his Portuguese journal in 1787, 'the fresh smell of my pines at Fonthill
seemed wafted to me in my dreams. The bleating of my sheep and
lowing of herds in the deep valley of Lawn Farm faintly sounded in my
ears. ... shall I banish myself forever from these happy scenes of my
childhood?'[36] If he were going to be ostracized, he decided it would be
on his own terms. Throughout the countryside of this large estate he
could find another challenge to his artistic imagination. It began with a
tower as a feature in a landscape, then gradually developed into a work
of art on a grand scale with a magnificent Gothic residence as the crown
in a well-conceived setting and whose scenic interior, displaying some
of the most impressive works of art ever to be gathered in one place,
combined with the exterior scenic effects to create a total aesthetic
experience that made Fonthill not only a sensation in its day but one of
the major contributions to the visual arts in nineteenth-century
England.

2
Cultivating a Taste for the Picturesque

It is important to recognize at the outset that Fonthill began as a land-scape design and that any structure that was considered within it, whether a tower or a ruin, was to be a feature of a broader artistic plan. This is not surprising when one considers the important role of land-scape architecture as one of the 'sister arts' in eighteenth-century England and the extent to which cultivated gentlemen before Beckford, from Alexander Pope to Horace Walpole, carried out garden experi-ments on their own estates. Both Stourhead and Longleat, neither of them far from Fonthill, had achieved notoriety as examples of this art. It is significant of Beckford's interest in gardening that he often purchased land to accommodate his landscape plans, that he continued his gardening and building efforts throughout his later years in Bath, and that he told his first biographer, Cyrus Redding, that his greatest artistic achievement was the creation of the picturesque wilderness about the Abbey.

It is clear that Beckford from a very early age was drawn to the beauty of the natural landscape. The knowledge of painting he obtained as a young man gave him insight into the possibilities of 'nature unadorned' as a subject of pure aesthetic enjoyment. His early travels continued to educate his eye by providing him with opportunities to analyse European scenery, often in relationship to his knowledge of eighteenth-century landscape paintings. Like many of his contem-poraries, he appreciated the beauty of the asymmetrical line. Formal patterns and geometric design, he would complain, dulled his senses and 'yawned' his 'soul out'. Although he never formulated a systematic theory of landscape gardening, it is clear from his letters and travel books, where he commented on the gardens of others, and from his own practical experiments, that he believed garden composition should be created by subordinating art to nature, while the natural elements of the layout had to be carefully massed and shaped into a harmonious whole in accordance with the basic principles of composition in painting.

There is evidence that Beckford received some formal training in the principles of architecture and landscape design under the tutorship of Sir William Chambers. He told an artist friend later in life that he was a 'pupil of Sir W. Chambers when he was building Somerset House'.[1] Chambers, whose professional accomplishments had led to his appointment as Comptroller of the Works in 1769, began work on Somerset House in 1775 when he was known to be one of the busiest architects in England, and this has led to some dispute over the possibility of his having enough time to tutor the young Beckford.[2] Certainly Chambers's contribution to Beckford's architectural education may perforce have been limited, but there is no reason to doubt Beckford's account. There is, furthermore, an additional piece of documentation that Beckford's biographers have overlooked and that is a presentation copy of the second edition of the *Dissertation on Oriental Gardening* (1773) which Chambers gave to Beckford. It contained the inscription 'From the Author, 19th March 1773',[3] which supports the existence of a relationship. Chambers could also have provided additional inspiration for Beckford's later interest in garden design since it was in the 1770s that he was expressing his strongly held views on the art of laying out grounds in contradistinction to the work of Lancelot 'Capability' Brown and his followers. Beckford's own knowledge of the principles of architecture developed as he became more widely read in this area and had an opportunity to examine various building styles on his travels. Over time, he amassed a respectable collection of architectural books and prints as an academic reference library. While it would be unrealistic to claim that his knowledge of architecture ever reached a professional level, he could claim at least a scholarly knowledge of the subject and came to be known as an individual who was quite capable of producing competent architectural drawings. A contemporary architect, who once shared with him a plan for a public building, conveyed his own astonishment at Beckford's understanding of architectural principles. 'I should have thought him', he exclaimed, 'a regular architect! When he saw the ground plans, he told me in a moment the intended size of all the apartments.'[4]

Following the tradition of naturalism in garden design, Beckford criticized the taste illustrated by the formal gardens of the Restoration and supported a freer, more open style of garden planning. When he visited the country house of Count Bentinck in The Hague in 1780, he complained that 'the walks and alleys have all that stiffness and formality our ancestors admired'; and on the road between Amsterdam and Utrecht, he recorded scornfully, 'We beheld no other objects than endless avenues and stiff parterres, scrawled and flourished in patterns, like the embroidery of an old maid's work-bag.'[5]

Seven years later he discovered examples of a similarly abhorrent architectural style in Portugal. A garden attached to the Pagliavam villa moved him to write:

> A great flat space before the garden-front of the villa is laid out in dismal labyrinths of clipped myrtle, with lofty pyramids rising from them, in the style of that vile Dutch maze planted by King William at Kensington, and rooted up some years ago by King George the Third. Beyond this puzzling ground are several long alleys of stiff dark verdure, called *ruas*, i.e. literally streets, with great propriety, being more close, more formal, and not less dusty than High-Holborn.[6]

For Beckford excessive art was too fastidious and disciplinary to be pleasing. His typical reaction was that it 'suffocated him'. He felt strongly enough about this subject to make it a central theme in his first published work, *Biographical Memoirs of Extraordinary Painters*, where he attacked Dutch and Flemish painters for their strained and artificial mannerisms.[7] He also complained in the opening chapters of *Dreams, Waking Thoughts and Incidents* about the 'whimsical buffoonery of a Dutch imagination', and even chastised Rubens for becoming 'lost in the flounces of the Virgin's drapery'.[8] Behind these criticisms was Beckford's preference for breadth and freedom, which he often found in the natural landscape and sometimes in a garden, like that of the Negroni in Rome.

> There I found, what my soul desired [he wrote], thickets of jasmine, and wild spots overgrown with bay; long alleys of cypress totally neglected, and almost impassable through the luxuriance of the vegetation; on every side, antique fragments, vases, sarcophagi, and altars, sacred to the Manes, in deep, shady recesses; which I am certain the Manes must love. The air was filled with the murmurs of water, trickling down basins of porphyry, and losing itself amongst over-grown weeds and grasses. Above the wood, and between its boughs, appeared several domes, and a strange lofty tower.[9]

In extreme reaction against the formal garden, some eighteenth-century landscapists, particularly Capability Brown and his followers, had laid too much stress on simplicity and smoothness in the garden scene. Beckford disliked both extremes. On this issue he was in agreement with Chambers, who argued in *Dissertation on Oriental Gardening* (1772) that 'neither the artful nor the simple style of gardening is right: the one being too much refined and too extravagant a deviation from nature; the other, like a Dutch picture, an affected adherence to her without choice of judgment.'[10] Beckford clearly disliked gardens designed in the style of Brown, such as the one he saw in Aranjuez in 1795 near the Casa del Labrador:

> I was sorry to see many, very many acres of unmeaning shrubbery, serpentine walks, and clumps of paltry flowers, encroaching upon the wild thickets upon the banks of the Tagus. The King, the Queen, the favourite, are bitten by the rage of what they fancy to be improvement, and are levelling ground, and smoothing banks, and building rock-work, with pagodas and Chinese railing. The laburnums, weeping-willows, and flowering shrubs, which I admired so much seven years ago in all their native luxuriance, are beginning to be trimmed and tortured into what the gardener calls genteel shapes. Even the course of the Tagus has been thwarted, and part of its waters diverted into a broad ditch in order to form an island, flat, swampy, and dotted over with exotic shrubs, to make room for which many a venerable arbele and poplar has been laid low.[11]

What was essential for a beautiful design, Beckford felt, was a proper mixture of both art and nature. Bare nature often lacked sufficient variety to amuse the spectator, so a limited assistance of art was needed to include in the plan the provocative elements of surprise and contrast. 'No one', Redding once observed, 'understood the force of contrast better than Mr. Beckford.'[12] In the case of the royal gardens of Aranjuez where nature was 'methodized', Beckford would follow Uvedale Price's dictum of 'knowing where to leave off'.

> If they would but let Aranjuez alone, I should not care. Nature has lavished her with charms most bountifully on this valley; the wild hills which close it in, though barren, are picturesquely-shaped; the Tagus here winds along in the boldest manner, overhung by

crooked willows and lofty arbeles; now losing itself in almost impervious thickets, now undermining steep banks, laying rocks bare, and forming irregular coves and recesses; now flowing smoothly through vast tracts of low shrubs, aspens and tamarisks; in one spot edged by the most delicate greensward, in another by beds of mint and a thousand other fragrant herbs.[13]

Beckford's ideas on the landscape garden were not particularly unique or extraordinary in the 1780s and 1790s. His specific disdain for the formal garden as an illustration of false taste, his belief in the principle that nature must ever be followed, and the view that a good landscapist was essentially a painter were, after all, major themes in the rise and development of the informal garden in the eighteenth century.

In terms of his specific interest in landscape gardening, Beckford was familiar with the works of almost every garden theorist, both French and British, in the seventeenth and eighteenth centuries. Of the books related to gardening theory, some containing his own ms. notes on the fly-leaves, the following were in his libraries at Fonthill and Bath: Batty Langley's *New Principles of Gardening* (1728); A. J. De Lille's *Les Jardins* (1732); J. Serle's *A Plan of Pope's Garden* (1745); William Chambers's *Dissertation on Oriental Gardening* (1773); Joseph Heeley's *Letters on the Beauties of Hagley, Envil and The Leasowes* (1777); Horace Walpole's *Essay on Modern Gardening* (1785); Thomas Whately's *Observations on Modern Gardening* (1793); William Gilpin's *Three Essays: On Picturesque Beauty; on Picturesque Travel; and on Sketching Landscape* (1794); R. P. Knight's *The Landscape* (1794); Humphry Repton's *Sketches and Hints on Landscape Gardening* (1794); and George Mason's *An Essay on Design in Gardening* (1795). This is only a partial list; he owned many others that were equally important in the history of the movement.[14]

Besides these specialized treatises, one of Beckford's interests had always been literary descriptions of 'Fortunate Isles' and other paradisiacal gardens. Not restricting himself to the classics, he also studied the descriptions of legendary gardens in Milton's *Paradise Lost* and Ariosto's *Orlando Furioso*, and the enchanted gardens and palaces in Tasso, Spencer, and Camoens.[15] He used to cite the following passages from Tasso and Milton as direct sources of inspiration for his ideas on garden design:[16]

Faire trees, high plants, strange herbes and flowrets new,
Sunshinie hills, dales hid from Phoebus' raies;
Groves, arbours, mossie caves, at once they view,
And that which beautie most, most wonder brought,
No where appear'd the arte which all this wroughte.

So with the rude, the polisht mingled was
That natural seemed all and every parte;
Nature would crafte in counterfeiting pas,
And imitate her imitator, Arte.   [Tasso]

Flowers, worthy of Paradise, which not nice Art
In beds and curious knots, but Nature's boon
Pour'd forth profuse on hill, and dale, and plain,
Both where the morning sun first warmly smote
The open field, and where the unpierc'd shade
Embrown'd the noon-tide bowers.   [Milton]

But to a man of Beckford's taste the direct appeal of these descriptions was, of course, in their insistence that nature was most attractive in its wild and unadorned state, and that the real serpent in the garden was art that was obvious, such as was represented in the clipped hedge, the geometrically shaped tree, or the embroidered parterre. This is not to say that Beckford believed that art had no place in garden design, but only that it should never be intrusive.

It was this view of 'professed art' as an encroachment upon the living landscape which ultimately led Beckford, as it did other early romantic artists, to the recognition that the integrity of a specific landscape must never be violated. Once irregular nature was appreciated for itself, without the intrusion of excessive art, the respect for the 'character' of an individual scene was inevitable and led to the study of topography as a prelude to landscape design.[17] There are no surviving statements by Beckford addressing this approach to laying out a landscape, but Redding furnished an example of how an appreciation of the topography of an area on the Fonthill estate became the basis for achieving a unified effect. Describing a section of the estate near Hindon that Beckford developed, Redding wrote: 'The character of the scenery here its owner had studied to render as wildly natural as possible. All was rustic. Even the lodges were common, and the twisted trees, meeting overhead, carried on the deception, until, emerging on a sudden, the

Abbey, in all its imposing mass, came suddenly upon the eye.'[18] In rela-
tion to the history of the gardening movement, this course of action
represented an important shift away from the neo-classical technique
of creating gardens according to a pre-established formula towards the
more romantic approach of allowing the character of a particular
setting to dictate the design. Interestingly, it was Alexander Pope who
laid the groundwork for this important principle of garden design in his
'Epistle to Burlington' in 1731:

> Consult the Genius of the Place in all;
> That tells the Waters or to rise or fall;
> Or helps th' ambitious Hill the heavens to scale,
> Or scoops in circling theatres the Vale;
> Calls in the Country, catches opening glades,
> Joins willing woods, and varies shades from shades;
> Now breaks, or now directs, th' intending Lines;
> Paints as you plant, and, as you work, designs.

One of the essential characteristics for a garden setting that Beckford
always insisted upon and took advantage of was its natural advantages
for a prospect. He was aware of the possibilities a good location
provided for an extensive view and considered it a principal ingredient
in the garden design. All four of Beckford's residences containing
garden scenes were located in elevated regions with commanding views.
In Portugal, he resided at Ramalhão in 1787–8, about twelve miles
from Lisbon, 'on an eminence under the pyramidical rocks of Sintra, an
exposed situation over-looking a vast stretch of country bounded by the
ocean'.[19] He selected Monserrate in 1794 for its lovely grounds and
views. The Fonthill Abbey estate was located in one of the highest
regions of Wiltshire, and the tower he had constructed as part of his
garden in Bath, the residence of his final years of life, provided an
extended view of the surrounding countryside. 'I am partial to glancing
over a wide horizon,' he once told Cyrus Redding, 'it delights me to
sweep along an extended landscape. I must elevate myself to do this.'[20]

Beckford's interest in prospect was inextricably involved with his
passion for towers. A tower presented an image of both authority and
seclusion for Beckford – an appropriate symbol that expressed the way
he saw himself and that he transferred to the central character of his
major literary work, the Caliph Vathek. At an exhibition of paintings,
he always ran first to look at those works that contained towers. The

drawings he made of landscape scenes or from imagination invariably had in them a tall tower perched on a mountain-top overlooking a deep valley below.[21] We have already pointed out how the essay-letter to Cozens in 1777 manifested the same obsession with the sweeping prospect from a lofty tower, where he and the artist could look down upon the world below. It was a compelling interest that remained with him throughout his life. At least five years after he left Fonthill he could not resist making note of the arresting character of a tower in a landscape, as he revealed in his copy of Gilbert L. Meason's *On the Landscape Architecture of the Great Painters of Italy* (London, 1828)[22] where he recorded in the fly-leaf the following passages that captured his interest in the book:

> Among the paintings found at Pompeia are some supposed to be of villas, each of which has its tower of safety hard by

> A tower was a necessary appendage to the vinyard or garden, in the east, at the most remote aera

> On the reverse side of a silver coin, fished up from the Euphrates, close to the ruins of the palace of Babylon, are five embattled towers, and one outward wall

> In the villa of Ventidus Bassus, the tower was sixty paces square; that of the palace of Maceanas was still larger

> Attached to the palace of the Duke of Braschi on the lake of Nemi, is a tower of great antiquity. It is one hundred and twenty feet high, thirty feet in exterior diameter, and the wells are five feet in thickness

A visitor to Beckford's tower in Bath once asked him how he managed to adjust to the loss of his great estate at Fonthill. His eyes brightened as, sweeping his fingers across the Welsh mountains, the Severn estuary and the rolling downs of Wiltshire, he answered: 'This! this – the finest prospect in Europe.'[23]

Beckford's need for a 'view' as an important element in the garden plan was a natural outcome of his years of European travel, but it also developed from his knowledge of painting. His early studies in painting, as already mentioned, had helped him to observe nature with the careful eye of the painter. Thus, when he walked through the garden attached to the Elector's residence in Bonn, it was the prospect that he highlighted and went on to describe because it reminded him of one of Alexander Cozens's landscapes:

> It was so dusky, that I was a minute or two seeking in vain the entrance of an orangery.... At length I discovered it; and passing under an arch, found myself in the midst of lemon and orange trees, now in the fullest blow, which form a continued grove before the palace, and extend, on each side of its grand portal, out of sight. A few steps separate this extensive terrace from a lawn, bordered by stately rows of beeches. Beyond, in the centre of this striking theatre, rises a romantic assemblage of distant mountains, crowned with the ruins of castles, whose turrets, but faintly seen, were just as you would have created to compleat a prospect.[24]

As this interest in the natural landscape grew, he inevitably recognized the essential interrelationship between gardening and painting: he came to understand that the basic principles of the one art readily applied to the other. This picturesque orientation ultimately manifested itself in his own highly visual style of writing, in his obsessive interest in collecting books with engraved illustrations, and, most dramatically, in his landscape designs.

Beckford never elaborated any technical theory of the picturesque, but it is clear from his writings that he understood the doctrines espoused by the picturesque theorists. He often spoke of himself as a man with 'a picturesque eye', and, like William Gilpin and Uvedale Price, he believed that certain objects had intrinsic qualities which made them picturesque. 'The situation is striking and picturesque,' he wrote in Verona, 'a long line of battlement-walls, flanked by venerable towers, mounts the hill in a grand, irregular sweep, and incloses many a woody garden, and grove of slender cypress.'[25] He described exposed tree-roots as 'picturesquely fantastic'.[26] Old, gnarled trees, ruined fountains, mutilated statues 'variegated by the lapse of years with innumerable tints of purple, green and yellow' were 'picturesque beauties'.[27] In his little-known satire *Modern Novel Writing* (1796) he portrayed Lord Mahogany's seat as essentially picturesque, utilizing a lengthy passage from his half-sister Elizabeth Hervey's novel *Melissa and Marcia; or the Sisters* (1788) to provide the descriptive details. From the beginning of this description, Beckford employed Hervey's exact words but where she identified 'Brown' as the improver of the estate in her book, he substituted the name of Brown's adversary – Richard Payne Knight – in his work. 'In the distribution of grounds,' Beckford wrote, ' the hand of KNIGHT had assisted but not forced nature; each masterly stroke of his art had only served to bring to light beauties that lay concealed before.'[28] The substitution of 'KNIGHT' in full capital letters could have been done in recognition that the park Hervey described (essentially based upon scenes around the Fonthill Splendens estate) as 'beautifully irregular; wild and diversified' was more in accord with Knight's taste than Brown's:

> A gradual descent carried you from the house, through a winding path irregularly planted with firs and forest trees, skirted with laurels and flowering shrubs. Here and there the eye caught thorns in all the pride of blossom; their reign of beauty is but short, yet they stood alone on distinguished spots and wreathed their trunks into many fantastic shapes.
>
> The purple lilac in lovely clusters, and the unsullied white, vied with the Portugal laurel, and gelder rose, in beauty. Here festoons of libernum, and there the elegant acacia pleased the eye, while the air was perfumed with the united fragrance of sweet-briar and violets... .
>
> In wandering thus through a labyrinth of sweets, sometimes you caught a view of the adjacent country, and saw the water glitter through the trees; but often the closing branches confined the eye to the delightful spot around. As you advanced, the shrubs gave way entirely to forest trees – majestic oaks, elms, chestnuts, and beeches formed into a spacious grove. At first their tall straight stems appeared like columns set at convenient distances from each other; by degrees they pressed together; their bright tints disappeared; the deep recesses of the grove were darkened with the solemn gloom of cedars, and mournful cypresses, now quite impervious to the rays of the sun [II, 66–8].[29]

Beckford could also have been using this opportunity to allude to the controversy between the Brown-Repton school of landscape practice and the adherents of the picturesque led by Knight and Price. Only two years before the publication of *Modern Novel Writing*, Knight launched a strong invective against Brown's 'levelling' and 'clumping' in his poem *The Landscape* (1794).

Beckford returned to this subject in his next satire, *Azemia*, published in 1797. Here he described the simplicity and utility of the grounds surrounding a vicar's country seat in opposition to the more dominant taste in the 1790s for the picturesque landscape:

> There are neither rising grounds nor hedge rows to relieve the wearisome uniformity of common fields on one side; on the other the eye turns with disgust from a dreary moor, intersected by sluggish streams, and apparently the abode only of the otter and the heron; discouraging as these appearances are, the general character of the country is that of fertility. It would have suited the taste of Dr. Johnson; but the poet, the painter, or the enthusiast in picturesque beauty, would undoubtedly travel through it as fast as they could.[30]

It is not surprising, then, that when Beckford set about engaging in the practical activities that he followed the principles of picturesque design – not in any strict academic sense but as a concomitant quality of his own individual style. His early travels, his training with Cozens, his knowledge of painting, his predilection for painting landscapes in prose, and a writing style with a strong visual accent – all helped to shape his taste for a landscaping style that would culminate in the creation of a dramatic landscape composition on his own property at Fonthill. At the age of twenty-one, when he assumed proprietorship of Fonthill, he had a sophisticated grasp of the important visual principles of separation, selection, and composition, possessed a strong feeling for colour and contrast, and understood how all of these elements could be carried into practice working with the canvas of the living landscape.

3
Beckford's Early Landscape Experiments

The vast estate of which Beckford became proprietor when he reached his majority in 1781, together with his own purchases of surrounding land, comprised an area of almost 6,000 acres. On its long side, the ground stretched from the village of Fonthill Bishop southwest along the downs as far as Knoyle Corner, where it turned southeast and proceeded to Castle Town. From there it moved in an irregular north-easterly direction to unite again with Fonthill Bishop. On the western side of the boundary lay the original estate, the mile-long river, and the family mansion, called Fonthill Splendens (fig. 4). The major approach to Splendens was by way of a public road which passed through the grounds from Fonthill Bishop on the way to Semley. Following this route, the visitor first came upon the grand stone gateway (fig. 5), said to be modelled after a seventeenth-century design by Inigo Jones and constructed by an unidentified architect in the mideighteenth century on the orders of Alderman Beckford. From this point one could see the 400-foot façade of Fonthill Splenden, nestled to the left of a hill which led to higher ground and to the scene of Beckford's later endeavours.

The mansion, constructed in the Palladian style, consisted of a main body with a classical portico, resembling Houghton Hall in Norfolk, flanked by two elliptical colonnades with square pavilions at each end. It was situated near a river, at a right angle to it, facing south. The river, crossed by a very large stone bridge with five arches, passed the east wing in a slight curve before losing itself in the distant woods. There was also a vaulted boathouse contemporary with the entrance gateway at the north end of the park. A large stone quarry, which provided some of the materials for the construction of the mansion, lay partially concealed by trees and shrubs on the eastern shore of its banks. For almost twelve years Beckford restricted his landscaping activities to this comparatively small family estate called Old Park.

It is not well known that Beckford engaged in landscaping activities on his father's estate. Boyd Alexander, for example, believed that Beckford's gardening activities at Fonthill began in 1793 with the construction of a barrier wall which enclosed the Abbey estate and that his contributions to landscape features were confined to this area.[1] But there is documentation to show that Beckford was heavily involved in planting activities before he turned his attention to the Abbey and its surrounding grounds. In a letter he wrote on 9 March 1787, revealing the extent to which he paid attention to such matters, he directed his agent to enhance the conservatory at Splendens in support of planned improvements by securing plants at an forthcoming auction of the collection of Princess Amelia, the daughter of George II: 'Let me enjoin you, as you love Fonthill & believe in the excellence of its conservatory, to buy fifty or a hundred pounds worth of the grandest orange, oleander & myrtle trees.'[2]

Furthermore, an important article entitled 'Account of the Works Now Executing at Fonthill', published in February 1797 by the editor of *The European Magazine and London Review*, reveals that Beckford had been actively engaged in making improvements on his father's estate 'from the time he attained majority in 1781'.[3] This report was actually a follow-up to a previous account of Christmas festivities at Fonthill, published in January 1797 by an unidentified 'correspondent' who was present at the affair. This correspondent was obviously an insider, possibly John Lettice, whom the editor considered to be an authoritative source of information about Beckford's activities. At the end of the correspondent's piece, the editor inserted the following paragraph announcing his forthcoming account 'through the same channel by which we have procured the above account':

As some interesting circumstances relative to Fonthill, and the works which have been carrying on there for these last sixteen years, are little known to the public, much the finest parts of the place being never shewn but to Mr. Beckford's particular friends, and the primary motives of these great projects being little understood, we hope to be able, in our next, to gratify our readers, through the same channel by which we have procured the above account, with a communication of some particulars, which will, perhaps, be thought more valuable, as they are of a less temporary nature than those we have now presented.[4]

In the next issue, the editor began by indicating that the 'following details will, as their authenticity may be depended upon, not appear unworthy of attention, nor ill calculated to gratify that curiosity which is still much alive on the subject of Fonthill.' The importance of this account lies in the fact that it documents some of the significant improvements Beckford made on his father's estate prior to his later efforts on the Fonthill Abbey grounds.

It is clear from the information available that Fonthill Splendens was never developed as a unified composition of house and grounds. While the mansion was a magnificent piece of architecture, strikingly displayed against a background of dark hills and rising forests, the surrounding grounds in conjunction with the building did not form a well-harmonized composition. There were several reasons for this incongruity. John Rutter, in his study of Fonthill, noted that the grounds were not 'constructed upon one pervading principle of art; but have in many parts a wild and uncultivated character, and derive their attraction from the beauty of their situation, rather than from the taste of their embellishment.'[5] William Gilpin, on one of his picturesque tours, expressed displeasure with the 'sumptuous bridge' that crossed the river. 'If the bridge had been more simple,' he observed, 'the scene about it would have been more pleasing.'[6] Another problem was the intrusive public road which passed in front of and close to the residence itself. Adjacent to the road was a river, looking more like a canal from the engraved views of the period. Rutter also reported that the view was 'circumscribed in its limits, and though beautiful, extremely monotonous in character'.[7] Then there was the matter of the white stone quarry, near the shoreline, which was used in the construction of Fonthill Splendens. Several acres had been left open upon completion of the mansion, leaving 'large naked masses of white stone and ugly excavations'.[8] Earth was brought in to fill in the excavations and cover the exposed stones. Trees and shrubs were also planted to mask this unsightly area. However, this area, the imposing stone bridge, public road and the serpentine river failed to blend with the stately simplicity of the Palladian mansion. Based on the record provided in *The European Magazine and London Review* and some other contemporary accounts, it is evident that Beckford attempted to correct some of the glaring faults of this situation after he assumed proprietorship, and his experiments during this time provide an interesting prologue to his later work on the Abbey estate.

One of the first changes Beckford made was to fill in some of the barren, unplanted areas throughout Old Park with trees, exotic plants, and shrubs to avoid the monotonous effect of the flat, rolling style of landscape that Capability Brown had made so popular. This effort continued every year after 1781 on a grand scale in conjunction with other improvements. Some years he planted as many as 'several hundred thousand trees'; other years he planted 'not less than a million'. [9] He removed the bridge that Gilpin had found so unsightly around 1781, [10] and thereafter ordered a partial damming of the river to enlarge it into a lake. The result was a larger, deeper body of water which greatly enhanced the beauty of the place. All of these changes constituted an effort to 'harmonize Fonthill', as he explained to Sir William Hamilton in 1796. [11] Even after 1797 Beckford was still planning to enlarge the lake further and to vary its form. [12] Years later, after the completion of the Fonthill Abbey estate, *The Times* reported that 'there is nothing at all about the grounds of the Abbey to compare with the broad lake which flows in front of the old mansion'. [13]

An undated landscape design by James Wyatt among the Beckford Papers reveals a more ambitious plan for Old Park than has been hitherto known. [14] This drawing shows an attempt to eliminate the public entry from the grand stone gateway through the property and to create an alternate route east of the existing road on the opposite side of the lake with the new road proceeding south and then crossing the water over a new iron bridge, whereupon it would run directly past Splendens and reconnect with the original public road (fig. 6). The elimination of a great part of the public road would not only create more privacy in the park but would also provide the opportunity for a more unified natural design in relationship to Splendens. Included in this configuration was an approach to the house from the bridge that Wyatt sketched 'in case the present road ... cannot be made private'. Other new features included a cascade on the western side of the lake and a series of small islands in the lake, one of which was identified as a 'Stew for Fish in the middle of a large island', a holding place for keeping fish fresh for the table. Wyatt also provided sketches for additional plantations and described the eastern side of the lake as a 'Marsh Common'. Another less detailed landscape sketch by Wyatt in the Beckford Collection at the Beinecke Library at Yale shows a three-arched stone bridge crossing a body of water with two roads, one to the house and the other to rejoin the public road. [15] On the back of the Yale drawing is a note to Wyatt from Beckford and Beckford's London address as '12 Wimpole

Street'. Since Beckford moved to Portman Square from Wimpole Street sometime during the spring of 1782, these drawings were very likely made in 1781 as possible replacement designs for the original bridge that was removed in the same year. This appears to be corroborated by John Britton who, in 1801, referred to a 'plan drawn by Mr. Wyatt' involving a 'fishing seat'.[16] Neither of these designs was ever carried out, but they underscore the extent of Beckford's interest in landscaping his father's estate. His failure to obtain the privacy he sought in Old Park may have been a factor in his decision in the end to construct another residence more removed from the eye of the public.

Looking at the lake more closely, it is evident that Beckford was committed to naturalistic effects in the way he insisted on heavy planting all the way down to the edges of the lake to avoid the hard line between water and land. When Britton first saw it, he pronounced it a superior achievement in the beauty of irregular design: 'The lake, which always produces the most brilliant and captivating effect in a landscape, is here a beauty of the superior order. Free from the formality of straight outline, its banks are thickly wooded, and its head concealed by clustered islands.'[17] While there is no record of the actual dates of initiation and completion of this particular project, Beckford seems to have made an allusion to it in two letters to Samuel Henley in May and July 1784, encouraging him to come to Fonthill to view the results of recent work. In the first he wrote: 'If you are to visit D[evon] this summer I trust you will not pass by Fonthill without casting an eye upon my rocks and water, which is wonderfully expanded.' And in July he followed up with a similar reference: 'I should not have let your last kind letter have remained so long unanswered had I not been engaged with packing up & preparations for Fonthill, where I now am amidst hay & roses perfectly tranquil and solitary. If you could stretch your excursion as far as Fonthill you would greatly oblige me, & we should enjoy my new creation of wood and water.'[18] While Henley is known as the individual who translated *Vathek* into English for its first publication in 1786, he was also a student of picturesque design and would have been keenly interested in Beckford's creation. He was sufficiently sophisticated in this area to have conducted a correspondence on the fine points of the principles of the picturesque with William Gilpin in the late 1760s, following the appearance of *The Essay on Prints* in 1768.[19]

Further indication of Beckford's gardening interests in Old Park was

6 Landscape Plan for Old Park, c. 1781. Drawn by James Wyatt.

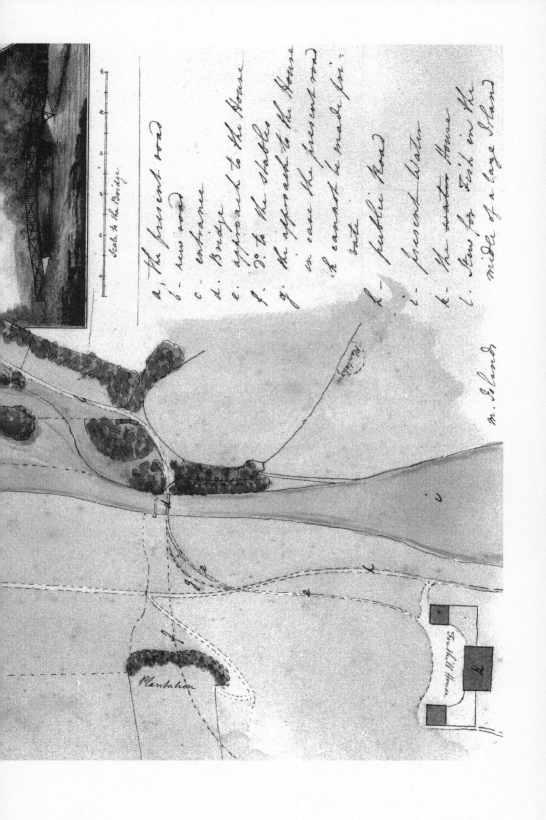

Scale to the Bridge.

a, the present road
b — new road
c — entrance
d — Bridge
e — approach to the House
f — Do. to the stables
g — the approach to the House
m — case the present road
— it cannot be made pri-
vate
h — public Road
i — present Water
k — the water House
l — stew for Fish in the
middle of a large Island

Plantation

m Islands

Scotch House

the creation of a new kitchen and flower garden in a protected area north-east of the house 'upon a scale four times larger than the old one'. As the editor of *The European Magazine and London Review* wrote: 'The Hot Walls, Pineries, Conservatories, quantity of glazed Frame-work, the Gardener's House, importation of soil for this extensive spot of many acres, with its plantations and nurseries, and an extensive inclosure of handsome brick-wall round the whole, have altogether concurred to render this work almost as unrivalled in magnitude and convenience, as it must have been in matter of expence.'[20]

Beckford's taste for picturesque effects in landscaping was also evident at this time in the type of improvements he advocated for the quarry scene on the eastern shore of the lake. Beckford's father had taken steps to conceal the exposed stones and excavation marks with soil and plantings of beech, larch, and fir and even allowed some of the rough-hewn pieces to show through the foliage to improve the scene.[21] According to *The European Magazine and London Review* article, Beckford capitalized on this situation by considerably extending this plantation 'along the adjoining hills which hang over the Lake'. By 1797 the quarry area, with the wood having attained a considerable growth, produced a scene that in 'point of beauty and original effect' would 'challenge any garden scenery in the kingdom'. [22] He also insisted, as in the case of the shoreline, that the edges of any walkways that were added in this area should be broken with flowers and shrubs so as to eliminate any signs of regular lines. In these cases the improve-ment was always dictated by Beckford's own sense of design and taste. How successful he was can be measured by Britton's comments in his description of this part of the Fonthill estate in 1801. He found the 'many bold inequalities' of this particular part of the estate captivating to the eye:

Mr. Beckford, in a very early stage of his minority, discovered that feeling for the picturesque, for which he is so much celebrated, and caused this ground to be planted with every sort of forest wood; adventitious soil was brought in, where natural earth was wanting. This plantation having wonderfully succeeded, and after some years attained a most luxuriant growth, walks and scenes of lawn, rocks, etc. were opened in several parts, where the nature of the place suggested that improvement. These first walks, and consequently the more open parts, were made of sufficient width to admit of borders of flowers and exotic shrubs, so adapted to each season as to delight the spectator with their successive bloom and fragrance through eight or nine months in the year.[23]

These grounds became known as the 'Alpine Garden' in 1796, when new walkways were added and additional planting executed under the supervision of John Lettice.[24] This work was carried out, according to Britton's account, for the purpose of procuring the pleasing effects of successive contrasts 'between the lowest, the intermediate and the highest ground'. Openings were made to emphasize particular views of the estate and the whole was so managed 'as to present to the moving spectator a continual variety of scenes, each marked with a different, and generally some striking character', and all designed to inspire particular sentiments or emotions in accordance with the new aesthetics of the romantic landscape garden.[25]

The idea of developing the Alpine Garden in the 'savage manner' could have been influenced by Beckford's maternal great-uncle, Charles Hamilton. Hamilton was considered one of the great landscape gardeners of the century. His garden at Painshill was considered a masterpiece of 'savage gardening', which Horace Walpole characterized as that 'kind of alpine scene composed almost wholly of pines and firs, a few birch, and such trees as assimilate with a savage and mountainous country'.[26] During a tour of England in 1779, Beckford visited Hamilton who was then living in Bath and at the age of eighty still busy with landscaping ten acres of land there. Redding noted later that the sight of Hamilton's landscaping accomplishments 'strengthened that love of rural economy and gardening which was afterwards so marked a trait in Mr. Beckford's history'.[27] It is not known whether Beckford ever saw Painshill, but it is not without significance that he hired Josiah Lane, a native of Tisbury, to construct a romantic grotto on his own estate in imitation of the one his father, Joseph Lane, had made at Painshill.[28]

Lane appears to have been at work on the lakeside grotto project as early as the fall of 1784, as is evident from a letter Beckford wrote to Henley in October: 'Mr. Lane is rockifying, not on the high places, but in a snug copse by the river side, where I spend many an hour.'[29] The finished work, on the eastern shore of the lake in the area of the Alpine Garden, was called 'one of the most striking beauties upon the old part of the demesne', and described years later in *The Times*:

Lying against, or rather cut into, the belly of the hill, it consists of two divisions, the one above the other. In the upper department, amidst a labyrinth of small caves and passages, a rude basin of rock, surrounded by crags, and overhung with lofty trees, receives the drizzlings of a tiny stream, called the 'Petrifying Spring'; the range of cave below is divided into three arched chambers; and, from the centre vaults of these there is an opening to the lake, which flows up a miniature creek, half way into the apartment. There is something, in fine weather, very delightful about the place. The vaulted roof of this last centre cavern we mentioned runs low towards the front that opens upon the water, so that the stranger's prospect (standing erect) scarcely reaches across the lake; the basis or little creek in the mouth of the apartment is as clear to the bottom as a Fonthill vase of crystal; and the trout which lie concealed among the roots about its margin shoot away with the speed of lightning at the approach of a human figure.[30]

In his description of Fonthill in 1801, Britton observed that the grotto, 'a work of the well known Lane', was 'ornamented within by grotesque petrifactions, stalactites, madrepores, &c. aquatic plants and flowers shooting from the crevices. Its large interior space resounds with perennial springs trickling from various parts, and through channels here visible, and there unseen, hurrying along till lost in the waters of the lake'.[31]

A remarkably close description of this grotto appeared in Elizabeth Hervey's *Melissa and Marcia*, which Beckford incorporated in *Modern Novel Writing* as one of the features of Lord Mahogany's country estate:

The paths became more numerous and intricate, till they brought you to some irregular steps cut in a rock; the light insensibly stole upon you as you descended; and at the foot of the steps you found the entrance of a spacious cave. All here was hushed and silent, save that the trickling drops of a purling rill struck your ear, while it softly bent its way toward the parent stream. A broken arch opened to your view the broad clear expanse of the lake, covered with numerous aquatic fowl, and weeping willows adorning its banks.

Round this cave no gaudy flowers were ever permitted to bloom; this spot was sacred to pale lilies and violets. An outlet, at first scarcely perceived in the cave, carried you through a winding passage to an immense amphitheatre, formed by a multitude of irregular rocks; some bold and abrupt, others covered with ivy, periwinkles, and wall-flowers. One of these grottos was destined for a bath, and ornamented with branches of coral, brilliant spars, and curious shells. A lucid spring filled a marble bason in the centre, and then losing itself for a moment under ground, came dashing and sparkling forth at the extremity of the cave, and took its course over some shining pebbles to the lake below [II, 68–70].

Beckford also engaged Lane to construct another series of caves on higher ground above the lakeside grotto on the same side of the lake. While it is difficult to provide a precise date for when this work began, Beckford referred to this activity in a letter to James Wildman of 5 August 1790 in which he wrote: 'My works at Fonthill, buildings, planting etc. are going on very briskly. I have been raising towers and digging Grottoes.'[32] In addition, there is a tablet carved in the stone of one of these caves that displays the inscription ' J. L. 1794', which Lane may have placed there himself.[33] We also know that the grotto existed by this time since Henri Meister, a French visitor to Fonthill in 1793, while describing his walk along the banks of the lake, referred to a temple dedicated to Hercules 'built on a small eminence almost disjoined from the other hills'.[34] Meister's description derived from the existence of a large statue of Hercules inside the grotto. The broken remains of a muscular statue can still be seen there.

While evidence exists that Beckford directed the development of grottoes on the east bank of the lake, the artificial constructions of a hermitage and a tunnel under the public road on the west side cannot as yet be attributed to his design. The hermitage itself was originally constructed as an evocative feature along the lakeside in the style of mid-eighteenth-century gardens and consisted of a dark cave with two openings. The cave in its early stage was occupied by a statue of a hermit, presumably in lieu of hiring a hermit as Charles Hamilton had done at Painshill.[35] Not far from the hermitage were the remains of a monolith which Rutter identified as a 'Cromlech'.[36] Nearby also was a grotto-like tunnel underneath the public road to Semley which may have been the work of Josiah's father, Joseph. Rutter described it as 'hewn in the rock' formed with great boldness of 'very considerable dimensions, and possessing all that gloom and mystery' that gave it the character of 'romantic magnificence'.[37] While these features were in accord with Beckford's taste, there is nothing to preclude the possibility that they were done after Alderman Beckford had ordered the construction of a vaulted boathouse at the northern end of the lake. In other words, they could have been designed as elements of the picturesque scenery to be indulged during a boat ride to a landing site created on the east side directly across from the hermitage.

It is significant of Beckford's interest in landscape gardening that he also carried out extensive landscaping activities during his year of residency at Monserrate, beginning the summer of 1794. Much of his work there served as preliminary design work that he then carried over to Fonthill. In his recent study, *The English Garden Abroad*, Charles Quest-Ritson notes that Monserrate played an important role in the history of English gardening primarily because Beckford conducted landscape improvements there.[38] Quest-Ritson points out that Beckford rebuilt a chapel that was destroyed in the earthquake of 1755 in the shape of a ruin and moved it to a visibly prominent location as an evocative feature that dominated the view of the forest from the house. It is significant that the creation of this ruin was done during the same period of time when Beckford was contemplating constructing a similar feature at Fonthill. José Cornélio da Silva and Gerald Luckhurst also attribute the construction of a cromlech at Monserrate and a circle of stones to Beckford, noting that the latter feature was recorded by Thomas Cargill in 1870:

> Above the Poet's stone, a winding way
> Few paces thence removed doth pleasant veer,
> Leading the pilgrim to a circle grey
> Of ancient stones... .
>
> Memorial this of Vateck's taste and love
> For Beauty wheresoever her devious steps may rove.[39]

Cargill also attributed to Beckford a dramatic element in the landscape scene, consisting of a large arch constructed of massive boulders set in a romantic bower covered by laurel, identifying it as 'Vateck's Rocky Bouldered Arch', a feature which still exists today:

> This choicest spot doth end, I ween,
> In a deep-sheltered cool retreat,
> Shadowed all oe'er by Laurels green,

> Here Vatek sat, and did he use,
> Oft in the sultry noon to muse
> In this fastidious bower y-wove
> Of circling rock, and leafy grove,
> His own creation: mortals now
> Spread oft their rural banquets here
> And pour libations free their vow
> To Bacchus, and to Ceres, cheer
> Grateful in summer's thirst! Oh! Green
> Retreat, all laurel-canopied
> Sun-shielded, charmed circle wide,
> To mirth devote![40]

Beckford's most important improvement, however, was the 'rock cascade where a stream bursts out over a great cataract and then races down a dark ravine, breaking and turning over boulders in a succession of different movements',[41] reminiscent of Charles Hamilton's cascade at Bowood that Josiah Lane was involved in creating. Beckford's extensive landscaping work at Monserrate has not been well known, but his development of the estate provides additional confirmation of his commitment to what has become known as the English or natural style of gardening which he would bring to fruition at Fonthill.

These, then, were the landscape experiments Beckford carried out on his father's estate and at Monserrate prior to the development of a more grandiose scheme on the Fonthill Abbey estate. As a prologue to his later work, these early activities are significant because they exhibit the same taste for irregular beauty and concern for topography, the same love of contrast and sense of composition, and the taste for evocative elements that were to become the hallmarks of the new Fonthill.

4

The Design and Development of the New Fonthill

The idea of designing a landscape garden that would bear the stamp of his own imagination and one that would be constructed as a work of art separate and distinct from Old Fonthill did not receive Beckford's earnest consideration until the early 1790s. It began in rudimentary form with a proposed building project, the erection of a solitary tower on the summit of the highest hill on the estate, called Stop's Beacon, in an area west of Splendens. The triangular foundation had been laid already by his father after the design of Alfred Tower at Stourhead, and Beckford felt that he should complete what had been started.[1] The earliest reference to this project appears in a letter he wrote to Lady Craven in January 1790. Here he explains that an unexpected windfall from one of his Jamaican estates would be put to this use. 'I am growing rich,' he wrote, 'and mean to build Towers and sing hymns to the powers of Heaven on their summits.'[2] Shortly thereafter he called upon James Wyatt, who had achieved some acclaim for his work in the neo-Gothic style at Lee Priory in Kent and the restoration of a number of Gothic cathedrals in England, to provide him with some possible designs by the summer of 1791. Wyatt, who had a reputation for being dilatory, neglected to give this task his proper attention and the delay frustrated Beckford, forcing him to follow up with a letter to Wyatt in October just before a planned trip on the Continent.

Dear Sir, I have been waiting for you the *whole* summer: if my plans would allow me to wait the *whole* winter also, I might perhaps still afford a month or two's patience; but in a fortnight I have agreed to move, and therefore, should you still retain any idea of coming again to Fonthill, let me beg and intreat you to give me an opportunity *within the ten days of the present date* of assuring you that, notwithstanding the disappointment it has been your pleasure to afflict me with, I am ever, dear Sir, your faithful and obedient Servant, William Beckford.[3]

It appears that Wyatt did not respond in time, and Beckford left on his trip in November and remained abroad until May 1793. It was during this period, however, that Beckford began to conceive of a work on a larger scale of which a tower would be a part.

The new scheme was marked upon his return by ordering the construction of a seven-mile wall, twelve feet high, to enclose 519 acres of the area surrounding Stop's Beacon, which provided the outlying acorn-shape form of the new estate (fig. 7). It was built of 'hewn stone', gathered from the area, and 'finished with a strong painted paling, inclined outwards, as a *chevaux de frize*'.[4] He told Cyrus Redding that building the wall was prompted by the number of hunters he found trespassing on his land in the summer of 1793. But he also explained to Lady Craven shortly after the wall was completed a year and a half later, that he planned to spend some time in his new enclosure. 'In process of time,' he explained, 'when my Hills are completely blackened with Fir, I shall retreat into the center of this gloomy circle like a spider into the midst of his web. There will I build my tower and deposit my books and my writings and brood over them till it please Heaven to ... open the doors of a pleasanter existence.'[5]

After contracting to have the wall constructed, Beckford left for a trip to Lisbon in November 1793. A month later he displayed his own talent for architectural design by outlining a plan for a house in Lisbon that contained many of the features of the future Fonthill Abbey (fig. 8). The drawing, dated 28 December 1793, showed an uninterrupted vista through a series of rooms, a central octagon, a sanctuary devoted to St Anthony of Padua, and even a fountain court outside the building.[6] He sent the Lisbon plan to Wyatt in April 1794 for his advice, explaining that 'my appetite for humouring St. Anthony ... is still so keen that I cannot live without a little tid-bit of a sanctuary'. He then went on to explain what he was planning for the Lisbon house:

> I want a new oratory, a sort of tabernacle with curtains and lamps and two candelabra and 6 altar candlesticks. All these holy implements may be made in Portugal at a very trifling expense – the lamps of bronze with the candelabra of wood – provided you will settle the proportion and design. As I have some beautiful straw-coloured silk ready, I have thought of hanging round the whole

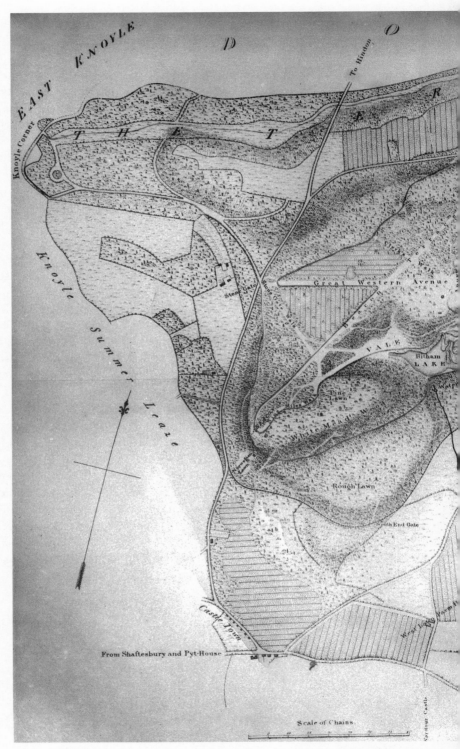

7 Map of Fonthill. From Rutter, *Delineations of Fonthill and Its Abbey*, 1823.

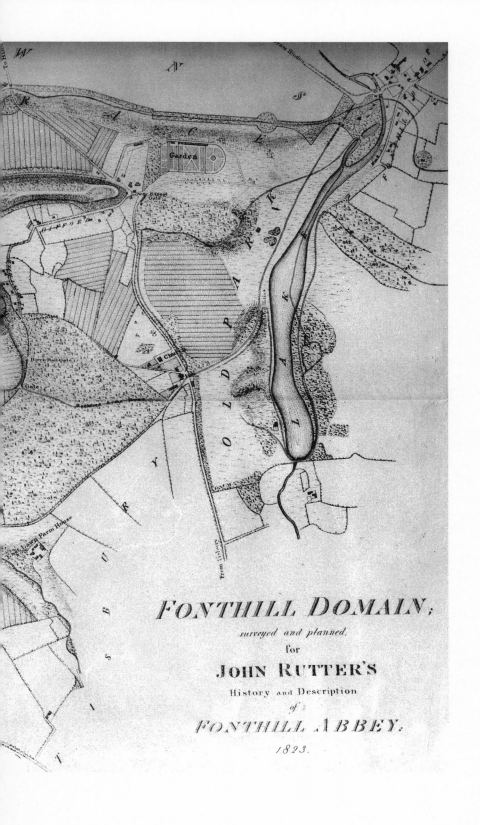

FONTHILL DOMAIN;

surveyed and planned,

for

JOHN RUTTER'S

History and Description

of

FONTHILL ABBEY.

1823.

room with curtains of these materials. The recess, I rather think, should be of another colour, perhaps lilac; but upon this also I beg your advice.[7]

At this stage these features were restricted to the planned Lisbon house, but it was only a matter of time before they would become essential elements in the designs being crafted by Wyatt at home for Fonthill.

While the record of Wyatt's efforts to put Beckford's ideas down on paper is sketchy, it is clear from the same letter that another project was in the works and that Beckford had already received from the architect a 'magnificent plan' for a 'chapel upon Stop's Beacon', which he hoped Providence and his financial situation would allow him to carry into execution.[8] No additional description of the new structure is provided. However, Beckford ended the letter by saying that 'we may still live to erect the buildings both grecian and gothic you designed for Fonthill.'[9] John Rutter, in his own description of the origin of Fonthill Abbey in 1823, described this chapel, in perhaps a slightly more advanced stage, as a 'convent' which would be a striking decorative feature in a garden scene made picturesque by being partly in ruin (fig. 9). It was to contain a suite of rooms large enough to make possible 'the enjoyment of a day, whether of sunshine or of shower'. According to Rutter, the final drawing showed the 'chapel, the parlour, the dormitory, and one small cloister alone' as having survived the ravages of time, while the 'refectory, the kitchen, and every other part of the edifice' were buried in 'one common ruin'.[10] Beckford felt it was a 'magnificent plan' but it was never carried into execution; instead it served as the germinal design, melded with the plans for the Lisbon house, for a larger structure, the future Fonthill Abbey, to be built on the ridge north-east of Stop's Beacon, called Hinkley Hill.

In the meantime the construction of a separate tower on Stop's Beacon remained a viable element in the design as late as February 1797.[11] Joseph Farington provided a sketch of it in July 1796, based on his conversation with Wyatt. The drawing, at that time, showed a tower that was 75 feet square at its base and elevating in three stories to a height of 175 feet.[12] There was a living storey on the second level containing dressing rooms, bedchambers, and a gallery. The upper storey was to be a single room lighted by a lanthorn at the top. Farington went on to explain that Beckford directed that he be buried 'at the top of the lanthorn'. A slightly different description of the tower appeared in *The Gentleman's Magazine* in September 1796:

> William Beckford, Esq., of Fonthill, is collecting the materials for a building of wonderful grandeur and utility. It is to consist of a tower to be erected on Stops' Beacon, near Fonthill, the loftiest scite in the neighbourhood; it is to have a square of 80 feet clear, within the walls, at the base, and to be 280 feet high, with a lantern at the top, so that it will command a view of near 80 miles every way, and the lantern to be seen by night at a greater distance. It is to be furnished as an observatory, and, notwithstanding its immense height, is to be so constructed as that a coach & six may be driven with ease and safety from the base to the top, and down again. This stupendous work will probably employ hundreds of the neighbouring poor for near ten years.[13]

It is difficult to determine precisely when the plan of the 'convent' became the plan of the Abbey with the separate tower scheme merging with a larger conventual structure, but Britton believed that a foundation was laid in the fall of 1795. While this is possible, it could not have represented at that point in time the final design of the building since Wyatt continued to make modifications at Beckford's behest. We do know that building and planting projects began to accelerate following his return to England in June 1796. In a letter of 5 October 1796 he noted that the 'Convent advances'[14] and seven days later wrote: 'Wyatt has been doing wonders according to custom, and he has given the great Hall another push 20 feet or so; we shall reach Knoyle before we have done. You will see Wyatt and converse with him upon all subjects, and arrange by all means some plan of getting forwards with the Convent more rapidly. The windows should be put into the painters hands without delay.'[15] The 'great Hall' was the western wing of the building which Beckford originally conceived of as a dining hall or refectory. In November he wrote to his mother that 'I have extended the front of the Abbey in the Woods from the dimensions you saw us working upon, to near two hundred feet, and a good part of the building has already reached the first floor.'[16] He also added that he was attending to the grounds:

> The Conservatory and flower Garden, which are to surround it, are begun. My Walk, which you will recollect is, according to the

Plan, to be carried out considerably more than twenty Miles thro' and round the Woods (to which I have just made an addition of ground by the completion of a new purchase) has already proceeded to nearly the length of nine Miles. The Season proves admirable for my planting, and, if it continues as open till Christmas, I think Vincent will by that time, with all the hands allowed, have got above a million of Trees into the Ground for this Year's work.

By February 1797, furthermore, work had proceeded rapidly enough for Beckford to report that the 'pleasure building in the shape of an abbey' was '*already half finished*'. 'It contains appartments', he added, 'in the most gorgeous Gothic style with windows of painted glass, a chapel for blessed St. Anthony – 66 ft. diameter & 72 high – a gallery 185 in length, & a tower 145 feet high.'[17] These dimensions correspond to the report in *The European Magazine* with the chapel of St Anthony being located in the unfinished octagon room.[18] Rutter recorded that during the winter of 1796–7 Wyatt was completing a series of designs 'comprising the grand octagon of the present structure, and the whole of the buildings to the south and west of it' that represented the basic form of the structure minus the north and east wings, or as they became known in time, King Edward's Gallery and the Eastern Transept. Rutter wrote about these early architectural plans in 1823 that the 'style and archetype' of the original plan was built upon but never lost sight of in the various and progressive additions.

The general arrangement of the plan in these designs is therefore nearly the same as we now find it in the Abbey, though a few of the apartments may have changed their destination, and some others their names. The Western Yellow Drawing Room and Gothic Cabinet were then the chamber and dressing room of the proprietor; the Great Octagon was a chapel, and the Western Entrance a dining hall, having no communication with the Octagon, except that a tribune or gallery overlooked it, from whence it might be presumed the lectures were to be delivered, as was usual during meals in all monastic establishments.[19]

Some of the extant early designs of the Abbey tower, however, differ significantly from the final design.[20] One shows a squat tower and spire emanating from the centre of the structure. A pen and wash sketch by

Wyatt exhibiting this feature is currently in the collection of the Royal Institute of British Architects. There is also a watercolour perspective from the south-west by Turner in the Bolton Museum and Art Gallery (fig. 11). This work shows the same squat tower configuration and appears to be made from Wyatt's design modelled after the monastery of Batalha. Wyatt was familiar with the Batalha design even before 1795 and adapted it for the tower he constructed at Lee Priory in Kent in the 1780s. J. C. Murphy's book on the Batalha architectural designs was also published in 1795 and Beckford was one of the subscribers. It may well be, as has already been suggested, that the squat design was the first tower under construction for the Abbey and the version that Wyatt exhibited at the Royal Academy in the summer of 1797.[21] It appears that the taller tower came into play by the end of the summer of 1797. At that time Farington reports seeing 'designs for Beckfords Gothic building – which is now much enlarged', and then in November described the change as a spire 300 feet high.[22] What prompted the shift in design might have been a collapse of a part of the tower as it was under construction. Rutter reported that the first tower was run up too quickly before the base was sufficiently secure to support it. Consequently, one day in the winter of 1796–7, a strong wind caught a large flag which had been attached to a scaffold pole on the tower and the force of it brought this structure down.[23] When Beckford gave the orders to resume construction, he could have used this opportunity to expand the original design to incorporate a taller spire and rebuild the base.[24] The RIBA collection also includes a second-stage drawing, a west view, showing a higher octagonal tower and a spire rising from it.[25] This elevation appears to have served as the basis for the watercolour often attributed to Turner, now in the Yale Center for British Art, showing a view from the north-west with an elongated tower rising triumphantly from the octagon with a flight of stairs at the end of the northern wing projecting west (fig. 12). A contemporary label on the verso of the painting makes it clear that this is the composition that Wyatt exhibited at the Royal Academy in the summer of 1798, matching, as it does, the title of exhibit no. 955: 'North West view of a building / Erecting at Fonthill at Wiltshire / the Seat of Wm. Beckford Esq / in the Style of a Gothic Abbey / James Wyatt R.A.', which brings into question the Turner attribution.[26]

Wyatt also drew a third-stage sketch elevation, a north-west view, whose spire was even taller than the second-stage design and for the first time he included all four legs of the final cruciform plan. This latter design was likely the one Wyatt exhibited at the Royal Academy in 1799, entitled 'View of a building now erecting at Fonthill, in Wiltshire, the seat of William Beckford Esq. in the style of a Gothic abbey' (no. 1016).[27] Beckford liked this painting well enough to hang it on the wall of the Duchess of Hamilton's Chamber in the Abbey. It ultimately sold as lot 724 in the furniture segment of the Fonthill sale of 1823. While the catalogue described this lot in sparse terms as 'a fine drawing as originally planned for *Fonthill Abbey*', a report in the *Morning Chronicle* about the sale provided a detailed description which makes the identification possible.[28] This report described the drawing as a 'watercolour' by Wyatt. It then proceeded to consider the substantive differences between this design and the final one:

> The edifice, as it at present stands, is in some respects materially different from the original design, particularly in the eastern wing, where the two towers that terminate the Baron's Hall were intended to be balanced by two others of similar dimensions to the west. The northern wing is also different, as the Lancaster turret was designed to project, and to have an external flight of steps, which is not the case at present. There are several other minor discrepancies, but the principal distinction is, that in the drawing the great tower is surmounted by a lofty spire.

This description matches a design by Wyatt in the RIBA collection showing a an even taller tower than the second-stage design with a flight of stairs this time facing south (fig. 13). The *Morning Chronicle* description of the dimensions of this new design differ from Farington by defining the height of the spire itself as 124 feet and then describing 'the whole altitude from the ground' as 400 feet, 'or about 60 feet higher than St. Paul's Cathedral'. At this height the spire would have matched Salisbury Cathedral's altitude from the surface. There also exists in the Victoria and Albert Museum another watercolour rendering of the Abbey with a sky-kissing spire by the artist Charles Wild after Wyatt's third-stage design.[29]

The construction continued to advance in stages as ideas flowered in Beckford's mind. By November 1797 he considered for the first time the possibility of demolishing Splendens and transforming the Abbey into his home. As Farington recorded: 'Beckford yesterday told Wyatt that He had an intention of taking down *Fonthill House*, which is badly situated – and in that case enlarge the Gothic building now erecting to be His Mansion House.'³⁰ He began to think of his new home as a repository for his books, expensive furniture, and a place that could display great works of art, particularly by Englishmen, setting himself up to become a patron of the arts in the tradition of other wealthy landowners of his time. One of his first steps was to hire Joseph Nollekens, John Flaxman, J. C. F. Rossi and Richard Westmacott to carve four Gothic statues for the place. Before long Beckford provided commissions to Benjamin West, William Hamilton, Henry Tresham, Ozias Humphrey and Turner to contribute original works to the enter-prise. Farington noted this celebratory role for the Abbey in his diary entry of 16 November 1798:

> The Abbey to be endowed, & Cathedral Service to be performed in the most splendid manner that the Protestant religion will admit – A gallery leading from the top of the Church to be deco-rated with paintings by the works of English Artists. Beckfords *own tomb* to be placed at the end of this gallery, – as having been an encourager of Art.³¹

Farington seems to limit the encouragement of art to 'paintings' by English artists, but Beckford actually had a grander scheme in mind, one that would incorporate within the walls of his new structure many other forms of art that were not as appreciated by his contemporaries. In time the Abbey would become a repository for examples of art that tended to be devalued in favour of sculpture and painting, the tradi-tional higher forms of art. In other words, Beckford took a more liberal approach to the arts than was characteristic of other owners of great estates in his day by including outstanding examples of craftsmanship in furniture, china, glassware, carvings and other objects of virtu. Abbé Macquin touched upon this rationale for Fonthill as promoting a democratization of the arts in an essay published in the *Literary Gazette* in 1822. He emphasized that as a museum Fonthill Abbey provided an 'enlarged view' of the state of the fine arts from the fifteenth to the early part of the nineteenth centuries than had been traditionally the case:

> We here see how the talents of great Artists were often employed. In our times pictures and statues only are deemed deserving of the hand of Genius. A modern *Artist* would probably throw a teacup

or a nautilus-shell at his patron's head, or at least let them fall (in astonishment) and break at his feet, if he were asked to exercise his ingenuity in painting them: In fact, such productions have been degraded from their station; and the successors of the famous chasers, designers, carvers, embossers, of former times, have sunk into a mechanical class. Under such a change, it is not a little striking to contemplate the minute and painful labours of those worthies whose fortunes flourished and whose immortality was achieved on the handles of vases and the embellishments of tankards. A multitude of their most remarkable performances are comprised in the collection at Fonthill, and may be very advantageously studied as works of fertile invention, high fancy, rich taste, and extraordinary execution.[32]

Beckford himself provided an additional motive for the Fonthill project in a letter to his mother, dated 29 November 1796, in which he explained that he intended to realize a humanitarian goal as a major employer for the poor and the needy in the adjacent villages. 'I have the satisfaction', he wrote, 'of giving constant Employment to some hundreds of People in one way or another.' This use of his wealth, he believed, was more meaningful than to devote his time to 'bumpering port and Madeira with Country Squires, in running for the Sweepstakes at Salisbury Races, figuring at a Country Ball, or a Mayor's Feast'.[33]

Another rationale for Beckford's decision to choose a grander design for his Gothic abbey was identified in the *European Magazine* in February 1797. The editor explained that Beckford's father during the period of his ownership ordered the demolition of a medieval church, dedicated to St Nicholas, because it was located too close to the principal mansion. This church contained monuments to the Mervyn family, one of the original owners of the Fonthill estate and ancestors of the Beckfords. The Lord Mayor had a new church built – this one in a square, classical style with a domed cupola – further removed from his mansion at a more convenient site on the Hindon-Tisbury road. But the monuments in the original church, which were examples of expert sixteenth-century workmanship, became 'exposed to the open air' and 'neglected till their ornaments became mutilated and their inscriptions effaced'. The construction of Fonthill Abbey, then, would be an opportunity to redress a debt of the past while paying homage to his ancestors: 'Mr.

Beckford has designed his Gothic Abbey as a memorial tribute ... to this ancient family. Their Arms, in regular series, and with their different Quarterings, are to be painted on the windows of this edifice, and the names and dates of each successive member of the family inscribed on mural tablets, in the galleries and cloysters of the Abbey.'[34] To accomplish this task, Beckford hired Sir Isaac Heard, the Garter King at Arms, who was already busily engaged in January 1797 in preparing 'Armorial Sketches for the Windows etc.', but, as he wrote to Beckford, '[I] have not yet been able to complete the proofs of all the descents.'[35]

The new structure finally received its name as 'Fonthill Abbey' by July 1798.[36] The scope of the operating plan for the building at this point can be gleaned from the list of dimensions published in the 24 December 1798 issue of the *Salisbury & Winchester Journal*:

To the top of the great spire	450 feet
The Octagon tower	225 feet
The spires of the eight octagon towers	264 feet
The great Octagon within	120 feet
Ditto wide	66 feet
Choir	140 feet long
	56 feet high
	28 feet wide
Length of long gallery	308 feet
From the West Door to the end of the Choir	284 feet[37]

These dimensions correspond to Wyatt's third-stage design with the spire now being 50 feet higher than the 400 feet reported by the *Morning Chronicle*. The height of this spire would now reach beyond Salisbury Cathedral and St Peter's at Rome (at 437 feet). While making allowances for the reliability of a second-hand report, these dimensions do reflect the final cruciform design of the Abbey. The 'long gallery' of 308 feet approximates the final exact length of the north and south galleries combined. The mention of a 'Choir' is the first reference to the east wing, whose dimensions cited here in combination with the west wing came to within fourteen feet of the final measurement from the door of the west wing to the end of the east wing. The use of the word 'Choir' may explain why Farington wrote that the Abbey would be 'endowed, & Cathedral services to be performed in the most splendid manner that the Protestant religion will admit'.

It was on the second level, above the choir or chapel, that Beckford was planning a gallery to display the works of English artists, his own tomb, and the Revelation Chamber, containing paintings from the Apocalypse by Benjamin West. In a conversation with Wyatt in December 1798, Farington recorded additional details about this gallery:

> Wyatt told me that Mr. Beckfords Gallery which is to lead to the *Revelation Chamber*, in the Abbey now building, is to be 125 feet long and 12 feet wide. It is to be wainscotted with Ebony, and in compartments are to be Historical Pictures by English artists.... . Tresham is to paint four pictures for one of the Compartments. The largest of them 4 feet 3 Inches wide. – The Revelation Chamber is to have walls 5 feet thick in which are to be recesses to admit coffins. Beckfords Coffin is to be placed opposite to the door. The room is not to be entered by strangers, to be viewed through wire gratings. The floor is to be Jasper. This Gallery and room are to be over the Chapel. West is to paint all the pictures for this room, and is now limited to £1000 a year while he is proceeding with the pictures.[38]

We have suggested that the idea of a Revelation chamber was inspired by the mausoleum at Batalha, but it was also reinforced by Beckford's association with Benjamin West and the artist's taste for apocalyptic subject matter in his paintings. West was a prestigious figure at this time. He was not only President of the Royal Academy, but he had ready access to George III, who had appointed him as his history painter. West's interest in portraying dramatic scenes from the Bible in his 'Dread Manner' coincided with the sombre religious character of the Abbey, and Beckford was impressed by the first picture West did for him entitled *Michael Casteth out the Dragon and his Angels*, which was exhibited in the spring of 1797. What followed was a series of paintings depicting scenes from the *Book of Revelation*, three of which were done for Beckford in 1797, before any mention of a Revelation Chamber in the Abbey, suggesting the possibility that the room was set up to accommodate West's works.[39] West's paintings would set the right tone for a room where the body of Beckford as an encourager of the arts would be entombed and forever memorialised. Beckford ultimately abandoned such an elaborately oppressive scheme but reserved a small apartment for West's paintings which was called the Revelation Chamber. Eventually West did seventeen paintings for Beckford, including six works after scenes in the *Book of Revelation*.

Paintings displaying historical and religious subjects were in keeping with the character of a Gothic abbey and would dominate the rooms of the structure. In a letter to the bookseller Robert Bowyer on 5 July 1798, Beckford rejected an offer of two paintings by Jacques de Loutherbourg as too modern and not in keeping with character of the place. 'Subjects of a grave, religious Cast,' he explained, 'will in general best suit the solemnity of its character, & except for the Decoration of Windows and of certain Scenes of a peculiar Sort in the Abbey, modern Painting will not answer my views & I shall be obliged chiefly to turn my Researches toward the old School of Italy.'[40]

An important part of the interior of the Abbey were the stained glass windows. Beckford turned to highly skilled artists to accomplish this work. The first was James Pearson who had introduced an improvement in the colouring of painted glass and had done the east window of Salisbury Cathedral. Pearson, who often worked with his wife Margaret, was under consideration to copy some of West's works, but he was too expensive and seems to have been limited to one work by West, the painting entitled *St Thomas à Becket*.[41] However, the Revd James Dallaway, in an historical essay on stained glass in England published in 1817, in which he praised the work of Pearson and his wife, suggested that they made additional contributions to Fonthill, noting that 'they have been much employed for bordures and mosaics at Fonthill Abbey for Mr. Beckford, and usually selected subjects from the best Italian masters'[42] James Storer noted in 1812 that the armorial bearings of the Mervyn and Latimer families in the window of what became the Oak Library were 'beautifully executed by Pierson [*sic*]'.[43] In a letter to Isaac Heard on 3 July 1798, Beckford asked Heard to speak to Wyatt about ten shields 'intended for the great window to be painted by Pearson with the Effigies of our Lady, the Holy Virgin, St. John the Evangelist, St. Michael the Arch Angel, blessed St. William, blessed St. Nicholas & the glorious Martyr St. Thomas of Canterbury'.[44]

The rest of the glass in the Abbey was done by Francis Eginton and his son William Raphael Eginton.[45] Francis revived the art of glass painting in England in the 1780s and was hailed for his work in St George's Chapel, Windsor and for his contributions to a number of windows in Salisbury Cathedral. The article on him in the *Dictionary of National Biography* indicates that he did 32 windows at Fonthill for which Beckford paid him £12,000. Since most of the glass in the Abbey is gone, it is difficult to assess the accuracy of these figures. Among the Beckford Papers, however, is a copy of a bill from Eginton, dated 24 April 1799, indicating the total cost of the glass 'finished' as £954. 4s with a description of where the glass was located:

8 Windows for South Front	210	
6 Large Windows for the Great Hall	312	18
4 Coats Arms for the Windows that are alike in the Gallery	25	4
2 Coats of Arms for Windows over the Chimney	12	12
3 d[itt]o for what was called the Revelation Window	18	18
2 large Crests for d[itt]o, d[itt]o, d[itt]o	8	8
8 Large Figures for the great Window in the Library	210	
Rich Ornamental Window for the Slip	84	
Mr. Jordans Bill for small Frames for 6 of the Arms	3	3
Messrs. Keir [?] Co. for Iron Frames	63	4
Mr. Smiths d[itt]o for packing Cases	5	17[46]

It has also been pointed out that Beckford collected ancient glass which he also had incorporated into the windows of the Abbey.[47]

The most reliable information that exists on the design and the progress of the building by the end of 1799 can be found in the detailed sketchbooks of Turner, now in Tate Britain.[48] The sketchbooks contain various perspectives of the Abbey under construction and were made in preparation for a set of watercolours of the building in its setting commissioned by Beckford. Turner spent three weeks on the estate at the end of summer in 1799[49] and exhibited five finished watercolours at the Royal Academy in the following summer (fig. 14). The original sketches Turner made show the upper structure of the octagon tower in the process of completion, along with the west and south wings. It is not yet evident from these views that the spire design had given way to the final great central tower plan. Turner's drawings clearly display the fragility of the tower at this stage, with the interlacing timbers rising above the rest of the building in a ghost-like filigree.

It is not known with certainty how high the tower rose in the Wiltshire sky at this time, but *The Times* reported that it was '120 feet above the stone work'.[50] Furthermore, the *Morning Chronicle* explained years later that the lofty spire that was under construction was made 'entirely of wood' and therefore subject to an early fate.[51] The result was that on 17 May 1800 a strong gale brought the upper storey with boards, beams, and scaffold poles falling inside the tower with a loud crash, constituting a second collapse of the tower. This time the newspapers reported the mishap, with *The Times* taking the lead in a report on 20 May:

> On Friday a heavy gale of wind came on from the S. W. which ere the dawn of Saturday morning had increased to a tempest: the tower of the famous Gothic Abbey, just erected at Fonthill, stood exposed to all its fury, and at three o'clock a considerable portion of this famed building came down with such a tremendous crash as to alarm the country for a considerable distance around. Thus, in a moment, perished the labour of hundreds of feeble mortals bestowed for years on this once favourite object, and the expence of very many thousands.[52]

A week later, after receiving additional information, *The Times* published a correction indicating that they overstated the amount of destruction. It was a costly event, but the rest of the building escaped damage:

> Fonthill Abbey has not been injured by the late storm to the extent reported. The damage has been confined to the timber frame which had been erected about 120 feet above the stone work; but no other part of this stupendous building has sustained the least injury.[53]

It was the *Morning Chronicle* report on the event, however, that had an impact on Beckford and remained in his mind as he described to others what happened. They first reported the damage in the issue of 22 May, explaining that the 'Tower of Fonthill-abbey, a capricious building which Mr. Beckford has been erecting on the summit of a hill at an enormous expence, was blown down by the high wind on Monday last.'[54] They then followed up with a more humorous report: 'The *damage* done by the late high wind to the *tower* of *Fonthill Abbey* is greatly to its advantage. It now looks like what it was intended to be, and more resembles an *ancient Gothic* edifice than ever!'[55]

Beckford was furious, blaming Wyatt for the shoddy work and failure to be on the job providing close supervision. 'Determined to sink no longer from disappointment to disappointment,' he wrote to the architect, 'I give you this plain and decided warning. If you take it as it is meant I shall soon see you at Fonthill. If not – the whole shall be stopped, every workmen discharged, the reasons which have compelled me to adopt so violent a measure stated at large in the [*Morning Chronicle*] and every other Chron. Morn. Or Eve. which appears in London.'[56] These were strong words that seem to have had an effect on Wyatt because a great stir of building activity followed. Beckford, it seems, was determined as ever to move forward. It may have been this occasion that led him to decide to forego the spire design. 'We shall rise more gloriously than ever,' he wrote to Heard, 'provided the sublime Wyatt will graciously deign to bestow a little more commonplace Attention upon what is supposed his favourite Structure. The Crash and the Loss sound magnificently in the Newspaper, I neither heard the one, nor feel the other.'[57] More than a year later, the tower was still not secure and never would be.[58]

Work on the building and grounds continued throughout the remaining months of 1800 but reached a fever pitch by the winter in preparation for an elaborate reception Beckford held in honour of Lord Nelson in late December. Nelson arrived on the 20th with Sir William Hamilton and Emma Hamilton. Benjamin West was present, along with John Walcot, Henry Tresham, Wyatt and an assortment of ladies and gentlemen. Tresham wrote an account of the event in the *Gentleman's Magazine*.[59] The *pièce de résistance* of the festivities was a visit to the Abbey, a memorable event for Nelson and all of the guests. Beckford had designed a series of lighting effects with lamps in the trees along the path through the woods with the slow-moving carriages lit by flambeaus (fig. 15). The lighting effect was heightened by the sounds of drums placed at different points among the surrounding hills and by music echoing through the dark woods. The grand display was the Abbey standing in the darkness but illuminated by the blaze of lights for dramatic visual effect, revealing sections of the walls, battlements, turrets and the great tower vanishing into the gloom above it. Tresham provided a description of the interior of the Abbey as well, which constitutes a record of the way it looked at this stage of its development:

The parties, alighting in orderly succession from their carriages, entered a groined Gothic hall through a double line of soldiers. From thence they were received into the great saloon, called the Cardinal's parlour, furnished with rich tapestries, long curtains of purple damask before the arched windows, ebony tables and chairs studded with ivory, of various but antique fashion; the

whole room in the noblest style of monastic ornament, and illuminated by lights on silver sconces. At the moment of entrance
they sat down at a long table, occupying nearly the whole length
of the room (53 feet), to a superb dinner, served in one long line
of enormous sliver dishes, in the substantial *costume* of the
antient abbeys, unmixed with the refinements of modern cookery. The table and side-boards glittering with piles of plate and a
profusion of candle-lights, not to mention a blazing Christmas
fire of cedar and the cones of pine, united to increase the splendour and to improve the *coup-d'oeil* of the room. It is needless to
say the highest satisfaction and good-humour prevailed, mingled
with sentiment of admiration at the grandeur and originality of
the entertainment. It should not be omitted, that many of the
artists whose works have contributed to the embellishment of the
abbey, with Mr. Wyatt and the President of the Royal Academy
at their head, formed a part of the company. These gentlemen,
with the distinguished musical party beforementioned, and some
prominent characters of the literary world, formed altogether a
combination of talents and genius not often meeting at the same
place.

Dinner being ended, the company removed up stairs to the
other finished apartments of the abbey. The stair-case was lighted
by certain mysterious living figures at different intervals, dressed
in hooded gowns, and standing with large wax-torches in their
hands. A magnificent room hung with yellow damask, and decorated with cabinets of the most precious japan, received the
assembly. It was impossible not to be struck, among other objects,
with its credences, (or antique buffets) exhibiting much treasure
of wrought plate, cups, vases, and ewers of solid gold. It was from
this room they passed into the Library, fitted up with the same
appropriate taste. The Library opens by a large Gothic screen into
the gallery; which I described to you in a former letter. This room,
which when finished will be more than 270 feet long, is to half
that length completely fitted up, and furnished in the most impressively monastic stile. A superb shrine, with a beautiful statue of St.
Anthony in marble and alabaster, the work of Rossi, placed upon
it, with reliquaries studded with brilliants of immense value, the
whole illuminated by a grand display of wax-lights on candlesticks and candelabras of massive silver gilt, exhibited a scene at

once strikingly splendid and awfully magnificent. The long series of lights on either side of the room, resting on stands of ebony enriched with gold, and those on the shrine all multiplied and reflected in the great oriel opposite, from its spacious squares of plate-glass, while the whole reflection narrowed into an endless prospective as it receded from the eye, produced a singular and magic effect.

As the company entered the gallery a solemn music struck the ear from some invisible quarter, as if from behind the screen of scarlet curtains which backed the shrine, or from its canopy above, and suggested ideas of a religious service; ideas which, associated as they were with so many appropriate objects addressed to the eye, recalled the grand chapel scenes and cere-monies of our antient Catholic times. After the scenic representa-tion a collation was presented in the library, consisting of various sorts of confectionary served in gold baskets, with spiced wines, &c. whilst rows of chairs were placed in the great room beyond, which had first received the company above stairs.

Shortly after the event West expressed his admiration for the impos-ing edifice and its creator and the impact the whole event had on him:

When I reflect on the progress, which the combination of arts have made, directed by true taste, since I first rode on the ground on which the Abbey stands – I am lost in admiration – and feel that I have seen a place raised more by majick, or inspiration, than the labours of the human hand: this is the sensation which the exami-nation of that elegant edifice produced on my feelings; and when the part which remains to be finished, is accomplished, must raise a climax of excellence without an example in the European world – and to give an immortality to the man whose elegant mind has conceived so vast a combination of all that is refined in Painting, Sculpture, and Architecture.[60]

It was soon after Nelson's visit that Beckford decided to make the Abbey more suitable as a residence. He made a major decision to move forward with these plans by ordering the demolition of the colonnade and wings of the Fonthill mansion. The stone gathered from the pile could be used at the Abbey. Surplus furniture, pictures and other belongings that would not be suitable for transference were sold in two separate auctions, the first in August 1801 and the second in February and March of 1802. While the stage was set for making the Abbey more habitable, some serious financial losses surfaced in 1802 that caused a delay. Beckford found himself faced with sudden reduction of income through the loss of some profitable West Indian property, which had been in his family for six decades.[61] A dispute over the title had been going on for years, but the property was finally removed from his ownership by a decree of the Court of Chancery. In addition, some unscrupulous agents and bad management deepened Beckford's losses at this time, forcing a necessary retrenchment. He decided to cease all work on the building for a period of three years.

In the meantime, Lady Anne Hamilton, daughter of the ninth Duke of Hamilton and a guardian of Beckford's daughters, visited Fonthill in September 1803 and provided an invaluable record in her unpublished diary of the state of construction of the Abbey building.[62] Based on the information she left behind, it is evident that many of the interior rooms had been fitted up for residence. Among these, for example, was the 'Abbot's Parlour' on the ground floor of the south wing, later called the Brown Parlour or the Oak Parlour because of its dark oak wainscoting. This would serve as Beckford's dining room. Lady Anne described the dimensions of this room as 54 feet long by 20 feet wide with a height of 13 feet. She noted that it was adorned with scarlet and purple curtains and observed that the views through the windows of the near and surrounding countryside provided an 'admirable Effect,' while the upper section of the windows were filled with stained glass paintings of kings and saints (the work of Eginton). Lady Anne also described the southern wing as 136 feet long ending with an altar and a statue of St Anthony of Padua holding a child 'surrounded by 36 wax lights in Gold Branches and Candlesticks'. This corroborates other reports placing the chapel at this stage of the Abbey's development in the Octagon room. Her diary also included dimensions of the Great Western Hall with the entrance door described as 30 feet high and the height of the Great Hall Entrance as 62 feet. She recorded that the Octagon Hall was 145 feet high and that the Great Tower rose at this time to a height of 250 feet, though this latter figure is lined out and 300 feet written in next to it by what appears to be another hand. She identified the proposed north wing as the 'Picture Gallery' and noted that combined with the south wing and 'Octagon Hall' it would produce a vista of 312 feet in length. Recognizing that the tower may not have reached its final height, Lady Anne's figures are very close to the final dimensions of the Abbey as identified by Rutter in 1823.

Work on the Abbey resumed in 1805 but proceeded slowly in light of the continuing economies. The construction of the tower continued to pose a major problem when it was discovered that the compo-cement Wyatt had used to build it was now crumbling rapidly and threatened to bring the whole structure down again. This resulted in hiring a number of workmen from London in the summer of 1805 to dismantle a great part of the tower and rebuild it in stone, adding considerably to the building costs and causing another long delay. The workers were still engaged in making this repair in December 1806, as an anonymous letter in the *Gentleman's Magazine* reported:

> To the instances of failure of *compocementing*, noticed by An Architect in p. 1005, the disgusting appearance of the handsome elegant tower of Fonthill abbey, in this neighbourhood, might have been added. It is the property of William Beckford, esq. M. P. and an entirely modern structure, on which a number of workmen from London have been employed during the summer in taking down a great part of it, from the decay of the cement, and still remain to prepare the materials for restoring it with stone, at an immense expence, though seven years have not yet elapsed since its completion.[63]

A major economy move was made by November 1806 with a decision to demolish most of the rest of the family mansion, leaving only one of the pavilions. It is also evident from a letter Beckford wrote at this time that he now had a complete model in his possession of Fonthill Abbey in its final form. 'If you could see the model of the entire Abbey,' he wrote, 'and were asked – will you, for the sake of a good common House in an uncommonly bad situation – renounce the execution of such a plan – I think you wd. give way and join with me and Wyatt in full accord.'[64] This *papier-mâché* model, which has survived,[65] shows the tower without a spire, an extended northern wing to balance the southern extension and an imposing eastern transept completing a total asymmetrical design.

Beckford finally moved into the Abbey in the summer of 1807. Interior finishing work would continue for years, particularly with the plans for additional wings. The interior walls of the great Octagon Hall were not completed until September 1808, followed by the incorporation of

windows and fan vaulting.⁶⁶ The tower itself remained a web of scaf-
folding until the fall of 1809.⁶⁷ We learn from a letter to Beckford's secretary, Franchi, in June 1810 that the carpet for the 'ante-sanctuary' had
not yet been laid – the first indication that the sanctuary would be relo-
cated to the end of King Edward's Gallery.⁶⁸ While there is no record of
when it happened, the west wing appears to have received its final con-
version from a banquet hall to grand entrance during the period
1809–10 with the addition of a massive flight of stairs leading up to the
Octagon Hall. Disguised as a labourer, William Bankes gained access to
the grounds in 1811 and reported seeing the finished stone stairs and
the great entrance hall looking 'very much like those of some large Col-
leges, with windows on both sides & a rich Oak roof very much gilt'.⁶⁹
Construction of the north wing, King Edward's Gallery, named after
King Edward III, began in 1808 and was sufficiently finished to be
included in James Storer's published description of the Abbey in 1812.
In this account Storer also refers to the planned eastern wing: 'We are
told it is the intention of Mr. Beckford to build a superb chapel, directly
opposite to the great hall.'⁷⁰ Beckford's correspondence for this period
indicates that the foundation for this new venture, the Eastern Transept,
was laid in August 1812.⁷¹

The construction of the Eastern Transept was a major undertaking
and, in the end, never completed. Beckford initiated this fourth wing
in spite of urgings from his lawyer to economize. His compulsion to
build could not be controlled even when the additional expense would
add to a growing burden of debt. As he wrote in August 1812: 'Some
people drink to forget their unhappiness. I do not drink, I build. And
it ruins me. It would be cheaper to find another distraction... .'⁷² The
outer walls went up at a furious pace with Wyatt on hand to supervise
the work, but in September of the following year the architect died in
a carriage accident, leaving the major portion of the supervisory work
in Beckford's hands with the assistance of George Hayter, the Clerk of
the Works at Fonthill, and occasional assistance from Wyatt's nephew
Jeffrey, who would change his name later to Wyattville. The instabil-
ity of the structure as a consequence of Wyatt's careless work continued to be a major concern and the hired labourers devoted almost two
years to rebuild various parts of the Abbey with stone to forestall
another major collapse. Franchi provided some specific information
on the state of affairs at Fonthill in 1814 in a letter to Beckford's son-
in-law:

You ask me for details about the Abbey. I would like to give you satisfactory ones, but that is impossible if I tell you the truth. Almost all that the villainous Bagasse [Wyatt] built has been dismantled (to forestall finding ourselves buried in its rotten ruins); all the walls in the in the Fountain Court have been very solidly rebuilt in stone; the chimney-flues have been changed, together with a thousand other errors which sooner or later would have damaged the edifice – this is the work upon which we have been engaged for the last two years. The kitchen has been finished, and with its adjoining offices it is the finest bit in the Abbey.[73]

In 1815 the roof and the turrets of the two towers were added to the Eastern Transept. The interiors of some rooms were finished on the first floor in 1817–18, but Beckford's enthusiasm for completing the wing began to wane in the absence of Wyatt and as structural problems multiplied. The Eastern Transept would have to remain unfinished, and he now began to consider seriously the possibility of giving up the entire venture. 'My resolution to abandon the theatre of so much useless labour', he wrote in October 1817, 'is fortified every hour that I stay here, experiencing blasts of wind, blasts of cold, blasts of rheum and financials blasts in this uninhabitable place.'[74]

The death of Hayter, who had been supervising the building repair and interior work of the Abbey, in December 1818 caused Beckford serious concern and had dire consequences for the future of Fonthill. A new Clerk of the Works was appointed almost immediately, but the inevitable end was in sight. By January 1819 Beckford was beginning to consider with extreme reluctance the sale of Fonthill. The steady decline of sugar prices in England over the years had drastically reduced his income from his West Indian estates. Annual interest on the mortgages on his Fonthill properties and an accrued indebtedness that reached £145,000 finally forced Beckford's hand.[75]

The final cost of the Abbey remains something of a mystery. Beckford told Cyrus Redding years later that the total outlay was £273,000, but Macquin, who was in a position to know, indicated in 1822 that it was £400,000.[76] Beckford made a desperate attempt to recoup by suggesting to his son-in-law, the Duke of Hamilton, that he liquidate a large portion of the debt in return for the guaranteed inheritance of the Fonthill estate and all of his possessions. Hamilton, however, was unwilling to become entangled in Beckford's financial affairs, and so

Fonthill was to be sold by auction in the fall of 1822, including all its buildings, land, and the valuable contents of the Abbey. The announcement of such a sale would come as a shock to a society that had come to believe that Beckford, as Byron had dubbed him, was 'England's wealthiest son'. As one contemporary writer reflected: 'The vast wealth which he expended here, one would have thought, was a stream from an exhaustless source; but the golden tide has had its ebb; the uncalculated treasure, which in its effects rivalled the power of enchantment, is dissolved like Cleopatra's pearl.'[77]

5
The Fonthill Abbey Landscape

While the construction of Fonthill Abbey was an enormous under-taking, complicated by structural problems and costly delays, the laying out of the grounds surrounding the building was equally chal-lenging in scope and central to Beckford's total artistic scheme. From the outset, Beckford planned a landscape garden in which the Abbey would be a central feature. Begun as a convent in ruins, graduating thereafter to a neo-Gothic museum of the arts and then to a residence, the building was always seen within the context of a landscape compo-sition in the tradition of the English garden. Beckford's landscape would not be in the formal style that had been characteristic of some of the great estates that preceded Fonthill. This landscape garden would bear the mark of his own particular artistic taste and reflect the ' new' aesthetics of the picturesque as expounded by such theorists as Uvedale Price and William Gilpin. Consistent with their theory, the picturesque landscape garden represented an attempt to apply the principles of landscape painting to the laying out of grounds surrounding an archi-tectural focal point. The accent was on the visual aspects of the garden scene presented as part of a whole composition. Various points of view were incorporated in the design to facilitate appreciation of the land-scape scene, as one would appreciate a landscape by Salvator Rosa or Gaspar Poussin in the gallery of a museum.

That Fonthill was recognized early in its development as more than a neo-Gothic structure is apparent from Humphry Repton's interest in playing a role in the development of the grounds surrounding it. One of the most famous landscape architects of the day, Repton offered to contribute to its design in 1799. Beckford was flattered, but he preferred to play that role himself.

It is impossible [he wrote to Repton] not to be flattered with an offer to contribute to the Ornament of my place from an Artist of your Eminence and Celebrity; but Nature has been liberal to

1 Fonthill Abbey in Its Setting. Drawn by Henry Gastineau, engraved by R. Havell & Son, 1823.

2 Monserrate, Portugal. Drawn by James Bulwer, engraved by F. Nicholson, 1828.

3 William Beckford, c. 1800, by John Hoppner

4 Fonthill Splendens. Drawn by John Britton, engraved by James Storer.

5 Entrance gateway to the park at Fonthill Bishop

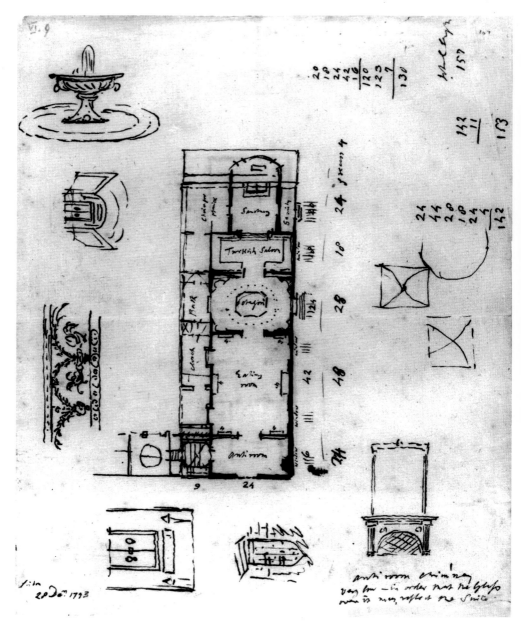

8 Beckford's architectural design for his Lisbon house, 1793

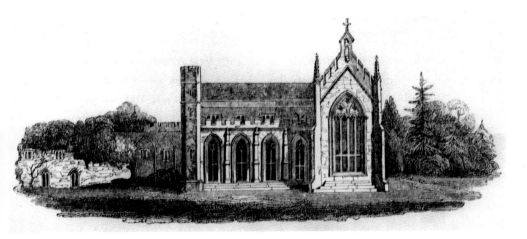

9 ABOVE *The Convent in Ruins*, c. 1796–7, engraved by T[homas] H[igham]

10 RIGHT James Wyatt, portrait by M. C. Wyatt, engraved by C. Turner, 1809

11 Early design of Fonthill Abbey; watercolour by J. M. W. Turner, c. 1797

12 Design of Fonthill Abbey with a spire; watercolour by James Wyatt, c. 1798

13 Charles Wild's conjectural watercolour after a c. 1799 design by James Wyatt

14 East View of Fonthill Abbey, c. 1799; watercolour by J. M. W. Turner

15 LEFT *Lord Nelson's Reception at Fonthill*; from *The Gentleman's Magazine*, April 1801
16 RIGHT *Fonthill Abbey from the American Plantation*, by James Storer, 1812

Fonthill, and some Embellishment it has received from Art, has fortunately gained so much the Approbation of my friends that my Partiality to it in its present state will not perhaps be thought altogether inexcusable. I am, nevertheless, much honoured and obliged in your having thought Fonthill considerable enough to merit your attention.[1]

The major landscaping projects at Fonthill were begun in the early part of 1795, when the barrier wall was receiving its finishing touches. Between this date and February 1797 they reached a fever pitch. During this period Beckford purchased an additional 1,700 acres of land and hired over a hundred persons to work on the ground improvements alone, with astonishing results.[2] Under the direction of his gardener, James Vincent, a conservatory and flower garden were begun, nine miles of a twenty-seven-mile ride were completed and more than one million trees planted. Furthermore, a variety of walks and avenues were formed, each of considerable length and width and all laid in smooth turf, the most impressive of which was a broad straight walk, later called the Great Western Avenue. This stretched from the entrance of the Abbey to the barrier wall, where it connected by 'means of a bridge over a road, with a bold terrace, four miles and a half in length.'[3]

It was evident from the initial improvements that Beckford was striving for naturalistic effects in his garden plan. Laying out the small walks and pathways, for example, he made every attempt to avoid strict regularity. He generally made their lines winding in gentle curves through various sections of the woods to avoid the sharp turns which had become so common in the formal gardens of the eighteenth century. When he did make the walkways straight, he broke the formality of their lines by planting flowers, shrubs, and trees close to the edges. According to John Rutter, they all appeared to be 'ordinary features of woodland landscape.'[4] As for the newly planted trees, Beckford avoided the kind of obvious clumping that had become an artificial characteristic of gardens in the style of Capability Brown. Rutter observed:

The ornamented grounds of Fonthill, though unequalled in extent, contain very few objects that will admit of individual description. The great principle upon which this labyrinth of groves has been constructed, is that of exhibiting an union of the wildest and the most ornamented scenery, the picturesque and the beautiful, in close society. The utmost profusion of expense has been bestowed, not to amaze the senses by some rich and magical effect of art, but to keep the mind in a perpetual enjoyment of the most striking beauties, and richest decorations of nature.

Citing a passage from Tasso, Rutter added: 'No where appear'd the arte which all this wroughte.'[5]

The most obvious illustration of Beckford's avoidance of the straight line could be seen in the construction of the Great Western Avenue, the central approach to the Abbey (fig. 17). Approximately one hundred feet broad and almost a mile in length, it was made along the top of a high wooded ridge, which declined on both sides into deep valleys, the sides of which were covered with fir trees that contributed to the impression of an Alpine scene. Unlike a formal planner who would have been satisfied with a broad formal avenue leading up to a central residence, Beckford made a deep depression about half way along the avenue to vary the surface and to give it a natural effect. He also gave the avenue an air of informality by bounding its sides with a variety of trees and undergrowth, planting them at irregular intervals. Finally, he carpeted the avenue with a fine, close turf, thereby avoiding the formal character of the gravel surface.

The use of turf as a replacement for gravel in the laying out of his central avenue was a master stroke in informal design, a solution to a problem of composition that was plaguing the major picturesque gardening theorists. Brown had banished all avenues from the landscape in his severe reaction against the formalism of the geometric garden. Knight, Price, and Repton brought them back in their attempts to modify Brown's extremism, but they did so with some reluctance. Repton believed, for example, that the 'great mischief of an avenue' was that it divided the park into separate parts and destroyed 'that unity of lawn or wood which is necessary to please in every composition.'[6] Price felt that although 'a broad dry walk near the house is indispensable to the comfort of every gentleman's habitation', the pared formal edges of a gravel walk produced a poor effect in the foreground.[7] Beckford solved the problem with turf and by planting approaches 'composed of a thick elastic body of various kinds of evergreen moss, low ground-fern ... wild thyme, and numerous sweet-smelling ground-flowers; the whole matted and interlaced together by a network of wild strawberries', which blended well with a lawn and eliminated the necessity for the 'horror' of the straight line.[8]

Beckford understood that a smooth relationship between building and grounds was important for a unified design. He also recognized that a structure of the size he was contemplating would serve as a focal point of interest to which everything else was related. Ordinary builders too often disregarded the role of the *l'architecto-pittore* and prepared their structures without regard for the general landscape, but Beckford took steps to ensure that the Abbey was integrated into the garden design.

That Fonthill was to be his personal creation was evident in the extent to which he participated in the landscape projects and oversaw the entire scheme. As the editor of *The European Magazine* wrote in 1797,

> All these splendid works are not merely effected in consequence of Mr. Beckford's orders, and by means of his fortune; but his own genius, whose comprehension and activity appear equal to any undertaking, has been the informing spirit of the whole; every one of the ... projects, whether of use or ornament, having originated from himself, and their plans, of whatever kind, having been assisted or corrected by his own pure and classic taste. One of his principal amusements at Fonthill consists in attending and frequently directing the superior workmen in the execution of his schemes; and such is the ardour with which he is carrying forward his favourite building, the Abbey, that the frost and snow of the present winter were never suffered to stop any part of the work which could still go on, nor to prevent his own daily excursions to the spot.[9]

By the winter of 1800–1, in time for Lord Nelson's visit, Beckford completed one of the most important elements in his scheme, a lengthy, winding drive, composed of the Nine Miles Walk and a carriage ride, both located within the boundary walls and both made of turf. It was this feature which provided a vantage point to almost every interesting view of the Abbey and the surrounding landscape which could be commanded within the estate.

A study of the Nine Miles Walk, as it looked in 1823,[10] shows how essential the elements of variety and contrast were to the design. Along its entire length, within the barrier wall, were planned a sequence of pictures that guided a person from a bright open view to the contemplative dark, covered woods. If a visitor crossed the southern lawn near the Abbey, he was presented, at the very beginning of the walk, with a striking landscape scene. Here the closely shaved lawn, bordered by plantations of oak, fir and hawthorn, and the reflective waters of Bitham Lake, combined with the wood of the middle distance and the terrace of Wardour Castle rising along the distant horizon, to form a beautifully balanced scene. Following the walk from this point as it proceeded in a north-easterly direction around Hinkley Hill, the scene shifted from this open view to a closed, heavily wooded path. For approximately two miles, 'an impervious fence of oak, elm, beech, hazel, and fir almost completely shuts out the distant landscape', giving it the quality of 'perfect seclusion'.[11] With such a long stretch of walk there was inevitably the risk of monotony, but Beckford managed to maintain interest by undulating its surface at various intervals along the way and by carpeting the walk with moss of varied tints and colours. This kind of variety was also heightened by the different character of the trees as the 'sparkling and feathery birch' succeeded the 'dark and solemn pine,' or as the humble hawthorn followed the lofty ash. Not until the end of this first arm of the walk, in the area of one of eight gates on the Abbey estate, called the Lower Street Gate, did the eye so long imprisoned in the thickly planted avenue range freely over the distant hills beyond Chilmark.

The second arm of the walk, which extended south-west from the Lower Street Gate to the summit of the Great Western Avenue, was designed, in contrast to the first, to be more open. A thinner tree line now afforded occasional glimpses of the Abbey, which served to stimulate curiosity until an open area brought it suddenly into view. Rutter noted that after passing beyond the Lower North Terrace a beautiful view of the south-western side of the Abbey was presented at the intersection of the Nine Miles Walk and a long 'natural' avenue called the Clerk's Walk.[12]

From the Clerk's Walk the drive pursued a winding course through an enclosure of pine and Scotch fir until it reached the western extremity of the Great Western Avenue, the beginning of the third arm, where, upon turning east, the Abbey burst into view in 'all the huge splendour of exalted height and magnificence'.[13] Proceeding in an easterly direction towards the Abbey, the walk followed the Great Western Avenue until it was intersected by an avenue which ascended south to the top of Beacon Hill, where the original tower was to be erected. It was here that Beckford created a terrace that cut across the whole breadth of the garden, a distance of approximately two and a half miles, providing striking views of the Abbey in its setting as well as the surrounding countryside. Beacon Terrace, as it was called, contributed to the unity of the total design by being 'bounded in an irregular line by every variety of forest tree and garden shrub' in keeping with the other walkways and avenues on the estate.[14] As a finished work in 1814, Beckford thought it was superior to the formal terrace at Stourhead: 'Believe me, the terrace at Stourton is no longer comparable to that at Fonthill: the lines too straight, the ground not undulating, a repetition of pyramids, larches planted regularly everywhere like the *fleurs-de-lis* on the royal robe which used to be at St. Denis. I don't like it, I can't admire it.'[15]

The next striking view of the Abbey could be seen as one descended eastward from Beacon Hill along the final section of the walk. Over a long measure of ground 'varied by gentle undulations and studded with clumps of trees, displaying a rich assemblage of glowing and luxuriant tints', the Abbey appeared, 'forming a grand mass of embattled towers, surmounted by the lofty octagon' and backed 'by an elevated woodland of a sombre aspect, which by contrast heightens the striking and brilliant effect of the edifice'.[16] As one continued down the hill, the focus of interest shifted to a series of alternating scenes designed to keep the eye stimulated. The uneven pine lawn on the right opposed in texture and colour the rolling turf on the left, while the tall stately White Mead Wood which followed gave emphasis to the depth of Bittern Vale, a few steps beyond. Passing through the open light of valley, the scene again shifted to the broken lights and shadows of the trees and thickets surrounding Bitham Lake.

Bitham Lake, one of the finest landscape features on the Fonthill estate, was a testimony to the principles of picturesque landscaping (fig. 18). While the creation of it through damming predated Beckford, he did capitalize on its potential for strong visual effects.[17] This was most evident in the way in which the deliberate arrangement of coves and inlets of various sizes and the heavy planting along the edges concealed any lines of definition and broke the uniformity of the banks – reminiscent of the treatment of the lake in Old Park. With the 'luxuriance of the shrubs and trees', wrote John Britton, ' the wildness of some spots contrasted with the smoothness and softness of others', and the 'shape and undefined borders of the lake' rendered the entire scene attractive, particularly to the 'artist and botanist.'[18] James Storer felt that it looked like 'the crater of an ancient volcano', whose shape was such that its 'stretching and meandering' contributed to the illusion of a greater size than it really possessed.[19] In some places, moss-covered stones and knotted tree-roots were allowed to remain exposed because they mixed well with the different coloured soils and the tints of vegetation, while the overhanging trees, shrubbery, and sky reflected in the water enhanced the quality of the scene. From its southern side, the lake and its surroundings formed a perfect foreground to an almost theatrical view of the Abbey (fig. 16). A writer in the *Morning Chronicle* recorded the palpable effect of this vantage point on an occasion when the Abbey was bathed in the soft radiance of a moonlit night:

> At night I had an opportunity of seeing the effect of a serene and beautiful moonlight sky upon the Abbey and the surrounding scenery... where there is a better combination of circumstances for a well composed picture of this kind than any I have yet seen. The mellow lustre and broad shadows which fall upon the majestic towers, the rugged battlements, the shafted oriels, and arched recesses of the Abbey, destroy all the detail of those parts which, in the broad-day, appear confusedly heaped together, and force upon the spectator the idea of disproportion and incongruity. The antique form of the edifice takes its full effect both on the eye and the imagination. The newness of its colour is not then at variance with the ancient character which its formation assumes. It does not seem to be an usurper upon the realms of antiquity, but a legitimate inheritor of the honours that are paid her. Entrenched in gloomy grandeur in its woody heights, tinged with the silvery flickering lights, which give a deeper tone to its solitude, and reflecting its broad masses in the calm transparency of the lake below, on which sometimes the wild bird raises his lonely cry; it seems the throne of ancient superstition, which has stood amid the storms of ages, and overlooked the revolutions of time... [20]

As for the tone of this section of the garden, it was in keeping with the general character of the place, 'tranquil and secluded'. For Beckford it was a *tour de force* in naturalistic design. 'The lake looks as if God had made it, it is so natural, without the least trace of art; I don't say it is marvellous, for its banks are too flat, but it spreads itself grandiosely

[98]

and the swans look as if they are in Paradise'.[21] The beauty of the lake was enhanced in 1810 by the completion of an American garden on the northern end, the last major landscape feature as the visitor walked up a steep incline to the southern lawn where the nine-mile excursion finally ended.[22]

The carriage drive within the Abbey estate extended approximately four miles, starting from the eastern side of the building, running down through the southern portion of the grounds, and skirting north around Beacon Hill to the Stone Gate, located at the beginning of the Great Western Avenue. We know this drive was finished in 1801 because Beckford used it to show Lord Nelson the estate in a horse-drawn phaeton. As the story goes, Beckford pursued the drive at such a spanking pace that Nelson became nervously agitated and asked him to stop, saying 'This is too much for me – you must set me down.' They then walked the rest of the way with Beckford later expressing amazement that the brave hero of the Nile could be so emotionally fragile.[23] Actually, this carriage drive was part of a longer ride, connecting with it at Stone Gate, which traced the outer boundaries of the entire Fonthill domain, a distance of almost twenty-three miles.

The design of the section inside the Abbey grounds was similar to that of the Nine Miles Walk. The first mile was bounded and shut in by a thick plantation of pine, fir and larch, with wild underwood and flowering shrubs filling the spaces between trees so that the extent of their thickness could not be judged. With the exception of an unexpected opening about a quarter of the way along its length, this first stretch moved in a winding course almost entirely through deep and solemn shadows. At any one time it was not possible to see more than a hundred yards ahead until a point was reached near the Eastern Gate where the drive turned abruptly to the right and passed through an irregular line of more open woods.

To maintain interest along the ride remaining inside the barrier wall, its course was planned to curve by the southern bank of Bitham Lake to take advantage of the special view of the Abbey that Storer liked so well. A rough lawn was added farther south to oppose the darkness of White Mead Wood on the hill to the north of the drive. The drive then curved north past the Norwegian Lawn on the left where Beckford had constructed a Norwegian Hut, a log house in keeping with the Alpine character of the trees growing in this area and on the slopes of Beacon Hill. It then proceeded almost directly north past the Laurel Walk on the left before reaching its terminal point inside the Abbey grounds at Stone Gate.

The prevailing characteristic of the design of the carriage drive was once again naturalistic: another example of the planned informality of the grounds. It was like reading a page from Price's *Essay on the Picturesque*:

> The banks [were] sometimes broken and abrupt; sometimes smooth, and gently but not uniformly sloping; now wildly over-hung with thickets of trees and bushes; now loosely skirted with wood; no regular verge of grass, no cut edges, no distinct lines of separation; all is mixed and blended together, and the border of the road itself, shaped by the mere tread of passengers and animals, as unconstrained as the footsteps that formed it: even the tracks of the wheels ... contributed to the picturesque effect of the whole.[24]

As in the case of the Nine Miles Walk, the carriage drive seemed not to be the consequence of artful design but cut through the woods by the forces of nature, so that it was possible to appreciate its design in accordance with Price's theory – 'not from what *had*, but from what had *not*, been done'.[25]

After the completion of the Nine Miles Walk and carriage drive in 1800, Beckford concerned himself with additional improvements on the estate. 'I love building, planting, gardening,' he told Cyrus Redding later, 'whatever will keep me employed in the open air. I like to be among workmen.'[26] Macquin reported that even the royal works of St George's Chapel, Windsor were set aside, during the time that Wyatt was serving as Surveyor-General, to allow 460 men to be employed at Fonthill, working in shifts by day and by lamp at night and on week-ends as well, regardless of weather conditions, to expedite the work, whether on the grounds or the building.[27] Beckford at this time, wrote Macquin, was on constant watch 'surveying the work thus expedited, the busy levy of masons, the high and giddy dancing of the lights, and the strange effects produced upon the architecture and woods below ... wasting the coldest hours of December darkness in feasting his sense with this display of almost superhuman power'. He then observed that 'these singular traits of character will not surprise those who have made mankind their study.... . The minds most nearly allied to genius are the most apt to plunge into these extremes: a Beckford builds a Babel by torchlight, a Byron writes a Cain with exultation; and Eratastratus burns the Temple of Diana to gain an immortal though infamous celebrity.'

With this kind of activity much was accomplished in creating the setting for the Abbey in the years that followed: the extension of the twenty-three-mile drive around the entire domain outside the Abbey estate's barrier wall, the completion of the American Garden in 1810 and Beacon Terrace across the breadth of the Abbey estate in 1814. The problem of handling the transition between the Abbey and the immediately surrounding grounds was solved, and the horticultural work carried out almost automatically every year. The construction of the Abbey with its inherent structural problems was costly but the creation of the surrounding grounds and the formidable ongoing tasks to maintain so vast an area were a constant drain on Beckford's financial resources.

One of the few visitors to gain access to the estate during this period of development was William Cobbett, whose keen interest in horticulture motivated the visit. He examined the grounds in August of 1808 and was impressed with what he saw:

> Well, we saw Fonthill, but, even if I had the talent to do justice to it in a written description, ten such sheets as this would not suffice for the purpose. When I see you, I will at times give you an hour's account of it. After that sight, all sights become mean until that be out of the mind. We both thought Wardour the finest place we had ever seen, but Wardour makes but a single glade in Beckford's immense grounds and plantations. The grass walks at Fonthill, fifteen feet wide, if stretched out in a right line, would reach from there to London, upwards of ninety miles; there are sixty-five men and ten horses constantly employed in the pleasure-grounds, a thousand acres of which, being the interior and more private part, are enclosed within a wall of squared stone from ten to twelve feet high, with an oak palisade at top pointed with iron. Scarcely any soul is permitted to enter here, and, from what we had heard, we had not the least expectation of it. ... But not to see the house, which no one as yet has seen the inside of. The outside we approached very near, and, like the rest, it sets description at defiance.[28]

Three years later, after being committed to Newgate prison for his criticism of the military, Cobbett wrote to Beckford to obtain seeds for his own estate at Botley:

Colonel Johnston, who has, I understand, lately been at Fonthill, has, by what he has told me of your disposition to oblige me in the *planting way*, emboldened me to give you this trouble. He did, indeed, bring me a message from you, that you should have pleasure in directing your gardener to furnish me with anything that I might want that you had to spare... .

To you, who know so much about planting, and who have, of course, so often experienced the disappointments, arising from seeds got from those most faithless people the Nurserymen (I mean *false*, for they may have as much *belief* as the rest of this most believing nation); to you I need not describe the vexations that I have suffered from the same cause. The fact is, that I have lost so much time and labour from this cause, beside what I have suffered in the way of vexation, that I have almost made a vow never to trust to a Nurseryman's seeds again. It is a principle with me, that, when a man begins to beget children, he ought if possible, to begin to plant, or sow, trees. I did so the moment I had a foot of land for the purpose; and the greatest pleasure I have in the way of occupation (next after giving good hard blows to despotic rulers) is in raising trees of all sorts, but particularly timber-trees. This is but a poor apology for plaiging you, but it is the best I have to offer.

What I would beg leave to ask of you is this: that you would have the goodness to direct your gardener whom, I believe I saw in 1808, and who appeared to be a very clever man, to cause to be collected for me, at the proper time, the following things.

12 Bushels of Larch Cones
12 Bushels of Spruce fir cones
12 Bushels of Scotch fir Cones
 6 Bushels of Weymouth Pine Cones
 2 Bushels, or any *Smaller Quantity*, of any other sort of fir Cones, and of as many sorts as he can
 4 Bushels of *Sycamore Seeds*
A Gallon of Acacia Seed
A Gallon of Laburnum Seed
 2 Bushels of Horse Chestnuts

and a small quantity of any other *Tree* Seed that it may be convenient for him to collect... .[29]

Beckford responded to Cobbett by indicating that because of a
recent thinning of the woods around the Abbey that it would take
'some years to come at least to produce any quantity of seeds worthy
your acceptance'.

Among the changes at this time, the horticultural work on the estate
deserves some special attention. The role of plants in the Fonthill landscape design rank in importance with some of its other features. As
early as 1803, Lady Anne Hamilton was impressed by the plants during
her visit, noting that a 'finer feast for the botanist than this Noble place
is, cannot be'.[30] The Fonthill landscape restored the status of the individual plant in the garden scene which in the extreme formal garden of
the eighteenth century had been almost totally neglected. For years the
individual plant had been an insignificant element in a mathematical
scheme, one that was shaped, cut, or treated at the architect's whim.
For a similar reason, flowers had been rarely used because they tended
to grow in a free, unrestrained manner without regard to artificial form.
But Beckford recognized their importance for colouring, contrast, and
variety and incorporated them eagerly into his plan. He often sought
new varieties of plants and took special care to avoid the excesses of
botanical exhibits.

The horticultural experiments for Fonthill were performed on a
portion of an eight-acre kitchen and flower garden, belonging to the old
estate, approximately a mile and a half north of the Lower Street Gate.
This extensive project, hidden by a row of lofty pines, was completed
before February 1797, when a detailed description of it appeared in the
European Magazine article.

> Mr. Beckford's next undertaking [the editor wrote] was the forma-
> tion of a new Kitchen and Flower Garden, contiguous to each
> other, in a more convenient site, under a warmer aspect, and upon
> a scale four times larger than the old one. The Hot Walls, Pineries,
> Conservatories, quantity of glazed Frame-work, the Gardener's
> House, importation of soil for this extensive spot of many acres,
> with its plantation and nurseries, and an extensive inclosure of
> handsome brick-wall round the whole, have altogether concurred
> to render this work almost as unrivalled in magnitude and conve-
> nience, as it must have been in matter of expence.[31]

Within the vicinity of the Abbey, Beckford would later add a small hothouse for Piero, his dwarf-servant, and a herb garden, 'containing such plants as we may suppose the monks might have cultivated to use in medicine'.[32] Near the end of the Nine Miles Walk, he half-concealed a Chinese garden, surrounded by a light iron fence and 'particularly appropriated to the culture of the rarest flower'.[33] John Claudius Loudon, the landscape garden historian and encyclopedist, recorded after a visit to Fonthill in 1807 the existence of a 'rose-ground' and 'thornery' treated in a naturalistic manner so as not to appear as obvious contrivances,[34] while Storer described in 1812 a mile-long path next to the Clerk's Walk that presented during the spring and summer a 'fascinating display of flowers of spontaneous growth, of luxuriant shrubs and variegated hollies'.[35]

It is evident that Beckford seems to have been well aware of the problem of clumping plants as displays foreign to the landscape and totally without connection to the layout as a whole. The way he used exotic flowers as by-scenes in the woods to curb this problem has already been mentioned, but the American garden at Fonthill, created on the northern margin of Bitham Lake by Beckford with the help of his gardener, Mr Milne, may serve as another example. It consisted of a great variety of American flowers and shrubs. Its winding paths led the visitor through rhododendrons, some places fifteen feet high. In his description of it, Rutter noted that the 'deep pink flowers shed an universal glow over an extensive declivity – here and there the beautiful magnolia displayed the exquisite whiteness of its large blossoms – while clusters of azaleas mingled with these loftier exotics in the richest harmony of colour and fragrance; the Carolina rose profusely studded the walks with its gorgeous blossoms – the allspice of the same region shed its exquisite perfume over the whole extent of these gardens – and the arbutus luxuriated in groups as lofty and as branching as the Portugal laurel.'[36] The whole display added considerable colour to the scene and provided a dramatic contrast to the monochromatic character of the Gothic Abbey and the dense, gloomy woodland.

The American plantation also created in Beckford's words, a 'great effect' because of its 'unusual arrangement'.[37] The flowers and shrubs were so carefully 'disposed in groups and thickets that it appeared that they had sprung up naturally'.[38] To ensure coherence of design every step was taken to make the foreign plants seem native to their setting. 'In this spot', wrote a visitor, 'the formality of gardening is absolutely lost. These enormous exotic plants mingle with the oak, the beech, and the pine, so naturally that they would delight a landscape painter.'[39] Here, as throughout the Abbey estate, 'the usual natives of the forest, the heath and the garden', wrote another visitor in 1823,

> meet together in one spot, and form one beautiful and happy family; and all flourish and bloom together, by mutual consent. Roses blush from out the bosom of the heath furze; rhododendrons fling their gorgeous flowers at random among ferns and forest shrubs; the frail woodbine hangs its dependent clusters upon the everlasting laurel; and on the ground all sorts of rich (so called) *garden* flowers group themselves with those gentle families of the earth which we... have chosen to banish from our presence into the fields and hedges, and denominate *weeds*.[40]

Thus, whether laying out drives, avenues and walkways, or planting woods, shrubs and flowers, Beckford made every effort to avoid the artificial extravagances of the architectural garden, favouring instead a freer design based on the irregularity of natural landscape. Following the tradition of the late eighteenth-century naturalistic designers, he incorporated variety and asymmetry into his garden plan, and, in doing so, as one unidentified visitor to the grounds in 1822 discovered, he was eminently successful:

> How little and contemptible is the taste displayed in the vaunted gardens of Versailles compared with that which has formed these beautiful grounds, where the only ambition of art has been to follow nature. Here no absurd artifices remind us of the geometrical gardener, with his compasses and his diagram, binding and torturing native charms in one chain of ostentatious formality. Nature has not here by barbarous refinement been dislocated out of her proper graces; she did not appear tight-laced and in a hoop petticoat, without the merit of simplicity, or the fascination of true elegance. In the grounds of Fonthill all beauty has been cultivated on so just a principle, that it seemed the spontaneous effect of natural fertility. From the lighter sprinkling of verdure, to the deepest gloom of almost impervious foliage, all partakes of the freedom of untrained production, and whether 'by hill or valley, fountain or fresh shade', the votary of nature may feel himself under the influence of her acknowledged supremacy. The diversity

of situation and circumstance is also very great. Here are extent, repose, and majesty for the pencil of Claude; the rugged grandeur that would attract R[u]ysdael, and the deep and savage wildness which suited the genius of Salvator. Here might Collins indulge in the dreams of fanciful enchantment, Gray soar upon the eagle wing of an ardent ambition, and the classic Thomson 'lie at large, and sing the glories of the circling year'.[41]

6

A Triumph of the Eye

If planting in a seemingly random fashion was essential to the Fonthill design, so also was the handling of the area immediately surrounding the Abbey. Recognizing the need for underlying unity throughout the garden, Beckford ensured that the grounds close to the building were in harmony with it and received appropriate formal treatment. In doing so, he agreed in principle with such garden theorists as Chambers, Walpole, Repton, and Price, who argued that 'a house is an artificial object, and, to a certain distance around the house, art may be avowed'.[1]

Although in the vicinity of the Abbey the area appeared clear in contemporary illustrations, J. C. Loudon during his visit in 1807 noted that there was in one angle, formed by two projections of the building, a small flower-garden, a sundial and a fountain.[2] Not far off was the herb garden, then a range of exposed workmen's sheds, Beckford's carriage shed, and stables for ponies. The formal features here were limited in number, but they combined with a wide, smooth and almost unbroken lawn, which encircled the house for some distance, as accompaniments of art. The graded lawn then melted by degrees into the forest to serve as an appropriate bridge between the Abbey and the wilds. Without this transitional element, a shift from art to unadorned nature would have been too sudden, the design would have lacked that 'gradation and congruity' which Price felt was 'so necessary in all that is to please the eye and mind'.[3]

Besides the formal areas close to the house, there were other ways the Abbey as a central feature was integrated into the landscape scheme. Its Gothic style of architecture, considered in Beckford's day as an important element of picturesque requirements, reflected, with its sudden breaks, variations of form and enrichments of surface, the irregular patterns of the outlying grounds. For this setting, Gothic was more appropriate than Grecian because it was more rugged in appearance and more picturesque. A Grecian structure would have been too symmetrical, its surfaces would have been too smooth and even. 'Mr.

Beckford', wrote an anonymous author in *The Gazette of Fashion*, ' has judiciously chosen the Gothic style of architecture, which harmonizes delightfully with the surrounding scenery of rock, river, and wood; the severe beauty of the classic Greek models, or even the more redundant grandeur which characterized the Roman temple, would not so well accord with English landscapes as the Gothic Abbey.'[4]

> Gothic architecture [Price observed in terms relevant to Fonthill] is generally considered as more picturesque, though less beautiful, than Grecian; and, upon the same principle that a ruin is more so than a new edifice... . In Gothic buildings, the outline of the summit presents such a variety of forms, of turrets and pinnacles, some open, some fretted and variously enriched, that even where there is an exact correspondence of parts, it is often disguised by an appearance of splendid confusion and irregularity... . Every person must be struck with the extreme richness and intricacy of some of the principle windows of our cathedrals and ruined abbeys. In these last is displayed the triumph of the picturesque; and its charms to a painter's eye are often so great as to rival those of beauty itself.[5]

Beckford appreciated Grecian architecture as a classical form of beauty, but, as he once explained to Cyrus Redding, 'his associations were with the North and the country to which himself and his father belonged'. The models for Fonthill, Redding further explained, were the examples Beckford 'found in our ruined abbeys and existing cathedrals'.[6] It was in keeping with this interest in authenticity that Beckford set aside a special library on the second floor of the Abbey called the 'Board of Works' (Oak Library), where the artists and craftsmen employed in the building designs of the Abbey could consult an authoritative collection of books and plates in the fine arts as they attempted to recreate some of the characteristics of the traditional style of Gothic architecture.

The asymmetrical plan of Fonthill Abbey also linked it to the landscape setting (fig. 19). When completed in 1818, it took the shape of a huge cross, 312 feet long from north to south and 270 feet from east to west, in the centre of which rose the great, octagonal tower, which was said to be 276 feet high.[7] H. A. N. Brockman concluded in his study of the Abbey that by 'planning in cruciform, with West and East as comparatively short and stubborn buttressing elements and with North and South galleries to afford length (seen from almost any angle), which helped the building "lie" gracefully, Wyatt had, for his share in this partnership, undoubtedly achieved one of his finest architectural massings.'[8] The result was the formation of a well-balanced architectural grouping that echoed the balanced irregularity of the basic garden plan. This was especially evident from Stop's Beacon, looking towards the south-west side of the building, where the display of 'a variety of forms and members, of studied dissimilarity', as Britton observed, combined successfully to constitute a pleasingly picturesque whole (fig. 23).[9] This was not true of every perspective of the Abbey. The south-east view, for example, suffered from the disproportionate size of the Eastern transept with its massive walls 95 feet high and twin octagonal towers, each 120 feet high, which tended to diminish the loftiness of the central tower and dwarf the size of the southern and northern wings of the Abbey. Britton noted the 'want of combination and harmony' here, but believed that Beckford had planned to counteract the imperfection. 'This part of the building was to have been enclosed by an embattled wall,' Britton explained, ' with a tower gateway, and other architectural appendages: these were to have extended from the mansion to the north, where a mass of coach houses, stables, and other buildings were also to have been erected in a style corresponding with, and apparently forming part of the Abbey.'[10]

The interior of the Abbey also tended to blend harmoniously with the external landscape to create one of the most important examples of the picturesque interior for this period. The long corridor-like galleries created by the cruciform plan reproduced the landscape effect of a tree-lined avenue. This was particularly evident in St Michael's Gallery, the south wing of the Abbey (fig. 20). It was a long fan-vaulted chamber, extending for 112 feet with a width of over 13 feet, and a height of 15 feet.[11] The first half of this gallery from the Octagon was lit by five arched windows on the west side, four of which had plate glass in the lower section and stained glass in the upper. The fifth was a copy of one of the windows in the transept of York Cathedral. The second half of the gallery had three oriels on the east side, two of which were filled entirely with stained glass, so that throughout the day the direct light alternated with the more subdued, producing a soft contrast similar to that which could be found as one walked through some of the winding paths of the estate.

From the angel corbels on both walls of St Michael's Gallery, the mouldings rose in succession and expanded into intricate fan-tracery over the entire length of the ceiling, creating the effect of interlacing trees on forest avenues. This internal landscape was then united with the external grounds at the southern extremity of the gallery, where a large oriel window provided a magnificent view of the lawns and rising forests (fig. 21). As a final touch to the landscape effects in this wing of the building, an uninterrupted vista of 307 feet was provided from the south oriel looking up the aisle to the Octagon through which the perspective was continued to the Oratory at the very end of the northern wing of the Abbey. The long perspective, in Brockman's view, provided another link to the Gothic past. As he explained: 'These long, corridor-like galleries were the cheapest and quickest means of attaining the internal "landscape" effect of an avenue of trees which Beckford was undoubtedly echoing by this attenuated inward projection. The "bare ruin'd choirs" of Shakespeare and, indeed, in the minds of many who still thought that the origins of Gothic were to be found in the interlacing trees of forest avenues, were there reflected.'[12]

The gradations of red tones throughout this room also contributed to its impressive visual effects while simultaneously serving the purpose of emphasizing the blue-blood lines of Beckford's ancestry. The floor was covered with a crimson carpet marked with white heraldic cinquefoils in recognition of his Hamilton background. The walls were pink in tone, and throughout the gallery the windows contained stained glass by Eginton that displayed Beckford's ancestral bearings, royal crests and the effigies of historical and religious figures – all dominated by red and purple colouring. Where there were no window openings, the walls were lined with recessed bookshelves and marble-topped ebony cabinets concealed partly by long double drapes. The colour of the outer curtain for the recessed areas and the windows was purple (though it appears dark blue in the coloured engravings of the interior) with gold trim, in contrast to the prevailing colour of crimson in the gallery. The inner curtains were scarlet. It was a colour scheme designed to cultivate a sense of repose as the eye contemplated the rich décor that served as the setting for the furniture, candle stands, and tables made of carved ebony and tortoiseshell, the impressive piece of sea-green medieval porcelain known today as the Gaignìeres vase, along with the dazzling metalware, ewers, japan and other art treasures on display in the gallery.

The chamber that composed the second half of this long perspective, King Edward's Gallery, extended for a distance of 127 feet, with a width in the principal section of nearly 17 feet, and a height of almost

18 feet (fig. 22).[13] It consisted of a main chamber and three compartments opening out of each other, known as the Vaulted Corridor, the Sanctuary, and the Oratory respectively. Looking up the gallery, Rutter described the view as 'another of those picturesque effects, for which Fonthill Abbey is so justly remarkable'. Like St Michael's Gallery, it was designed to promote heavy visual accents in a composition of colour and contrast. 'As in an excellent picture,' Rutter added, 'the light and shade, the composition and the colouring, have been carefully and successfully studied. The powerful aid of association has been called in, and the united influence of the excitement of the mind and of the imagination is fully felt.'[14] Beckford's appreciation for colour and its effects was well known among his close associates. This was particularly evident in his use of the draperies in this room. To control the strong light emitted through the large windows, the inner scarlet curtains would be drawn, causing a 'general magical tint' to be projected throughout the gallery – a warm harmonious light that Beckford liked so well. Redding wrote about Beckford that he studied the theory of colour as he studied music and 'felt the art of pleasing the ear and eye with true judgement'.[15] Well before the creation of Fonthill, Beckford spoke of the powerful role of drapery in creating a picturesque effect.

'I have often wondered', he wrote in 1787, '[why] architects and fitters-up of apartments have not availed themselves of the powers of drapery. There is no ornament I like so well or that admits of more variety.'[16]

For 68 feet of its length, the ceiling of the northern gallery appeared to be quite different from that in St Michael's Gallery, being flat and of oak. Yet the two galleries were thematically linked in their spatial unity and in the continuation of the dominance of the crimson colouring, contrasted by the purple and gold accents, and by the repetition of the religious and genealogical motifs. The ceiling of this gallery was laid out in square panels containing the Latimer cross, an allusion to Beckford's claimed descent from the first Lord Latimer. Below it for further enrichment ran a cornice of oak whose frieze contained quatrefoils with emblazoned shields of seventy-two Knights of the Garter whom Beckford considered to be ancestors. A flowered red damask covered the walls, while a crimson carpet with flower prints covered the floor. As in the case of St Michael's Gallery, purple and scarlet curtains adorned the windows. In the middle of the eastern wall there was an alabaster chimneypiece flanked on either side by three recessed bookcases, all of which continued the horizontal emphasis of the ceiling. Above the bookcases were six portraits: John of Montfort, Alphonsus V, John of Gaunt, King Edward IV, King Henry VII, and the Duke of Montmorency. A large portrait of Edward III occupied a central position directly over the chimneypiece, the founder of the Knights of the Garter that this gallery was designed to commemorate. To avoid the mathematical repetition of identical patterns, however, Beckford applied the same pictorial principle he used in laying out the grounds. Preferring to give added unity to the scene by balancing different patterns, he made certain that the horizontal lines of the chimney-piece and the six bookcases were offset in the opposite wall by seven tall pointed windows whose linearity was markedly vertical. These lofty windows combined with the long narrow curtains, which hung on each side from the ceiling to the floor, and with a row of single candles, which rested conspicuously on high slender stands, to furnish a vertical emphasis sufficient to give the scene visual equilibrium and relieve what would otherwise have been a formal and flat effect.

Moving beyond the gallery proper, through folding plate-glass doors, the wing narrowed suddenly to a width of 14 feet by means of internal false walls, whereupon the scene shifted from light to dark. Finished in oak with gilt mouldings, the Vaulted Corridor was without windows, but there were on each side three pointed doorways with perforated bronze doors which allowed dim light to filter through from the narrow windows of clear glass in the outer walls, modelled after Henry VII's Chapel in Westminster Abbey. This dim corridor, designed to be an appropriate prelude to the solemn mood of the Oratory, was then succeeded by a square Sanctuary, elevated by a single step. The ceiling here was done in oak, with gilt mouldings and bosses 'covered with a reticulation of lozenge work', in contrast to the vertical ribbing of the Vaulted Corridor.[17] The walls were covered with crimson damask, but the absence of oak ribbing allowed a stronger indirect light to pervade the room, providing another contrast along the way. The wing terminated finally in the Oratory, a five-sided apse, each angle of which contained a slender gilt column, from whose capital rose a 'fan-work reticulation of burnished gold, spreading upward over a ground of deep crimson (fig. 24)'.[18] At the intersection of the mouldings was a gilt boss from which was suspended a golden lamp created for Beckford by the goldsmiths Green and Ward of Ludgate Hill.[19] At the east end was the altar spread with a Persian tapestry of patterned silk, on which stood a marble statue of Beckford's patron saint, St Anthony of Padua, executed by the sculptor John Charles Felix Rossi. For lighting effects in this room, silver candelabra, containing giant tapers, were placed on either side of the altar, the golden lamp provided a subdued light, and two small lancet windows filled with stained glass emitted a glimmering and multicoloured illumination which alternately threw touches of light and shadow on the carved projections and recesses of the statue, and along the face of the gilt mouldings, all designed to produce the effect of repose and harmony.[20]

Turning around at this point to look down the long architectural vista from the north end back to the oriel window at the southern end presented, in Rutter's words, an astonishing scene:

> To reach us, the distant light of the southern oriel has to traverse the Vaulted Corridor, King Edward's Gallery, the Grand Saloon, and the Gallery of St. Michael, every receding step of which is marked by some splendid architectural feature, by some brilliant meuble, by a burst of light, a breadth of shade, or a glow of colour, in varied and almost infinite succession. It is from this point, that the mind of the spectator receives its deepest impressions of the grand conception, the successful execution, the poetic taste, and the commanding wealth of the possessor of Fonthill.[21]

Since the interior of the Eastern Transept was never completed, it is difficult to discuss its aesthetic relevance to the Fonthill plan as a whole. It was originally designed as a chapel and then evolved on the second floor into a baronial hall to commemorate the barons who had signed the Magna Carta, from whom Beckford claimed he was descended. Internal architectural effects were almost totally absent in this wing, as Rutter noted, even as late as 1822, when the estate was sold.[22] This was not true, however, of its counterpart on the west, which was occupied by one grandiose feature, the Great Western Hall. Begun originally as a banqueting hall, it was converted in 1809–10 into the principal entrance when its enormous size precluded the possibility of adequate heating. The Tribune, originally conceived as an elevated gallery to give readings during meals in the manner of early monastic establishments, and an enormous fireplace, both of which separated the hall from the Octagon, were removed to provide direct access to the centre of the building.

The entry to the hall from the outside was by way of massive double doors 35 feet high, hung upon four hinges which were supposed to have weighed more than a ton and cost £1,500.[23] The hall itself was 68 feet long by 28 feet wide. Above the entrance was a roofed niche, surmounted by a cross, which contained a statue by Joseph Theakston of St Anthony of Padua. Crossing the threshold, the dimensions of this grand portal and the extreme height of the archways inside must have caused surprise and astonishment (fig. 26). Seventy-eight feet from the floor was a hammer-beam roof painted in imitation of old oak, which displayed a frieze moulded and arranged into ornamental forms. Above the entrance was a Minstrels' Gallery or Music Loft. The walls of the hall were finished to look like stone, with oak wainscoting on each side to a height of 11 feet. On the south side were three arched windows, and on the north were three recesses in the same form filled with crimson curtains. In the centre recess stood J. F. Moore's full-length marble statue of Beckford's father in his robes as Lord Mayor of London, depicted in the act of making his famous reply to the King. A wide flight of twenty-nine stairs led to the higher level of the Octagon floor, making the Octagon Hall or saloon the focal point of the whole building where all four wings could be seen.

As in the case of the other principal wings of Fonthill Abbey, visitors to the Great Western Hall found the carefully planned effects of light and shade particularly masterful. Rutter felt that the 'the atmosphere of the coloured light, and the solemn brilliancy of the windows' produced an effect closely associated with the contemporary theory of the sublime and combined with the dark colour of the roof, the massive piers of the great portal and the general contour of the noble archway to contrast powerfully with 'the light, the freshness, and the depth of the "marble air", and the delicate colouring and simple outline of the external scene'.[24]

The centrepiece for all four divisions of the Abbey was the Octagon Hall, which ultimately became known as the Grand Saloon. Measuring 35 feet in diameter, it rose to the height of 132 feet where a sixteen-sided lantern hung from a vaulted roof. In each of the eight walls was a pointed arch 80 feet high. In four of them were purple curtains which hung from the top of the arch to the floor and gave access to the four wings of the Abbey. The other four contained curtains 50 feet high, above which were stained glass windows modelled after windows in the Batalha monastery in Portugal. Three of them contained a pattern of a crimson Lancastrian roses with yellow centres, each surrounded by a quatrefoil of mazarine blue bordered with gold. The fourth was a dim sea-green colour. James

Storer observed in 1812 that the 'light emitted through the painted windows of the octagon presents a most enchanting play of colours, and the effect produced by the sombre hue of twilight, contrasted with the vivid appearance at different hours of the day, is indescribably pleasing and grand'.[25] A correspondent from *The New Monthly Magazine* reported the visual effects of the Grand Saloon during various times of day as unrivalled in his experience:

> For ourselves we have experienced its effects under every variety of circumstance; in the stillness of the fresh morning, when the sun was visiting it with his first rays – in the glare of mid-day, when gazing crowds were pacing it, looking upward and around in empty admiration, and not daring to speak, lest they should put to flight the superb silence that seems to be the presiding Genius of the place – in the gloaming of evening, when the receding light seems reluctantly to leave its gorgeous windows, majestic arches, and mysterious recesses – and finally, in the still darkness of midnight, by the guiding ray of one glimmering lamp, we have wandered through its 'visible darkness', and explored the dim vestibules and vaulted corridors, and winding turrets, that adjoin to it, till the spirit of old Romance became young again within us, and we have yearned to act over again *The Mysteries of Udolpho!*[26]

Above the arches was an open gallery, called the Nunneries or Nun's Walk, which connected with a series of apartments. Above this gallery was the fan vaulting that rose to support the great lantern. The dramatic effect of this room was its upward thrust, creating a sense of awe particularly in visitors who entered from the lower northern and southern galleries. Rutter noted that the colossal height of this room emulated the length of the horizontal views elsewhere in the Abbey and that it was constructed on a design executed from a sketch by Beckford himself. Wyatt's taste, in Rutter's mind, would not have produced such a bold effect. 'The colossal height of its dimensions,' Rutter wrote, 'the defiance of all common-place or ordinary arrangement, and the daring originality of its design, were probably far beyond the range of his professional architect, whose *forte* lay in the production of the elegant, rather than the sublime.'[27]

The Grand Saloon also supplied a final scenic effect that should be mentioned. From the top of the side stairs looking down through the entrance hall, as an anonymous visitor described it in 1823, one became aware of the way in which the romantic interior of Fonthill Abbey blended with the exterior grounds to create a totally unified scene:

> Instead of looking along a level, as in the preceding views, the eye, immediately on reaching the extremity of the octagon, or saloon, descends down a spacious staircase, which terminates in a grand entrance-hall, built in the old baronial style; which hall opens of the great western Avenue, or lawn, by a pair of arched gothic doors, more than thirty feet in height.... . The effect of the view through this door, up what is called the Great Western Avenue, is highly characteristic and impressive; and it is imagined in fine taste – blending together, as it does, the outer domain with the inner, and forming them into one stately and magnificent whole [fig. 27].[28]

These then were the principal interior arrangements of the wings of the cruciform, planned in keeping with the style of the whole Fonthill scheme as it evolved over time. Other rooms too numerous to describe in detail were also designed to have a strong sensory impact. Indeed, so important was sensory appeal and visual richness in the decorative context that Beckford created inside the Abbey, namely the theatrical effects of light and colour throughout the rooms augmented by the beauty of the fine and applied art, the fine bindings of the rare books on display, the dominant religious and ancestral symbols in the stained glass and elsewhere, that even domestic comfort was sacrificed. Thus, the dining room, called the Brown Parlour, located in the south-west corner of the Abbey, was the farthest apartment from the kitchen, which lay below the Octagon Hall on the ground floor. The offices on the same floor were cold, poorly lighted and without means for baking, washing, or brewing. Equally impractical were the eighteen bedrooms about the Abbey, thirteen of which were not readily accessible and lacked light and ventilation. The other five had no dressing room. Beckford's own bedroom, the Gallery Cabinet, on the second floor of the south-west tower, was nothing but an unheated cell with one small window and a narrow bed without hangings, certainly a dramatic contrast to the sumptuousness of the rest of the Abbey and another piece of evidence to show that at Fonthill function and comfort gave way to pictorial effect.

Beckford created a memorable Palace of Art, a magnificent scenic effect in a magnificent setting, but beneath the beauty of its surface appeal there was its inherent fragility and insubstantial character that would have dire consequences in time.

7

Bursting upon the Public View: The Sale of Fonthill in 1822

While the Abbey grew in size and expense, rumours about Beckford's financial difficulties began to float about in public. Benjamin West, who was close to the situation, was the source of some of them, having shared them in detail with Joseph Farington in 1807. We learn from Farington's diary, for example, that Wyatt's poor work habits and use of shoddy materials had cost Beckford an unnecessary £30,000. Farington also indicated that the Jamaican estates were losing money and that legal battles over contested ownership of some of these properties had forced Beckford to dispose of property in Bedfordshire and St Pancras. 'Nothing now remains to Him', he wrote, 'but His unproductive Jamaica estates, & the Fonthill estate which is reckoned at £10,000 a year: more might be made of it were the extensive park & grounds turned to greater advantage. Upon this income He knows it is impossible to keep up His former establishment, & He has accordingly reduced it to a very limited scale compared with what it had been.' Farington continued: '[Beckford's] carriages & Horses have been sent away for sale, & Coachmen, Grooms & attendants discharged. He also desired West to assist Him in disposing of His valuable collection of pictures and drawings, saying at the same time He would feel much at parting with them as they never could be recovered by Him.'[1]

Beckford also decided to take up residence in the south wing of the Abbey in the summer of 1807. The north and east wings were yet to be completed, but he had ordered the final demolition of his former residence, Fonthill Splendens, to be carried out in the same year, thereby forcing the shift to the new residence. Dismantling the body of such a magnificent Palladian structure provided visible evidence that 'England's Wealthiest Son' needed to retrench, lending even more credence to the rumours about the state of his financial affairs being bantered about in drawing rooms throughout England. Yet, despite these preliminary signs, it still came as a shock to English society when the papers announced that the contents of Fonthill Abbey were to be sold by Christie's in September 1822:

> MR. CHRISTIE has the Honor very respectfully to inform the Nobility and Publick (the Connoisseurs and the Lovers of Virtú in particular), that on TUESDAY the 17th of September, and nine following Days (Sunday excepted), he will SELL by AUCTION, at FONTHILL ABBEY – The MAGNIFICENT ORNAMENTAL CONTENTS of that distinguished Mansion: including the Collection of PICTURES, ancient and curious GOLD and SILVER PLATE, CABINETS, JAPAN, AGATE, PORCELAIN, and a multitude of costly and precious ARTICLES, no less remarkable for their intrinsic value than for the fine taste with which the whole have been selected.

The Pall Mall firm, headed at this time by James Christie, the younger, had handled four earlier sales for Beckford, the most recent being in 1817, a sale of pictures, drawings and furniture. It is significant that the 'contents' of the new sale did not include the library, though there were in excess of 20,000 volumes on the shelves in the Abbey at the time. While he was willing to forego some remarkable paintings, furniture and *objets d'art*, Beckford's attachment to his books was such that he would dispose of them only as a last resort. It was an exceptional library that in many respects diverged from the more typical collection of Greek and Roman classics. It also bore his personal imprimatur since many of the volumes were arrayed in his armorial bindings and contained pencil notes he was in the habit of writing in the fly-leaves.[2] He was not yet ready to make this supreme sacrifice – financial problems notwithstanding. It was for this reason that when Christie issued the pink wrapper catalogue in July the books were conspicuously absent.

For the first time in its history the Abbey estate was open to the public. The admission tickets issued with the catalogue for a guinea granted multitudes access to the building and the grounds and perhaps even a glimpse of one of the most renowned recluses in England. Once the gates were open for visitors on 1 July 1822, a pilgrimage to the Abbey became a major social event, and the reaction to the experience was often described in hyperbolic terms. 'Since the days of Harry the Eighth', announced the *Morning Herald*, 'there has been nothing in

England that might be compared with the scenes to which the opening of this edifice has given rise.'³ 'It is impossible', explained another report on the event in *The Gazette of Fashion*,

> to do justice to the extraordinary beauty and splendor of Fonthill; so long jealously secluded from the world's gaze, it now bursts upon the public eye like a region of enchantment. We behold all the wonders of nature and of art, the richest and most precious materials, decorated with still more costly workmanship; wealth that would prove the ransom of an emperor, added to the laborious occupation of the longest span of life. The painter, the sculptor, and the architect, have exhausted the treasures of their genius; and the bodily strength of the mechanic, the sweat of the brow, and the waste of the limb, have been called forth to aid the designs of the most exquisite talent. We have here the work of ages past, and the touch of yesterday; and we require the recollection, that dust is all that is left of many of the sublime artists whose resplendent contributions form a miracle and a wonder, to prevent us from exalting human beings to a level with the gods, when we behold the perfection of beauty, the gorgeousness and the elegance which the hand of man assembled at Fonthill.⁴

Beckford himself fully enjoyed the public attention.

> The Holy Sepulchre [he wrote] has at last become one of the most animated spots in England. People go to it as to the waters; they admire it, they devour it with their eyes, they vanish into its thickets, doubtless regretting not yet being able to *retire* behind West's great dauberies. Yesterday seventy waggons, each drawn by several horses, followed by innumerable gigs, deposited at the foot of the Great Portal several dozen insipid personages of that diversity of persuasions in which we glory in this blessed Isle.⁵

Captivated by Beckford's acknowledged reputation as a connoisseur and by the impenetrable secrecy of his pleasure dome, the public found itself afflicted by the 'Fonthill Fever,' as Thomas Dibdin characterized it in a series of six articles about the event which he published in *The Museum* under the pseudonym Cuthbert Tonstall. 'The FEVER raged without control,' he wrote. 'The whole country seemed to feel, in a *social* degree, what the earth would, in a *physical* degree, if a slight shock of an earthquake had agitated it. Across the country, in all directions, for some 50 miles, parties were in a perpetual state of locomotion.'⁶ Symptomatic of the rage to participate in the 'view,' letters, essays and poems about the Abbey and the grounds appeared in numerous newspapers and magazines throughout the country. The excitement surrounding the event also spawned a number of entrepreneurial ventures. One of the earliest of these was hatched by John Rutter, who hastily produced a guidebook to Fonthill that ran through six editions before the end of the year. George B. Whittaker joined in with his descriptive account to capitalize on the event, while James Easton chose this opportune time to reissue his Salisbury guide, with an expanded section on Fonthill Abbey. At least two of these guides borrowed from James Storer's book on Fonthill, so it is not surprising that Storer himself decided to reissue it with eight engravings in a royal octavo and large quarto format.⁷ Many artists seized the opportunity to produce original drawings which were then engraved to accompany the written accounts that were published at the time.⁸ Some individuals reacted by writing poems celebrating Fonthill as an astonishing artistic creation. The contemporary drawings and written accounts which appeared in 1822 and 1823, many done by prominent figures of the day, serve as historical testimony to the keen interest in and popularity of Fonthill and remain of significant value in forming an estimate today of one of the enduring icons of the Romantic period.⁹

As soon as the gates were opened in July, the roads leading to the estate were crowded with pilgrims from all levels of society. The press fuelled the intensity of the event by printing the names of prominent citizens who came to pay homage. The Duke of Gloucester, the King's brother-in-law, spent a night at the Beckford Arms on the estate to have sufficient time to examine the contents of the Abbey and was impressed by what he saw. He was followed by the Duke of Wellington who after his visit declared that nothing could be compared to Fonthill anywhere in Europe. The Dukes of Buckingham, Beaufort, and Devonshire also came, as did an array of lesser-titled individuals. The newssheets noted that Romeo Coates, the actor, spent three nights at the Lamb Inn to indulge himself in the experience, living up to his motto 'While I live, I'll crow'. Many visitors came in private coaches, others on horseback, and still others on foot to see first hand what had only been the stuff of rumour or daydreams. Kendell and Richardson's public coach service ran three days a week to carry passengers from Salisbury to Fonthill on the road that became the main thoroughfare to the Abbey. Once at the Abbey, the *Morning Herald* observed, 'there is no idea of rank. A Marquis's equipage is obliged to wait until a tax-cart full of the farmer, his wife, his grown-up daughters, and his whole nursery, have passed in.'[10]

Rooms in nearby Hindon, Tisbury, Mere and the surrounding towns were impossible to come by, a source of inevitable frustration. 'He is fortunate', *The Times* reported, 'who finds a vacant chair within twenty miles of Fonthill... . Falstaff himself 'could not take his ease' at this moment... . The beds throughout the county are literally doing double duty – people who came in from a distance during the night must wait to go to bed until others get up in the morning.'[11] Every week the numbers swelled until a total of more than 7,200 people were admitted to the grounds. Fonthill became an attraction that even drew people from outside of England. *The Times* commented: 'The languages of France, of Holland, and of Germany; the peculiarities (in tongue) of Scotland and Ireland, the broad dialect of Somersetshire, the tinkling accent of Wales, and the more polished tones of metropolitan residents, are all, at the same moment, heard clashing and contending together.'[12] Author and publisher Charles Knight would later recall that in the year 1822 'the world went mad about Mr. Beckford's wonders. No profane eyes had ever looked upon his towers and pinnacles – his domes and galleries. There was mystery, then, to combine with what was really worth seeing at Fonthill. Its exhibition and its auction produced as much excitement as a Crystal Palace upon a small scale.'[13]

Throughout the acclaim, Beckford was elated. He relished the attention and knew that in the end this mania would serve the sale and his financial interests. He could hardly contain himself in a letter to his son-in-law, the Duke of Hamilton:

The rage is at its height. They dream only of the Abbey, they talk only of it. I doubt whether since the beginning of printing they have ever uttered such extravagances. Semiramis, Babylon, Persepolis no longer count for anything: they proclaim that Vathek and his tower have surpassed them... In short, it is a veritable Rage, and buyers present themselves from all sides.

... Before the most attractive object in the whole world (according to the frenzied impression of the day) is for ever lost to us, come and glance at it, try to glide one fine Sunday up to the demonstrator of the magic lantern, our faithful and well-beloved Franchi. He will tell you what is passing, what has passed. He will relate a thousand anecdotes which would make a fortune if one cared to print them – for the avidity with which they swallow everything which people choose to scribble about Fonthill is unexampled.

The strange things which are passing in my affairs do not cast me down. The Saint who inspired me with the Abbey will also arm me with supernatural courage to do without it, and perhaps even to erect yet another monument to his glory. It will not be for a modest sum, you may be very sure, that I will deprive myself of the fruit of so much labour and so much trouble, in fact of an object which all England beholds agape. It seems that they believe in Fonthill as blindly as in pious times they believed in the most inconceivable legends.

If by any chance the *Literary Gazette,* the *London Museum,* the *Gazette of Fashion,* the *Observer, Morning Herald, Chronicle* etc. etc come into your hands, read them and you will hear only once voice and one acclamation, and that voice the most sonorous and that acclamation the most deafening that was ever raised. And all this only costs me the trouble of reading the most ridiculous declamations and the most high-flown phrases, for neither I nor any of my satellites have paid a sou for puffing. On reading them I have cried a hundred times 'The dog star rages, Bedlam is let loose.' And so will you ...[14]

It is evident from his letter that Beckford was angling for a private arrangement that would allow him to dispose of the entire estate at an attractive price. In the end, the Christie sale became the bait to attract the right buyer. The Duke of Somerset, the brother-in-law of the Duke of Hamilton, was interested, as was Harriet Mellon, the actress and recent widow of the wealthy banker Thomas Coutts. Others, like Earl Grosvenor, flirted with the idea but were unwilling to pay the £300,000 Beckford wanted to close the deal. The puffery in the press was more than Beckford anticipated, but he nevertheless continued to spin his own web behind the scene to extricate himself from a difficult financial situation. He was aided initially by a member of his inner circle, Abbé Ange Denis Macquin, who contributed to the promotional effort by providing a series of four articles, an original drawing and a poem celebrating Fonthill and its creator in the August and September issues of William Jerdan's *Literary Gazette*. The poem concluded with lines that undoubtedly helped to nourish Beckford's rising celebrity status:

> Through the blazoned halls,
> The storied galleries and princely rooms,
> A bright galaxy of heraldic stars,
> Long lines of noblest ancestry, declare
> Who planned, who raised the splendid mansion, where
> Above the puny jarrings of the world,
> Above the strife for glory and power,
> Wrapt in his cloak of learning and of wit, –
> A mind of fire, a deeply feeling heart, –
> A founder stands aloft – a stranger to our sphere![15]

Macquin was a miscellaneous writer and a professor of rhetoric and belles-lettres in France before coming to England in 1792. A frequent resident of the Abbey, he assisted Beckford as librarian for the Fonthill collection and as an occasional genealogist. Beckford's entrepreneurial instincts had to play a role in Macquin's delineations of the Abbey and its contents in the articles published. Macquin would also have shown the manuscript to Beckford for any last-minute changes to ensure accuracy in the details, thus making these articles important authoritative sources of information on Fonthill.

If the celebratory nature of Macquin's pieces were not enough, Beckford approached Macquin in August and proposed that Sir George Beltz, the Lancaster Herald, prepare an informative article on the armorial bearings in the Abbey. This led to the lengthy work that appeared in several issues of the *Gentleman's Magazine* in the fall of 1822.[16] Beckford understood the importance of timing and the role the 'rage' would ultimately play in serving his personal interest, as he made clear to Macquin: 'Now is the moment. I think the public will gladly swallow it up, for they are beginning to busy themselves with the Abbey, and they even seem disposed to panegyrize everything about it.'[17]

The original date for the auction was set for 17 September but then postponed to 1 October and then delayed again until 8 October. No cause for the delay was given to the public. Most assumed that it was due to the constant stream of visitors to the estate that seemed to increase on a weekly basis rather than diminish. What was not known was that negotiations were taking place behind the scenes to sell the entire estate to the wealthy merchant John Farquhar (fig. 25). Farquhar, a Scot, who was represented in the negotiations by the auctioneer Harry Phillips, was a native of Aberdeen. He had made a great deal of money by manufacturing gunpowder and selling it to the Government. He was also a partner in the London agency house of Basset, Farquhar & Co. and a major shareholder of Whitbread's brewery. He was known to have a weakness for speculation and found Phillips's argument compelling that the purchase of Fonthill would elevate his social position instantly as owner of one of the great estates in England.

The deliberations remained a secret until an agreement was reached on 5 October 1822, three days before the auction was to begin. James Fownes, Beckford's solicitor from the London firm of Fownes and White, drafted a memorandum of agreement entitled 'Argument for the Sale & Purchase of the Fonthill Abbey Estate & Effects'.[18] Various maps, plans, and surveys were supplied by James Still, Beckford's land steward. James Christie was now out of the picture, but his catalogue was a document of record in the agreement. Beckford identified certain lots in the catalogue that he wanted set aside for himself.[19] Farquhar, a serious book collector in his own right, wanted the library to be included among the effects. This was a sore point for Beckford, but he ultimately relented after negotiating the retention of one-third of the 'bound Books, Works in letter press, Manuscripts, Books of Prints, Prints and Drawings' and incorporating a carefully written arrangement in the agreement to govern the selection process, which read: 'The said William Beckford or his Nominee, having the first choice, and the said John Farquhar, or his Nominee, the second and third choice (each choice to apply to the full extent of each individual Work so chosen) and so on till the whole shall be divided as aforesaid.'[20] Beckford also excepted the unbound books, all of the articles in his bedroom, the wines and plate not in the catalogue, the useful china in the custody of the kitchen maid, the family portraits, the japan and other objects within the closet of the Yellow Room, along with a portrait of a woman in a striped dress and a carved ebony chair, the statue of St Anthony from the Oratory, two green China jars in the 'new Book Room', and all of his writings, private papers, and account books. He also set aside two riding horses and for his devoted secretary at Fonthill, Chevalier Gregorio Fellipe Franchi ,'one Horse and Gig'. In the end Beckford agreed to accept the sum of £275,00 for the estate and an additional £25,000 for all remaining effects.

So secret were these negotiations that not even Christie was informed that they were taking place. It was only when he arrived at the Abbey on Monday, 7 October, that he learned that he would not preside over the sale. Dismayed and undoubtedly feeling undercut by his competitor, Harry Phillips, Christie dashed off a letter to the *Salisbury and Winchester Journal* in which he made it clear that he was not a party to these deliberations:

> As the Advertisements for the Sale of Effects at Fonthill Abbey were sent by me to your Journal, and have appeared under my name, I consider it due to the many respectable individuals who have quitted their homes to attend this sale, the greater number of whom I conclude are at this time readers of your Journal, that through the same medium I express my concern at the disappointment they must have experienced, a disappointment in which I in some degree partake, and to which I have been unintentionally (if) instrumental.
>
> I arrived at the Abbey on Monday at one o'clock, to undertake the sale, in consequence of the latest notices I had been directed to publish up to the time of my departure from London on Saturday. – It was then only that I was informed of orders that had been received, forbidding further proceedings and the admission of company.
>
> I am sensible that in every transaction of business I have a duty to fulfill to the public, as well as to my employer, and the discharge of my public duties is never unmixed with private feeling. I deem it most unfortunate in the present instance, that I have been allowed such imperfect means of performing the first of these, and that the last, as far as the public are concerned, is to me extremely painful. I feel persuaded, however, that the very unexpected and sudden disposal of the whole Estate has alone induced the Proprietor to determine on a measure, which involved so much disappointment to the public, and to avoid which, he had formerly rejected an offer made to him for the private purchase of the whole of the articles contained in the catalogue of sale.
>
> I am, Sirs, Your very obedient humble servant,
>
> JAMES CHRISTIE
>
> Amesbury, Tuesday, Oct. 8, 1822[21]

Christie was obviously worried about a negative public reaction to him and his auction house and seemed to hint at an earlier offer he had made to buy the contents of his catalogue *en bloc* which was rejected. Some dealers and connoisseurs felt duped by what they ultimately perceived to be a shrewd marketing scheme. Reports also followed in the press about the possibility of some legal actions initiated by individuals to recoup the expenses incurred from travelling long distances to the Abbey. Another spurious account indicated that Beckford was so financially embarrassed that the Sheriff had actually taken entire control of the contents of the Abbey, disguising his own officers as servants during the view, to ensure liquidation of the indebtedness.[22] But rumours and strident complaints faded quickly as winter approached and as the Fonthill rage abated.

Meanwhile, Beckford expressed his relief that he was finally free from his debts. 'Let me announce a great piece of news,' he wrote at the time, 'Fonthill is sold very advantageously. I am rid of the Holy Sepulchre, which no longer interested me since its profanation; I am delivered of a burden and of a long string of insupportable expenses. At present I have only to distribute my funds prudently and await the outcome of events. For twenty years I have not found myself so rich, so independent or so tranquil.'[23] Tranquil he was not for very long. The selection clause involving the identification of the property to be divided between Beckford and Farquhar proved to be contentious, causing an extended delay of the legal transfer and the final payment from Farquhar. Beckford's book agent, William Clarke, and Chevalier Franchi participated in these negotiations as Beckford's representatives. Farquhar hired the bookseller George Lawford to provide assistance with the division of the books and prints. The wrangling was almost inevitable.

By December, with these matters not resolved, Beckford was beginning to have second thoughts about the entire contract with 'old Filthyman,' as he dubbed Farquhar. In advance of a scheduled meeting to obtain agreement, Beckford urged Fownes to find a way to cancel the contract. 'They ought not to quit the Cabinet', he wrote, 'without a signed paper authorizing the specific offer required for the annihilation of the agreement *in all its branches*. This, if obtained, would give me more heartfelt joy than all the 100,000s in the miserable old Reptile's Den.' The loss of Fonthill was troublesome – 'a place I can never forget' – but the loss of his library that he spent years collecting was particularly galling:

All the collective importance of the Library is destroyed. The gaps in every class are so wide that the repurchase of 10,000 volumes would hardly fill them. O that the galling contract was dissolved & my books restored! ... How cheerfully would I pay all incurred expences & square matters so as to exist upon capital till the sale of effects, gutting of the Abbey, disposal of Hatch & of Jamaica the 1st favourable moment, came to my assistance. God send the miserly old Man one ray of intelligence. What a dreadful load would he take off his own shoulders & what a burden of eternal regret from mine.[24]

It was too late, of course, to turn back. The negotiations at that meeting must have been successful because a report surfaced in the press in January that a final agreement had been reached which was 'either agreeable to the original contract, or in consequence of subsequent purchase'.[25] The same report made clear that that the 'purchase money' had not yet been paid because of title complications involving the 'houses and land in Hindon and the neighbourhood, together with a moiety of the Representation of the Borough'. Furthermore, it was noted that Farquhar would have his own sale before the end of the year. In fact, final settlement of the Fonthill sale did not take place until after 25 March when Beckford sent a letter to Farquhar expressing relief that the protracted negotiations were 'upon the eve of final settlement' and offering him as a present the 'fine works of plate [which] still remained at Fonthill Abbey'.[26]

The conclusion of the Fonthill proceedings enabled Beckford to establish permanent residence in Bath by the purchase of houses in Lansdown Crescent in the summer of 1823 where before long he would build another tower amidst a landscape garden on a much smaller scale than Fonthill. The loss of two-thirds of his library would remain a permanent source of discontent, and he spent the rest of his life buying back 'Fonthills', as he called the books he lost in the sale, and when he could not afford to take them in, he would have his bookseller run up the price at an auction to 'teach them the immense value of the worst books from the F[onthill] Library'. [27] The other loss he lamented was the role he played as the major employer of the poor and needy in the population surrounding Fonthill. Despite the rumours about his imperious manner, he was known to have been a generous landlord. There were frequent notices in the press acknowledging

Beckford's contributions as a major employer of the poor in his neighbourhood, as in the case of a correspondent of the *Morning Chronicle*, who characterized the expenditure of monies on Fonthill as a patriotic act:

> This interesting sale, which will take place in a very few days, has given occasion to a great variety of remarks in the public prints, and to some animadversion on the large sums that have been expended by the Proprietor in extravagant projects. It should, however, be considered, that the judicious employment of a princely fortune is a happy art which few have able to attain. In cases where an income may exceed what is necessary for the individual happiness of the owner, the most fastidious objector must surely admit, that calling forth the genius of the architect and the artist, and the labour of the artisan and the husbandman – that constructing a palace where not a shepherd's hut stood before – that clothing with woods a heath or a sheep down, and distributing a large portion of this wealth among the many who co-operate in such works – is true patriotism There are some persons who have attained more than a competence by partaking of the sums so expended in this instance, and hundreds are thereby now enjoying a livelihood in comfort.[28]

In a letter Beckford wrote in January 1823 to John Still, the rector of Fonthill Gifford, he asked that a man caught stealing wood on the estate be released from responsibility. 'This perhaps may be the last opportunity I may have in my power to lessen the sum of misery in my former neighbourhood,' he wrote. 'I shudder to think of the distress which is impending over it.'[29] This was one of Beckford's last acts as proprietor of Fonthill. His reign had come to an end. It was Sir Richard Colt Hoare, long captivated by the Abbey and its owner, who wrote the epitaph for the *Gentleman's Magazine*: 'The pleasing vision is now past, and the noise of the Auctioneer's hammer will not be heard - silence pervades the long-drawn ailes – the lofty portal is closed – and the Abbot is returned to his Cloysters, with thanks to his Patron Saint, St. Anthony, for the numerous Pilgrims who have been attracted to his shrine. But with a farewell look he will shortly bid adieu to his cloistered walls, and extensive solitudes, which are now doomed to greet a second Abbot.'[30]

8

'Sic Transit Gloria Fonthill':
The Sale of 1823

Farquhar, motivated more by speculation than genuine interest in the valuable contents of the Abbey, decided to put the collections up for auction a year later. Phillips, as a reward for assisting Farquhar in the original purchase of Fonthill, was hired to preside over the sale of the 'effects' scheduled to begin on 9 September 1823. Tickets for viewing on any two days sold for a guinea each; tickets with sale catalogues admitted three persons every day, except Sundays, during the view and sale, for 5 guineas each. On 16 June the estate was open to the public for inspection and once again they flocked to it in great numbers. By 8 August newspaper reports indicated that over 5,000 people had visited the estate. The Beckford Arms and the Lamb, Swan, and Crown Inns of nearby Hindon were filled to capacity. This time William Dore of the White Lion Hotel in Bath provided spirits and food all day long in the Fountain Court on the west side of St Michael's Gallery (fig. 28), and the remaining pavilion of Fonthill Splendens was fitted up with beds for overnight accommodations. Rooms in the Abbey that had been closed the previous year were opened to indulge the curious. The unfinished Eastern Transept was set up under the direction of the architect Stedman Whitwell as the site of the auction to provide ample room to display to advantage the objects of virtu, paintings, furniture and books for sale. The walls were covered with a tapestry, while the rafters and joists above were cloaked with a false ceiling made of striped muslin. The auction rostrum stood in the middle of the floor surrounded by a range of wooden benches which rose from the floor in amphitheatre effect to the upper sections of the walls. The auction of some of the paintings and other items took place in the Oak Parlour and the Crimson and Yellow Drawing Rooms. This time there were no postponements, with the sale commencing on 9 September at 1 o'clock in the afternoon.

The first ten days, devoted to the sale of a portion of the books, were surprisingly uneventful, with attendance lower than expected. On the opening day of the auction Phillips made it clear that there would be no reserve on any of the lots offered for sale. The first lot, *Memoirs of the Rev. Alexander Geddes*, sold for 12 shillings. Any books containing Beckford's notes in the fly-leaves drew great interest and were quoted extensively in the press, much to the enjoyment of the readers. One of the volumes, which received the most attention, was Walpole's *Life of the Late Charles James Fox*, containing Beckford's notes about Fox that were reproduced in detail in the published accounts. Before long, a caustic anonymous response to these remarks followed in *The Times*: 'Several papers have published a heap of loose memoranda from a manuscript by Mr. Beckford, of Fonthill, abusive of the character of the late Mr. Fox. We suppose that few persons care to know what Mr. Beckford thinks of Mr. Fox: if Mr. Fox had ever thought it worth while to express an opinion concerning Mr. Beckford, that, indeed, might be a matter of interest and curiosity.'[1]

The prominent London booksellers, Rodd, Lawford, Triphook, and Longman, were among the heaviest buyers. Mr J. Upham, a bookseller from Bath, outspent many bidders. Clarke was present as Beckford's representative doing his master's bidding and took in thirty lots the first day of the sale. But many of the books were knocked down to private individuals, including Sir John Wrottesley, William Miles, son of a Bristol merchant and banker, and the Earl of Arundel. The ubiquitous Richard Heber was there, taking in items at his usual rate. Members of the nobility and other prominent members of society could also be seen on the grounds or examining the treasures of the Abbey. Lord and Lady Lansdowne spent the night entertained by the strains of Mr Goodall, the organist to the Earl of Arundel, who played by candlelight in the Grand Saloon and elicited the admiration of the listeners with a piece called 'The Storm,' and the music of the witches' scene in *Macbeth*. Lord F. Leveson Gower was at the sale, as was Sir James Mackintosh. Sir Henry Wilson made the most ostentatious entrance by arriving in a coach drawn by six horses.

It was not long into the sale before a controversy broke out accusing Phillips of adding books and paintings that were never owned by Beckford. The strongest onslaught came from the *Leeds Intelligencer*. Following a comparison of the paintings listed in Christie's catalogue with Phillips's a year later, the *Leeds Intelligencer* drew attention to the fact that while Christie had listed 115 paintings, Phillips's catalogue included 415 pictures. Where Christie had one work by Teniers for sale, Phillips offered twenty-two. This published report also went on to argue that a man of Beckford's taste would not have owned some of the books in listed in Phillips's sale catalogue:

> We should deserve to be scorched to a cinder by the terrible eye of the Caliph Vathek, if we could bring ourselves to believe for a single moment that Mr. Beckford, of Fonthill, who spared neither pains nor expense in the collection of his books, could ever have been prevailed upon to admit within the precincts of his splendid library, 'A Dictionary of Painters, bound in sheep, to imitate morocco!' or triplicate copies of such publications as the following, which we notice among a vast many more of the same quality in Mr. Phillips' Catalogue: –
>
> > Watt's Views of the Seats of the Nobility and Gentry, 3 copies!
> > Angus's Views of the Seats of the Nobility, 3 copies!
> > Rogers's Imitations of the Old Masters, 3 copies!
>
> These copies, the triplicates of which are, as may be supposed, introduced at respectable distances from each other, are all of precisely the same quality and appearance. Of the last book each copy is differently designated – a system which is pursued in numerous other instances throughout the catalogue. The object of thus varying the titles 'cannot be mistaken'. That the *genuine* Fonthill library should have comprised three sets, none of them proofs, of such common trashy Auction Mart works as the above, is perfectly incredible; and almost equally so, that it should ever have contained duplicate and triplicate copies of such rubbish as
>
> > Beaumont's Travels through the Leopontine Alps.
> > Smith's London and its Environs, folio.
> > Deuchais' Etchings, folio.
> > Marchant's Gems (one of the sets *framed* and *glazed*.)
>
> There are a vast many other items hardly more worthy of preservation, which it would be an insult to common sense to consider as a part of the collection of Mr. Beckford.[2]

Some of the booksellers present at the sale labelled the added books 'foists', believing that the sale was 'made up' from rakings from the stalls of London. Another accusation claimed that the prices Beckford recorded on the inside cover or fly-leaf for each book he bought had been altered in an effort to push up the prices artificially. The *Literary Gazette* provided further fuel to the controversy by hinting that the bookseller Lawford was involved in the scam and identified the libraries from which many of the books supposedly came.[3] Lawford responded with a letter to *The Times* in which he attacked the *Literary Gazette* and defended himself:

> Availing myself of the liberal offer with which you prefaced an article appearing in your journal of the 22d inst., purporting to be copied from an obscure publication, called the *Literary Gazette*, (although I should not have considered it worthy of notice, had it remained in its narrowed limits), but being copied in so respectable a channel, I feel it due to my character, to give it that refutation which it deserves, by broadly asserting it a falsehood; and allow me, Sir, through your medium, to assure such noblemen and gentlemen who have favoured me with their commissions, that in defiance to such invidious calumny, I shall be found to discharge my duties to them with that integrity that I hope shall entitle me to their future patronage ...
>
> Seville-passage, Sept 25   G. Lawford[4]

Needless to say, these reports caused tongues to wag and led to reprintings of the accusatory article throughout England, including an appearance in *The Times*. Alaric Watts, who was the editor of the *Leeds Intelligencer* at this time, recaptured the controversy his own newspaper created in a lengthy poem, 'The Sale at Fonthill A Fragment,' published in the November issue of the *Literary Museum*:

> Here a black-letter hero, with rat-smelling air,
> Tipping winks full of meaning, squats down in his chair,
> The veteran of many a Book-auction is he,
> And he'll not be bamboozled, we think, Mr. P.!
> If the item is genuine, away goes his nod,
> And if cheap, is knocked down with, 'tis your's Mr. Rodd.'
> If a 'foist,' and his glance of contempt is enough,
> Why he dives for his snuff-box and only takes snuff![5]

Copies of the Leeds article circulated freely at the sale and in the local inns to the dismay of Phillips who protested his innocence from the podium, chastised Thomas Barnes, the editor of *The Times*, for reprinting the damning piece and attempted to shift blame to Longman by pointing out that he was the proprietor of both the *Leeds Intelligencer* and the *Literary Gazette*. He did allow that Farquhar had added some furniture and valuable effects from the Marshal Bessières estate in Paris, but he believed that this was the prerogative of the new owner of Fonthill. Thomas Adams, a Shaftesbury bookseller who attended the sale, characterized the atmosphere that had evolved, claiming that he 'never was at a Sale where so much suspicion and jealousy reigns'.[6]

The sale of books continued, nevertheless, with the finest items being readily identifiable by the knowledgeable buyer. But just when the dust had settled, a new, more dramatic flap occurred involving one of the most highly touted works of art in the collection. This was lot 1567, described as a topaz cup with a dragon handle of enamelled gold, set with diamonds and mounted on a tripod stand, and said to have been made by Benvenuto Cellini as a wedding present for Catherine Cornaro. Phillips offered it for bidding on 23 October, the thirty-second day of the sale, whereupon its authenticity was immediately challenged by Kensington Lewis, a London silversmith and antiquities dealer. The *Salisbury and Winchester Journal* reported the dramatic details:

A singular scene took place in the sale-room at Fonthill Abbey on Wednesday last. The magnificent Topaz Cup, which has been so long considered as one of the chief objects of curiosity in the Abbey, and on which Benvenuto Cellini lavished all his skill, was put up for sale. A Mr. Lewis, a London silversmith, declared it was not a topaz, but a chrystal! This assertion, so unhesitatingly made, seemed to startle the company who were assembled to witness the disposal of this celebrated gem. Mr. Phillips expressed his astonishment at the boldness of the assertion, and declared that he would not only undertake to sell it as a topaz, but would realise his description of it. The cup, he said, had been for many months submitted to public view, during which time it had been seen by many scientific men, none of whom had ever ventured to express a doubt upon it. Mr. Beckford, whose refined taste and judgment were so well known, and so infinitely superior to Mr. Lewis's, never entertained any other opinion than that it was a topaz; and he (Mr. Phillips) thought Mr. Lewis presumed too far, in declaring it to be a chrystal, considering the very limited acquaintance he had with the article. He desired Mr. Lewis to understand that long before he was born, it was his (Mr. Phillips's) practice to sell nothing under a false description, and that if his sense of honesty did not prompt him to do this, his conditions of sale would bind him to do so. (Applause)[7]

While managing to sway the crowd in the room, Phillips was still anxious about being undercut in a way that would deflate the hammer price of the item. He appealed to Robert Hume, Beckford's London agent, who was on the scene, and Hume declared that Beckford had always considered it to be a topaz. A heated argument followed wherein Phillips suggested that Lewis's motive was to try to buy the cup himself at a depreciated price and threatened to secure redress if the 'cup should be injured by his unjustifiable attack upon it'. The cup was finally put up for sale at 300 guineas and sold for £630, a sum that was considered far below its value. Still agitated, Phillips cited William Buckland, who held the chair of mineralogy at Oxford, as an authority who had examined the cup earlier and declared it to be his conviction that it was formed of a block of genuine Hungarian topaz. The report in the *Salisbury and Winchester Journal* concluded that the 'highest credit is due to Mr. Phillips for the great coolness and spirit with which he conducted himself, and we do not envy the reproof which Mr. Lewis received'.

The Times, keeping an ever-watchful eye on activities at the Fonthill sale, republished a great portion of the article from the *Salisbury and Winchester Journal* on 28 October, which drew a detailed response from Lewis a few days later in which he defended himself and continued to question Phillips's integrity over the conduct of the sale.[8] Notably, he pointed to the fourth condition published in Phillips's catalogue: 'The lots to be cleared away, with all faults and errors of description, at the purchasers' expense, without reference to the identity of subject or master.' Lewis found this clause too obviously self-protective. 'Surely,' he continued, 'if Mr. Phillips never sells under "false descriptions", or, as his duty demands, without first satisfying himself as to the "identity of subject or master", this condition must have been unnecessary, and I am quite satisfied would not have been included by any other auctioneer... . As to his threat of legal proceedings against me, he may be assured that I shall meet him in Westminster-hall, where, perhaps, I may have an opportunity of exhibiting a little more of his "practices, sense of honesty, and manner of doing business".' This was a strong personal attack against Phillips that might have been dismissed as intemperate, but then Lewis provided some provenance of the cup that continued to cast a shadow over its authenticity:

And now, Sir, for the history of this topaz (which I have taken some time and trouble to ascertain) – I have traced it originally to have been in the possession of Mr. Stanley, of Bond-street, who offered it twice for sale by auction for about £300, but was unable to obtain that bidding, and ultimately sold if for considerably less. I have Mr. Stanley's authority for stating, that the vase was in his possession for a year and a half at that price; and that during that time he repeatedly offered it to the trade, including Mr. Farmer, of Tavistock-street, and Mr. Foster, who are well-known dealers in articles of vertu, without being able to obtain a purchaser. It ultimately got into the hands of Mr. Baldock, of Hanway-street, who sold it to Mr. Beckford for less than £300.

Lastly, Sir, permit me to repeat my opinion, that the vase is not a topaz; and to state that my judgment has been since supported by some of the most experienced jewellers, and dealers in articles of vertu, in London; including Mr. Hawley, of the Strand; Mr. Jarman, of St. James's-street; and of Mr. Farmer and Mr. Foster, whose names I have already mentioned.[9]

Lewis's history of the ewer appears to be credible, based as it was on his own familiarity with the principal dealers and auctioneers in the trade. Beckford did in fact buy the ewer in 1819 from Edward Holmes Baldock, a prominent antique dealer of 7 Hanway Street, London. There is a document among the Beckford Papers entitled 'Description of Vase of Topaz of Saxony – Work of the Celebrated Benvenuto Cellini', which Beckford received from Baldock when he purchased it. The document outlines its spurious history from the time it was executed as a wedding present when Georgio Cornaro married Elizabeth Morosini and then from the Cornaro family to the ducal family of Gonzaga of Mantua and then to London sometime in the eighteenth century.[10] It eventually ended up in Lord Rothschild's collection where it remained until it was sold to Jack and Belle Linsky of New York. From the Linsky collection it went to the Metropolitan Museum, where it remains today.

Lewis's mineralogical assessment that it was rock crystal instead of topaz also turned out to be correct. The most recent evidence indicates that the rock crystal bowl was probably carved in Prague in the seventeenth century, while the mounts appear to date from the early nineteenth.[11] There is no record of Beckford's reaction to Lewis's charge, but he was aware of the possibility that it was not an authentic Cellini and was attempting to investigate its provenance. As he wrote to Chevalier Franchi in 1819, 'You may admire the Zenobia [a sardonyx gem portrait] as much as prejudice permits; for my part I prefer the Cornaro – if it is the Cornaro. I've searched in vain so far for any information about this real marvel in the writings of Benvenuto Cellini. In his treatise on the goldsmith's art he talks a good deal about enamelling, but I can't see that he ever quotes this vase as an example.'[12] So it is evident that Beckford was not deceived into believing that it was an authentic Cellini work. He bought it as a beautiful work of art: 'I'll return to this research another day, though it matters little whether or not I find the answer – the object in itself deserves the most wholehearted eulogy.' He admired its craftsmanship and rich beauty, calling it a 'sublime *objet d'art*' and noting that its 'diamonds, topaz and enamel – everything glitters in a magical way'.[13]

Phillips's reaction did appear in *The Times*. In his response he distanced himself from any responsibility by saying that he relied on the Christie catalogue for the description which was 'precisely that which was given Mr. Farquhar when he purchased it'. ' If,' he added, 'contrary to my expectations and the deliberate judgment of many eminent mineralogists, it should prove to be any thing but an Hungarian Topaz, it will be returned to Mr. Beckford, as not answering the description he gave of it when he sold it.' He then concluded with the following defence:

The assertion which I made respecting Professor Buckland's opinion of it, whether true or false, could have no possible influence on the sale of it, as it was not made till *after* the Cup was knocked down, when it was communicated to me for the first time, by authority which I could not doubt... .

Some allusion has been made to one of my conditions of sale. I have only to remark, in reply, that it is a condition which I have used for many years, and which is to be found, in effect, in every catalogue that ever was published, and is in many instances much more summary and decisive, being frequently summed up in these very comprehensive words – 'The lots to be taken away with *all faults.*'

My conduct and character have been long before the world, and the large share of its favour which I have gratefully received, seems to render any defence of them unnecessary; but I think the explanation I have given is due to those friends and patrons with whose confidence I have been honoured.[14]

The controversy over the authenticity of the Cellini ewer diminished as the sale continued for thirty-seven days. There were, after all, many spectacular works of art to consume the interest of the insatiable collector or his representative. Among the furniture, for example, there were the chairs that once belonged to Cardinal Wolsey from his palace at Esher; the ebony state bed of Henry VII with its crimson damask hangings and purple quilt worked with gold; the massive table, about nine feet long and over four feet wide, inlaid with marble, jaspers, and oriental onyx, from the Borghese Palace; the Holbein cabinet designed for Henry VIII; the Japanese lacquer chest once owned by Cardinal Mazarin; Japanese cabinets from the Duc de Bouillon's collection; and the secretaire made by Riesener for Marie Antoinette. There were silver plate of various designs, a Miessen dinner service of 363 pieces made for the Prince of Orange, the Rubens vase, Limoges enamel reliquary, the Van Diemen Box owned by Marie Antoinette, and the Cellini nautilus. There were also 424 paintings, which took four days to sell, including works by Rubens, Rembrandt, Teniers, Dürer, da Vinci, Dow, van Eyck, and Gainsborough, among others. In short, the Fonthill sale offered a dazzling array of rarities that makes it difficult to accept William Hazlitt's judgement at the time that Beckford's taste was meretricious and the Abbey a 'desart of magnificence, a glittering waste of laborious idleness, a cathedral turned into a toy-shop, an immense museum of all that is most curious and costly, and, at the same time, most worthless in the productions of art and nature.'[15]

The fact is that for many of Beckford's contemporaries Fonthill lived up to its mythic reputation. The attention in the press, whether positive or not, spurred interest in the event and made participating in the actual 'view' of Fonthill even more irresistible. The sale of the books and prints, which occupied twenty days, had the lightest turnout, with reports estimating approximately fifty people in attendance each day. The numbers swelled to sometimes 200 a day for the paintings, furniture and other works of art. Beckford did not personally attend, but his agent William Clarke bought over 640 lots in the book portion of the sale. In the end Farquhar realized £43,869.14s from the sale. Phillips also conducted a separate sale of the choice and valuable wines and liqueurs in the Abbey cellars on the last two days of October, but the total amount realized from these proceedings is not known.

In one of his final acts before the closing of the sale on 29 October, Farquhar ordered the illumination of the Abbey at night and invited the public to the spectacle. The event took place on the evening of 22 October, with a large crowd in attendance. On hand for the event were Lord and Lady Arundel, Richard Heber and the poet Thomas Moore and his wife, among other prominent figures. For the occasion all of the heavy curtains were pulled aside in the Abbey to expose the incandescent glow of candlelight flickering in every room. Light poured out through the windows radiating the colours of the stained glass portraits and the array of rich heraldic symbols. The lantern in the tower streamed its radiance against the dark sky to the silent amazement of those individuals stationed outside on the lawn who 'gazed as intensely as Leander when he looked up to the turret of Hero for the signal-torch which was to guide him to the possession of happiness'.[16] The doors of the Abbey were then thrown open to the onlookers who passed through the rooms to indulge more intimately the fully illuminated spectacle inside. To enhance the visual effects, the grand organ filled the air with its 'high and holy harmony'. The play of light inside the Grand Saloon was particularly impressive as a correspondent from the *Morning Chronicle* observed: 'The light playing along the shafted arches which lead off to various parts of the structure, and flickering upon the enriched work of the interior of the tower, the height and symmetry of the poetic architecture – the splendour of the lanthorn – all whose stained windows were in a blaze of coloured radiance – the clear brightness of the circular windows beneath, and the deep relief of draperies of solemn richness, all produce the effect of a magical illusion.' Looking up and down St Michael's and King Edward's galleries was an equally imposing sight. 'The lengthened streams of light, along which the eye had an indistinct vision of glittering and accumulated ornaments which yet decorate the walls, gave the impression of a place where genii held their fanciful dominions, or reminded one of those depositories of the treasures of Eastern Caliphs, in which gold and jewels are surrounded by spells, mystery, and enchantment.' It was a fitting farewell for this palace of enchantment, a Keatsian event that Beckford himself would have appreciated and indulged.

The villagers of Hindon and Tisbury expressed their own farewell to Beckford as the landlord of Fonthill on 29 September, when they celebrated his birthday. A band played throughout the day in Hindon, bells rang, and the air was rent with exclamations of ' Beckford forever,' 'Good luck to Beckford,' and 'May he last forever *till the world is without end*'. Guns were fired in his honour, while revellers who were voters proclaimed that they would never vote for anyone but him or for the candidate he supported.[17] Contrary to various reports, which appeared in the press from time to time, that Beckford mistreated the people he employed, this occasion was indicative of the goodwill and gratitude they felt towards him as a generous benefactor, feelings that continued throughout the years that followed. Beckford expressed his own gratitude to the workers on the Fonthill estate by continuing to pay the annual bounty to them in 1823, long after he had any obligation to do so.

As the second Fonthill sale came to a close, the woods and pathways of the estate once again fell quiet and the new Abbot proceeded to settle down to refurnish the Abbey to reflect his own taste and interests. It was not long thereafter, however, that Farquhar received word that the structural weakness of the Abbey was a threat to its survival and a danger to the inhabitants. The information came from Beckford, who had been summoned to the deathbed of Wyatt's Clerk of the Works and learned from him that, although money had been supplied, he failed to provide an adequate foundation for the octagon tower according to the established specifications. Consequently the tower was unsafe. Beckford felt it was his duty to report this incident to Farquhar who accepted the information with a cool indifference, saying that he felt the tower would last a lifetime.

Farquhar might, in fact, have known about this possibility after living in the Abbey for a while. Whenever a strong wind was up, it creaked, groaned, and whistled, which once led Beckford to say that he feared that someday he would be crushed like a lobster in his shell. Charles Knight was in residence one night in 1823, along with Stedman Whitwell and the artist George Cattermole, and reported an alarming experience during a storm that drove the guests who were lodged in the dormitories of the tower to seek safety on the main floor of the building. 'The wind rose,' he recollected, 'the storm grew louder and louder;

the frail structure rocked, as Gulliver's cage rocked in the eagle's beak. The terrified guests rushed down the broad stairs, and sat directly in the dark saloon till the daybreak gave them assurance of safety.'[18] Well before the sale of Fonthill there was also public awareness that Wyatt had created a perilous situation through his failure to provide a solid foundation for the tower. For example, a writer in the *Gentleman's Magazine* observed in December 1821 that 'the tower is acknowledged to be a weak and dangerous structure, and so tottering are the eight surmounting pinnacles, that they are held on their bases by strong iron bars, to the no less disparagement of the building than of the builder.'[19]

The tower did collapse on 21 December 1825, at three o'clock in the afternoon, falling into the fountain court, destroying the Octagon and a major portion of St Michael's and King Edward's galleries and the Great Western Hall. Intact were the great organ in its established place and the statue of Alderman Beckford in its niche, 'as if it remained to point to the ruins of his son's ambition'. Sir Richard Colt Hoare published a farewell to the passing of Fonthill in the *Gentleman's Magazine* a few months later – 'Sic transit gloria Fonthill' – and arranged to have John Buckler do a dramatic picture of the Abbey in ruins as a historical record of the event (fig. 29).[20]

Fortunately, no one was hurt. The most detailed account of what happened appeared in the *Gardener's Magazine* ten years later.[21] According to an eyewitness, Farquhar, who was in ill health at the time, was wheeled out in a chair in the front of the building to examine the deep cracks in the tower which was already tilting off centre towards the south-west. Once again, he dismissed the possibility of its coming down, but just after he had been taken back inside, it toppled, causing an immense rubble below as it fell on other sections of the building. Oddly, neither the servants working in the kitchen nor Farquhar heard the crash, though the dust cloud it created could be seen as far away as Wardour Castle. The witness described the fall as very beautiful as the weakened tower descended in slow motion before his eyes: 'It first sank perpendicularly and slowly, and then burst and spread over the roofs of the adjoining wings on every side, but rather more on the south-west than on the others. The cloud of dust which arose was enormous, and such as completely to darken the air for a considerable distance around for several minutes. Such was the concussion in the interior of the building, that one man was forced along a passage, as if he had been in an air-gun, to the distance of 30 ft., among dust so thick as to be felt.'

Once Farquhar realized what had occurred, he observed in his usual cool manner that he was glad it fell, for now the house would not be too large for him to live in. Beckford was supposed to have responded with equal aplomb when he learned of the incident, exclaiming that the tower had made a bow to Farquhar that it had never made to him. From that time on, according to Redding, the relationship between Beckford and Farquhar grew closer, to the point where Farquhar considered bequeathing Fonthill back to Beckford, 'for he frequently observed he had a great inclination to do so'. When Beckford was asked whether he would have liked this legacy, he replied, 'Good heavens, yes, I should have been in an extacy at it, for it would have falsified the old proverb, "You can't eat your cake and have it too".'[22]

In the end Farquhar did not follow through on what would have assuredly embellished the Fonthill legend. Plagued by ill health and uninterested in restoring the Abbey, he moved instead to sell the Abbey remains and the land within the enclosure, including land in the parish of Fonthill Gifford and Tisbury, the total amounting to 2,975 acres, to John Bennett of Pyt House, MP for Wiltshire. A second portion, which consisted of 1,400 acres, was to go to Henry King of nearby Chilmark.[23] No sale price was agreed upon for these properties before Farquhar died of apoplexy in July 1826 at his house in London. Since he left no will, the final terms of these sales were not decided until 1838. Farquhar's nephew, George Mortimer, acquired in a transfer that was later disputed, the lower grounds with the remaining wing of the old mansion and 1,200 acres of adjoining land, the value of which was established in court to be £19,700. He proceeded in 1827, in a triumph of utilitarianism over aesthetics, to build a cloth factory at the end of the lake in the lower park. During the same year Farquhar's library was disposed of by auction at Sotheby's.[24] Mortimer then, on 29 October 1829, divided this property into three lots which he sold by auction through George Robins. The first portion, including the pavilion and the park, consisting of 1,000 acres, was knocked down for 40,500 guineas; the second portion, involving the cloth mill, 24 cottages and 39 acres, went for £12,000. Legal complications over the estate, however, prevented transfer. These two lots eventually went by private treaty to James Morrison. The third lot, which included Lawn Farm and 107 acres of land, sold for £4,900 and shortly thereafter was sold to John Bennett for £5,000. Again the deeds of purchase, because of family legal squabbles involving a Chancery suit, were not signed until

1838. Oddly enough, Fonthill Abbey remained in ruins throughout Beckford's lifetime. The rubble was finally removed in 1844, the year of his death, after Earl Grosvenor, later Marquess of Westminster, contracted with Bennett to buy the estate. Only a small section of King Edward's Gallery was left after everything was removed from the site. It remains standing today, consisting of the Lancaster Tower and the Oratory, Sanctuary, and Vaulted Corridor on the main floor, the Lancaster State bedroom on the next floor above it, and on the second floor of the tower, the Upper Lancaster Room, which was used as a billiard room in Beckford's day (fig. 30).

Few individuals sought entry to the Fonthill estate in the years that followed the ruin of the Abbey. But there was at least one occasion when Beckford himself certainly returned. It was on 19 July 1835 that he decided to ride his horse from Bath to Fonthill after being away for twelve years. In a draft to an unidentified person, he recorded the experience, revealing the sense of distance he now felt from the Fonthill phase of his life: 'T'other day I rode all over Fonthill – the woods are still magnificent, & one point, of the ruins – sublime. Mephistopheles could not have contemplated the whole scene more impartially or with greater composure.'[25] Alfred Morrison, son of James, claimed that one day in 1843, as he was out walking on the estate, he was surprised to discover an old gentleman – 'sitting on a small grey cob, motionless and absorbed' – contemplating the ruins. ' It was William Beckford,' according to Morrison, 'come over from Bath … to have a last look at the remains of that stupendous folly that he had built' – one year before he died.[26]

Another very important record and the most complete account of the ruins was left by the Bath artist Henry Venn Lansdown, who visited the remains on 28 October 1844, after Beckford's death and before the broken structure was dismantled and hauled away.[27] Upon gaining access to the grounds, he walked to the site and stood in awe before the extensive assemblage of ruins. There stood the Eastern Transept, still imposing with its twin towers rising 120 feet into the air but now roofless and completely open to the elements. The remains of the Great Western Hall were covered with briars and brambles. The lofty painted windows, the heraldic symbols, and the heavy thirty-foot doors were gone. Theakston's statue of St Anthony was in its place still holding out his right hand 'as if to protect the sylvan and mute inhabitants of these groves', but tottering in the wind and soon to be a victim of time.[28]

Reaching the Octagon, Lansdown observed that two sides remained. As he looked above, he could still see two windows of the four nunneries. 'And what is more wonderful than all,' he wrote, ' the noble organ screen, designed by "Vathek" himself, has still survived; its gilded lattices though exposed for twenty years to the "pelting of the pitiless storm", yet glitter in the last rays of the setting sun.' The only room that seemed to survive the desolation was the Brown Parlour. The eight windows remained intact with William Hamilton's designs of thirty-two figures of kings and knights from whom Beckford was supposedly descended. But even this room, the site of elegant dinners in the glowing light of the silver candelabra, was showing the effects of an insecure roof, with the floor now covered in a pool of water. Despite the battering over time, King Edward's Gallery revealed something of its former glory. Lansdown noted that the ceilings of the consecutive rooms were still beautiful and as fresh as if just painted, with the cornice still preserved and its three gilded mouldings. But the seventy-two emblazoned shields that were a part of the frieze had been torn off by vandals, as were other ornaments throughout the remains that they could carry away. The oratory still gleamed with purple, scarlet and gold as if recently painted, but the elegant golden lamp was missing and the floor in the southern end of the gallery had been removed exposing unsightly beams. Looking back down King Edward's Gallery, Lansdown saw the alabaster chimneypiece was still in place but suffering a deep crack in the centre. The recesses for the books with sliding shelves were still there; on the opposite side, however, the window frames and glass windows had been removed, exposing the interior to the harsh elements. Finally, Lansdown climbed the circular staircase in the Octagon, entered a remaining apartment and ultimately reached the balcony that overlooked the Octagon where he could view the whole desolate scene at once. 'How deep were my feelings of regret at the destruction of the loftiest apartment in the world,' he wrote. 'Twenty years ago this glorious place was in all its splendour. High in the air are still seen two round windows that once lighted the highest bedrooms in the world.' He then walked away from the building lamenting the loss of the 'gem and the wonder of earth'.

9
The Contemporary Reception of Fonthill

Any assessment of Fonthill today must rely to a great extent on the early nineteenth-century published accounts of the estate since it no longer exists as a whole composition – that is, the Abbey and its landscape setting. These contemporary appraisals are of significant historical value because they were based on the first-hand examination of the building and the grounds when the estate was accessible to the public during the sales of 1822 and 1823. They also remain an important testimony to the impact Fonthill had on the collective imagination of the age, giving dramatic expression to the new aesthetic currents, including the solipsistic character of its artistic expression, the nostalgia for religion, the taste for the beauty of the irregular line and the celebration of the animating qualities of the picturesque and the sublime. Nikolaus Pevsner's observation that Fonthill was 'the first neo-Gothic building to create sentiments of amazement, of shock, even of awe' is borne out by the many essays, poems, and graphic works that have been left behind in response to the experience of visiting the Abbey and by the celebration of its image in an array of ceramic souvenirs in the nineteenth century.[1]

Since the Abbey was located in one of the highest regions in Wiltshire, its commanding height set it off to particular advantage and contributed to the awe of visitors who saw it rising towards the heavens for the first time. It was an unusual setting for a building of this type as a perceptive writer in the *Morning Chronicle* noted.[2] In England, abbeys or ruins of abbeys were usually situated in valleys or plains surrounded by woods. Valle Crucis or Tintern Abbey, for example, had romantic and tranquil settings, but did not hold commanding views. The elevation of Fonthill Abbey set it apart from similar structures, giving it a singular and arresting character. Such a prominent structure standing in the midst of a magnificent wooded setting communicated a sense of 'seclusion with authority.' As the writer in the *Morning Chronicle* explained: 'While it seems to withdraw from the surrounding world, as in conscious superiority, looks down upon it. Thus a lofty sternness appears blended with a mysterious retirement, and like as in the character of Becket or Wolsey, the spectator does not know whether to admire most the real ambition or the assumed sanctity.' In a few sentences this writer captured the essential symbolism of Fonthill Abbey and the basis of its appeal to many contemporaries. Mirroring the increasing secular trends of the age, it was a church devoted to human creations rather than to divine. It drew its sanctity not from any religious associations but from the boldness of its conception and the self-asserting authority of its creator.

What particularly impressed those visitors who were familiar with the Abbey property before Beckford began developing it was the astonishing transformation of the grounds. Some had remembered sections of barren or sparsely planted land, especially along the broad front of the hill where the Abbey was located, which can be seen in Turner's watercolours of the building under construction in 1799. But by the time of the first sale, the entire area was covered with plants and shrubs of all varieties, and towering pine, Scotch fir, and oak. Looking south over the hill from the Abbey tower, an unidentified observer in 1823 stood in wonderment of what had been accomplished over a thirty-year period. 'Here we stand', he mused, ' on the summit of this far-famed tower, overlooking a spot which, even within the memory of most of us, was a barren heath – an interminable extent of bare *down*, with scarcely a tree upon it; and which now, by means of one man, and under the inspection of one superintending assistant, has become what we now see it – a magnificent domain, including nearly all the natural beauties that can belong to a spot of the kind, and crowned by a building of unrivalled extent and grandeur.'³

Its rich and abundant growth amidst the smooth, rolling downs of Wiltshire prompted some visitors to call Fonthill 'a paradise amidst the wild',⁴ and 'an Eden rescued from a desart'.⁵ Rutter felt that the cultivation of this terrain was an extraordinary achievement for one man to have accomplished. 'We as constantly feel the presence of the creative power of unbounded wealth and exquisite taste,' he wrote, 'in rendering these woods what poetry might depict of the woods of Arcadia; where the kindliest soil and the most genial climate should strew the earth with every sweet, and a garden should bloom in every wilderness. The luxuriant imagination of Milton has painted a part of that scene, which has been almost realized, under the greatest natural disadvantages, by the

[145]

enterprising spirit of unlimited wealth.'[6] The remarkable metamorphosis of Fonthill explains why so many visitors described it as a fairyland, a place, as Richard Colt Hoare wrote, 'raised more by majick, or inspiration, than the labours of the human hand'.[7] The age of necromancy has not passed away, explained a report on Fonthill in *The Gazette of Fashion*: 'The Genii of the Ring and the Lamp, under the more modern names of Wealth and Taste, can raise structures equalling, in the richness of their architecture, the fairy palace of Aladdin and convert barren heaths to gardens of delight, rivalling in beauty the oriental splendours of the happy valley.'[8]

Equally remarkable was the interior of Fonthill. Visitors were struck by the powerful effect of the *ensemble* of art as they toured the various rooms. It was noticed that care was taken not to display the art objects in the 'monotonous uniformity of a nun's rosary'. Instead, one visitor wrote: 'The genius of combination has here been exerted with the happiest effect; and with such harmony are the most costly treasures disposed that each article, besides its separate lustre and attractions, serves towards some general design. The mind is thus diverted and relieved from the painful repetition of but one action, the exercise of but one faculty. The imagination is thus roused from the individual wonders of the scene to the contemplation of the grand *ensemble*. In this consists the secret of true taste, and of the witchery of Fonthill.'[9] Indeed it was Fonthill considered as a total aesthetic experience that impressed many individuals who participated in the viewing. In a letter from published in the *Morning Chronicle*, a writer explained that wandering through the rooms of Fonthill with their arranged lighting effects, dazzling display of exquisite works of art and vivid interior décor was so awe-inspiring that it could best be described as 'a self-annihilating experience'. It constituted an achievement that extended beyond the reach of ordinary mortals: 'Here is a palace ready-made and worthy of a King. All that is awful in the Cathedral, all that is magnificent in the modern style of architecture, all that is superb in fitting up, and most of what you find interesting in various museums, all is concentred in this place.'[10] The multifaceted sensory impact achieved through the artistic presentation of interior and exterior scenes promoted an immersion, explained another correspondent in the *Morning Chronicle*, that was deeply moving:

The long galleries, now thronged, now sprinkled with company, display a fantastic moving picture; while the perspective, inter-spersed in the distance with Lilliputian variegated forms, either retires into solemn gloom, or opens upon the brilliant and glad-some landscape without. Every moment some new object strikes the attention; at every step the feet, the eyes, are entangled in the folds of luxury.... In most collections some one object prevails to the exclusion of every other: here Art wooes us in all her shapes; Taste holds a hundred mirrors, a hundred magic sceptres in her hand, and shews the glittering treasures of the world around her.[11]

For this individual, Fonthill in its entirety constituted an aesthetic experience unequalled anywhere in Europe: 'There is nothing equal to the interior of Fonthill in Germany, in Italy, or even in *la belle France*; and the grounds, which include nineteen hundred acres, present a greater variety of beautiful landscapes, wood and water, than we ever saw within the same circumference. Every English man that can ought to visit Fonthill.'

Many contemporaries who recorded their reactions to Fonthill viewed the translation of raw nature into a luxuriant landscape scene as a measure of Beckford's artistic inventiveness and credited him for masterminding it. It was one thing, they felt, to improve with success an already existing landscape garden, as was Humphry Repton's forte, but it was quite another to bring one into existence from humble begin-nings. The artist Constable, who lived in nearby Gillingham, was among the curious who reacted this way. ' I was at Fonthill yesterday', he explained to his wife, 'to see that extraordinary place... on the whole it is a strange, ideal, romantic place; quite fairy-land.' Such a model of elegance and taste seemed almost out of place, as he explained in an earlier letter, 'standing alone in these melancholy regions of Wiltshire Downs'.[12] William L. Bowles used the same subject as the theme of his poem 'Lines on a First View of Fonthill Abbey', which appeared in the *Gentleman's Magazine*:

> The mighty master wav'd his wand, and lo!
> On the astonish'd eye the glorious show
> Bursts, like a vision; SPIRIT OF THE PLACE,
> Has the Arabian wizard, with his mace
> Smitten the barren downs far onward spread,
> And bade th' enchanted Palace tower instead?
> Bade the dark woods their solemn shades extend?

High to the clouds yon spiry tow'r ascend?
And, starting from th' umbrageous avenue,
Spread the rich pile magnificent to view?
... ...[13]

Abbé Macquin, in his longer poem published by the *Literary Gazette*, described the sun as it rose in the east over the tower of Salisbury Cathedral and shed its rays on the woods of Beacon Hill. He then noted the 'sedgy banks' of Bitham Lake, listened to the 'deep groanings' of the water wheel in the southern ravine, inhaled the perfume of the American gardens and observed the Abbey 'in full display', like Atlas with the heavens on its shoulder:

No Gorgon's direful face,
No secret talisman, nor fairy wand,
These wonders wrought; - but Genius, Taste, and Power
Combined, conceived the whole, and bade it rise
Magnificent – its bosom to contain
What plastic Nature and what skilful Art
Could e'er achieve.
... ...

The whole astonishing scene, he concluded, was created by a man with a 'mind of fire'.[14]

Amidst all this praise, some of which was no doubt exaggerated, there were dissenting voices, and one in particular, William Hazlitt's, was sufficiently influential to have shaped a negative view of Fonthill to the present day. Hazlitt's first account of Fonthill, which was published in the *London Magazine* in November 1822, denounced the Abbey and its collections as all 'tinsel, and glitter, and embossing'. It was, he felt, a 'system of tantalization' and a 'fret-work of imagination'.[15] He paid no attention to the exterior of the building, the interior design, or the library. Instead, Hazlitt seemed more intent on characterizing Beckford's taste as given to collecting objects that were expensive trifles - admittedly often unique but basically ephemeral in quality. While many of Beckford's contemporaries praised him as a generous patron of the arts, Hazlitt characterized him as 'an industrious *bijoutier*, a prodigious virtuoso, an accomplished patron of unproductive labour, an enthusiastic collector of expensive trifles – the only proof of taste (to our thinking) he has shown in this collection is *his getting rid of it*' (p. 406).

If Hazlitt found no relic of imagination among the *objets d'art*, he was equally relentless in his criticism of the collection of paintings in the Abbey, labelling them 'mere furniture-pictures, remarkable chiefly for their antiquity or painful finishing, without beauty, without interest, and with about the same pretensions to attract the eye or delight the fancy as a well-polished mahogany table or a waxed oak-floor' (p. 405). He complained that there was no painting that made the spirit soar – no 'heir-loom of imagination'. Or, as he explained in another piece on Fonthill a year later: 'It is obviously a first principle with him [Beckford] to exclude whatever has feeling or imagination – to polish the surface, and suppress the soul of art ... to reduce all nature and all art, as far as possible, to the texture and level of a China dish – smooth, glittering, cold, and unfeeling!'[16] What hung on the walls of Fonthill, according to Hazlitt, lacked the eminence and imaginative power of some of the old masters, such as Titian's *St Peter Martyr* which received a great deal of attention in the 1822 essay. Instead, not 'one great work by one great name, scarce one or two of the worst specimens of the first masters, Leonardo's Laughing Boy, or a copy from Raphael or Correggio, as if to make the thing remote and finical – but heaps of the most elaborate pieces of the worst of the Dutch masters, Breughel's Seahorses with coats of mother-of-pearl, and Rottenhammer's Elements turned into a Flower-piece' (pp. 405–6). Hazlitt continued in this vein throughout the article, but then in the very last paragraph, almost as if sensing that he had gone too far, managed to muster praise for some of the cabinets, specifically the Princess of Bavaria's triple jewel cabinet. He also admired Cellini's nautilus shell, a cup by Magnus Berg, a work by John of Bologna, and the Borghese table in King Edward's Gallery. After making positive comments about works by Ludovico Carracci, Gerard Dow and Nicolaes Berchem, he concluded by conceding that the 'grounds, which are extensive and fine from situation, are laid out with the hand of a master' (p. 410).

Beckford reacted strongly to Hazlitt's attack in a correspondence on the subject with Macquin.[17] While Beckford's letters pertaining to this subject have not come to light, their content can be inferred from two letters written by Macquin on 8 and 9 November 1822, shortly after the appearance of Hazlitt's piece. In the letter of 9 November, Macquin revealed Beckford's feelings on the subject and his desire to fight back: 'You seem to want to have M[onsieur] H[azlitt] flogged.' The nature of the flogging turned out to be a well-crafted retaliation in the press by

Macquin which Beckford supported with the proviso that no mention be made of 'either the abbey or its creator'. Macquin felt that this restriction would tie his hands in any attempt to mount a counter-attack. At the same time, he stood ready to defend his friend, describing Hazlitt's critique as a 'rambling tirade, insolent in the extreme, which proves that the author combines the grossest ignorance of works of taste with the impudence of a hack journalist'. As to preparing a published response, however, Macquin was more circumspect, fearing that it would only provoke further reactions. 'I am convinced', he wrote to Beckford, 'that the scorching breath of a critique as biting as it would be just would have no other effect than that of suddenly hatching a new race of vipers a hundred times more venomous than their mother.' 'Let us not allow him to think', he added, 'that he has achieved his aim. He deserves nothing but the profoundest contempt. Let us not give him the satisfaction of thinking that he has caused one moment of anxiety to anyone who loves you or that he took up two minutes of the sublime imagination of the founder of Fonthill Abbey. His arrows will never reach this extraordinary man.' Beckford must have recognized the wisdom of these remarks because in the second letter Macquin repeats one of Beckford's favourite statements of postured indifference when-ever he wished to distance himself from the fray: 'Since you assure me that it is all one to you – and I believe you', and then he added by way of conclusion: 'Whichever way this thing ends, I am confident I will not disappoint you.' Macquin, of course, was being diplomatic in his care-ful phrasing while clearly signalling to Beckford that a critique of Hazlitt's views would not likely to be forthcoming from his pen; and none in fact ever did appear.

What may have motivated Hazlitt's sweeping diatribe against the Fonthill collection? Part of it may have been a consequence of Hazlitt's personal feelings about Beckford. There was a decidedly moral cast to Hazlitt's assessment which might have influenced his artistic judge-ment. He clearly viewed the collection as a sybaritic display of self-indulgence, a squandering of great wealth for the narrow purpose of tantalizing the senses. While he spoke highly of *Vathek* as a 'masterly performance', that work represented a younger Beckford. In Hazlitt's mind the creator of Fonthill was now a 'volcano burnt-out' whose talent was vitiated on gathering 'frippery and finery'. It is interesting to note that the *New Times,* edited by Hazlitt's ex-brother-in-law John Stoddart, published an anonymous article in September 1823 attacking

Beckford directly on moral grounds, explaining that no person in the rank of a gentleman would enter Fonthill because there was a 'moral impediment' against doing so. Alluding to the 'original criminality' of the Powderham scandal of 1784, the author wrote:

> The question is, whether a person once excluded from society, for imputations never disproved, shall be indirectly sought to be restored to his former eminence – and we say, No: the purity and honour of our social intercourse forbid it. It is essential to the maintenance of our English delicacy, in considerations of this kind, that the leper be *for ever* cast out of the camp – that the disgraced character remain *for ever*
>
> > 'A fixed figure for the hand of scorn
> > To point his slowly moving finger at.'
>
> And the richer, the prouder, the most ostentatious he is, the more inexorably should he be kept in the state of an Indian *Pariah*, the object of general aversion and contempt.[18]

Moral pronouncements about Beckford and his lifestyle were common fare during his day,[19] but what is particularly puzzling about Hazlitt's review of the Fonthill collection is what he left out. Boyd Alexander has already pointed out that Hazlitt skipped over many important works of art in his assessment. In pointing to the contents of the Christie catalogue to make his case, Hazlitt paid too much attention to the items listed in the first two days of the proposed sale, while ignoring the seventh day where the important pictures were listed.[20] He said nothing, for example, about Bellini's *Doge Loredan*, Rembrandt's *Rabbi*, Perugino's *Virgin and Child with St John*, and Cima da Conegliano's *St Jerome*, among others. Absent also were such treasures as the Rubens vase, the Limoges reliquary, and the many distinguished pieces of fine French furniture. It may be that Beckford's taste was ahead of his time, leading to the purchase of items that were unimportant to Hazlitt who was operating with a different set of standards. It is interesting to note that so much research now devoted to works of art once in the collections at Fonthill and in Bath has affirmed the quality of Beckford's connoisseurship, identifying him as one of the outstanding collectors and patrons of the arts in the nineteenth century.

Clive Wainwright's most recent studies on the contents of the Fonthill collection, for example, concluded that 'the Abbey as a whole housed one of the most important collections of paintings ever assembled in this country', ranging from modern works commissioned by Beckford to a wide range of old masters.[21] Wainwright believed that Beckford was not modelling his collection after the mid-eighteenth-century antiquarian, such as Horace Walpole in search of medieval relics, but rather on late sixteenth- and seventeenth-century prototypes that were outside the artistic scale of values of many of his contemporaries, including Hazlitt. 'Beckford bought objects', Wainwright explained, 'primarily as works of art or virtuoso craftsmanship in precious and exotic materials. These objects had naturally often been owned by or created for celebrated historical figures, but for Beckford this was an extra bonus and not the main reason for their acquisition.'[22]

On many occasions Beckford established the provenance himself after he purchased the object, which lends support to the view that his primary interest was the artistic quality of the object, with the historical association a secondary matter, as in the case of the controversial Cellini ewer. Beckford's interest in craftsmanship was also evident in the fact that he would create designs based on research in his Board of Works Library and then have Franchi show the design and the original books and prints from which they were derived to the artists executing the work. Franchi would be in constant attendance as the work progressed to ensure that it met the highest standard of quality. As the famous wood carver William G. Rogers recorded as a common occurrence with Franchi: 'He would come into the carvers workshop with a volume of Holbein or Aldegraver, select a spoon or handle and have them executed in ivory or ebony as high as he could get talent to bring them, would watch the progress of work day by day, and the question would often be – 'if you spent another day on it could you get it finer?'[23] All of this effort may have constituted a preciousness of manner and style that Hazlitt could not abide.

Beckford's wealth assuredly played a role in sharpening Hazlitt's criticism of the Fonthill collection. Four years after the sale to Farquhar, he made it clear that in his mind Beckford's expenditures on Fonthill were lavishly excessive. He wrote scathingly in 1826 that 'thirty pampered domestics sat down in the servants' hall at Fonthill Abbey, to dine on Westphalia hams boiled in Madeira wine, and other luxuries of the same stamp, while old age staggered under its load of labour, or sickness fainted for want of a glass of wine or a morsel of bread in the neighbourhood.'[24] The luxury Hazlitt witnessed at Fonthill must have been particularly grating at a time when he was in serious financial straits and had suffered the humiliation of being arrested for debt in February 1822. Furthermore, recent research has led to the discovery of two more essays on Fonthill by Hazlitt that underscore his financial desperation and which raise additional questions about his professional integrity as an art critic at least in regard to his treatment of the Fonthill collection.[25]

Harry Phillips, it seems, in an effort to counteract some of the bad publicity surrounding the possibility of adding scourings from London shops in the 1823 sale, approached Hazlitt and offered him fifty guineas to puff the Fonthill pictures in the press. The offer was too attractive to be refused, particularly in the face of his indebtedness, so Hazlitt decided to accept the commission from Phillips even though he had already publicly sacked the collection. The artist Benjamin Haydon heard about the arrangement, commenting in a letter of 26 September 1823 that 'Hazlitt was up last week from Fonthill, where Phillips has fixed him to write up for fifty guineas, what he wrote down from his conscience last year.'[26] Needless to say, it was a considerable challenge to the art critic under the circumstances, but he attempted to be true to his artistic principles, while appearing to praise the Fonthill pictures, by being subtly ironic throughout the anonymous article that appeared serially in four succeeding issues of the *Morning Chronicle*.[27] Keeping in mind Hazlitt's aversion to literal detail and high finishing, the double-edged character of the article is apparent at the outset when he says about Karel du Jardin's *A Riding Horse*: 'The trees in the back-ground (if *back-ground* it can be called, where the objects are seen close upon the eye) are exquisitely touched, with every leaf almost detailed, and yet the masses are finely rounded off. You might fancy the air to have stirred their branches just before, but they had stopped while the artist was painting them – so accurately is every thing expressed, at the same time with "such happiness and pains", that you hold in your breath while looking at it, as if you could hardly examine with sufficient care, nor admire long enough.'[28] In the second article, 'The Science of a Connoisseur', Hazlitt, seemingly to assuage some of the discontent he experienced for his duplicity, returned to his more direct attack of the previous year in a dramatic piece involving a conversation between a 'friend' and a 'connoisseur', designed to expose a taste for triviality as represented by the Dutch paintings Beckford owned, with specific attention being paid to Metzu's *Woman Cleaning Fish*. As Hazlitt wrote:

There, Sir – a perfect specimen of the art and the master. They talk of their Ostades, their Mieris's, and their Gerard Dows, give men the ease and nature of Metzu. The *pensive Selima* – the expression is in Gray – look at that kitten on the top of the brass pan, watching the operation of scraping the fish - demure, devout, cautious, expressing the very soul of the feline tribe, and looking as if a turn of the brass pan on which she has perched herself might suddenly upset all her speculations – and then the pencilling is actually of fur.

FRIEND – I don't think it at all like a cat.

CONNOISSEUR – (*doucement*) – You are fastidious! But what do you say to the face of the woman? Is it not charming? – Such an easy air, such an arch expression, such clearness of tone, such freedom of touch; and then the fish seem absolutely alive! If you observe, all is done here that can be done by the art of man, and it is done without any appearance of labour. Facility of execution is what charms me most in a picture... . Mr. Beckford must be allowed to have been a judge in this style of art.

FRIEND – But did not his taste run too much on merely high-finished and furniture pictures? There are, I grant, a number of capital and indeed first-rate specimens of minute and elaborate workmanship; but are not the productions of the grand historical style of art a very indifferent description – heavy, lumbering, ooarse, and uninteresting?[29]

Fonthill would remain in Hazlitt's mind as an exemplar of false taste, a smouldering irritant that would rekindle from time to time, as it did again in 1828. As he wrote about the Abbey then: 'This quaint excrescence in architecture, preposterous and ill-contrived as it was, occasioned, I suspect, many a heart-ache and bitter comparison to the throng of fashionable visitants; and I conceive it was the very want of comfort and convenience that enhanced this feeling, by magnifying, as it were from contrast, the expense that had been incurred in realising an idle whim.'[30]

The legacy of Hazlitt's appraisal of Fonthill, particularly in view of his own reputation as a distinguished nineteenth-century critic, cannot be underestimated. It accounts, to a great extent, for the tendency today to treat Fonthill lightly, even contemptuously, as an example of a silly rich man's whim. As Boyd Alexander explained in 1962, 'Hazlitt's vitriolic attack on the art treasures which Fonthill housed and the taste which it displayed has left an uneasy memory of triviality and meretriciousness.'³¹

While Hazlitt was at Fonthill during a second visit in 1823, a close friend of his, Peter G. Patmore, was also present preparing his own article on the pictures for his series 'British Galleries of Art' in the *New Monthly Magazine*. The two men spent some time together visiting other estates in the area, so it is likely they shared their respective views on Fonthill. Patmore's own analysis seems to have been written with Hazlitt's criticism in mind since he covers some of the same territory and even refers to the excesses of 'Flemish finishing'. But Patmore's views were not entirely in accord with Hazlitt's. In fact they seem to be directed at providing an antidote to the art critic's venom. Striving to give a fair impression of the character of the Fonthill collection, he singled out Albrecht Dürer's *Virgin and Child* as a 'rich little gem', a 'perfect specimen of what *finishing* ought to be – of how far it ought to be carried, and at what point it should stop'.³² Whereas Hazlitt trashed Metzu's *Woman Cleaning Fish*, Patmore pronounced it 'without exception the very best' of the specimens he had seen of the Flemish school of finishing whose object, he explained, was to produce 'natural impressions'. 'The little work before us', he added, 'is the most purely *natural* effort of the pencil that I have ever seen; so much so, as to have required nothing less than *genius* to produce it' (p. 405). Patmore also found at Fonthill other noble specimens of art, citing Ludovico Carracci's *Sibylla Lybica* ('merits to be called the grand style in art'), Teniers's *Temptation of St Anthony*'('a force of conception, a vividness of imagination, and a truth and facility of hand, that have never been united in any other person'), Berchem's *L'Embarquement des Vivres* ('the most faultless work of the whole collection'). Of the Flemish school of finishing that Hazlitt so generally deplored, Patmore found some pictures of extraordinary merit, including Mieris's *A Lady Feeding a Parrot*, Dow's *Poulterer's Shop*, and Philippe de Champaigne's *Adoration of the Shepherds*. Patmore felt that among over 400 pictures, exhibiting such a great diversity of technique and subject matter, there are bound to be varying levels of quality – some fine and some mediocre – and even some bad canvases. In his view it was a mistake to try to build a great collection by limiting price rather than the number of paintings. With the space that Fonthill offered and £100,000, one could a create a private gallery finer than any in existence. 'The late Mr. Angerstein', he concluded, 'was known all over Europe, and will not soon be forgotten, for no other reason than that he possessed ten of the finest pictures in the world!' (p. 408).

While neither Hazlitt nor Patmore devoted attention to the artistic qualities of the Abbey as a building or to any extended examination of the landscape design, there were published contemporary accounts that addressed these matters. On occasion these accounts were written by individuals who brought professional expertise to bear on their critical assessment and who tried to provide some balance between strengths and weaknesses in their accounts. One such work appeared under the title 'Candid Critique on the Architecture of Fonthill Abbey' in the *Gentleman's Magazine*.[33] It was signed with the initials 'W. G.' This was William Garbett, surveyor to the Dean and Chapter of Winchester Cathedral for twenty-five years and the person who supervised the architectural repairs of the cathedral from 1812 to 1828. John Britton, who knew Garbett well, shared this article in manuscript form with Beckford shortly before publication.[34] His reaction to it is not known, but it is likely that he would have concurred with Garbett's sentiments. Beckford did examine the architectural work of William's son Edward at Theale, Berkshire, considered to be one of the first churches of the Gothic revival designed in the Early English style, and he was quoted as having 'passed the highest encomiums on the taste of the architect, in having selected the purest style of pointed architecture'.[35]

William Garbett understood the difficulties any architect faced in an attempt to revive the authentic Gothic style of the medieval period. In the first place, he believed that the original ecclesiastical structures were built without any consensus regarding the underlying principles of construction. He also noted that extant examples of the buildings in England and elsewhere often exhibited the same disparities that critics were fond of pointing out as weaknesses in revival Gothic. His own work in the field led him to believe that the slavish adoption of ancient models would be unsuited to the present age because the 'improved conveniences of modern times' required substantive changes in both structure and design. In his view, any attempt to revive an architectural style could only be accomplished in an evolutionary manner, building upon the stylistic refinement that developed from the actual practice of creating new buildings or modifying old ones. But in the end, as with other ancient architectural styles, the Gothic style had to address the practical needs of the current age and therefore would never be completely recreated.

17 *View from the End of the Western Avenue.* Sketch by Thomas Higham, engraved by J. Thompson 1823.

18 Bitham Lake, photograph by author

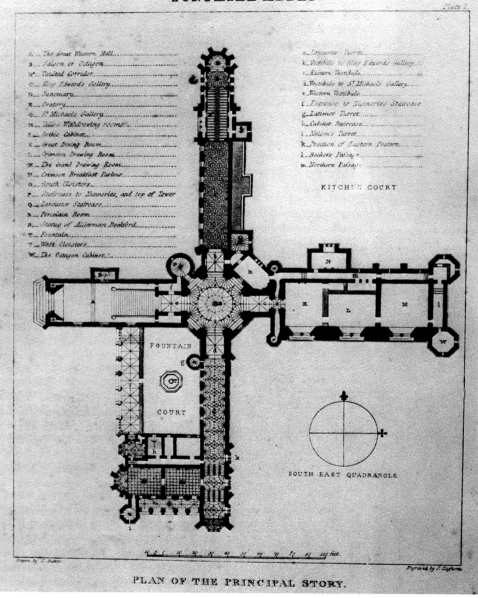

FONTHILL ABBEY.

Plate 2

A... The Great Western Hall.................
B... Saloon or Octagon.....................
C... Vaulted Corridor.......................
D... King Edward's Gallery.................
E... Sanctuary.............................
F... Oratory...............................
G... St Michaels Gallery..................
H... Yellow Withdrawing rooms............
I... Gothic Cabinet........................
K... Great Dining Room...................
L... Crimson Drawing Room...............
M... The Grand Drawing Room.............
N... Crimson Breakfast Parlour............
O... South Cloisters.......................
P... Staircase to Nunneries, and top of Tower
Q... Lancaster Staircase...................
R... Porcelain Room.......................
S... Statue of Alderman Beckford..........
T... Fountain..............................
V... West Cloisters........................
W... The Octagon Cabinet.................

a... Lancaster Turret......................
b... Vestibule to King Edward's Gallery...
c... Eastern Vestibule......................
d... Vestibule to St Michaels Gallery......
e... Western Vestibule.....................
f... Entrance to Nunneries Staircase.......
g... Latimer Turret........................
h... Cabinet Staircase......................
i... Nelson's Turret........................
k... Position of Eastern Postern...........
l... Beckers Passage.......................
m... Northern Passage......................

KITCHEN COURT

FOUNTAIN

COURT

SOUTH EAST QUADRANGLE

Drawn by J. Rutter.

Engraved by J. Cleghorn.

PLAN OF THE PRINCIPAL STORY.

19 Fonthill floor plan. Drawn by John Rutter, engraved by John Cleghorn, 1823.

20 St Michael's Gallery. Drawn by W. Finley, engraved by John Cleghorn, 1823.

21 Southern Oriel Window. Drawn by George Cattermole, engraved by M. Dubourg, 1823.

22 King Edward's Gallery. Drawn by C. F. Porden, engraved by R. Havell & Son, 1823.

23 The 'Studied Dissimilarity' of the Abbey. Drawn by C. V. Fielding, engraved by S. Rawle, 1819.

24 LEFT St Anthony in the Oratory, from Storer, 1812 25 RIGHT John Farquhar; engraved by W. T. Fry and published by T. Boys, 1823

26 The Great Western Hall. Drawn by George Cattermole, engraved by J. C. Varrall, 1823.

27 Blending the Interior of the Abbey with the Exterior Grounds. Drawn by H. Gastineau, engraved by R. Sands, 1823.

28 Fountain Court as public refectory. Drawn by S. Whitwell., engraved by J. Boosey & Co, 1823.

29 Fonthill Abbey in Ruins. Drawn by John Buckler, engraved by Thomas Higham, 1828.

In his examination of Fonthill Abbey, Garbett identified structural weakness as the central problem with the building. He attributed this considerable deficiency to the fact that the Abbey was not constructed from a well-planned design but evolved over time as Beckford moved from his original conception of a tower design to a grander conception of a Gothic residence. Looking at the Grand Saloon, Garbett felt that it lacked solidity as a base for the tower, that the walls were too thin to provide the necessary support. With thicker walls and the addition of flying buttresses, he explained, the 'cloud-capt' spire that Beckford originally conceived would have been possible. He also believed that Wyatt had sacrificed 'rational symmetry' to 'picturesque effect' in the lack of height and width of the northern and southern galleries, 'more particularly in the upper spaces within their roofs, and in the diminutive upper windows'. This became more noticeable when the Eastern Transept was viewed in relationship to the two galleries, since its gigantic size tended to emphasize their more diminished character. While recognizing that the Eastern Transept was never finished, Garbett further observed that the three large and imposing windows on the south side cried out for the creation of an ancient hall 'appropriated to the hospitable purposes of the banquet', following the model of Hawksmoor's work at All Souls College, Oxford (p. 493).

In the interest of authenticity and further structural support, Garbett would have added buttresses to both the eastern and western wings. In addition, the lack of ornamental detail on the vast surface of the wall of the Eastern Transept seemed to him to be out of harmony with the rest of the building, as were the 'perforated parapets' which were too light in character to harmonize with the 'general tenor of the design' (p. 493). The paucity of decorative detail on the surface of the Abbey was also taken up by a critic in the *Morning Chronicle* who believed that the embellishments of the interior called for a more 'florid style' in the surface of the exterior, 'enriched with the most elaborate decorations of quaint devices and antique imagery'.[36]

Proceeding to the interior of the Abbey, Garbett itemized some deficiencies in workmanship, such as the fan work supporting the lantern in the Octagon, which he believed lacked the elegance of other parts of the Abbey but which might have been corrected had Wyatt lived long enough. The Brown or Oak Parlour, a long low room on the ground floor with foreshortened windows, he found out of keeping with the Gothic style, but he was highly complimentary about other rooms: 'When we come to the [Great Western] Hall, the Octagon, and the South and East Oriels, we find the style approximates much nearer to ancient models; the Lobbies to the Brown Parlour, the Green Cabinet Room, and the West and South Arcades, approach still nearer to perfection; and finally, the Galleries forming the library, combined with the Sanctuary and Oratory, merit the highest commendation, as well for general effect as for elegance of details' (p. 494). In other instances, where critics might have issued condemnations as deviations from 'abstract notions of correct and congruous style', Garbett was more liberal, willing to embrace the superiority of aesthetics over rules. Where some might be critical of the extreme height of the western entrance hall, he felt that any diminution of it 'would destroy one of the finest effects produced on this stately edifice, particularly when viewed from the perspective of the Octagon'. If others argued that the arches of the Octagon were too 'acutely pointed' to satisfy the true Gothic style, Garbett answered that 'the piers supporting the Tower, being evidently elevated to the utmost admissible proportion, the acute shape of the arches rising from them will, in the eyes of those who prefer pleasing forms to fancied rules, appear a beauty rather than a defect'. While the cavilling critic might make the charge of an inappropriate mixture of the modern with the Gothic in the absence of mullions and tracery in the windows of the Octagon, Garbett argued that this would have diminished the quality of light infusing this hall and prevented the stained glass from creating the splendid effect of light that was felt and commented upon by almost every visitor (p. 491). In short, these qualities showed that Wyatt was not insensible to the 'grace surpassing rule and order'.

So in the end Garbett leaned in favour of the overall aesthetic qualities of Fonthill despite the faults he observed as an experienced architect. He found that the Abbey could not be judged simply as an imitation of an earlier style and according to some perceived rules of old. Indeed the fusion of elements of the modern with the ancient was not only inevitable but necessary. 'It must therefore be pretty obvious', he concluded, 'that the most fastidious architectural critic of the present age would be as little pleased to inhabit a mansion built after the exact model of one of the fourteenth century, as the most discontented political reformer would be with the precise constitution of the same period. When all these circumstances are duly considered, it must remain for ever questionable, whether any other person would have conducted the same undertaking with greater success than the deceased Architect of Fonthill' (p. 494).

Another important architect, Charles C. Cockerell, visited Fonthill in August 1823 and recorded his observations in an unpublished album entitled 'Ichnographica Domestica'.[37] His analysis was not as extensive as Garbett's, but significant enough to cite as another example of an assessment by a contemporary practitioner and theorist. Cockerell, undoubtedly influenced by rumours that he had heard, had anticipated a patchwork quilt at Fonthill, but was surprised to find instead an interior layout that exhibited an overall controlling purpose and orderly design. He was particularly impressed by the way the Octagon Hall served as an axis of communication with the major wings of the Abbey. 'I was agre[e]ably surprised at Fonthill, not finding it as I had supposed a monstrous caprice. The system of the plan seems to me judicious, as you arrive by the vestibule at once into the centre, which is the means of communication to & from the various apartments of the House, which lies ... round it. How much preferable is this to the quadrangle as at Blenheim, Wooburn or even as at Blenheim, Luton (& my Wellington Plan) when there are two small courts as at Kedleston.' Cockerell's review also stressed the Abbey's iconographic character and, unlike some visitors, emphasized a lighter tone in the interior environment rather than the more typical emphasis on the pervading sombre lights and hues of the Abbey in the evening or the magical tints and colours caused by the stained glass in the late afternoon. Walking through the Abbey on this day, Cockerell observed the daylight quality of the radiating wings. 'In the history of ichnography', he wrote, 'Fonthill ranks as a highly interesting example, as novel & excellent in many respects, the considerable plan offering great cheerfulness, light, and greatest possible facilities of communication.' Interestingly, Cockerell focused almost entirely on the structure, believing that there was no apparent relationship between the building and the exterior grounds and prospects. Instead, he tended to view the Abbey as a 'studious abstraction for persons living indoors delighting therefore in that respect'. In his mind the Abbey was a monument to self-sufficiency, lending itself to the cultivation of habits that do not lead to or require the open air. The breathtaking scenes were all within the building – 'hence these vistas of 330 feet, this octagon Hall 130 feet high – this bold elevation & vastness.' 'It is evidently the production of a sedentary literary person,' he continued, 'a poet & composer of Vathek who proposed to pass his life in the Cloister Gallery of 300 feet & in the contemplation of this vast tower.'

The two major illustrated books by John Britton and John Rutter respectively provided a broader evaluation of Fonthill, incorporating the Abbey in a grander artistic scheme by considering it within the aesthetic context of a landscape garden. Both volumes have stood out over time as important written and visual records of Fonthill. As a prescient writer in the *Salisbury and Winchester Journal* observed in 1823, ' Whatever may be the destiny of FONTHILL ABBEY, – whether its lofty head may defy the loud blast of Boreas, and remain an object of admiration to future ages; or like certain edifices renowned in story, it may fall a sacrifice to the raging storm or devouring flame – neither the enterprising genius of its founder, nor the skill of its architect, will be lost to posterity, so long as a faithful description and accurate delineation of the Abbey shall remain in the library of the virtuoso.'[38] Both volumes can also be considered major authoritative works that document the history and conception of Fonthill because of Beckford's willingness to provide assistance as a source of information to both writers. To a significant extent these books can be considered Beckford documents.

Of the two writers Britton was the established antiquarian and topographer, having already published the first two volumes of *Beauties in Wiltshire* in 1801, jointly authored with Edward W. Brayley *The Beauties of England and Wales* from 1801 to 1816, and having begun his own fourteen-volume series *The Cathedral Antiquities of England*, the publication of which ran from 1814 to 1835. Britton visited Fonthill Abbey in 1817, and he and his wife Mary Anne were guests there for a month at the height of its celebrity in 1822. During this stay Britton prepared the notes that would serve as the basis for *Graphical and Literary Illustrations of Fonthill Abbey*, which he published by subscription the following year. In addition to his wife, he was also accompanied by George Cattermole, who made many of the drawings for the illustrations in Britton's book. As the leading publicist of the Gothic architectural style after John Carter and collaborating at the time with Augustus Pugin on *Specimens of Gothic Architecture*, Britton naturally wanted to write about Fonthill. Just prior to his visit in late August and early September, he had already published an anonymous piece in *The Museum* in which he referred to the Abbey as a 'unique specimen of the triumph of modern skill and genius over the difficulties of construction presented by the Gothic style'.[39]

Britton was impressed with Beckford and eager to seek his favour. He seemed to be in awe of his strength of mind, the quick wit and breadth of knowledge he exhibited in conversation, and of his artistic accomplishments. He told Beckford in 1835 that when he first met him in 1799 he was 'astonished & terrified' by his 'splendours & powers'.⁴⁰ Mary Anne Britton's letter of appreciation for being treated so graciously during their stay at Fonthill mirrored her husband's sentiments:

> ... All around me seems like the work of enchantment, and I can only gaze and gaze, and wonder how the mind of man should have projected so gigantic a structure and still more, how the mind of man *could* have so far, almost, outstretched itself, as to have organized and arranged each and every part in such true and perfect order & harmony.
>
> 'Twas for you – and you alone: for your capacious mind and refined taste and judgement to have accomplished a task, which does, and *must* and *ever will* be the astonishment of the world.⁴¹

From the beginning Britton was concerned not only about pleasing his subscribers but Beckford himself. In July 1823 he wrote to Beckford expressing delight that he was willing to look over the proof sheets of the book ('I most cheerfully submit some of them to your keen eye: although I feel much trepidation at the ordeal')⁴². Later he consulted with him about the inclusion of genealogical tables of the Beckford family, a portion of which George Beltz had published in the *Gentleman's Magazine* in the fall of 1822. It is also a measure of his desire to impress Beckford that he worked so painstakingly on the frontispiece for the volume. For this plate Britton personally designed an ornate presentation of armorial bearings of Beckford's ancestors. It took the form of an architectural design composed of parts of other ecclesiastical edifices in England in which he saw some stylistic relationship with Fonthill. Thus part of the design was copied from a screen in the nave of Wells Cathedral; the 'arch mouldings, spandrils, and trefoil suspended arches' were drawn from a monument in the north transept in the same church. The six compartments of tracery that enclosed the shields came from Norwich and Winchester Cathedrals, while other elements of the design were copied from specimens in St. George's Chapel, Windsor and Exeter Cathedral. It is a remarkably detailed and intricate construction that associates Fonthill Abbey with some of the major examples of Gothic architecture in England while simultaneously paying homage to its creator and to his connection with a revered past through his celebrated lineage. He also incorporated in the lower panel of the design two of the most valuable objects from the Fonthill collection, namely a fourteenth-century Chinese porcelain vase on the left side and a vase on the right that was once owned by Rubens. Britton also intended to incorporate in the centre niche a medieval Limoges chasse from the collection but copied the wrong chasse by mistake.[43] Beckford appears to have noticed the error and brought it to Britton's attention but to no avail. 'I observe that the glaring error in the herald title page', he wrote to Britton, 'remains uncorrected – at least in all the sm[all] paper Copies I have yet seen.'[44]

Britton admitted to having written his Fonthill book hastily, usually after 9 o'clock in the evening, after a day of meeting other professional obligations. This may explain, in part, the lengthy preamble that burdens his account, beginning with an address to subscribers, a five-page explanation of the frontispiece, the lengthy description of the plates, a Preface, and then a wordy dedication to John Broadley. Once into the body of the text, Britton presented Fonthill within the context of other great country estates in England and followed the established formula for guidebooks of his time by dividing his discussion into four major parts: a description of the architectural style of the house, an examination of the grounds and prominent features surrounding it, the details of the building's interior provided on a room-by-room tour, and finally the genealogical history of the owner. He also provided some variation of the pattern by interlacing his account with embellishments, such as the description of Lord Nelson's visit in 1800 and a brief review of the reaction of the press and the public during the 'view' of 1822. Beckford also permitted him to publish two of his poems, 'A Prayer' and 'The Last Day'. His most significant departure from the usual guidebook format was exhibited in his tendency to avoid describing the valuable contents and works of art in each room, which may have been a decision resulting from the excess of this kind of coverage in other venues. Instead, he attended to the heraldic shields and armorial bearings that permeated the rooms and stained glass windows of the Abbey. Consistent with his interest in the Gothic style of architecture and the ethos that brought it into being, Britton appreciated Fonthill for its nostalgic appeal, specifically the way in which it promoted in the mind of the observer associations with antiquity through the monastic character of its architecture and its commemoration of royal ancestry. 'It is evident', he wrote, 'that Fonthill Abbey is an unique building; that it is large and lofty, of varied forms, styles, and character; that many of its parts are designed more for effect than mere domestic utility; and that externally and internally it presents a succession of scenes which cannot fail to produce powerful impressions on the imagination.'[45] There was also its 'seraphic influence', which Britton described as having experienced in the Abbey, when the play of light and shadow against the walls and gilt mouldings combined with the fragrance of eastern perfume permeating the air and the deep tones of the organ echoing throughout the galleries to produce a total immersion of the senses as if one were transported to another time and place.

It was Fonthill's affective qualities that Britton seized upon because he was well aware that the quality of its construction could not measure up to other specimens of Gothic architecture that he had written about and studied. Form could not completely compensate for the functional problems embedded in the heart of the building, but for these he held Wyatt accountable. Beckford, he felt, provided the wealth and the grand conceptions. It was up to Wyatt to realize this vision in an edifice that would challenge the vicissitudes of time. Britton believed that Wyatt failed to capitalize on the opportunity that was provided him.

> The architect of Fonthill [he wrote] had free and full scope for the exercise of *all* his professional talents: and had these been as considerable as frequently ascribed to him, and had he been impelled by laudable ambition – had he bestowed but common industry on the subject – had he felt that enthusiasm which the occasion demanded, and acted with that inflexible perseverance which his munificent employer had a right to expect, we should then indeed have seen an edifice of surpassing magnitude, beauty, and grandeur; one calculated to prove the fallacy and folly of the common notion, that all excellence and merit in the ecclesiastical species of architecture was extinguished with the dissolution of monasteries... . Every incentive and every opportunity appear to have been afforded to the surveyor of Fonthill Abbey; but he was either insensible to their call or incapable of employing them to great and eminent results. ... The present hall has been rebuilt, of nearly double its first dimensions: and the central tower is the third that has been raised! Such things ought not to have occurred.[46]

William H. Harrison once asked Beckford if Fonthill was built on his plan. 'No,' he answered. 'I have enough sins to answer for, without having that laid to my charge. Wyatt had an opportunity of raising a splendid monument to his fame, but he missed it.'[47] Similar criticism of Wyatt found its way into the press, pointing out that 'Mr. Beckford's conceptions were not adhered to, and he subsequently often blamed the plan and execution of Mr. Wyatt.' This prompted a vigorous response from his son, Benjamin Wyatt. It took the form of a letter in which Benjamin pointed out that Fonthill did not spring from a pre-determined plan nor was it modelled after any pre-existing building. Instead, he explained that it evolved from its original conception as a 'Convent', so there could be no original plan to which his father failed to adhere:

...When the building now called Fonthill Abbey was first begun, the project was confined *exclusively* (as I can prove by a variety of evidence in my possession), to that small portion of it, which now constitutes the south eastern wing, and which was then denominated by Mr. Beckford ' the Convent.'

I am aware that great efforts have lately been made to suppress the publication of this fact, and thereby to mislead the public as to the merits of my late father as connected with the designs for Fonthill Abbey...

The autograph letters of Mr. Beckford to my late Father, now in my possession, contain, in many parts, expressions of the most enthusiastic admiration of the talents displayed by my father at Fonthill, as well as the most implicit reliance on his skill and experience; avowing, in reiterated instances, on the part of Mr. Beckford, the utter impossibility to proceed without my father's guidance; and, in short, upon the whole, furnishing the most irrefragable truth of feelings and relations, between Mr. Beckford and Mr. Wyatt, as employer and architect ...[48]

Benjamin made an admirable defence on his father's behalf. He was also accurate in conveying Beckford's admiration for the architect, but the serious issue of the structural integrity of the building was not mentioned despite previous notices in the press about it, and there Wyatt has to assume responsibility, as Britton observed.

One of the most valuable aspects of Britton's book were the twelve engraved illustrations he included with the textual material. Here he called upon some of the most eminent topographical artists and engravers of his day to assist him. They included two watercolourists,

Henry Gastineau and George Cattermole – the latter having worked with Britton on the *Cathedral Antiquities of England*. Cattermole was responsible for the north- and south-west views of the Abbey for the volume as well as the impressive south end view of the oriel window in St Michael's Gallery, one of the two coloured engravings in the book (fig. 21). Gastineau worked up a more refined drawing of a Cattermole sketch of a striking view, looking down the steps of the Great Hall and out upon the Great Western Avenue (fig. 27). John Martin, considered to be a dramatic and an original historical and landscape painter, provided an impressive distant south-west view of the Abbey in its setting. Among the engravers, the most prominent was Henry Le Keux who had contributed his artistry to Britton's *The Beauties of England and Wales*. Also involved were Thomas Higham and John Thompson, the latter considered to be the most distinguished wood engraver of this time. Then there was Henry Shaw, architectural draftsman, engraver, and a scholar of Gothic architecture in his own right, who did the fine drawing for the coloured engraving of the east window in St Michael's Gallery.

Britton himself was not entirely satisfied with the quality of some of the illustrations, believing that overall they did not measure up to the quality of the plates in his *Cathedral Antiquities*.[49] He was particularly unhappy with some of Cattermole's contributions and conveyed to the artist his dissatisfaction with the drawings of the ground plan and some of the external views. Beckford, on the other hand, found Cattermole's interior drawings to be 'beautiful, correct and full of feeling, particularly his fine perspective of Ed 3rd Gallery and the view from the Hall down the great avenue'.[50] But so concerned was Britton about a potentially negative reaction from the subscribers to the volume's illustrations that he moved to distance himself from any criticism by declaring at the conclusion of his list of plates that no one could 'feel and lament their imperfections' more than himself and that he hoped the reader 'will not attribute the blame to the author', explaining that the 'author and the publisher of an embellished work is necessarily at the mercy of others: and as all persons have not the same feelings – the same zeal – and the same responsibility, it is not surprising that there be carelessness in one – want of judgment in a second – defective taste in a third – and dishonesty in a fourth' (pp. 13–14). Britton then had seven of the eleven copper plates for the illustrations destroyed to ensure, he said, the perpetual value and integrity of the engravings in the book, but he also added that he took this step because his well-established friends and patrons will 'see an inferiority in some of the plates' (p. vii). The fact that five of the seven were based on drawings by Cattermole further underscores his dissatisfaction with the artist. It could not have helped to reduce his distress when Beckford, on receiving his copy, wrote to Britton that the 'observations you so candidly make on y[ou]r own work, the plates etc., are strictly true & there is nothing so delightful as Truth'.[51]

Underlying Britton's dissatisfaction with Cattermole was a deeper anxiety that began when he learned that Rutter was going to publish a rival work on Fonthill. Britton considered Rutter's move an act of treachery and a direct threat that could only undermine the sale of his own book, with bleak financial implications if he could not recover the money he had already invested. He immediately wrote a stinging letter to Rutter, accusing him of being dishonourable as a tradesman for planning this publication when he knew that there was already a volume on the drawing boards. Things became worse when he discovered that Cattermole and Higham had also been hired to contribute to Rutter's book, which helps to explain some of Britton's bad feelings towards Cattermole and perhaps his dissatisfaction with his work. The correspondence on this matter reveals that Britton, in near desperation, tried to enlist outside aid in obstructing Rutter. He started with Chevalier Franchi and tried to convince him to prevent the promotion of Rutter's book at the Abbey. Franchi refused but tried to placate Britton with encouraging words regarding Beckford's support. 'I can't prevent the sale at the Abbey of Mr. Rutter's Descriptions & advertisements,' Franchi wrote. 'As for plans & views, perhaps he has already stuffing enough for all his purposes. You know how active he is. However his work, I think, will never be sanctioned or encouraged by M[onsieur] Beckford .'[52]

The situation for Britton worsened when Farquhar bought the estate because Rutter was then granted free access to the Abbey. The thought of Rutter being granted this privilege rankled Britton, and he hoped Franchi would come to his assistance. But, once again, Franchi reported that he had little control over the matter: 'I have seen several persons here making drawings for Rutter & some very good. Rutter has permission from Mr. Farquhar to do as many as he likes – therefore I could not interpose in any way his progress – he appears very sanguine upon the results.'[53]

This report of Rutter's optimism about his book must have stung Britton. He went on to express to a number of correspondents his bitterness over Rutter's intrusion into his perceived publishing territory, but not all were sympathetic. Richard Colt Hoare, for example, did not feel that Britton's grumbling was justified. He reminded Britton that the quality of the final work was what really mattered and that he intended to buy both books. 'I think you are not warranted to complain in such bitter terms as I hear you have done,' he wrote, 'as to myself, I shall take *both*, & whichever is the *best*, will succeed *best*.'[54]

Britton's book finally appeared at the end of August in 1823 as a limited subscription edition of 806 copies, including 6 in royal folio, 300 imperial quarto, and 500 medium quarto. He offered the six royal folio copies to Beckford, including one with the original drawings bound in. In the end Britton sold the entire edition but not without leaving some wreckage of personal relationships behind. It is perhaps a mark of the differences between the two rivals that in Rutter's case the architect C. F. Porden and publisher Charles Knight gave Rutter a 'Congratulatory Dinner' at a London hotel on 22 October 1823, in celebration of the publication of his Fonthill book and 'to express their sense of the liberal manner in which he has acted to all parties'.[55] Britton, on the other hand, issued his own invitation for a celebratory dinner on 19 January 1824 at the same hotel.[56] Cattermole was not on the invitation list. Of the sixteen people who attended, most were booksellers or magazine editors. The artists who contributed to his work either were not invited or did not attend.[57]

While Britton was a well-known figure in England, Rutter was new on the scene, a young upstart of twenty-seven, brought up as a Quaker, who entered the bookselling and printing business in Shaftesbury in 1818. It is not known precisely when he met Beckford, but it had to be before he brought out his first guidebook for the Christie sale in 1822. He did indicate in the Preface to *Delineations of Fonthill* that 'from the earliest hour that the interesting mansion which is the subject of the following pages, became accessible to the world, the author felt a dawning ambition to prepare a description of it for the public eye' and that he actually visited the estate 'at a time when the rarity of such permissions made it more than an ordinary favour', which suggests the possibility of access earlier than 1822.[58] Because new rooms were opened for the 1823 sale and some rearrangements of the contents made under Farquhar's direction, Rutter brought out a new portable guidebook for the occasion that reflected these changes, thereby continuing to demonstrate his entrepreneurial skills and laying additional groundwork for his *magnum opus* on Fonthill.

A question arises as to how much information in Rutter's book was directly from Beckford. Boyd Alexander believed, for example, that the material in Chapter IV, dealing with the description of the grounds within the barrier wall, came from direct contact with Beckford. He felt that Rutter would not otherwise have known the literary quotations from Tasso, Chaucer, and Uvedale Price used in that chapter. Furthermore, Rutter used the same six lines from *Paradise Lost* that Beckford had recited to Henri Meister in 1792.[59] If this is the case, then Rutter's book becomes a very important document as a primary source of evidence for Beckford's original conceptions of Fonthill. Beckford's friend, Chevalier Franchi, and particularly the scholarly Abbé Macquin, must have played important roles as additional sources of information as satellite figures for Beckford. It was Macquin, as we have noted, who wrote and published a series of four papers and a long poem on Fonthill in the *Literary Gazette* in 1822. It is also interesting that a Latin epigram on Fonthill that Macquin included in his third paper was quoted by Rutter on the title page of his abbreviated guidebooks to Fonthill in 1822 and 1823. Beltz provided the genealogical information for the volume. Sir Richard Colt Hoare was the source for the historical material on the manor of Fonthill Gifford, while Farquhar allowed Rutter ready access to the Abbey for observation and study. Just prior to publication, Rutter was also granted access to Wyatt's papers, plans and memoranda which enabled him to include in Appendix B the important piece on the 'Origin and Progress of Fonthill Abbey'.[60] Rutter's knowledge of architecture was admittedly limited, but he persuaded Stedman Whitwell to provide the necessary professional assistance. Whitwell was an experienced architect who had designed Brampton Park in the Gothic style for Lady Olivia Sparrow in 1820–1.

Still, Rutter was not without his own capabilities and expertise, and they show in the production of this elegant guidebook, particularly in the area of topography in which he had a professional interest. Indeed he wrote and published other guidebooks, including his *Historical and Descriptive Sketch of Wardour Castle and Demesne* in 1822, the *Westonian Guide* in 1828 and *A Guide to Clevedon* and *Delineations of North-West Somersetshire*, both in 1829.

By all accounts Rutter produced a better book than Britton. Rutter seems to have appreciated the dominance of Fonthill's pictorial impact. He therefore interleaved his descriptive text with thirteen engraved illustrations, three of which were in colour, but then added fifteen woodcut vignettes illustrating special points of interest inside the Abbey, such as the arranged group of virtu which included the Cellini ewer, the silver lamp in the Oratory, and the corbel of the South Oriel as well the Fountain Court, the American gardens, the entrance gateway to old Fonthill and other architectural elements in the grounds outside the Abbey. Cattermole and Martin, serving no particular master, also made contributions to Rutter's volume, though with different perspectives from those they did for Britton. For Rutter, Martin provided a dramatic north-west view of the Abbey from the end of the Clerk's Walk, set off by a background of turbulent clouds. Cattermole reversed his perspective of the interior of the Great Western Hall, capturing the majestic vertical thrust to the baronial ceiling that visitors experienced as they passed through the massive doors of the entrance (fig. 26). His other work, a distant view of the Abbey from Beacon Terrace, seemed placid in comparison to Martin's more romantic depiction from the same perspective in the Britton volume. Rutter also employed two lesser-known artists, C. F. Porden and W. Finley, who made impressive contributions. In particular, Porden's drawing of King Edward's Gallery and Finley's interior of St Michael's Gallery, both in colour with the engraving of the one and etching of the other by John Cleghorn, stood out in terms of artistic quality. Among the engravers commissioned by Rutter, William Hughes was considered to be one of the most prominent wood engravers of the time, having done previous work for *Dibdin's Bibliographical Decameron* (1817) and Ottley's *History of Engraving* (1816). Responsible for most of the vignettes, Hughes was well known for his careful and precise execution. One of the most valuable aspects of Rutter's book, however, was the fold-map of the Fonthill domain surveyed by S. Paull, drawn on stone by B. R. Baker, and printed by T. Boosey of London. Here Rutter provided a detailed display of all of the central features, walks, and rides of Fonthill, leaving an invaluable historical record of the original layout of the entire estate.

The quality of the graphic work was praised by contemporary reviewers and seen as superior to Britton's book in terms of both execution and subject matter. Britton recognized, though grudgingly, that his own work did not measure up to Rutter's. He wrote to Beckford: 'I presume you have seen the modest quaker's book. I cannot doubt but *you readily* perceive its merits & defects. It surpasses my expectations in many points ... . Though mine shrinks by its side in quality of paper, quantity of Engravings & printing, I hope it will not lose by comparison in matter or manner. Some of its plates are also much better & *all* should have been so had my Artist done his duty.' Beckford's response was very brief, noting that he had seen the 'Quaker's grand Catalogue' and, then in an apparent attempt to muster something negative as a sop to Britton, explained that he found it at times too methodical in its treatment – 'in some parts furiously *déraisonné*'.[61]

Unfortunately for Britton, the body of Rutter's work – both in 'matter or manner' – turned out to be more skillfully handled, better organized and more comprehensive in treatment. It was an advantage that Rutter achieved by keeping the reader in mind as he prepared his work. He divided his material into roughly six major parts, beginning with a description of the approaches to the estate travelling the roads from London, Bath and Shaftesbury and recording at what points the Abbey could be seen from a great distance. If you were taking the Great Western Road from London, for example, just outside Salisbury the Abbey could be seen from a distance of almost twenty miles 'as an object of extraordinary height and magnitude, rising out of the side of one of the highest hills on the horizon' (p. 2).

Part two of the book was devoted to a description of the interior of the building. Here Rutter provided a descriptive account of each room in a systematic manner, but separated general commentary from the specific details respecting the architecture, furniture, pictures and heraldic ornaments of each room. It was a novel approach that subdivided the technical, decorative and historical matters under the headings of A (Architecture), F (Furniture), P (Paintings), and H (Heraldry), thereby allowing readers the option of reading the running account of the various rooms without being diverted by genealogical symbols and other specific details. Part three directed the visitor to examine the exterior of the Abbey from different vantage points, both close-up and from a distance. Part four consisted of a detailed description of the grounds inside and outside the barrier wall, concluding with the grand ride around the entire domain of Fonthill. Rutter then concluded his account with parts five and six devoted respectively to historical information on the building of the Abbey and the former Fonthill mansions and ending with the inclusion of the genealogical tables based on Beltz's research.

Rutter's treatment of the architectural merits of Fonthill Abbey, derived to a great extent from Whitwell, was more balanced than Britton's in that it was spiced with occasional criticism. In his description of the Oak Parlour, for example, he observed that the general impression of it was 'rather unpleasing, from a want of proportionate height in the ceiling and windows; from a deficiency of harmony between the cold pink ground and pale yellow mouldings of the ceiling, compared with the warm and rich colour of the wainscoting of the walls; and from a discrepancy in the style of this wainscoting, and the pointed heads and tracery of the windows' (p. 11). He also made some suggestions for improvement: 'If the Tribune were re-opened into the Chintz Boudoir, what still more extraordinary emotions would agitate a spectator entering from the Western Lawn' (p. 62). But then he praised the architectural achievement of the Oratory, Great Western Hall, and the Southern Oriel and singled out the Grand Saloon for its incomparable artistic effects: 'In one or two royal palaces in the world, there may be single scenes of greater extent and grandeur, than any one at Fonthill Abbey; but among them all, has Invention yet produced any thing to be compared with the grand Saloon, its four-fold vistas, its purple light, and superb altitude!' (p. 62).

There were knowledgeable visitors who felt that the interior of the Abbey suffered from too much compositional variety and that this detracted from the unity of its effect. Aware of this criticism, Rutter argued that architectural irregularities were inherent in the Gothic style as it developed over time and that 'additions of successive ages in their own characteristic styles are to be found in all of them' (p. 64). Moreover, while admitting that Fonthill was an example of revival Gothic, Rutter did not believe that it should be judged entirely as an imitative work. 'There is', he wrote, 'no sickly affectation of fidelity', or slavish adherence to pre-existing models. So he ended up concurring with Britton that Fonthill was unique and not to be judged by common rules:

The Abbey is no *Frankenstein*, built up of the actual head of one individual, the arms of another, and the body of a third, forming a disgusting and unnatural whole. There is a tower; but it is not the tower, *faithfully copied*, of Canterbury, nor of Gloucester, nor of any tower extant. Its interior is in the ecclesiastical manner, as decidedly as that of any Abbey existing; but where is its exact prototype? Confessionals, and Sanctuaries, and Oratories, have been raised over all Christendom; but when before did genius so temper the light, and conduct the perspective? When did taste so spread the decorations with such inimitable effect! St. Anthony might have had lodgings of larger dimensions at Padua, but he was certainly 'enshrined' at Fonthill [pp. 64–5].

Consequently, Rutter placed Fonthill within the context of Romantic aesthetics in that as a work of domestic architecture Fonthill was unsurpassed in its originality and, when contemplated, stimulated emotions 'that have never been excited by any building erected by any private individual in our times' (p. 78).

Moving from a discussion of Fonthill Abbey as an architectural achievement, Rutter once again surpasses Britton's account by emphasizing Beckford's view of Fonthill as a landscape garden governed by the principles of England's picturesque movement. His frequently uses controlling terms – 'picture', 'composition', 'balance', 'breadth of chiaro-oscuro', 'light and shade', 'perspective', 'middle distance', 'line of horizon' – which imply that the rendering of Fonthill was closely allied to the technique of landscape painting. And when he writes that the most 'picturesque view' of the Abbey was obtained from Beacon Terrace, where 'the great masses from this point, under favourable circumstances of light, have a sufficiently intelligible outline, notwithstanding the excessive intricacy of the detail', and goes on to complain that, though the general effect was magnificent, there was 'a want of balance, harmony, and keeping in the great masses; no breadth of chiaro-oscuro, no repose, but a uniform sparkling of light from the number of facettes into which the surface is cut', this is essentially an assessment of Fonthill as a picture (p. 78). Of the Nine Miles Walk: 'The effects of light and shade... give the utmost richness and grace to the broad masses of hanging wood, and the occasional bursts of the distant landscape' (pp. 84–5). Then, in his analysis of the ingredients of the garden plan, he relates the two arts by observing the variations of line in the undulating or rugged surface, the varied tints and textures inherent in the smooth and rough lawns, the long perspective of the avenues leading to a terminal object, and the contrast of tone and verticality in the succession of dark pine and white birch, tall ash and short hawthorn (p. 86).

It is no coincidence that Rutter makes references to Price's *Essay on the Picturesque* to illustrate Beckford's work at Fonthill. Beckford was as familiar with Price's work as he was with the works of the major garden theorists of the seventeenth and eighteenth centuries. Parallels between Price's theory and the Fonthill landscape design have already been noted, but Rutter's use of the phrase 'general character of the place' in his survey of the Fonthill grounds is equally significant in light of the evolution of the picturesque gardening movement. By not finding any discrepancy in the general character of Fonthill, he was in effect confirming that Beckford had achieved a unity of design through a careful subordination of parts to a whole – a basic tenet of mature landscape design. This was the implication of his following observations:

> The ornamented grounds of Fonthill, though unequalled in extent, contain very few objects that will admit of individual description. The great principle upon which this labyrinth of groves has been constructed, is that of exhibiting an union of the wildest and the most ornamented scenery, - the picturesque and the beautiful, in close society [p. 83].

> The union of garden and the grove is almost universal; and it is impossible to imagine a more charming feature of the place, or one which more clearly indicates the care with which its scenery has been created, and almost matured, by one tasteful possessor [p. 84].

Rutter appeared to be aware that the subordination of detail to a general theme was the key to landscape composition, and he believed that the Abbey and its adjoining buildings were integral features of the garden plan and in harmony with it:

> In the greater number of our walks about Fonthill we have felt strongly impressed with the care by which the buildings of the Abbey have been made to harmonize with the general scenery. In this particular, we know no modern erection which deserves such unqualified praise. We too often behold our ordinary builders abandoning the character of *l'architecto pittore*, and preparing their elevations without the slightest notice of their relation to the general landscape. It is not so at Fonthill. The Abbey and its accompanying scenery were produced under the direction of one superintending mind; the building, therefore, and its surrounding woods have an equal character of security and seclusion. We feel,

in our romantic moods, that the Abbey is a place dedicated in its grandeur to the most impressive of religions [pp. 86–7].

It was unity of design that led Rutter to conclude that the 'grounds of Fonthill exhibit the true spirit of English gardening carried to its utmost extent of a bold and varied simplicity' (p. 84).

J. C. Loudon visited Fonthill in 1807 and in 1833 to examine the Abbey estate for its merits as a landscape garden. Besides being a landscape gardener himself, he had studied the works of the popular eighteenth-century landscapists and understood the development of the theory of the English informal garden from Sir William Temple and Batty Langley to Repton and Price. Their influence is reflected in his belief that 'the principles of landscape-gardening' were 'derived from nature, as developed by the principles of landscape painting; and, as recognised by a poetic mind, or a mind alive to those general beauties or associations universally felt in civilised society'.[62] His *Encyclopedia of Gardening*, an invaluable historical record for students in the field, first appeared in 1822. From 1826 to his death in 1842, he published the monthly *Gardener's Magazine*, and in 1842 he edited the *Encyclopedia of Trees and Shrubs* and an edition of Repton's *Sketches and Hints on Landscape-Gardening*.

It was in the September issue of the *Gardener's Magazine* in 1835 that he published his findings on Fonthill. In Loudon's judgement, Fonthill was more than a work of architecture, it was a modern example of an English landscape garden that brought together a taste for the picturesque with a taste for the Gothic as a unified composition. 'This place', he began, 'well deserves to be visited by every person who takes an interest respecting, or is desirous of improving himself in, landscape-gardening; because it is the only one in England in which he will find the most perfect unity of character preserved throughout the grounds.'[63] The term 'character,' as Loudon applied it here, was synonymous with a controlling theme or underlying design to which all parts related in order to produce a unified composition. He then proceeded to identify the 'character' of Fonthill as 'belonging to an age long since past in this country, and only now to be found in certain mountainous regions of Catholic countries on the Continent. The chief object of Mr. Beckford seems to have been to impress this character on all the great leading features of Fonthill' (pp. 441–2). Again, as Loudon approached from the open downs on the Hindon side, he observed that 'the occasional glimpses caught of Fonthill ... surrounded by woods and without a single human habitation, a fence, or a made road appearing in the landscape, convey to a stranger a correct impression of the character of the place; viz, that of a monastic building in a wild, hilly, and thinly inhabited country, such as we may imagine to have existed three or four centuries ago' (p. 441).

To obtain the best impression of the Abbey and its surrounding scenery, Loudon felt that it was necessary to approach from the Stone Gate at the end of the Great Western Avenue. As he walked up the main avenue leading to the Abbey, he was moved by the 'solemn solitary grandeur of this scene', recalling 'the associations which we have formed of monasteries in alpine countries'. He found the use of turf particularly suitable to the design: 'This avenue is naturally of that fine close turf peculiar to elevated regions and chalky soils; and, in Mr. Beckford's time, it was kept smoothly shaven: the work being always performed during the night, in order that the prevailing character of solitariness might not be interrupted during the day' (p. 442). Near the Abbey the avenue widened, leaving a broad area in front that was broken by scattered trees so as to appear as 'having been cleared by the founders of the abbey from the native forest'. 'At the distance of a few yards, there was a range of humble sheds, in which workmen of different kinds were employed, hewing and carving for continuous additions of improvements; and this was also quite in character with the scene, as such was often the case with ancient monastic establishments.' (p. 443) In short, everywhere Loudon looked throughout the estate – the paths, drives and gardens – he saw evidence of naturalistic design carried out on such a large scale and in such a free manner 'as never once to excite the idea of art or formality'. He continued to make these observations as he walked about the entire estate, and they inform his final conclusion: 'We admire in Mr. Beckford his vivid imagination and cultivated mind, and that good taste in landscape-gardening which produced the perfect unity of character which pervades the grounds at Fonthill.' (p. 449)

An Artistic Tout Ensemble:
The Legacy of Fonthill

Almost fifty years before Fonthill, Horace Walpole set up Strawberry Hill as a model for the Gothic style, but it was tame by comparison to Fonthill, partly because Walpole had an 'Augustan core', as Kenneth Clark put it, while Beckford possessed a greater penchant for risk-taking that enabled him to transcend the classic habit of mind. Beckford himself believed in Fonthill's superiority in terms of its more dramatic public appeal and immense theatricality, calling Strawberry Hill by comparison a 'miserable child's box – a species of gothic mouse-trap – a reflection of Walpole's littleness'.[1] Even Charles Eastlake, at the high point of interest in Victorian ecclesiology and the re-creation of authentic Gothic structures in England, concluded that Fonthill 'for its size, eccentricity of character and bold adaption of Gothic form was unequalled in importance by any which had preceded it'.[2] James Fergusson, Fellow of the Royal Institute of British Architects, concluded similarly in 1862 that, despite all its faults, Fonthill Abbey was the 'most successful Gothic building of its day, more Medieval in the picturesque irregularity of its outline, more Gothic in the correctness of its details, than any which had then been erected'.[3]

The appraisals of Fonthill by Eastlake and Fergusson gave it an important place in the history of the revival of medieval design in domestic buildings in nineteenth-century England. But today there is a growing tendency to view Beckford's Fonthill as it was originally conceived – as an artistic *tout ensemble* – more than a work of architecture and more than a landscape garden. The large body of original essays, poems, and engraved 'views' that it inspired during the period of its existence constitute an invaluable historical record of the popularity of Fonthill and the extent and impact of Beckford's artistic achievement. It is for this reason that some of the most important of these writings have been incorporated in the Appendices of this study as an anthology of writings on Fonthill published during its heyday. Equally important have been the numerous engravings which appeared in the guidebooks, periodicals and other descriptive accounts of the period. Having been more readily available than the newspaper and journal accounts, they provide a visual record of Fonthill and help to account for its persistence as a romantic icon. The combination of both the iconographic and written records make for a more objective and holistic assessment of Fonthill as a work of art even though it no longer exists in its original form.

With the contemporary historical record missing, the critical assessment of Fonthill in the first half of the twentieth century has often been limited in perspective, focusing on the exotic character of the Abbey building while neglecting the contents and the grounds, or on the personal and moral eccentricities of Beckford without attending to his artistic accomplishment. Since the revival of interest in Beckford in the early 1900s, it has become almost a fashion among modern critics to be dismissive in their treatment of Fonthill. Thus Charles Whibley, in the *Pageantry of Life* in 1900, characterized Fonthill as a capital example of 'insensate grandeur' and the 'monstrous Abbey' as 'an orgy of reckless Gothic'.[4] Margaret Jourdain, after quoting Whibley in her essay in *Memorials of Old Wiltshire* in 1906, argued that 'the creation of [Beckford's] extravagance, only too literally the "basic fabric" of a vision, left no trace behind it, and is hence of no more interest to us today than Nonesuch, another "Palace of Delight".'[5] In *The Drift of Romanticism*, Paul E. More concluded in 1913 that Fonthill was obviously the result of an attempt to satisfy a 'whimsical taste' and a 'disorganized fancy',[6] while Guy Chapman, one of Beckford's biographers, dismissed the Abbey in 1928 as 'one of the more striking monuments to man's vanity and presumption'.[7] These were harsh judgements, to be sure, but perhaps the most severe attack was lodged by John Steegman, who, in *The Rule of Taste* in 1936, omitted mention of the Fonthill landscape and condemned the building as an illustration of architectural sterility. 'Fonthill gave birth to nothing,' he wrote, 'and ... its features passed out of mind.' It was 'an unexpected piece of treasure-trove carried in on the tide of romanticism and crumbling as it struck the shore'.[8]

There is another kind of criticism that has contributed to the widespread impression that Fonthill is not worthy of serious consideration as an artistic work. Here is a writer who, after a visit to the grounds in

1954, made her evaluation with Beckford's moral character clearly in mind:

> As I crossed the wilderness of human wastefulness over which time and nature have drawn a decent pall, I could well believe the astonishing tales I had heard in the village of William Beckford and his palace, stories even more fantastic than appear in the textbooks but none the less likely to be true, and it was with something like relief that I turned away down the long drive and, back again in Tisbury, entered the clean, sweet atmosphere of its noble church.[9]

It is no coincidence that this same article opened with Hazlitt's denunciation of the Abbey and its contents as worthless and trivial. With only traces of the original design left and a fragment of the original structure, Hazlitt's dissenting voice has been and remains strong and influential.

An exception to this tendency to marginalize Fonthill was Kenneth Clark's pioneer book on the Gothic revival which first appeared in 1928. Clark tended to see Fonthill as an important expression of Romanticism in the 1790s and the 'epitome of eighteenth-century Gothic'. His concentration was less on the archaeological purity of the Abbey than on the 'effect' it had on the viewer and, in this sense, he judged it as a major achievement ranking with other important examples of romantic art of the time:

> All that the eighteenth century demanded from Gothic – unimpeded perspectives, immense height, the sublime, in short – was present in Fonthill, and present more lavishly, perhaps, than in real medieval buildings. Even we, who pride ourselves on classicism, cannot be quite dead to this sudden outburst of romantic rhetoric. We know very well that the plaster tower is mere trumpery, but its sudden vehemence sweeps away our judgement; as Berlioz may suddenly sweep us away from Haydn, and El Greco's nightmare vision of Toledo seduce our eyes from the judicious Poussin.[10]

Clark also understood that Fonthill was influential in the Gothic revival because of the fascination with Beckford the man. In the eyes of the public, Beckford had mythical status and the personal appeal of a romantic outsider. They were interested in him as an aloof, glamorous figure who had committed an unpardonable sin that served, among other things, to illustrate his unconventionality and enhance his appeal. Not surprisingly, there were contemporaries who saw him as the proto-type for Byron's Childe Harold. In Clark's view, Beckford's public persona invested Fonthill with its own empowering character, because by 'involving Fonthill in mystery, he made it a brilliant advertisement for the Gothic style'.[11]

Clark's emphasis on the 'scenic effect' of Fonthill and its 'romantic rhetoric' helped to foster a broader view of Beckford's achievement in the twentieth century. One of the first efforts to claim a place for Fonthill in a wider artistic scheme was J. W. Oliver, who published a biography of Beckford in 1932. Oliver argued that Fonthill Abbey should be considered as a 'magnificent feature in a magnificently conceived scheme of landscape gardening'.[12] He also placed Fonthill's landscape within the context of the aesthetics of the picturesque, and, while considering it extravagant, defended Beckford's work as the fash-ion of wealthy men of the age: 'Walpole's Strawberry Hill is an earlier example of the tendency, while Abbotsford is one of the latest, and Beckford should surely not be too severely ridiculed for succumbing to a weakness from which Scott himself, with all his sanity and humour, was not exempt' (p. 231).

H. A. N. Brockman's book-length study of Fonthill, published in 1956 under the title *The Caliph of Fonthill*, helped to provide a more balanced and less defensive assessment for the second half of the twen-tieth century. Brockman brought his architectural background to bear on his examination of Fonthill. He found that Wyatt was successful in recreating the atmosphere of a medieval monastery and stressed the need to examine the building as part of a romantic landscape ('The jewel in the setting was magnificent') since he recognized that Beckford was devoted to the art of landscape gardening. He believed that the design of the Abbey was also successful as an illustration of revival Gothic with all the appearance of authentic medieval models. It could not be expected to be compared to its models in any true archaeological sense, but it represented for Brockman a break from the classical tradi-tion and, though unsound as an architectural structure, possessed suffi-cient evocative power to align it with the new aesthetic trends of the Romantic age. As he concluded in his evaluation, 'the curious thing about it is that it really did *sing* as a building; it was frozen music of the most romantic and moving kind; it was, alone of all Wyatt's works, a thing of artistic genius.... Architecturally, it was wicked, but terribly attractive!' (pp. 183–4).

Anthony Dale, in his biography of Wyatt published in the same year, also discussed the merits of Fonthill. He concluded similarly that its main virtues were scenic and that the Abbey was sufficiently realistic in detail to be the 'greatest Gothic production of the eighteenth century, to shout defiance at [Salisbury Cathedral] its medieval rival'.[13] Dale also noted that as a consequence of Wyatt's work on the Abbey he was able to extend its influence during his lifetime by carrying out commissions at Windsor Castle for George III, the Parliament buildings at Westminster, and Ashridge.

While Wyatt was heavily criticized for his many Gothic restorations during his lifetime, he has now achieved the status of a 'torch-bearer' of the revolution that led to the Gothic revival in England, with Fonthill Abbey being considered the finest of his achievements in the area of domestic Gothic.[14] Other students of the period have found traces of the influence of Fonthill Abbey in Hadlow Castle, Coleorton Hall, Highcliffe Castle, Toddington Manor, Kinfauns Castle, Ravensworth Castle, Childwall, Eastnor, Lowther, and Eaton Hall,[15] all of which demonstrates its architectural longevity and impact. Across the Atlantic, the American actor Edwin Forrest built a castle on the Hudson River in 1852 and called it Fonthill Castle. While not similar in the exterior design, Fonthill Castle did consist of six octagonal towers with the central tower enclosing an octagonal rotunda reminiscent of the central octagonal tower at Fonthill. Forrest owned a copy of Rutter's *Delineations of Fonthill and Its Abbey* and used it as a guide for some of the interior design-work. This is evident in the fan vaulting of Forrest's drawing room, modelled after St Michael's Gallery, the oak webbing of the octagonal chamber, a bay window in the west side of the drawing room and in several other details.[16]

Boyd Alexander extended the discussion of Fonthill as a landscape garden in 1962, by illustrating how various aspects of the design of the grounds adhered to the principles of Uvedale Price's theory of the picturesque.[17] This treatment of Fonthill in a broader aesthetic scheme finally led to the inclusion of Fonthill in a history of gardens by Christopher Thacker in 1979. 'In practice,' Thacker wrote, 'William Beckford ... went furthest towards achieving a garden landscape which was wholly natural while remaining a garden.'[18] 'It marks the absolute limit of the English landscape garden,' he continued, ' and from this point a return to less absolute and less deeply philosophical garden convictions occurs' (p. 222). More recent assessments are beginning to recognize that the formal composition of Fonthill includes three areas of consideration: the Abbey as a neo-Gothic structure, its landscape setting, and the sequence of interior scenic effects as the elements of a calculated artistic totality.[19]

In this study we have added another dimension, stressing that as a landscape Fonthill represented the 'picturesque style' in a deeper, more sophisticated sense than simply the reproduction of scenes from popular landscape paintings of the day. Fonthill was also an important example of the successful application of the technique of landscape painting to the field of landscape gardening because it was based on Beckford's own educated sense of composition and training. The natural elements of its layout were carefully massed and shaped into a harmonious whole according to the basic principles of composition in painting, and there was in the end a definite unity of design to which both Rutter and Loudon gave special attention. Everything contributed to the 'solemn, undisturbed tranquility' of its monastic theme: the high enclosure wall, the density of its woods and groves, the lake, the American plantation, the enclosed walks and drives, and the Abbey itself rising in splendid isolation as the diadem of the scene. The subordination of these details to a single theme was the keynote to the Fonthill composition.

There was also a planned coherence among the various parts of the entire garden scheme. Everywhere the garden melted into the glade, so that all the individual parts could be linked to form a harmonious whole. This was particularly evident, as we have seen, in the connection between the building and the outlying grounds where the wide, smooth, and almost unbroken lawn blended by degrees into the forest beyond. This gradual shift provided the 'insensible transition' so esteemed by the progressive gardening theorists. In addition, the irregular style of its Gothic architecture, the asymmetrical floor plan, and the layout of the interior galleries were all appropriate to the external landscape. The result was a focal point of interest to which all other elements were subordinate, a fine centrepiece in an elaborate landscape setting.

Fonthill as a landscape garden was an original creation personally attended to and conceived by Beckford. He understood the importance of studying the topography of the estate as a prologue to design, a fundamental principle of modern planning. There were other important aspects of the Fonthill design that deserve attention as well: the consistency of naturalistic effect through the careful concealment of art, the restoration of the status of the individual plant to the garden picture, the blending of the different parts of the scheme to form a unified and coherent whole, and the skilful management of such important ingredients as texture, form, colour, light and shade to enliven the entire setting and provide the force of contrast. In these ways, Beckford's work at Fonthill represented a significant step towards modern design and was in this sense in advance of its age. 'Little had been said by the public about any part of Fonthill but the buildings,' Redding wrote, 'yet were the beautiful grounds there nurtured by his taste as superior to the gardens of Versailles as St. James's is inferior to the French palace of that name. The grounds were marvellously fine, no expense being spared in keeping them. They covered nineteen hundred acres within the wall, with three thousand more around it.'[20]

It is unfortunate that Fonthill no longer exists in the original state that made such a powerful impression, imaginatively and aesthetically, on all who wandered in its precincts. But the fact that it did not last is no diminishment of Beckford's accomplishment. Dr Gustav Waagen, Director of the Royal Gallery at Berlin, and one of the most accomplished European art critics of the day, examined Beckford's collections in Bath and discussed Fonthill with connoisseurs who had been there. When he left Bath, he recorded some very perceptive comments on the nature of the Fonthill experience as a total aesthetic immersion in a multidimensional artistic experience. He wrote:

> On the whole, I came away with the conviction that Mr. Beckford unites, in a very rare degree, an immense fortune with a general and refined love of art and a highly cultivated taste. Such a man alone could have produced a creation like Fonthill Abbey, which, from the picture that I am now able to form of it, must have realised the impression of a fairy tale. The extensive Gothic building, with a lofty, very elegant tower, from the views which I have seen of it, must have had, in the highest degree, the grandly fantastic character by which this style of architecture exercises so wonderful a charm. Conceive the interior adorned with ... important works of art, with the most elegant and costly furniture; conceive it surrounded by all that the art of gardening in England

can effect by the aid of a picturesquely-varied ground, luxuriant vegetation, and a great mass of natural running water; and you will have a general idea of this magic spot, which so far maintained this character that for a long time no strange foot was permitted to intrude. Accordingly, when Mr. Beckford... resolved ... to sell it with all its contents, the fashionable and the unfashionable world flocked from all parts of England to wonder at this 'lion', the greatest that had long been exhibited... . Unhappily, Fonthill Abbey has resembled also in its transitory existence the frail creations of the world of enchantment.'[21]

Fonthill in the end was a 'frail creation of the world of enchantment', but interestingly its legacy has transcended the physical character of the Abbey, its magnificent setting, and the works of art within its walls. Despite all the efforts to diminish its importance and to discredit it as a work of art, Fonthill has remained a fixed image in the minds of students of the Romantic period. It was a fantasy that became reality as memorable as the works of Gothic fiction writers and the likes of such prominent Romantics as Coleridge, De Quincey, and Edgar Allan Poe. Why this is so has something to do with the fascination with William Beckford the man, who possessed the allure of other great figures of wealth and singularity in history. In addition, Fonthill was bolder as an artistic totality, more adventurous than any similar work that preceded it. As an expression of Beckford's artistic genius and taste, it was transgressive and rose to a higher order of aesthetic interest. It represented the new Romantic aesthetics that had their roots in Milton's own powerful inversion that gave rise to the beauty of outlaw daring and free expression. It had the appeal of a work that broke through boundaries. In the manner of Piranesi and John Martin, Beckford created a work of art that achieved the status of the monumental sublime, where elements of the extraordinary and the vast mingled to create expressions of awe and wonder and produced an indelible image that continues to hold an important place in the realm of Romantic iconography now and for future generations.

Notes

CHAPTER ONE

1 Cyrus Redding, *Memoirs of William Beckford of Fonthill* (London, 1859), II, p. 146 and the unpublished manuscript of Redding's *Memoirs* etc., as quoted by Boyd Alexander, *England's Wealthiest Son* (London, 1962), p. 172.

2 [W. B. to Alexander Cozens], 24 November 1777, Lewis Melville, *The Life and Letters of William Beckford of Fonthill* (New York, 1910), p. 40.

3 *Hamilton Palace Sale* catalogue of the Beckford library. London, 1882–83, II, 2465; hereafter referred to as *H. P. S.*

4 [W. B. to Cozens], 3 October 1777, Melville, p. 32.

5 [W. B. to Cozens], 5 June 1778, *ibid.*, p. 52.

6 Alexander examined this document in unpublished form when he was custodian of the Beckford Papers. He gave it a working title of 'Fonthill Foreshadowed' and quoted from it in *England's Wealthiest Son*. The complete text has now been made available as an edited manuscript on the internet by Dick Claésson with a different title, 'The Transport of Pleasure' (1996) to reflect the broader characteristics of the work than did Alexander's title. This quotation is from p. 26 of the text. All quotations hereafter are from this text. Available: http://www.hum.gu.se/ ~litwww/TransportOf Pleasure.pdf

7 24 November [1777], Melville, p. 37.

8 *Idem.*

9 25 December 1777, *ibid.*, p. 41.

10 *The Vision* [and] *Liber Veritatis*, ed. Guy Chapman (Cambridge, 1930), p. 85.

11 For a further discussion of Beckford's writing within the tradition of picturesque aesthetics, see the Introduction to *Dreams, Waking Thoughts and Incidents*, ed. R. J. Gemmett (Rutherford, 1972), pp. 13–16. All references hereafter are to this edition.

12 Beckford's record of this experience is included as *An Excursion to the Grande Chartreuse, in the Year 1778* in my edition of *Dreams, Waking Thoughts and Incidents* (pp. 261–84), p. 263.

13 Cyrus Redding, 'Recollections of the Author of *Vathek*', *The New Monthly Magazine*, LXXI (June 1844), p. 153.

14 'William Beckford', *Dictionary of National Biography*, II, p. 84.

15 Kim Sloan, *Alexander and John Robert Cozens* (New Haven, 1986), pp. 138–57. For a more extended application of Sloan's findings to Beckford, see E. S. Shaffer's essay '"To Remind Us of China" – William Beckford, Mental Traveller on the Grand Tour: The Construction of Significance in Landscape', in *Transports: Travel, Pleasure, and Imaginative Geography, 1600–1830*, ed. Chloe Chard and Helen Langdon (New Haven, [1996]), pp. 207–42.

16 *Dreams, Waking Thoughts and Incidents*, p. 184.

17 As quoted by J. W. Oliver, *The Life of William Beckford* (London, 1932), pp. 89, 91.

18 *Vathek*, ed. Roger Lonsdale (Oxford, 1998), p. 4. All references hereafter are to this edition.

19 *The Travel-Diaries of William Beckford of Fonthill*, ed. Guy Chapman (Cambridge, 1928, II, p. 272. All references to *Recollections of an Excursion to the Monasteries of Alcobaça and Batalha* hereafter are to this edition.

20 Redding, *The New Monthly Magazine*, LXXI, p. 146.

21 In addition to the accusation of apostasy, this article, which ran for two consecutive issues of the *Sunday Times*, ranks among the most severe attacks on Beckford and his father ever published. It charged his father with deriving his wealth from a 'traffic in Negro slaves', which, it said, he 'pursued with more persevering ardour than those who laboured with him in the same wretched field'. Once the Lord Mayor died, the article continued, the 'whole mass of this evil-speaking gold devolved upon the present Mr. Beckford', who then squandered it on building Fonthill for the purpose of astonishing the world with the 'extent of his resources'. 'Fonthill Abbey – Mr. Beckford – and Vathek', *Sunday Times*, 28 September 1823, p. 4 and 5 October 1823, p. 1. For Beckford's extended reaction, see MS. Beckford, Bodleian Library, c 84, ff. 64–5.

22 'Conversations with the Late W. Beckford, Esq.', *The New Monthly Magazine*, LXXII (November 1844), pp. 419–20.

23 *Ibid.* (December 1844), p. 518.

24 *England's Wealthiest Son*, p. 135.

25 Charles Quest-Ritson, *The English Garden Abroad* (London, 1992), pp. 160–1.

26 W. B. to Charlotte Courtenay, 22 February 1781, Guy Chapman, *Beckford* (London, 1952), p. 82.

27 Written in 1838. Chapman, p. 69.

28 W. B. to Count Benincasa, 21 October 1780, *England's Wealthiest Son*, p. 76.

29 11 December [1780], Oliver, p. 52.

30 29 December 1780, *ibid*., p. 54.

31 9 January 1781, *ibid*., p. 55.

32 28 January 1781, *ibid*., p. 59.

33 For press citations on the scandal, see Chapman, pp. 185–6.

34 'Thoughts on a Late Biography', *The Monthly Visitor*, II (October 1797), p. 343.

35 Draft to Lady Craven, undated [between 1793 and 1796], *England's Wealthiest Son*, p. 122.

36 *The Journal of William Beckford in Portugal and Spain 1787–1788*, ed. Boyd Alexander (New York, 1955), p. 100. All references hereafter are to this edition.

CHAPTER TWO

1 'Conversations with the Late W. Beckford, Esq. Contributed by Various Friends', *New Monthly Magazine*, LXXII (November 1844), p. 419. This is the second of three articles signed 'H'. The author remains unidentified.

2 See James Lees-Milne, *William Beckford* (Tisbury, 1976), p. 41.

3 *H. P. S*., I, 1788.

4 William Gregory, *The Beckford Family. Reminiscences of Fonthill Abbey and Lansdown Tower*, 2nd ed. (London, 1898), p. 139.

5 *Dreams, Waking Thoughts and Incidents*, pp. 66, 73.

6 *Travel-Diaries*, II, 18.

7 For a discussion of this subject, see the Introduction to *Biographical Memoirs of Extraordinary Painters*, ed. R. J. Gemmett (Rutherford, 1969), pp. 26–31. All references hereafter are to this edition. See also R. J. Gemmett, *William Beckford* (Boston, 1977), pp. 61–2.

8 *Dreams, Waking Thoughts, and Incidents*, pp. 62–3.

9 *Ibid*., p. 257.

10 London, 1772, p. viii. Beckford's reaction to Chambers's essay was that it was 'florid' and 'exaggerated,' but it is not clear that he understood that the architect's real purpose for writing this essay was to present his own views on English landscape gardening rather than to extol the virtues of Chinese gardening. For Beckford's comments, see *Travel-Diaries*, II, pp. 265–6.

11 *Travel-Diaries*, II, p. 246.

12 *Memoirs*, II, p. 147.

13 *Travel-Diaries*, II, p. 247.

14 For the catalogues of Beckford's library, see *The Sale Catalogues of*

Libraries of Eminent Persons, Vol. 3, William Beckford, ed. R. J. Gemmett (London, 1972). I provide a more extensive list of books on gardening in Beckford's library in my unpublished dissertation 'William Beckford and the Picturesque: A Study of Fonthill', Syracuse University, 1967, pp. 252–6.

15 *England's Wealthiest Son*, pp. 177–8.

16 These citations appeared in chapter 4 of John Rutter's *Delineations of Fonthill and Its Abbey* (London, 1823), pp. 83–4. Boyd Alexander believed that these and the other poetical citations in Rutter's book came directly from Beckford. See *England's Wealthiest Son*, p. 173.

17 For an excellent discussion of the gardening movement in the eighteenth century, see Isabel Chase, *Horace Walpole: Gardenist* (Princeton, 1943), pp. 135–67; 178–9.

18 *Memoirs*, II, p. 147.

19 *Journal in Portugal and Spain*, p. 127.

20 *The New Monthly Magazine*, LXXI (June 1844), p. 149.

21 *Travel-Diaries*, II, 343. See also *England's Wealthiest Son*, p. 152.

22 This book was in the Beckford collection of James T. Babb, now housed in Yale's Beinecke Library.

23 Oliver, p. 295.

24 *Dreams, Waking Thoughts and Incidents*, p. 83.

25 *Ibid.*, p. 147.

26 *Travel-Diaries*, II, p. 239.

27 *Journal in Portugal and Spain*, p. 111.

28 *Modern Novel Writing, or the Elegant Enthusiast* (London, 1796), II, 63–4. All references hereafter are to this edition. Hervey wrote: 'In the distribution of the grounds, the hand of Brown had assisted, but not forced nature; each masterly stroke of his art had only served to bring to light beauties that lay concealed before.' (London, 1788), II, p. 204.

29 See Hervey, II, 204–11 for the full description of the grounds that Beckford used as the source for describing Lord Mahogany's estate.

30 *Azemia: A Descriptive and Sentimental Novel* (London, 1797), I, p. 142.

CHAPTER THREE

1 *England's Wealthiest Son*, pp. 172–3.

2 MS. Beckford, Bodleian Library, c. 15, f. 12. This is the collection of Amelia Sophia Eleanor Hanover (1711–86), who died the previous year.

3 *The European Magazine and London Review*, XXXI, pp. 104–7. The identity of the editor during this period has been a mystery. James Perry (1756–1821) was the founding editor, but he left the magazine in 1783. In an unpublished letter, John Lettice reveals that the functioning editor

at this time was Isaac Reed (1742–1807), who was also a proprietor of the magazine. While it is known that he denied being an editor (J. B. Nichols, *Illustrations of the Literary History of the Eighteenth Century* (London, 1848), VII, p. 48), he was a frequent contributor and Lettice addressed him as the editor in a letter requesting an editorial change in an article on Beckford, which appeared in the September issue of the magazine under the title 'William Beckford, Esq. of Fonthill', XXXII, pp. 147–50. On 11 July 1797 Lettice wrote to Reed: 'In the last period of my Account of Mr. Beckford sent to you Yesterday, I much wish the word *valued* to be substituted for *regarded*. To say the Laws of Nations might possibly be *little regarded* by the French Plenipotentiaries would admit a bad Construction; I mean an unsafe one.' Beinecke Library, Beckford Collection, Box 4, f. 96. Reed did incorporate the correction. The fact that Lettice authored this account of Beckford points to the possibility of Lettice being the 'correspondent' of the article on the Christmas festivities at Fonthill published in January 1797 and to Lettice being the source of information for the article in the February issue.

4 'Account of the Christmas Festivities at Fonthill by a Correspondent Who Was Present', *The European Magazine and London Review*' (January 1797), XXXI, pp. 4–6.

5 Rutter, pp. 92–3.

6 *Observations on the Western Parts of England Relative Chiefly to Picturesque Beauty* (London, 1798), p. 116.

7 Rutter, p. 107.

8 *The European Magazine and London Review*, XXXI, p. 105.

9 *Ibid.*, p. 104.

10 John Britton indicated that the bridge was removed in 1781, the year Beckford reached majority. *The Beauties of Wiltshire* (London, 1801), I, p. 248.

11 W. B. to Sir William Hamilton, 15 April 1796, Alfred Morrison, *Collection of Autograph Letters and Historical Documents, The Hamilton and Nelson Papers* (Second Series), printed for private circulation, 1893–4, I, 219. Hereafter referred to as *Hamilton and Nelson Papers*. Beckford is referring to the interior of Fonthill Splendens in this letter ('harmony is everything in pictures, furniture, &c. I have been trying to harmonize Fonthill – no easy attempt, I can assure you – wealth having done a confounded deal of mischief.'), but his remark applies to his exterior work as well.

12 *The European Magazine and London Review*, XXXI, 105.

13 'Fonthill Property', *The Times*, 4 October 1822, p. 3.

14 MS. Beckford, Bodleian Library, c. 84, f. 110.

15 Beinecke Library, Beckford Collection, Gen MSS 102, Box 6, f. 111.

16 *The Beauties of Wiltshire*, I, p. 246.

17 *Ibid.* I, p. 240.

18 W. B. to Samuel Henley, 19 May and 10 July 1784, Alfred Morrison, *Collection of Autograph Letters and Historical Documents* (Second Series), printed for private circulation, 1893, I, 192. Hereafter referred to as *Morrison Collection*.

19 Fraser Neiman, 'The Letters of William Gilpin to Samuel Henley', *Huntington Library Quarterly*, XXXV (February 1972), pp. 159–69.

20 *The European Magazine and London Review*, XXXI, p. 105.

21 *Idem.* See also Redding, *Memoirs*, II, 80 for corroborative information regarding the Alderman's work.

22 *The European Magazine and London Review*, XXXI, p. 105.

23 *The Beauties of Wiltshire*, I, p. 242. It should be noted that Britton's phrasing here is somewhat ambiguous on the matter of when Beckford became involved in planting. One could interpret his wording to mean he began before 1781, during his 'minority'. However, Britton may have intended a separation of time between the development of Beckford's 'feeling for the picturesque' which he discovered 'in a very early stage of his minority', and the major landscaping activities conducted later in the area of the Alpine Garden. The account provided in *The European Magazine and London Review* is clearer in identifying 1781 as the year Beckford's land improvements began.

24 Redding wrote: 'Soon after Mr. Beckford's return from seeing Aranjuez, his old tutor was at Fonthill, instructing the Misses Beckford, and he suggested that walks should be made of nearly a mile in extent, in order to render that wild spot pleasanter for the ladies, who seemed to have a partiality for it. Mr. Beckford, struck with the capabilities of the place, ordered the necessary workmen to be busy; and the end was achieved in what afterwards had the name of the "Alpine Garden".' *Memoirs,* II, p. 81. It should be noted that this published version differs from Redding's manuscript account of the *Memoirs*. In the ms. he overstated Lettice's role in the production of the Alpine Garden by saying that it was 'formed by Dr. Lettice' and then modified it before publication. MS. Beckford, Bodleian Library, c. 86, f. 33 and 34b. While Lettice played a role, it is clear from Britton's account and *The European Magazine and London Review* that considerable work had been done before Lettice's involvement. See also Laurent Châtel's reconstruction of the development of this landscape element in 'The Mole, the Bat, and the Fairy or the Sublime Grottoes of "Fonthill Splendens"', *The Beckford Journal*, V (Spring 1999), pp. 58–60.

25 *Beauties of Wiltshire*, I, pp. 242–3.

26 'Modern Gardening', *Anecdotes of Painting in England*, ed. Ralph Wornum (London, 1849), III, p. 807.

27 *Memoirs*, I, p. 148.

28 Redding wrote: 'A grotto was made by a workman named Lane, in imitation of one constructed many years before for Mrs. Beckford's uncle, the Hon. Charles Hamilton, of Pain's Hill, Surrey', *ibid.*, II, 81. Josiah Lane is often wrongly identified as the person responsible for creating the grotto at Painshill. See Norman and Beryl Kitz, *Pains Hill Park* (Cobham, 1984), p. 73. When the construction of it began in 1763, Josiah (1753–1833) was only ten years old. It therefore had to be the work of his father, Joseph (1717–84), who died the year Josiah began to create Beckford's grotto on the east side of the lake.

29 13 October 1784, *Morrison Collection*, I, 192–3.

30 *The Times*, 4 October 1822, p. 3.

31 *Beauties of Wiltshire*, I, p. 247.

32 Lot 255, Jamica Letter Books, Manuscript, Christie, Manson, Woods sale catalogue, *Important Autograph Letters*, 2 April 1975.

33 It is difficult to know with certainty that Lane was responsible for this inscription, particularly since this grotto, as I examined it, contains numerous carvings of initials and dates in the stone. The fact that it is a roundel, however, sets it apart from the others. Châtel, p. 58, has pointed out the initials J. L. could also stand for John Lettice, but it is difficult to see how Lettice's interest in overseeing the development of walkways in the Alpine Gardens could be associated with the construction of a grotto.

34 *Letters Written during a Residence in England* (London, 1799), pp. 304–5 [letter XIX devoted to Fonthill]. There have been some differences of opinion concerning the year Meister visited Fonthill. He does mention Beckford's age in this account as thirty-three which would place the year of the visit as either 1793 or 1794. However, Meister's description indicates that he actually met Beckford which would make 1794 impossible since he was in Portugal during that year. Internal evidence, involving seasonal references, suggests that Meister was there in the summer of 1793, a matter of months before Beckford's thirty-third birthday on 29 September.

35 Rutter described this feature as a 'building called a Hermitage, whose ruinous state indicates that the taste which presided over such erections is gone by'. Rutter, p. 95. A handbook for travellers published in 1869 recorded that the 'Hermit's Cave' was made by the 'younger Beckford' and described it as a 'circular cavern with 2 dark recesses in one of which lies the mutilated figure of the hermit'. *Handbook for Travellers in Wiltshire, Dorsetshire, and Somersetshire* (London, 1869), p. 153.

36 Timothy Mowl believes that this cromlech was really a viewing tower.

William Beckford (London, 1998), pp. 34–5. Châtel argues convincingly that this monolith is really a cromlech after all. *The Beckford Journal*, pp. 63–4.

37 Rutter, p. 96.
38 *The English Garden Abroad* (London, [1992]), p. 160.
39 *Sintra A Landscape with Villas*. Ediçöes Inapa, [1989], p. 67.
40 *Ibid.*, p. 64. A photograph of the stone arch appears on p. 66.
41 Quest-Ritson, p. 160.

CHAPTER FOUR

1 Rutter, p. 108.
2 *England's Wealthiest Son*, p. 157.
3 *Idem.*
4 *The European Magazine and London Review*, XXXI, p. 105.
5 This draft letter is undated, but, in view of a reference in it to the recently completed wall, it was likely written in the year 1795. See Oliver, pp. 257–8.
6 Reproduced for the first time in *England's Wealthiest Son*, p. 118.
7 Melville, p. 214.
8 *Ibid.*, pp. 214–15.
9 This passage was omitted by Melville. See *England's Wealthiest Son*, p. 282 n.6.
10 Rutter, p. 109.
11 *The European Magazine and London Review*, XXXI, p. 106 and Beckford's letter to Sir William Hamilton of 2 February 1797, *Hamilton and Nelson Papers*, I, p. 227.
12 *The Diary of Joseph Farington*, ed. Kenneth Garlick and Angus MacIntyre (New Haven, 1978), II, p. 612.
13 *The Gentleman's Magazine*, LXVI, pt. 2, p. 784.
14 To John Lettice, Melville, p. 243.
15 To Nicholas Williams, 12 October 1796, *England's Wealthiest Son*, p. 159.
16 29 November 1796, Melville, p. 221–2.
17 W.B. to Sir William Hamilton, *Hamilton and Nelson Papers*, I, p. 227.
18 *The European Magazine and London Review*, XXXI, p. 105.
19 Rutter, p. 109.
20 See John Wilton-Ely, 'Beckford, Fonthill and the Picturesque', in *The Picturesque in Georgian England*, ed. Dana Arnold (London, [1995]), pp. 37–9, and his earlier work 'The Genesis and Evolution of Fonthill Abbey', *Architectural History*, 23 (1980), pp. 40–51 and plates 28b, 30a, b, c, 31, 32a, b.

21 Wilton-Ely, 'Beckford, Fonthill Abbey and the Picturesque', p. 37. Wyatt's exhibit was no. 1143: 'Design for a building now executing at Fonthill, the seat of William Beckford, Esq. in the style of a Gothic abbey.'

22 *Farington Diary*, III, pp. 880 and 918.

23 Rutter, p. 110. There has been some question about how many times the tower collapsed under construction. Rutter is the only source that reported a fall this early. This could be considered a mistake, but Rutter obtained his information from Wyatt's personal notes on the history of the Abbey's construction which provides credibility to his account. We do know for certain that a dramatic collapse of the tower occurred in May 1800, and Cyrus Redding indicated that the tower was rebuilt three times. Redding, *Memoirs*, II, p. 158. Beckford's secretary and librarian, Abbé Macquin, also reported in his series of articles on Fonthill that the tower was once destroyed by fire, but he provides no date. Redding also recorded a fire at the summit of the tower, noting that a 'considerable expense was incurred in its restoration'. Redding, *Memoirs*, II, p. 156. Finally, John Britton reported that the tower had been raised three times. See 'Visit to Fonthill', *The Literary Gazette and Journal of Belles Lettres*, 24 August 1822, p. 527, and Britton's *Graphical and Literary Illustrations of Fonthill Abbey* (London, 1823), p. 52. In short, the evidence supports the occurrence of two collapses (one in the winter of 1796–7 and the other in 1800) and a fire at some indeterminate date during construction – all three occasions requiring raising the tower. But even after these three events, problems continued because Wyatt used a synthetic material called 'compo-cement' which had to be re-encased in 1806 – hence a fourth restoration. See *England's Wealthiest Son*, p. 14.

24 This could have been one of the occasions for Redding's comment that the Octagon Hall was 'twice built.' *Memoirs*, II, p. 158.

25 Derek Linstrum, *Catalogue of the Drawings of the Royal Institute of British Architects Wyatt Family* (Westmead, 1974), p. 38.

26 The contemporary label information kindly provided by Scott Wilcox, Curator of Prints and Drawings.

27 Linstrum reproduces all three early-stage drawings by Wyatt in figures 32, 33, and 34.

28 'Fonthill Abbey', *Morning Chronicle*, 3 October 1823, p. 3.

29 See II, A, 14, b in the Bibliography for details.

30 *Farington Diary*, III, p. 916.

31 *Ibid.*, III, p. 1091.

32 'Visit to Fonthill', *Literary Gazette and Journal of Belles Lettres*, 14 September 1822, p. 585.

33 Oliver, p. 235.

34 *The European Magazine and London Review*, XXXI, p. 106. The editor indicates that the medieval church was demolished after Fonthill House burned down in 1755. Actually, records show that the removal of the church took place earlier, sometime between 1747 and 1749. D. A. Crowley, *A History of Wiltshire, Southwest Wiltshire* (Oxford, 1980), XIII, p. 168. The church was already in a state of ruin by 1747. The foundation stone of the church he built still exists and is incorporated in the vestry of the current Fonthill Gifford church on the same site. It reads: '18 May 1748/ WILLm.BECKFORD/ESQR FOUNDER.'

35 ALS, 4 January 1797, MS Beckford, Bodleian Library, b 8, ff. 10–1.

36 *The Gentleman's Magazine*, LXVIII, pt. 2 (July 1798), p. 639.

37 As cited by H. A. N. Brockman, *The Caliph of Fonthill* (London, [1956]), p. 111. Farington recorded in his diary on 16 November 1798 that the spire would be '17 feet higher than the top of St. Peter's at Rome'. III, p. 1091.

38 *Farington Diary*, III, p. 1117.

39 A suggestion first made by Nancy L. Pressly, *Revealed Religion: Benjamin West's Commissions for Windsor Castle and Fonthill Abbey* (San Antonio, 1983), p. 58.

40 Draft copy, MS Beckford, Bodleian Library, c. 16, ff. 21–2. Robert Bowyer (1758–1834), bookseller and miniature painter, Historic Gallery, Pall Mall.

41 Rutter, 31. Pearson (c. 1742–c. 1840) is identified in the *Dictionary of National Biography* as having died in 1805, but he lived well into his nineties and, in 1815, published a letter in *The Gentleman's Magazine* in which he cited Beckford as one of a number of authorities who could confirm that the 'art of staining glass has been brought to perfection in England'. See LXXXV, pt. 2 (July 1815), p. 28. Pearson's window of Thomas à Becket has survived and is now in the Lord Mayor's chapel in Bristol.

42 'Progress, &c. of Stained Glass in England', *The Gentleman's Magazine*, LXXXVII, pt. 1 (April 1817), 315n. Dallaway (1763–1834), topographer and antiquarian, was the author of numerous works, including *Anecdotes of the Arts in England* (1800) and *Observations on English Architecture, Military, Ecclesiastical, and Civil … including Historical Notices of Stained Glass, Ornamental Gardening, etc.* (1806). This important essay was published anonymously, but it is obviously Dallaway's work. It is signed with the initials 'E. M. S.', which he often used for his anonymous pieces and which stood for Earl Marshal Secretary, a position to which he was appointed in 1797 and held for the rest of his life.

43 *A Description of Fonthill Abbey, Wiltshire* (London, 1812), p. 11.

44 MS. Beckford, Bodleian Library, c. 16, f. 20.

45 Rutter, p. 55.

46 MS. Beckford, Bodleian Library, c 30. f. 115.

47 See Clive Wainwright's excellent essay on the interior of Fonthill Abbey in *The Romantic Interior* (New Haven, 1989), p. 117.

48 A detailed description of these sketchbooks is provided in the bibliography. See also E. G. Cundall, 'Turner Drawings of Fonthill Abbey', *Burlington Magazine*, XXIX (April 1916), pp. 16–21.

49 *Farington Diary*, IV, p. 1277.

50 *The Times*, 27 May 1800, p. 3.

51 *Morning Chronicle*, 3 October 1823, p. 3.

52 *The Times*, 20 May 1800, p. 3.

53 *Ibid.*, 27 May 1800, p. 3.

54 *Morning Chronicle*, 22 May 1800, p. 3. The tower actually fell on Saturday, 17 May 1800.

55 *Ibid.*, 29 May 1800, p. 3.

56 Oliver, p. 238.

57 21 May 1800, Oliver, p. 237. There is some evidence to suggest that he never gave up entirely the notion of a spire that would be added to the tower. An article that appeared in the *Morning Herald* in 1822 stated that the tower 'lofty as it is, it is yet unfinished; the spire remains to be added, which, from the proportion, must be raised to least a hundred and twenty feet. It is to be surmounted by a cross, and the whole, when finished, will present a tower and spire, whose highest point will be four hundred feet from the ground. Some idea may be formed of the extensive view which the highest galleries will afford, when it is observed that the base of the tower is as high as the top of the spire of Salisbury Cathedral, which is remarkable for its altitude.' 'Fonthill, October 4', *Morning Herald*, 7 October 1822, p. 2.

58 Nicholas Williams to W. B., 11 September 1801, Melville, p. 263.

59 'Letter from a Gentleman, Present at the Festivites at Fonthill, to a Correspondent in Town', *The Gentleman's Magazine*, LXXXIX, pt. 1 (March, April 1801), pp. 206–8; 297–8.

60 To Nicholas Williams, 5 January 1801, Melville, p. 238.

61 Redding, *Memoirs*, II, pp. 132–4 .

62 MS. Beckford, Bodleian Library, e 4, ff. 1–15.

63 The letter was signed 'Observator' in *The Gentleman's Magazine*, LXXVI, pt. 2 (December 1806), pp. 1127–8. This repair of the tower confirms Redding's statement that the central tower was rebuilt 'three times'. Redding, *Memoirs*, II, p. 158.

64 To Marquess of Douglas, 28 November 1806, Oliver, pp. 247–8.

65 John Wilton-Ely provides photographs of this model and discusses

aspects of it in 'A Model for Fonthill Abbey', in eds. Howard Colvin and John Harris, *The Country Seat: Studies in the History of the British Country House* (London, [1970]), pp. 199–204. The model is currently in the possession of Neil Rimington, Stop's Farm, Fonthill Gifford.

66 Based on letters to Isaac Heard of 11 September and 11 October 1808, Oliver, pp. 249–50. See also letter of 25 September 1808, *Life at Fonthill ... From the Correspondence of William Beckford*, ed. Boyd Alexander (London, 1957), pp. 83–5.

67 Based on a draft letter to Lady Craven, 22 July 1809, *England's Wealthiest Son*, p. 165.

68 W. B. to Franchi, 22 June 1810, *Life at Fonthill*, p. 91.

69 Letter dated 23 December 1811 found and published recently in *The Beckford Journal*, I (Spring, 1995), Bankes (d. 1855), the eldest son of Henry Bankes of Kingston Hall, Dorset, represented the borough of Truro in Parliament from 1810 to 1812. A close friend of Byron, he later became MP for the University of Cambridge and the county of Dorset.

70 Storer, p. 8.

71 *Life at Fonthill,* p.128.

72 *Ibid.*, p. 128.

73 *Ibid.*, p. 150.

74 *Ibid.*, p. 226.

75 For details on Beckford's financial problems and his offer to the Duke of Hamilton, see *ibid.*, pp. 326–31.

76 'A Visit to Fonthill Abbey', *Literary Gazette*, 17 August 1822, p. 520.

77 'Fonthill Abbey,' *Morning Chronicle*, 26 September 1823, p. 3.

CHAPTER FIVE

1 24 July 1799, Melville, p. 256.

2 Letter to his mother, 29 November 1796 and to Sir William Hamilton, 2 February 1797, Oliver, pp. 234–6.

3 *The European Magazine and London Review*, XXXI, p. 106.

4 Rutter, p. 83.

5 *Idem.*

6 'Sketches and Hints on Landscape Gardening' in *The Art of Landscape Gardening*, ed. John Nolens (Boston, 1907), p. 26.

7 *Essays on the Picturesque* (London, 1798), II, p. 160.

8 'A Day at Fonthill Abbey', *New Monthly Magazine*, VIII (1823), p. 370. See also Boyd Alexander, 'William Beckford, Man of Taste', *History Today*, X (October 1960), pp. 693–4.

9 *The European Magazine and London Review*, XXXI, p. 107.

10 Based on Rutter's description in 1823.

11 Rutter, p. 86.

12 *Ibid.*, p. 88.

13 This was Sir Richard Colt-Hoare's description of the Abbey from a different vantage point. It appeared in an article he published under the pseudonym 'Viator'. See 'Fonthill Abbey. On Its Close', *Gentleman's Magazine*, XCII, pt. 2 (October 1822), p. 291. This article has often been erroneously attributed to Beckford. The files of the Nichols family, proprietors of *The Gentleman's Magazine* from 1778 to 1856, reveal that Hoare was the author. See James M. Kuist, *The Nichols File of the Gentleman's Magazine* (Madison, 1982), p. 80.

14 Rutter, p. 89.

15 *Life at Fonthill*, p. 158.

16 As described by Storer in 1812. Rutter omits these details. Storer, pp. 4–5.

17 The lake was created before 1639 by the Cottington family by damming a stream which flowed eastward to the Nadder river. Crowley, XIII, pp. 155–6. Beckford made clear his own involvement in the development of the 'sublime effect' of the lake in a letter of 1817, noting that it was accomplished by 'tree felling' and by 'the particular shape I have given to the shore on a grand scale'. *Life at Fonthill*, p. 234. The lake also had a utilitarian purpose. At the southern extremity of the lake, Beckford had an ingenious hydraulic system installed, involving a water wheel, a wooden trough and a series of underground pipes, that provided water to the Abbey.

18 *Illustrations of Fonthill Abbey*, pp. 35–6.

19 Storer, p. 5.

20 'Fonthill Abbey', *Morning Chronicle*, 17 September 1823, p. 3.

21 *Life at Fonthill*, pp. 97–8.

22 Lady Anne Hamilton's diary mentions the existence of the American garden in 1803. MS. Beckford, Bodleian Library, e. 4, f. 10. Milne could have been involved in additional planting here for the purpose of expanding it from when she saw it.

23 Redding, *Memoirs*, II, pp. 127–8.

24 London, 1794, pp. 20–1.

25 *Ibid.*, p. 277.

26 *The New Monthly Magazine*, LXXI, p. 149.

27 *Literary Gazette*, 24 August 1822, pp. 527–8.

28 To Dr Mitford, 29 August 1808, ed. A. G. L'Estrange, *The Friendships of Mary Russell Mitford* (New York, 1882), pp. 30–1.

29 Oliver, pp. 272–3.

30 MS. Beckford, Bodleian Library, e. 4, f. 11.

31 *The European Magazine and London Review*, XXXI, p. 105.
32 John Claudius Loudon, 'Notes on Gardens and Country Seats – Fonthill', *The Gardener's Magazine*, XI (September 1835), p. 444.
33 Storer, p. 6.
34 *The Gardener's Magazine*, XI, p. 444.
35 Storer, p. 3.
36 Rutter, p. 90.
37 *Life at Fonthill*, p. 90.
38 Loudon, XI, p. 443.
39 Henry V. Lansdown, *Recollections of the Late William Beckford of Fonthill, Wilts. and Lansdown, Bath*, ed. Charlotte Lansdown (Bath, 1893), p. 47.
40 'A Day at Fonthill Abbey', *The New Monthly Magazine*, VIII (1823), p. 379.
41 'Fonthill Abbey', *Morning Chronicle*, 13 September 1823, p. 3.

CHAPTER SIX

1 Repton, p. 132. See also William Chambers, *Dissertation on Oriental Gardening* (London, 1773), pp. 18–19; Horace Walpole, 'On Modern Gardening', III, 805; Price, London, 1798, II, p. 177.
2 Loudon, pp. 442–3.
3 London, 1798, II, pp. 134–5.
4 'Fonthill Abbey', *The Gazette of Fashion*, 31 August 1822, p. 65.
5 London, 1794, pp. 50–1.
6 *Past Celebrities Whom I Have Known* (London, 1866), I, pp. 315–16.
7 These figures represent exterior measurements as provided by Britton, p. 13.
8 Brockman, p. 112.
9 Britton, p. 11.
10 *Ibid.*, p. 12.
11 The exact dimensions, according to Rutter, were 112 ft. 4 in. long, 13 ft. 7 in. wide, 15 ft. 4 in. high. Rutter, p. 55.
12 Brockman, p. 112.
13 Rutter gives the dimensions of the Gallery as 68 ft. long, 16 ft. 10 in. wide, 17 ft. 10 in. high; the Sanctuary as 13 ft. long, 14 ft. wide, 16 ft. high; the Oratory as 12 ft. long, 14 ft. wide, 17 ft. high. He neglected to mention the measurements of the Vaulted Corridor. My estimate is that it was approximately 34 ft. long, 14 ft. wide, 17 ft. high. See Rutter, p. 36. Neither Rutter nor Britton identified the length of the vestibules leading into King Edward's and St Michael's Galleries. Each of these, utilizing the extant floor plans of the Abbey, appears to have been approximately

16 ft, 6 in. long. Thus, combined with the 35 ft. diameter of the Grand Saloon or Octagon Hall, the length of the vista from one end of the two galleries to the other would be 307 feet, as Rutter recorded.

14 *Ibid.*, p. 33.

15 *Memoirs*, II, pp. 53–4.

16 *Journal in Portugal and Spain*, p. 301.

17 Rutter, p. 36.

18 *Ibid.*, p. 37.

19 Goldsmiths identified by Lady Anne Hamilton; she also identified the '36 wax lights in Gold Branches and Candlesticks' that surrounded the statue of St Anthony in 1803 as by goldsmith Henri Auguste of Paris. MS. Beckford, Bodleian Library, e. 4, f. 4.

20 Britton, p. 47.

21 Rutter, p. 40.

22 *Ibid.*, p. 28.

23 Storer, p. 18.

24 Rutter, p. 24.

25 Storer, p. 17.

26 *The New Monthly Magazine and Literary Journal*, VIII (1823), p. 372. The poet Thomas Campbell (1777–1844) was the editor at this time. Cyrus Redding was serving as the sub-editor.

27 Rutter, p. 21.

28 *The New Monthly Magazine*, VIII (1823), p. 373.

CHAPTER SEVEN

1 14 December 1807, *Farington Diary*, VIII, pp. 3166–7.

2 For a further discussion of Beckford's book collecting tastes and interests, see *The Consummate Collector: William Beckford's Letters to His Bookseller*, ed. R. J. Gemmett (Wilby, Norwich, 2000), pp. 13 – 20.

3 'Fonthill Abbey', *Morning Herald*, 7 October 1822, p. 2.

4 'Fonthill Abbey', *The Gazette of Fashion*, 31 August 1822, p. 65. See also R. J. Gemmett, 'The Critical Reception of William Beckford's Fonthill', *English Miscellany*, XIX (1968), pp. 133–51.

5 7 August 1822, *Life at Fonthill*, p. 336.

6 Author attribution derives from John Britton, *Graphical and Literary Illustrations of Fonthill Abbey, Wiltshire* (London, 1823), who identified these articles as 'written by the lively and versatile pen of the learned author of several volumes on bibliography and bibliomania; and who, by his writings on the latter subject, has contributed more to increase than to cure the disease' (p. 15). Furthermore, a piece on Stourhead extracted from this extended review appeared under the pseudonym

Cuthbert Tonstall in *The Gentleman's Magazine*, XCII, pt. 2 (1822), pp. 388–91. The files of the Nichols family, proprietors of this magazine from 1778 to 1856, reveal that Tonstall was Dibdin. See Kuist, p. 56. These quotations are from the first and sixth essays. *The Museum, or Record of Literature, Fine Arts, Science, Antiquities, the Drama, etc.*, 5 October 1822, p. 379 and 9 November 1822, p. 456.

7 Rutter's book, a precursor to his more extended and elegant book on Fonthill published the following year, appeared under the title *A Description of Fonthill Abbey, and Demesne* (Shaftesbury, 1822); Whittaker's book appeared as *A New Guide to Fonthill Abbey* with an engraved frontispiece by William Read (Witham, Essex, 1822) and in a London edition with a frontispiece by Thomas Higham; Storer's book, *A Description of Fonthill Abbey, Wiltshire*, was published in London by Sherwood, Neely, and Jones and in Salisbury by Brodie and Dowding in 1822 and 1823. The first issue of *The Portfolio* (1823) contained Storer's description and interior views of the Abbey. Earlier editions of Easton's book, *The Salisbury Guide*, provided only a brief description of Fonthill Abbey.

8 For a census of the various engravings that appeared, see Jon Millington, 'Engravings of Fonthill', *The Beckford Journal*, VII (Spring 2001), pp. 47–58.

9 See Appendices I and II for a selection of some of the contemporary essays, commentary and poems dedicated to Fonthill.

10 'Fonthill', *Morning Herald*, 7 October 1822, p. 2.

11 *The Times*, 30 September 1822, p. 3.

12 *Idem*.

13 *Once Upon a Time* (London, 1865), p. 506.

14 2 September 1822, *Life at Fonthill*, p. 337–8.

15 Beginning with the *Literary Gazette* issue of 17 August 1822. These five contributions appeared anonymously. I have based this attribution on Jerdan who recorded that 'from Fonthill, in the autumn of 1822, he [Macquin] contributed... a series of papers giving an historical account of the Abbey, a biography of the family of Beckford, the author of "Vathek", and a fine description of the place and its contents previous to its sale. The second paper was illustrated by a drawing, of which I published a neat engraving. The fifth is in verse....' *The Autobiography of William Jerdan* (London, 1853), III, pp. 107–8. The poem appeared in the issue of 21 September 1822, pp. 602–3.

16 'Armorial Decorations at Fonthill Abbey', *The Gentleman's Magazine*, XCII, pt. 2 (September October, November 1822), pp. 201–4; 317–20; 409–14.

17 7 August, 1822, *Life at Fonthill*, pp. 337–8.

18 MS. Beckford, Bodleian Library, b 8, ff. 19–20.

19 The sale document lists only the lot numbers from *A Catalogue of the Magnificent Effects At Fonthill Abbey, Wilts.* 'to be sold by Auction, by Mr. Christie' (1822). The lots Beckford selected were: First day, Lots 18 'Two extremely rare BLACK AND GOLD JAPAN SALVERS with the Fung-Hoang and foliage. – N.B. *These fine pieces came from the collection of the Duc de Bouillon*'; 52 'A very singular [Japan tray], the ground *of a curious wood artificially waved*, with storks in various attitudes on the shore, mosaic border and avanturine back, from the museum of the Duchess of Portland'; 73 'Two fine illumined missal drawings in one black and gold frame'; 87 'An extremely curious enamel on copper, in three divisions, the centre representing the Descent from the Cross, and Daniel and St. Paul in the side compartments, in an ebony frame'; Second day, Lots 61 'BAUER. A fine and elaborate small drawing of figures disembarked, and architecture'; 62 'Three curious illumined miniature paintings of Saints of the Greek Church, in a black and gold frame, in 3 compartments'; 71 'A MINIATURE PORTRAIT, in water-colours of LOUIS XII. at his Devotions, with St. Louis, St. Michael, Charlemagne, and St. Denys'; 93 'A fine miniature drawing of Saint Charles Borromeo, in a very richly carved and gilt frame'; Third day, Lot 26 'A round CUP and COVER of ORIENTAL MAMMILLATED CALCEDONY undulated, mounted in sliver gilt, delicately engraved in the Persian style, the stem enriched with oriental rubies, set in gold, *most singularly beautiful*'; Fourth day, Lot 58 'A pair of beautiful silver gilt candlesticks, executed by VULLIAMY, *from an original design by Holbein*'; Fifth day, Lots 41 'A Circular Deep SALVER of LIMOSIN ENAMEL, on copper, embellished with a Procession of Diana and Nymphs returning from the Chace; the border of Raffaellesque device, the bowl of the salver also externaly [*sic*] decorated with masks and ornaments. The date is inscribed in enamel, 1563, P. R. It was made for Henry II. Of France, and was presented by him to Diane de Poictiers. It is mounted with a central boss bearing her cypher, a triple crescent, and inscription; and the border also enriched with monograms'; 46 'A VESSEL, of compressed oval shape, formed of a LARGE BLOCK of SARDONYX hollowed out, and the surface incrusted with vine leaves of good design and sharpest execution. A pair of Satyr's Heads are sculptured as Handles to the Vase; the bottom is externally carved with foliage, and affords reason for believing, that this rare and very curious article must have been executed by a GREEK ARTIST in ASIA MINOR. It is protected at the top by a rim of fine gold'; 58 'A Magnificent Large Oval CASSOLETTE, of Hungarian Agate, massively mounted in silver, engraved, chased and gilt, ornamented with masks of satyrs admirably

modelled, and of the first workmanship'; Seventh day, Lots 5 'Flemish A small Portrait of a Lady, with the date 1662'; 9 'Stothard Tom o'Shanter: from Burns's Poems'; 10 'Steenwyck Interior of a Cathedral, with figures'; 15 'Holbein A small Portrait of a Man with the Hands joined in Prayer – very beautifully finished'; 16 'Walckenberg The Building of the Tower of Babel, with a Multitude of small Figures. *See the Catalogue of King Charles's Collection*'; 25 'Breughel A Landscape with numerous Figures, and Christ bearing his Cross, with distant View of Jerusalem and Mount Calvary'; 34 'Siqueira The Reposo in Egypt, with Infant Angels – a very pleasing specimen of a distinguished Portuguese Artist'; 41 'Cima di Conegliano The Virgin, in richly coloured Drapery, holding the Infant in her Lap. In the distance, is a Landscape with view of part of the buildings of a fortified town, with a clear and brilliant sky. This beautiful specimen of one of the scarcest Masters of the early Venetian School, formerly belonged to Mr. Strange, and was originally in the collection of the Nuncio di Verona'; 53 'Breughel A small River Scene with Boats and Figures'; 76 'Wilson A small Landscape, View on the Tiber, with a Figure on a Timber Raft, and a Female reposing on the Front Ground. From Mr. Knight's Collection, undoubtedly, one of the most beautiful productions of the Master'; 81 'Peters A View of Ostend, and the Mouth of the Harbour, with Boats putting out – very fine and spirited'; 97 'West A Grand Mass in the Interior of St. George's Chapel at Windsor, in which are intro-duced the Kings of France and Scotland, when Prisoners at Windsor: cabinet size'; 98 'Poelemborg A Landscape, with Two elegant draped Female Figures; beyond which are others in a Pool of Water, half-concealed by the rising front-ground; rocky Masses and Ruins, with Wood, crown a Bank in the distance'; 99 '[Poelenburgh] A [Landscape] with Ruins, and Pastoral Figures, and an elegant Group of half-draped Females in the front-ground; finished with great delicacy'; 112 'G. Poussin A grand Landscape, composed of fine mountainous Scenery, and at the foot of it a woody Glade, where Figures are Reposing; a Conflagration of some Buildings on the half-ascent of the hills, is repre-sented with great spirit, and gives a lively interest to the scene'; 'either Lot 106 or 113 option, as to the said John Farquhar', Lot 106 'Berghem A small Landscape with Cattle feeding and reposing on a rising Pasture Ground; a Shepherd and Shepherdess piping on the left; with a hilly distance, and a very brilliant sky. This pure and exquisite bijou was formerly in the Cabinet de Praslin. Where it ranked high, as the Diamant de Berghem'; Lot 113 'Berghem The very celebrated Sea Port of the PRASLIN CABINET, termed the *Embarquement des Vivres*; and noticed in the Catalogue as one of the three principal ornaments of that Collection. It represents a group of Figures and Cattle on the Shore of the Gulf of Genoa, which is enlivened with Buildings and Shipping, painted in the finest style of the Master'.

20 MS. Beckford, Bodleian Library, b 8, ff. 19–20.

21 *Salisbury and Winchester Journal*, 14 October 1822, p. 4.

22 See the *Observer*, 13 October 1822, p. 4.

23 7 October 1822, *Life at Fonthill*, p. 340.

24 [December] 1822, MS. Beckford, Bodleian Library, c 30, ff. 122–3.

25 *New European Magazine*, 2 (January 1823), p. 83.

26 Draft copy, Tuesday 25 March 1823, MS. Beckford, Bodleian Library, c. 14, f. 55.

27 W. B. to George Clarke, 1 April 1832, *The Consummate Collector*, p. 134.

28 'Fonthill Abbey', *Morning Chronicle*, 24 September 1822, p. 3.

29 9 January 1823, Oliver, p. 289.

30 *The Gentleman's Magazine*, XCII, pt. 2 (October 1822), p. 291.

CHAPTER EIGHT

1 *The Times*, 12 September 1823, p. 2.

2 As quoted by *The Times*, 30 September 1823, p. 3.

3 *Literary Gazette*, 20 September 1823, p. 602 and 27 September 1823, pp. 617–18.

4 *The Times*, 26 September 1823, p. 3.

5 *Literary Museum and Register of Belle Lettres*, 1 November 1823, pp. 701–2. Watts served as editor of the *Leeds Intelligencer* from 1822 to 1825. This poem was published anonymously and reprinted as a broadside in 1824 as 'Fonthill Sale A Parody', signed with the initials A. A. W. I have been able to identify Alaric Watts as the author from a copy of the broadside in the Beinecke Library, Yale University. Watts sent this copy to John Britton, noting on the verso that there were errors in the first printing that he corrected. The broadside also contains a date hand-written at the top as '19 Jan 1824'. Beinecke Library, Beckford Collection, GEN MSS 102, Box 4, f. 100. Lewis Melville reproduced the broadside for the first time, but without author identification (pp. 315–19). This quotation is from the corrected broadside which appears in full in Appendix II.

6 AL, to John Britton, 6 October 1823, Beinecke Library, Beckford Collection, GEN MSS 102, Box 4, f. 71. Adams's letter also provides the details regarding Phillips's reactions.

7 *Salisbury and Winchester Journal*, 27 October 1823, p. 4.

8 *The Times*, 5 November 1823, p. 3. Interestingly, Lewis paid for the publication of his response as an 'Advertisement', probably to ensure its appearance.

9 The individuals identified in Lewis's provenance of the vase were George Stanley, auctioneer, 21 Old Bond Street, George Winyett Farmer, jeweller and silversmith, 32 Tavistock Street, Covent Garden, and either Edward Foster, 14 Greek Street, Soho, or Charles Foster, 6 Angel Court, Throgmorton Street, both London auctioneers. The other dealers Lewis mentions as supporters of his assessment included the firm of J. T. & C Hawley, 75 Strand, goldsmiths and watchmakers and John Boykett Jarman, goldsmith and jeweller, 30 St James's Street.

10 MS. Beckford, Bodleian Library, b. 8, f. 7. On the verso of this document is written in Beckford's hand 'Acct of the Topaz Vase'. There is no date, but the paper is watermarked 1810.

11 See Joseph Alsop, 'The Faker's Art', New York Review of Books, 23 October 1986, pp. 25–31 and Richard E. Stone, 'A Noble Imposture: The Fonthill Ewer and Early-Nineteenth-Century Fakery', Metropolitan Museum Journal, 32 (1997), pp. 175–206.

12 29 October, 1819, Life at Fonthill, p. 324.

13 28 October 1819, ibid., pp. 323–4.

14 The Times, 17 November 1823, p. 3.

15 'Fonthill Abbey', London Magazine, VI (November 1822), p. 405.

16 'Illumination of the Abbey', Morning Chronicle, 24 October 1823, p. 4.

17 'Fonthill Abbey', Morning Post, 1 October 1823, p. 3.

18 Passages of a Working Life During Half a Century (London, 1865), I, p. 311.

19 Signed 'A Passerby', The Gentleman's Magazine, XCI, pt. 2 (December 1821), pp. 495–6.

20 Signed 'H', 'Fonthill Abbey in Ruins', The Gentleman's Magazine, XCVI, pt. 1 (February 1826), 123. See also the letter, dated 21 December 1825, from a person on the scene, published in The Gentleman's Magazine, XCV, pt. 2 (December 1825), p. 557.

21 J. C. Loudon, 'Notes on Gardens and Country Seats, Visited, from July 27 – September 16, 1833', The Gardener's Magazine, XI (September 1835), pp. 446–7.

22 Memoirs, II, p. 258.

23 Crowley, XIII, 161; Sir Richard Colt Hoare, The History of Modern Wiltshire. Hundred of Dunworth and Vale of Noddre (London, 1829), p. 24. For additional details of these complex transfers, see John B. Nichols, Historical Notices of Fonthill Abbey, Wiltshire (London, 1836), pp. 32–4.

24 Catalogue of the Entire Astronomical, Chemical, and Philosophical Library of the Late John Farquhar, Esq. of Fonthill; including Six Volumes of Elaborate and Splendid Patna Drawings. Which will be Sold by Auction by Mr. Sotheby... on Thursday, the 1st of March, 1827 and four following days.

25 MS. Beckford, Bodleian Library, c. 14, f. 81.

26 Richard Gatty, *Portrait of a Merchant Prince, James Morrison 1789–1857* (Northallerton, [1976]), p. 111.

27 Charlotte Lansdown, *Recollections of the Late William Beckford of Fonthill, Wilts and Lansdown, Bath* (Bath, 1893), pp. 38–48.

28 It still exists today, though in a badly weather-worn condition, and can be seen in the garden of Wardour Castle.

CHAPTER NINE

1 'Foreword', Brockman, p. xii. Jon Millington has compiled an interesting exhibition catalogue of Fonthill souvenirs that demonstrates the keen interest in the Abbey during Beckford's lifetime. *Souvenirs of Fonthill Abbey* (Bath, 1994).

2 'Fonthill Abbey', *Morning Chronicle*, 17 September 1823, p. 3.

3 'A Day at Fonthill Abbey', *The New Monthly Magazine and Literary Journal*, VIII (1823), p. 376.

4 'Fonthill Abbey', *The Literary Chronicle and Weekly Review*, 19 October 1822, p. 666.

5 'Fonthill Abbey', *The Examiner*, 10 August 1823, p. 514.

6 Rutter, pp. 83–4.

7 *The Gentleman's Magazine*, XCII, pt. 2 (October 1822), p. 291.

8 *Gazette of Fashion*, 31 August 1822, p. 65. See also [John Britton], 'Fonthill Abbey', *The Museum; or Record of Literature, Fine Arts, Science, Antiquities, the Drama, &c.*, no. 19 (1822), pp. 300–1.

9 *Morning Post*, 22 August 1823, p. 3.

10 *Morning Chronicle*, 21 August 1823, p. 2.

11 'Fonthill Abbey', *Morning Chronicle*, 20 August 1823, p. 3.

12 Based on a transcription of the original letter of 29 August 1823, by Ian Fleming Williams and published in the *Beckford Newsletter*, ed. Jon Millington (Spring 1983), pp. 8–9.

13 *The Gentleman's Magazine*, XCII, pt. 2 (August 1822), p. 102.

14 'Fonthill Abbey', *Literary Gazette*, 21 September 1822, pp. 602–3.

15 'Fonthill Abbey', *The London Magazine*, V (November, 1822), p. 406.

16 'Pictures at Wilton, Stourhead, &c.', *The London Magazine*, VIII (October 1823), p. 359.

17 See Damian W. Davies and Laurent Châtel, '"A Mad Hornet": Beckford's Riposte to Hazlitt', *European Romantic Review*, X (Fall 1999), pp. 452–79. Macquin's letters in French are among the Beckford Papers. My quotations are from the translations provided in this valuable article.

18 'Fonthill and Its Late Owner', *New Times*, 23 September 1823, p. 2.

19 One of the most severe condemnations ran in two consecutive issues of the *Sunday Times*. The editor at the time was Daniel Whittle Harvey, known for writing hard-hitting lead articles to capture reader interest. The first of the two articles noted about Beckford that 'the story of his past life is reviewed with unyielding rancour – the wild caprices of his restless mind are arrayed as sins, and a frightful stain upon his moral character has rung across the land.' 'Fonthill Abbey – Mr. Beckford – and Vathek', 28 September 1823, p. 4 and 5 October 1823, p. 1.

20 'William Beckford, Man of Taste', *History Today*, X (October 1960), pp. 686–7.

21 Wainwright, pp. 121–7;131–6; 141–2.

22 *Ibid.*, p. 143.

23 *A List of Carvings and Other Works of Art* (London, 1854), p. 26, as quoted by Wainwright, p. 139.

24 *The Complete Works of William Hazlitt*, ed. P. P. Howe (London, 1933), XIX, p. 280.

25 Stanley Jones, 'The Fonthill Abbey Pictures: Two Additions to the Hazlitt Canon', *Journal of the Warburg and Courtauld Institutes*, XLI (1978), pp. 278–96.

26 F. W. Haydon, *Benjamin Robert Haydon:Correspondence and Table Talk* (London, 1876), II, p. 79.

27 'Notices of Curious and Highly Finished Cabinet Pictures at Fonthill Abbey', *Morning Chronicle*, 20 August, p. 3; 22 August, p. 3; 25 August, p. 3; 1 September 1823, p. 2.

28 *Ibid.*, 20 August 1823, p. 3.

29 *Morning Chronicle*, 30 September 1823, p. 2.

30 'The Main Chance', *The New Monthly Magazine*, XVII (February 1828), 120. In my 1968 article on Fonthill in *English Miscellany*, I mistakenly identified this essay as appearing in the *Literary Examiner* under the title 'Judging of Pictures' (p. 136, fn. 11).

31 *England's Wealthiest Son*, p. 170.

32 *New Monthly Magazine*, VIII (1823), p. 404.

33 *The Gentleman's Magazine*, XCII, pt. 2 (December 1822), pp. 491–4.

34 'I enclose a few remarks on the Abbey written by my friend Garbett, an Architect of Winchester, & intended by him for Gents. Mag.' Copy of a letter to Beckford, 23 October 1822, Beinecke Library, Beckford Collection, GEN MSS. 102, Box 8, f. 181.

35 *Salisbury and Winchester Journal*, 30 September 1822, p. 4.

36 'Fonthill Abbey', *Morning Chronicle*, 13 September 1823, p. 3.

37 John Harris, 'C. R. Cockerell's "Ichnographica Domestica"', *Architectural History*, XIV (1971), pp. 15–16.

38 *Salisbury and Winchester Journal*, 8 September 1823, p. 4.

39 'Fonthill Abbey', *The Museum; or Record of Literature, Fine Arts, Science, Antiquities, the Drama, &c.*, no. 17 (1822), p. 264. Britton was identified as the author of this essay in the August 1822 issue of *The Gentleman's Magazine*, pt. 2, XCII, where it was reprinted on pp. 100–3. See also Britton's abbreviated description of the Abbey in his *Beauties of England and Wales* (London, 1814), XV, pp. 265–8 for textual similarities. Beckford saw the manuscript before it was published and provided some emendations.

40 ALS, 13 July 1835. MS. Beckford, Bodleian Library, c. 27, ff. 32–3.

41 ALS, dated 'Fonthill', 5 September 1822 to Beckford at the Clarendon Hotel, London, MS. Beckford, Bodleian Library, c. 27, ff. 14–15a.

42 ALS, 30 July 1823, MS. Beckford, Bodleian Library, c. 27, ff. 16b–17.

43 The Chinese vase, now in the National Museum of Ireland, dated from circa 1300 and is today considered to be one of the earliest documented pieces of Chinese porcelain to have reached Europe. The Metropolitan Museum now owns the chasse. The rare Rubens vase is in the Walters Art Gallery in Baltimore. See Wainwright, 133–6 and Arthur Lane, 'The Gagnières-Fonthill Vase: A Chinese Porcelain of about 1300', *Burlington Magazine* CIII (April 1961), pp. 124–32. The chasse Britton substituted was owned by the antiquary Thomas Astle (1735–1803). Ironically, Britton noted the similarity between the two reliquaries in *Illustrations of Fonthill Abbey*, p. 55. Marie-Madeleine Gauthier provides a full history of the Beckford chasse in *Émaux Méridionaux: Catalogue international de l'oeuvre de Limoges*, I (1987), pp. 181–2.

44 ALS, 5 September 1823, Beinecke Library, Beckford Collection, GEN MSS 102, Box 1, f. 8.

45 *Illustrations of Fonthill Abbey*, p. 39.

46 *Ibid.*, pp. 51–2.

47 'Conversations of the Late W. Beckford, Esq.', *New Monthly Magazine*, LXXII (December 1844), p. 516.

48 The article he was responding to and quoted from here was 'Mr. Beckford Fonthill Abbey', *The Gleaner, or Weekly Historical Register*, 15 October 1823, pp. 407–9. For Wyatt's response, see *The Morning Herald*, 1 November 1823, p. 3.

49 Stephen Clarke addresses Britton's unhappiness with Cattermole's work in 'The Troubled Gestation of Britton's *Illustrations of Fonthill*', *The Beckford Journal*, VI (Spring 2000), pp. 58–74.

50 Copy of an ALS, W. B. to Britton, 3 October 1822, Beinecke Library, Beckford Collection, GEN MSS 102, Box VIII, f. 181.

51 ALS, 5 September 1823, Beinecke Library, Beckford Collection, GEN MSS 102, Box 1, ff. 7–8.

52 ALS, Franchi to Britton, 3 October 1822, bound in Britton's personal

copy of *Graphical and Literary Illustrations of Fonthill Abbey* (1823), Devizes Museum Library, f. 133.

53 ALS, Franchi to Britton, 9 November 1822, *ibid.*, f. 136.

54 ALS, [September, 1823], *ibid.*, f. 145.

55 Beinecke Library, Beckford Collection, Gen Mss 102, Box 9, f. 189.

56 *Ibid.*, f. 189.

57 Le Keux was invited but never responded. All of the other artists were not invited. There is a Shaw on the list, but it may not be Henry Shaw, who did the drawing for the east window in St Michael's Gallery.

58 *Delineations of Fonthill and Its Abbey*, pp. vii; ix.

59 *England's Wealthiest Son*, p. 284, n. 35.

60 *Salisbury and Winchester Journal*, 29 September 1823, p. 4.

61 ALS, 22 November 1823, MS. Beckford, Bodleian Library, c. 27, ff. 18–19; Beckford's draft, MS. Beckford, Bodleian Library, c. 27, f. 20.

62 John Claudius Loudon, *An Encyclopedia of Gardening* (London, 1824), II, p. 999.

63 *The Gardener's Magazine*, XI (September 1835), p. 442.

CHAPTER TEN

1 Redding, *The New Monthly Magazine*, LXXI, p. 308.

2 *History of the Gothic Revival*, ed. J. M. Crook (Leicester, 1970), p. 61.

3 *History of the Modern Styles of Architecture*, 2nd ed. (London, 1873), p. 360.

4 *Pageantry of Life* (New York, 1900), pp. 212–13.

5 *Memories of Old Wiltshire* (London, 1906), p. 116.

6 *The Drift of Romanticism* (Boston, 1913), p. 14.

7 *Travel-Diaries*, I, p. xliv.

8 *The Rule of Taste* (London, 1936), p. 85.

9 Katharine Ashworth, 'Tisbury's Ancient Secrets', *Country Life*, 4 November 1954, p. 1592.

10 *The Gothic Revival* (London, 1964), p. 75.

11 *Ibid.*, p. 77.

12 Oliver, p. 229.

13 *James Wyatt, Architect: 1748–1813* (Oxford, 1936), p. 157.

14 Michael McCarthy, *The Origins of the Gothic Revival* (London, 1987), p. 2.

15 James Lees-Milne, *William Beckford* (Tisbury, 1976), p. 52; James Macaulay, *The Gothic Revival 1745–1845* (London, 1975), pp. 148; 210; 297; David Watkin, *The English Vision: The Picturesque in Architecture, Landscape, and Garden Design* (New York, 1982), p. 108.

16 Reynolds, Donald M. *et al.*, *Fonthill Castle: Paradigm of Hudson-River Gothic* (Riverdale, 1976), pp. 13–15; 20–2; 24.

17 *England's Wealthiest Son*, p. 176.

18 *The History of Gardens* (Berkeley, 1979), p. 221.

19 Most notably John Wilton-Ely in 'Beckford, Fonthill Abbey and the Picturesque', pp. 35–44 and his essay 'Beckford's Fonthill Abbey: a Theatre of the Arts', in *The Beckford Society Annual Lectures 1996–1999*, ed. Jon Millington (Bristol, 2000), pp. 3–22. See also Wainwright, pp. 109–46.

20 *Memoirs*, II, p. 226.

21 *Works of Art and Artists in England*, III (London, 1838), pp. 129–30.

Contemporary Essays and Commentary on Fonthill

1797–1844

Account of the Christmas Festivities at Fonthill

BY A CORRESPONDENT WHO WAS PRESENT

Several of the first artists in the kingdom, whose talents, in their different branches, have been engaged for the plans and ornaments of an abbey, a noble specimen of Gothic architecture now erecting at Fonthill, being at present there to pass the Christmas holidays, Mr. Beckford chose this occasion to give an entertainment to the numerous body of daily workmen who have been, and will long be, employed on this edifice, or on the grounds and plantations where it is situated.

On Friday, Jan. 6, being Twelfth Day, the feast was given without doors; but so far was it from being confined to the workmen just mentioned, who amount to upwards of three hundred, that the poor in general of the two Fonthills, of the town of Hindon, and many other poor persons of the neighbourhood, all together near one thousand, received tickets to partake of it; not to mention that bread and strong beer were provided for ten thousand of the multitude of strangers, who were admitted into the park as spectators of the entertainment. The dinner, to the persons invited, consisted of an ox, and ten sheep, roasted whole. A very large square tent, or booth, coved in the roof, and covered with canvass, having seven long parallel tables, each receiving one hundred persons, was erected on the lawn, before the North front of the house, for the purpose of the dinner. At a proper distance, on one side of this capacious booth, a considerable length of brick wall, to support the necessary iron ranges, was reared for the occasion. Eleven great fires which supplied them, partly for the purpose of roasting the meat, and partly that of warming the air, may be imagined to have had a striking effect in the *coup d'oeil*. On the opposite side of the booth, and in front of the house, a portion of ground was fenced out, within which was pitched a Turkish tent, for the reception of Mr. Beckford, and a large of company of ladies and gentlemen. In the area, between this and the dinner-tent, two bonfires were lighted, and, at due distances from each, were placed two semicircular tables, to receive a number of children at dinner, chiefly belonging to the persons seated in the grand booth. Betwixt the bonfires sufficient space was left for the exhibition of several of the rural sports with which the company were entertained both before and after dinner. Prizes were given to the best wrestlers, runners, players at single stick, and those who excelled in various other performances. The game of foot-ball, on an open part of the lawn betwixt the scene already described and the lake, afforded admirable diversion. This engaged not only the two parties concerned in the match, but put ten thousand spectators, chiefly consisting of the peasantry of both sexes, in motion, all in high glee at the different turns of the game, and yet without riot, or any other disorder than a lively and continual change of place. This diversion formed to those who beheld it from high ground at some distance, taking in the occasional scenery, combined with the views of the house, its surrounding hills, woods and water, a spectacle altogether of singular interest, and, indeed, of curiosity. The bonfires and all the others, which remained burning all night, with their flames and long-wreathed columns of differently coloured smoke rising among the lofty firs and unleaved oaks in the neighbourhood of the tent, still crouded by a shouting multitude, dimly seen dancing round them, displayed to spectators in the house an effect equally picturesque and uncommon. Many gentlemen of the county, the Mayor, the Corporation, and other gentlemen of the city of Salisbury, having expressed a desire to pay their respects to Mr. Beckford on this occasion, a superb dinner, in the old stile of baronial hospitality, was served in the Grecian hall, which, with the colonades and passages leading to it, was beautifully illuminated. A chosen band of vocal and instrumental music entertained the company during the whole evening, and the greatest good-humour and hilarity prevailed beyond the earliest hours of the morning. The collection of songs, catches and glees, prepared by Mr. Corfe, and printed for the occasion, that books might be distributed to the whole company, was judiciously made, and the execution of them did equal credit to his taste and that of the Salisbury choir. The effect of some of the choruses, particularly that of *God save the King*, accompanied as they were by the organ, and the full band of military instruments, and these joined by hundreds of voices in the hall, and in the apartments contiguous, with those of persons who filled the colonades and surrounded the house, was inconceivably grand, and excited in the minds of many of the company a lively recollection of the first performances of Westminster Abbey.

The subsequent toasts and sentiments, among many others, were given, and followed by music, or by repeated cheers:

Chair.[Beckford]	1st. The King. *God save the King.*
	2d. The Queen and Princesses.
	3d. The Prince of Wales.
	4th. The Duke of York and British army.
	5th. The Navy of England. *Rule Britannia.*
Mayor of Salisbury.	6th. Mr. Beckford – and may his noble benevolence be as generally known and imitated in the world, as it is cordially felt by thousands this day at Fonthill.
Chair.	7th. The Mayor, Corporation and City of Salisbury.
Mr. Still.	8th. The County of Wilts.
Chair.	9th. The Archduke, and his army of heroes.
	10th. The Prince of Brazil, and his hundred and eighty thousand brave defenders of Portugal and of the common cause of the Allies.
Chair.	11th. The People of England, and may they never forget the value of order and good government.
Mr. West.	12th. Prosperity to Fonthill and the fine arts.
Mr. Wyatt.	13th. May the great work at Fonthill be successfully accomplished, and long enjoyed, by the present owner.
Chair.	14th. Christmas – Twelfth-day – old times and old names for ever and may the ears of John Bull never be insulted by the gipsey jargon of France.

On the same day, Mr. Beckford's tradesmen, tenants, and several other parties, dined in different apartments of the house; and the whole number entertained within doors, including his own family, amounted, at least, to four hundred persons. The whole entertainment on Twelfth-day (not to notice those which commenced with

Christmas) was characterised by that good order, picturesque arrangement, hospitality, and magnificence, which have on several occasions been witnessed at Fonthill.

The joy, gratitude, and contentment, expressed by repeated acclamations from such a multitude of the peasantry as assembled on the lawn, their neat appearance, and, above all, their orderly conduct throughout the day, were circumstances, in these times, highly to their credit, and serve to shew the vast influence which gentlemen of fortune and beneficent dispositions, residing on their estates in the country, can still maintain, in opposition to the effects of more modern habits and fashionable life, which, totally estranging the higher from the lower ranks of society, tend to increase the hardships and discontents of the latter, and, in their consequences, to hasten that levelling and confusion of all orders, which the higher ranks are so peculiarly interested, by their best exertions, to avert.

We cannot close this account without mentioning, what we have learned on good authority, that the Christmas festivities of Fonthill, which appear to have been conducted with such extraordinary hospitality, were begun by acts of the most substantial charity; Mr. Beckford having ordered two hundred blankets to be distributed among the poor families of both the Fonthills, with a load of fuel to each of them, besides considerable sums of money to the indigent of his own and other neighbouring parishes.

As some interesting circumstances relative to Fonthill, and the works which have been carrying on there for these last sixteen years, are little known to the public, much the finest parts of the place being never shewn but to Mr. Beckford's particular friends, and the primary motives of these great projects being little understood, we hope to be able, in our next, to gratify our readers, through the same channel by which we have procured the above account, with a communication of some particulars, which will, perhaps, be thought more valuable, as they are of a less temporary nature than those we have now presented.

EDITOR'S NOTE *The European Magazine and London Review*, XXXI (January, 1797), pp. 4–6. For the possible identity of the author of this essay, see editor's note in the following essay.

Account of the Works Now Executing at Fonthill

[ISAAC REED]

Such was the avidity of the Public for information upon the subject of the late Festivities at Fonthill, that our account in the last Month's Magazine was, we fear, considerably anticipated by details, not much unlike our own, which, in the course of the month, had been very generally circulated through the channel of the London and Provincial Papers. This present communication however, which we had encouraged our readers to expect, concerning Fonthill, is particularly consigned to the Editor of the *European Magazine*; and it will probably not prove the less interesting from the sort of connection it will be found to have with the late accounts just mentioned. These, we need not say, have left on the public mind the most advantageous impressions of Mr. Beckford's hospitality and munificence. As soon, therefore, as it was known that the noble spirit displayed on that occasion originated in the scheme of a Christmas entertainment to his numerous body of workmen, curiosity could not fail to be awakened respecting the objects on which the workmen have been, and are at present employed. We flatter ourselves, therefore, that the following details will, as their authenticity may be depended upon, not appear unworthy of attention, nor ill calculated to gratify that curiosity which is still much alive on the subject of Fonthill.

The present Proprietor of Fonthill, from the time he attained his majority, is known to have made it matter of principle, that some considerable work or other, at his chief family residence, should be continually carrying on for the sake of giving bread to the poor of an extensive neighbourhood, destitute of manufactures, and that through the laudable medium of their own labour and industry. In this principle will be found the motive of most of the works of this place;

and notwithstanding all the beautiful specimens of genius and talents which the first Artists have displayed there, or are engaged to produce, the world will have less satisfaction in contemplating the various works at Fonthill as monuments of Mr. Beckford's distinguished taste in the Fine Arts, than as a continued exercise of that generous and charitable disposition, which is ever rendering his princely fortune, in some way or other, subservient to the benefit or happiness of others.

Although parts of the original estate at Fonthill are covered with fine oak timber, yet some thousand acres of the ground purchased by Mr. Beckford's father, as well as by himself, the leases of which have been continually falling in, were unplanted. Not to mention the great plantation begun by the late Mr. Beckford, the present gentleman has been, every year since his possession, continuing them upon a grander scale. Several hundred thousand trees, and, some years, not less than a million, and those of all the different sorts of forest wood, and of various tribes of exotic plants and shrubs, often constitute the work but of a single season. As new purchases are continually adding large tracts of land to Mr. Beckford's domain, his plantations will probably proceed in the same stile for some years to come. As the planting at Fonthill may be considered as a kind of general undertaking always going forward in the proper seasons, a single work only in this way shall be particularly specified, because it was attended by some circumstances which gave it peculiar merit. – The stone of the present Fonthill House, built by the late Mr. Beckford, was taken from a quarry on the Eastern shore of the Lake, at an inconsiderable distance from the scite of the mansion itself. Several acres of rocky ground, which formed this quarry, continued after the completion of the building still open; and exhibiting nothing but large naked masses of white stone and ugly excavations, and those almost fronting the house, it was resolved to cover every part of this quarry, some picturesque features of rock excepted, with soil brought from a distance by dint of labour, and then to plant the ground with oak, beech, elm, larch, fir, &c. leaving green walks, bordered with shrubs and flowers, and such other spaces open, as good taste suggested, according to the nature of the ground. This plantation Mr. Beckford soon after considerably extended along the adjoining hills which hang over the Lake; on the side of which has been formed a Grotto trickling with perennial springs; the surface of its Rock-work variegated with many-coloured mosses, and its crevices filled with aquatic plants and flowers. This whole range of scenery, but particularly the quarry part, the wood having now attained a very considerable growth, may, in point of beauty and original effect, challenge any garden scenery in the kingdom.

That work, having employed a great number of hands for two or three years, was succeeded by an enlargement of the bed of the river, and the removal of a stone bridge of several arches, by which the water could no longer be crossed. The different form of the shores and extension now given to the breadth of the water have entirely changed its former aspect and character, and rendered it worthy of its present appellation of a Lake. The clearness and depth of this water, partly supplied by the river Nadder, and partly by those numerous fountains issuing from the high ground, and giving the appropriate name of Fonthill to the village, add greatly to the merit of this Lake, in respect to its volume and expanse, and entitle it to rank as one of the most interesting objects of the place. Further improvements, however, are in due time to be made upon this water; its size to be still enlarged, and its form more varied.

Mr. Beckford's next undertaking was the formation of a new Kitchen and Flower Garden, contiguous to each other, in a more convenient scite, under a warmer aspect, and upon a scale four times larger than the old one. The Hot Walls, Pineries, Conservatories, quantity of glazed Frame-work, the Gardener's House, importation of soil for this extensive spot of many acres, with its plantations and nurseries, and an extensive inclosure of handsome brick-wall round the whole, have altogether concurred to render this work almost as unrivalled in magnitude and convenience, as it must have been in matter of expence.

About three years ago was begun a Wall of considerable height and thickness, built of hewn stone, and carried circularly round near seven miles of the loftiest and finest part of the hills and woods of Fonthill. This has been finished with a strong painted paling, inclined outwards, as a *chevaux de frize*, which runs entirely round the top of the wall in order to secure this favourite inclosure from all intrusion. Hares, pheasants, partridges, and other game, with birds of song or of beautiful plumage, are the constant inhabitants of this secure region, and are, some or other of them, continually offering themselves to sight in the air or on the ground, half tame, and almost fearless, as if conscious of their privileged safety.

At the bottom of a wildly wooded hill, within this inclosure, is a natural Lake of the most transparent water and happily varied outline –

> Haud procul inde Lacus
> Panditur, et nemorum frondoso margine cinctus
> Vicinis pallescit aquis.

CLAUDIAN

On an elevated scite above this Lake, a space, converted into a Lawn, has been opened in the Wood, consisting chiefly, in this part, of larch and the various tribe of firs, with some mixture of holly and yew, for the erection of a Gothic Abbey, upon a very magnificent plan by Wyatt. This edifice, in which considerable progress is already made, extends to the length of 185 feet; one of its towers, an octagon of 64 feet in diameter, will rise to the height of 145 feet. They alone, who have seen the elevations of this edifice, and are acquainted with its characteristic situation, can form any adequate notion of the grand and striking effects which it will display within the place itself, or present to the surrounding country. It will naturally enough be asked, what suggested to Mr. Beckford the scheme of this building in the form of a Gothic Abbey: the following circumstances will explain the motive: – When this Gentleman's father, soon after the burning of the ancient house in 1755, began to erect the present noble mansion, he obtained a faculty to take down the old church, which stood too near it, and to build a new one in a situation more convenient. This venerable old structure, dedicated to St. Nicholas, contained a number of monuments, and some of splendid workmanship for the times when they were executed, in memory of the family of the Mervyns, formerly one of the most opulent and respectable in the county of Wilts. This family was descended, by an heiress, from the first Lord Latimer, who was summoned to Parliament in the reign of Edward I. Through the Mervyns, Mr. Beckford clearly traces his own lineal descent up the same source.[1] The above-mentioned sepulchral monuments of the Mervyns, who were not only Mr. Beckford's ancestors, but for several centuries the original possessors of the Fonthill estate, having been exposed to the open air on the removal of the old church, and neglected till their ornaments became mutilated and

---

1 The Writer of this Memoir had, very lately, inspection of the Table of this Descent, as drawn out with great precision by Sir Isaac Heard, Garter King at Arms. [Heard (1730–1822) assisted Beckford in the genealogical research into his family background that played such an important role in the schema of Fonthill Abbey. RJG]

their inscriptions effaced, Mr. Beckford has designed his Gothic Abbey as a memorial tribute, in their stead, to this ancient family. Their Arms, in regular series, and with their different Quarterings, are to be painted on the windows of this edifice, and the names and dates of each successive member of the family inscribed on mural tablets, in the galleries and cloysters of the Abbey.

Although it will be imagined that avenues and ridings cannot have been wanting in the vast extent of the woods and plantations of Fonthill, it should be particularly noticed in this account of works set on foot by the present Mr. Beckford, that a great variety of beautiful walks and avenues have been formed under his direction, particularly within the great walled inclosure. These, though each of very considerable length and width, are all laid in the smoothest turf, kept at great expence, and constantly mown in the manner of bowling-greens, and are almost all bordered on either side, within the lofty screens of the plantations with laurel, flowering shrubs and flowers in great variety and abundance. One of the approaches lately made to the Abbey is a broad straight avenue, in the same stile and keeping as of those just mentioned, and at its termination at the wall of the inclosure communicating, by means of a bridge over a road, with a bold terrace, four miles and a half in length. Besides this terrace, and the avenues here spoken of, a walk (for so it is called) was begun to be opened last summer, which is to be continued for at least twenty miles, and to wind about in easy curves over hills, valleys and levels, to every striking or interesting point of view which can be commanded within or without the whole extent of Mr. Beckford's sylvan domain. As the ground of this walk is to be smoothed throughout, and covered with the verdure of a lawn, a great deal of labour is necessary to its formation, and not more than five or six miles of it are yet entirely finished; but as an addition of labourers will be employed upon it, a very considerable progress may be expected in the course of another year.

With how little influence the motive of ostentation can be supposed to have operated on the mind of the Proprietor, in the greatest of these projects, may be concluded from the impracticability of shewing more than a small part of them to the numerous companies who are used to include Fonthill in the plan of their summer excursions. It is not only that some days would be requisite for parties on foot, but that no carriages, except garden chaises, with broad wheels, can, without injury, be admitted within the great walled inclosure.

As not less than three hundred men will generally continue to be employed on the present works, it is hoped that two years more may nearly suffice for their accomplishment. When they are finished, nothing, unless we mention another inclosure of about eleven hundred acres, the present bank-fence of which will be changed into a wall, will remain to be executed, except the great Tower on Stops-Beacon, of which an incorrect, though not exaggerated account, appeared last autumn in the Papers.[2]

Mr. Wyatt has already drawn some of the plans and an elevation of this edifice. The President of the Academy, and many other celebrated Artists, are at present engaged on the paintings and different objects of ornament for the Abbey, not to mention many others intended for the decoration of Fonthill-House; a great portion of which has been entirely new fitted up and furnished since Mr. Beckford came to age; and the whole, before long, will have undergone the like change and improvements.

It remains now only to notice one particular, which certainly claims regard in this Memoir. All these splendid works are not merely effected in consequence of Mr. Beckford's orders, and by means of his fortune; but his own genius, whose comprehension and activity appear equal to any undertaking, has been the informing spirit of the whole; every one of the above-mentioned projects, whether of use or of ornament, having originated from himself, and their plans, of whatever kind, having been assisted or corrected by his own pure and classic taste. One of his principal amusements at Fonthill consists in attending and frequently directing the superior workmen in the execution of his schemes; and such is the ardour with which he is carrying forward his favourite building, the Abbey, that the frost and snow of the present winter were never suffered to stop any part of the work

2 For example, *The Gentleman's Magazine,* LXVI, pt. 2 (September 1796), p. 784, carried the following announcement about Stops' Beacon: 'William Beckford, Esq. of Fonthill, is collecting the materials for a building of wonderful grandeur and utility. It is to consist of a tower, to be erected on Stops' Beacon, near Fonthill, the loftiest scite in that neighbourhood; it is to have a square of 80 feet clear, within the walls, at the base, and to be 280 feet high, with a lantern at the top, so that it will command a view of near 80 miles every way, and the lantern to be seen by night at a greater distance. It is to be furnished as an observatory, and, notwithstanding its immense height, is to be so constructed as that a coach and six may be driven with ease and safety from the base to the top, and down again. This stupendous work will probably employ hundreds of the neighbouring poor for near ten years.' RJG

which could still go on, nor to prevent his own daily excursions to the spot.

EDITOR'S NOTE *The European Magazine and London Review*, XXXI (February, 1797), pp. 104–7. The name of the editor during this period has been shrouded in mystery. James Perry (1756–1821), the founding editor, left in 1783. It is believed that Edward Dubois (1774–1850), lawyer and art critic, served as an editor prior to 1807, but it is not clear exactly when he assumed this role. Arthur Sherbo, however, has made a convincing case for identifying Isaac Reed (1742–1807), who was a proprietor of the magazine at this time, as also the working editor. See 'Isaac Reed and the European Magazine', *Studies in Bibliography*, XXXVII (1984), pp. 210–27. While it is known that he denied being an editor (J. B. Nichols, *Illustrations of the Literary History of the Eighteenth Century* (London, 1848), VII, 48), he was a frequent contributor and John Lettice addressed him as the editor in an unpublished letter to Reed requesting an editorial change in an article on Beckford that appeared in the September issue of this magazine under the title 'William Beckford, Esq. of Fonthill', XXXII, pp. 147–50, thus bolstering Sherbo's case and now adding another article to the list of works attributed to him. On 11 July 1797 Lettice wrote to Reed: 'In the last period of my Account of Mr. Beckford sent to you yesterday, I much wish the word *valued* to be substituted for *regarded*. To say the Laws of Nations possibly be *little regarded* by the French plenipotentiaries would admit a bad construction; I mean an unsafe one.' See Beinecke Library, Beckford Collection, Box 4, f. 96. Reed did incorporate the correction. The fact that Lettice authored this account also points to the possibility of Lettice being the 'correspondent' of the article on the Christmas festivities at Fonthill published in January 1797 and to Lettice being the source of information for the article in the February issue.

Lord Nelson's Reception at Fonthill

[HENRY TRESHAM]

As you are desirous of some account of the late[1] entertainments given by Mr. Beckford to Lord Nelson, Sir William and Lady Hamilton, at Fonthill, I will do the best I can, without pretending much talent for description to gratify your curiosity. But, previously to what passed at Fonthill, I cannot but mention the enthusiasm which was testified, at various places on the road, for the hero of the Nile; but particularly at Salisbury. The yeomanry cavalry of the city too, zealous in their respect to wait his arrival, went out to meet him at the distance of ten miles on the verge of the county, headed by their commanding officer, Captain Windham; one of the members for the county. The noble Admiral on his arrival was received at the house of one of the principal citizens; by whom he was conducted, with Sir William Hamilton, amidst the acclamations of a great multitude, to the Council-house, which was guarded by a corps of the Royal North British dragoons. His Lordship was received by the mayor and corporation, attended by their regalia, at the iron gates in front of the house, where, forming a procession, they introduced him into the great council-chamber. After a handsome speech from the mayor, his Lordship was presented with the freedom of the city in a box of heart of oak, embellished with a silver plate on which was engraven the vote of Council. His Lordship, having in energetic terms expressed a grateful sense of the honour he had received, partook of a cold collation with the body corporate, and departed shortly afterwards for Fonthill; being again escorted by the cavalry and their officers on the Wilton road, where he took his leave, politely acknowledging the flattering attentions they had shewn him.

As on such occasions every eye is naturally turned upon the distinguished person whom all delight to honour, nothing escapes notice:

---

[1] They commenced on the 20th instant.

eve[n] the least occurrence in which he may have concern, assumes some degree of importance. We eagerly observe the minutest action, listen to the slightest word, and dwell upon every tint or shade of character, which may furnish opportunity of tracing, in the favourite object, either resemblance or dissimilitude on a comparison with the ordinary class of men which every day presents. Admitting this reflection to be just, you will not be displeased if we do not proceed on the route to Fonthill, till I have mentioned an incident or two, which took place before Lord Nelson and his party quitted Salisbury. In the crowd before the Council-house he caught sight of sailor who had fought in the battle of the Nile. The recollection of a man, who had hazarded his life with himself for the glory of his country, associated with the idea of his having been one among the many humble instruments of his own exaltation, instantly touched his heart. He called him forward, and, after cordially expressing the satisfaction he should ever feel on meeting anyone who had borne a part in that proud day, instantly dismissed him with a handsome present. Another man, whether sailor or soldier I know not, presented himself, who, at the Helder point, had met a similar fate with his lordship of Teneriffe, in the loss of an arm. Every circumstance of greatness or distinction vanished, for the moment, from the brave Admiral's mind. He found himself in a like predicament with the poor man before him. His sympathy was awakened. The only difference it allowed him to recollect, was that of his own better fortune; a proof of which his fellow sufferer soon experienced in a generous token of the hero's feeling.

You will now think it an odd coincidence, that Lord Nelson should next discover, amidst the huzzaing multitude, a person who had attended him at the time he lost his arm, and had assisted at the amputation. The Noble Admiral beckoned him up stairs, and meeting him as he approached the room, took him by the hand with a present in his own, and with looks expressive of remembrance for the tender services he had experienced from him on that melancholy occasion. As the man withdrew, he took from his bosom a piece of lace which he had torn from the sleeve of the amputated arm; declaring he would preserve it to his last breath in memory of his late gallant commander, whom he should always deem it the honour of his life to have served. Lord Nelson bade him farewell, with an emotion which no effort could stifle. I have only to add to these circumstances attending his Lordship's passage through Salisbury, that he left, in the hands of the mayor, £20 for the use of the poor.

You, who are a great observer of characters, will, I know, thank me for these little anecdotes; as they serve to shew that, with the brilliant qualities of a hero, Lord Nelson unites a feeling and generous heart, a quick discernment of occasion, and popularity of manners.

You shall now accompany the noble Admiral and his party on their visit to Fonthill. As soon as they reached the lodge of the park, the Fonthill volunteers, already waiting, drew up in a double line. Their band of music consisting of thirty performers, playing 'Rule Britannia', the corps presented their arms, and marched on either side of the carriages in slow procession up to the house. Here Mr. Beckford, with a large company of gentlemen and ladies, received Lord Nelson and his party on the landing of the grand flight of steps in the portico before the marble hall. The volunteers now formed into a line upon the lawn in front of the house, and fired a *feu de joye*, while the band played 'God save the King'. The day, which had been thick and foggy, cleared up just before Lord Nelson's arrival; so that this military parade and salute, under the command of Capt. Williams, were performed with admirable effect. The company now entered the house, and about six o'clock sat down to dinner. After coffee, a variety of vocal pieces were finely executed by Lady Hamilton in her expressive and triumphant manner, and by Banti with all her charms of voice and Italian sensibility.[2]

The company, after some time, divided into parties of conversation, cards or music. Supper was served at twelve. Every sort of delicacy appeared upon table; the greatest elegance and taste were displayed in the desert. The supper, in short, was such as might worthily succeed the dinner. The two next afternoons and evenings passed in the same manner. The mornings were spent in seeing the house, the paintings, the library, and in such excursions out of doors as the weather admitted.

On Tuesday the 23d, the festivities were transferred from the Mansion-house to the Abbey. The company being assembled by five o'clock, a number of carriages waited before the house to receive them. The several parties, as arranged for each, took their places. Lord Nelson was loudly huzzaed by the multitude as he entered the first coach. They all proceeded slowly and in order, as the dusk of the evening was growing into darkness. In about three quarters of an hour, soon after having entered the great wall which incloses the abbey-woods, the procession passed a noble Gothic arch. At this point the

2 There were other eminent performers, vocal and instrumental.

company were supposed to enter the Abbot's domain; and hence, upon a road winding through thick woods of pine and fir, brightly illuminated by innumerable lamps hung in the trees, and by flambeaus moving with the carriages, they proceeded betwixt two solemn marches, the effect of which was much heightened by the continued roll of drums placed at different distances on the hills. What impression at this dark hour, the blaze of lights, partly stationary and partly moving, as reflected from the windows of the carriages or gleaming on the military armour, together with music echoing through the woods; what impression, I say, this *ensemble* of light, sound, and motion, must have made on those who could quietly contemplate it all at a distance, may be left to imagination without any attempt to describe it.

The company on their arrival at the Abbey could not fail to be struck with the increasing splendor of lights and their effects, contrasted with the deep shades which fell on the walls, battlements, and turrets, of the different groups of the edifice. Some parts of the light struck on the walls and arches of the great tower, till it vanished by degrees into an awful gloom at its summit; over which, mounted on a staff of 50 feet, the broad sheet[3] of colours could at some moments be discerned, by catching lights mysteriously waving in the air.

The parties, alighting in orderly succession from their carriages, entered a groined Gothic hall through a double line of soldiers. From thence they were received into the great saloon, called the Cardinal's parlour, furnished with rich tapestries, long curtains of purple damask before the arched windows, ebony tables and chairs studded with ivory, of various but antique fashion; the whole room in the noblest style of monastic ornament, and illuminated by lights on silver sconces. At the moment of entrance they sat down at a long table, occupying nearly the whole length of the room (53 feet), to a superb dinner, served in one long line of enormous sliver dishes, in the substantial *costume* of the antient abbeys, unmixed with the refinements of modern cookery. The table and side-boards glittering with piles of plate and a profusion of candle-lights, not tq mention a blazing Christmas fire of cedar and the cones of pine, united to increase the splendour and to improve the *coup-d'oeil* of the room. It is needless to say the highest satisfaction and good-humour prevailed, mingled with sentiment of admiration at the grandeur and originality of the entertainment. It should not be omitted,

3 The Vice-Admiral's flag, in compliment to Lord Nelson.

that many of the artists whose works have contributed to the embellishment of the abbey, with Mr. Wyatt and the President of the Royal
Academy at their head, formed a part of the company. These gentlemen, with the distinguished musical party beforementioned, and some
prominent characters of the literary world, formed altogether a combination of talents and genius not often meeting at the same place.

Dinner being ended, the company removed up stairs to the other finished apartments of the abbey. The stair-case was lighted by certain
mysterious living figures at different intervals, dressed in hooded gowns,
and standing with large wax-torches in their hands. A magnificent room
hung with yellow damask, and decorated with cabinets of the most precious japan, received the assembly. It was impossible not to be struck,
among other objects, with its credences (or antique buffets) exhibiting
much treasure of wrought plate, cups, vases, and ewers of solid gold. It
was from this room they passed into the Library, fitted up with the same
appropriate taste. The Library opens by a large Gothic screen into the
gallery; which I described to you in a former letter. This room, which
when finished will be more than 270 feet long, is to half that length completely fitted up, and furnished in the most impressively monastic stile.
A superb shrine, with a beautiful statue of St. Anthony in marble and
alabaster, the work of Rossi, placed upon it, with reliquaries studded
with brilliants of immense value, the whole illuminated by a grand display of wax-lights on candlesticks and candelabras of massive silver gilt,
exhibited a scene at once strikingly splendid and awfully magnificent.
The long series of lights on either side of the room, resting on stands of
ebony enriched with gold, and those on the shrine all multiplied and
reflected in the great oriel opposite, from its spacious squares of plate-
glass, while the whole reflection narrowed into an endless prospective
as it receded from the eye, produced a singular and magic effect.

As the company entered the gallery a solemn music struck the ear
from some invisible quarter, as if from behind the screen of scarlet curtains which backed the shrine, or from its canopy above, and suggested
ideas of a religious service; ideas which, associated as they were with so
many appropriate objects addressed to the eye, recalled the grand chapel
scenes and ceremonies of our antient Catholic times. After the scenic representation a collation was presented in the library, consisting of various
sorts of confectionary served in gold baskets, with spiced wines, &c.
whilst rows of chairs were placed in the great room beyond, which had
first received the company above stairs. A large vacant space was left in

the front of the seats. The assembly no sooner occupied them than Lady Hamilton appeared in the character of Agrippina, bearing the ashes of Germanicus in a golden urn, and as presenting herself before the Roman people with the design of exciting them to revenge the death of her husband; who, after having been declared joint emperor by Tiberius, fell a victim to his envy, and is supposed to have been poisoned by his order at the head of the forces which he was leading against the rebellious Armenians. Lady Hamilton displayed, with truth and energy, every gesture, attitude, and expression of countenance, which could be conceived in Agrippina herself, best calculated to have moved the passions of the Romans in behalf of their favourite general. The action of her head, of her hands and arms in the various position of the urn, her manner of presenting it before the Romans, or of holding it up to the gods in the act of supplication, was most classically graceful. Every change of dress, principally of the head, to suit the different situations in which she successively presented herself, was performed instantaneously with the most perfect ease, and without retiring or scarcely turning aside a moment from the spectators. In the last scene of this beautiful piece of pantomime, she appeared with a young lady of the company, who was to personate a daughter. Her action in this part was so perfectly just and natural, and so pathetically addressed to the spectators, as to draw tears from several of the company. It may be questioned whether this scene, without theatrical assistance of other characters and appropriate circumstances, could possibly be represented with more effect. The company delighted and charmed broke up, and departed at 11 o'clock, to sup at the Mansion-house. On leaving this strange nocturnal scene of vast buildings and extensive forest, now rendered dimly and partially visible by the declining light of lamps and torches, and the twinkling of a few scattered stars in a clouded sky, the company seemed, as soon as they had passed the sacred boundary of the great wall, as if waking from a dream, or just freed from the influence of some magic spell. And at this moment that I am recapitulating in my mind the particulars of the description I have been writing you, I can scarcely help doubting whether the whole of the last evening's entertainment were a reality, or only the visionary coinage of fancy.

EDITOR'S NOTE This article was published under the title 'Letter from a Gentleman, Present at the Festivities at Fonthill, to a Correspondent in

Town,' Fonthill, 28 December 1800, *The Gentleman's Magazine*, LXXXIX, pt. 1 (March, April, 1801), pp. 206–8; 297–8. Identification of the author is based on John Britton's attribution in *Graphical and Literary Illustrations of Fonthill Abbey* (London, 1823), p. 31 and the files of the Nichols family, proprietors of *The Gentleman's Magazine* from 1778 to 1856. See James M. Kuist, *The Nichols File of the Gentleman's Magazine* (Madison, 1982), p. 150. These editorial papers are now located at the Folger Library in Washington, D. C. Tresham (1749?–1814) was a historical painter and exhibited at the Royal Academy from 1798 to 1806. Beckford supplied the print that accompanied this article of the carriages making their way to the Abbey as they passed through a grand archway. See John B. Nichols, *Historical Notices of Fonthill Abbey, Wiltshire* (London, 1836), p. 18.

Fonthill Abbey

[JOHN BRITTON]

The public curiosity was a short time since excited in an extraordinary degree, by the exhibition of the house and furniture at Wanstead. Its vicinity to London, that vast hive of human population, rendered it singularly attractive; and thousands of the fashionable, idle and curious inhabitants of the metropolis and the surrounding country flocked to view the place, and lament its desecration and dissolution.

If Fonthill Abbey were equally near London, we might easily fancy what attractions it would possess for the same class of persons: for this edifice – its grounds – the acknowledged taste of its possessor – the impenetrable secrecy which has hitherto guarded its every avenue, must all conspire to stimulate the most latent curiosity, and rouse more sensitive admirers of the wonders of nature and art to the highest degree of excitement. A catalogue, of five shillings value, entitled its possessor to admission to Wanstead: but in order to view Fonthill it is necessary to produce a ticket, for which, including a catalogue, the charge is one guinea. Fonthill is likewise more than 100 miles distant from London. Hence it may be reasonably inferred, that the visiters to this place will not be so numerous as those to Wanstead. But it may also be concluded, that every person of taste and virtù will either see, or be anxious to see, this noted edifice, and its splendid contents.

Fonthill Abbey is situated two miles S. W. from Hindon, and fifteen West from Salisbury. This stately building – an unique specimen of the triumph of modern skill and genius over the difficulties of construction presented by the Gothic style – may justly be regarded as one of the wonders of the West of England. The mansion itself, its noble apartments, characteristically ornamented, and furnished with the most curious and costly productions of art are well calculated to astonish and gratify the spectator, and inspire admiration of the munificent spirit of the proprietor, and of the varied talent displayed in carrying into execution his princely designs. The circumambient secresy, which exhibits the plastic efforts of creative genius, must be beheld to be properly appreciated. Description can only assist the visiter of Fonthill, by particularly marking the points of view whence the mansion itself, and other prominent objects, may be most advantageously surveyed.

The natural and cultivated scenery of this place displays features which are bold, grand, and finely diversified. Nearly the whole of an eminence which gradually ascends from an open country on the north, and a fine inclosed country to the south, is covered with woods, some of which are of ancient growth but the larger portion of modern plantation. The inner grounds, around the mansion, are secluded from immediate observation by a lofty wall surmounted with *chevaux de frise*. On passing this barrier by an arched gateway, the road ascends through a dark wood of firs, remarkable for their lofty growth, to a path leading eastward of the Abbey, up the Hard Walk, or Hinkley hill. This path is skirted with laurels, and enclosed by tangled underwood: at intervals the Gothic Tower and turrets of the mansion appear on the left, between the trees. After traversing, the space of about half mile, the path is crossed by the Forest Lawn, a spot decorated with American and other exotic oaks; and affording from its front a distant view of the Beacon Tower. A quarter of a mile farther is the Clerk's Walk, which, on the left, passes the western front of the Abbey. A narrow mossy alley on the right, closely shaded, conducts to a path of considerable extent, bordered with the scarlet thorn, ornamented by the addition of evergreens and flowering shrubs; and during spring and summer affording an agreeable display of flowers of spontaneous growth.

These parts of the grounds are situated to the north of the mansion. Inclining to the north-west, we enter another path, called the Nine-miles'-walk, being part of a journey of two and twenty miles, which may be made within the enclosure, without retracing the same tract. Pursuing the winding course of this path we reach the summit of the great avenue; whence, turning to the east, the Abbey, with its towers and battlements, bursts at once on the view. Here folding gates open into the public road; crossing which, another gate leads to the terrace, a woody ridge extending about five miles from west to east. Continuing our course along the western boundary, the prospect becomes varied and extensive. Among the most prominent objects which it affords, are Alfred's Tower and the adjacent home grounds of Sir Richard C. Hoare at Stourhead; a domain, the decorations of which are strongly characteristic of the classic taste of its owner. Turning southward, and leaving on the left a deep dell, called Bitham Wood, through a narrow path we arrive at the spot already mentioned denominated the Beacon, one of the highest points in the whole range of hills for which this part of the country is remarkable. On the top of this lofty eminence is a plain, consisting of five or six acres, intended for the site of a magnificent tower. The foundations are completed, and the walls raised to the height of nine or ten feet. It is a structure of large extent, and of a triangular figure, having at each corner a circular bastion and being overgrown with shrubs and moss, so as to form a picturesque object.

Descending now towards the south-east near the foot of the Beacon, an interesting view presents itself, displaying amidst the sylvan scenery the Abbey surmounted by its Gothic Tower, and relieved by an elevated back ground of woodland landscape. Passing onwards to the valley, we come to a fine pellucid lake, whose glassy surface reflects the slopes, crags, and woods by which it is environed. Hence by a sheltered walk we reach the American Plantation, a spot dedicated to the culture of the hardier ornamental exotics, of lofty growth. Pursuing a south-eastern direction, we arrive at a small enclosure called the Chinese Garden, a spot appropriated to the rarest and most beautiful of the floral tribes. A little to the eastward is the kitchen-garden, including a space of eight or nine acres, sheltered from the northern blasts by a wood of lofty pines. From the garden a winding walk, between the trees, leads to an avenue by which the great western front of the Abbey is approached, affording a fine view of its grand outline and most striking features.

To attempt a particular and detailed description of this magnificent edifice, without the aid of graphic delineation, would answer little purpose. A few remarks on the situation and general appearance of this specimen of the modern gothic style of architecture may, however, prove not uninteresting.

From the summit of an eminence, amidst encircling woods, rises the lofty tower, turrets, pediments, and pinnacles of Fonthill Abbey, which assumes externally the character of an ancient monastic structure. It consists of a central tower of an octagonal shape, 276 feet high; a lofty transept, stretching from the tower eastward; and 2 other wings, branching off from the centre to the north and south. The exterior elevations of each of these portions of the building differ from the others, and display peculiar and appropriate features.

The part of the Abbey fronting the north is the least ornamented. The eastern side is distinguished by three square towers, between 2 of which is placed an oriel, richly sculptured and adorned with shields, armorial bearings, and other devices. The south side has a noble embattled front, at the eastern extremity of which, projecting from one of the square towers, is placed the south oriel, forming the termination of the long gallery, or library, and having below it a door leading to the lobby of the parlor. The western front presents, as its most striking feature, the superb chief entrance, through a door-way 3 5 feet high, terminating above in a pointed arch, ornamented with a moulding of a similar form, having crockets and a highly wrought finial. On the top of the pediment is a niche, containing a statue of St. Anthony of Padua, surmounted by a cross-fleury, the arms of William, the first Lord Latimer, from whom Mr. Beckford is lineally descended. The noble pair of Gothic doors, composed of oak, which close this entrance, are suspended on 8 hinges of cast brass, weighing more than a ton, but so constructed as to admit of the opening or shutting of the doors with the utmost ease. These hinges are said to have cost upwards of £400.

This building was erected from the designs of the late James Wyatt, Esq., aided and indeed materially directed by the acknowledged taste of the owner. In the embellishment of the interior, many of the most eminent artists of the country have been employed.

The manor of Fonthill Giffard (the proper denomination of Mr. Beckford's territorial domain) derives its name from a spring or fount flowing from the hill, and from its having been formerly the property of the family of Giffard. It was vested in this Norman family at the time Domesday-book was compiled. In the reign of King John it was surrendered to that monarch by the then proprietor Andrew Giffard, with the consent of his legal heirs. John Mauduit, summoned to Parliament among the barons of Edward the third, held Fonthill, and left it, with his other estates, to his grand-daughter Maude. It was then possessed by the Wests, Lords De la War, from whom it passed to William Lord Molins, who bequeathed it to his daughter Eleanor. The marriage of this lady conveyed Fonthill to the Hungerfords, from whom it was transferred to the ancient family of Mervin. An heiress of the Mervins brought the manor into the possession of George Lord Audley; and, on the attainder of Mervin Lord Audley, it was granted to Sir Francis, afterwards Lord Cottington. His heirs sold Fonthill to William Beckford, Esq., the patriotic alderman of the City of London, celebrated for the speech he made to his late Majesty, when Mr. Beckford, then Lord Mayor, presented to the King an Address, or Remonstrance, from the Citizens and Livery of London. ...

EDITOR'S NOTE *The Museum; or Record of Literature, Fine Arts, Science, Antiquities, the Drama, &c.*, no. 17 (1822), pp. 264–5. The title of this weekly magazine varied during its short life. When it was first published in April 1822, it ran for numbers 1–6 as the *London Museum*, then for numbers 7–66 as *The Museum etc.* and finally as *The Literary Museum and Register of Arts, Sciences, and General Literature* for numbers 67 – new series 7, concluding its publication in February 1824. The editor was P. Bayley. Britton was identified as the author of this essay in the August 1822 issue of the *Gentleman's Magazine*, pt. 2, XCII, where it was reprinted on pp. 100–3. See also Britton's abbreviated description of the Abbey in his *Beauties of England and Wales* (London, 1814), XV, pp. 265–8 for textual similarities.

Fonthill Abbey

FROM *THE GAZETTE OF FASHION*

The castle has a pleasant seat; the air
Nimbly and sweetly recommends itself
Unto our gentle senses. ....
.... The guest of summer,
The temple-haunting martlet, does approve,
By his loved mansionry, that the heavens' breath
Smells wooingly here: no jutty, frieze, buttress,
Nor coigne of vantage, but this bird hath made
His pendent bed, and procreant cradle: where they
Most breed and haunt, I have observed, the air
Is delicate.

It is an error to assert that the age of necromancy has passed away, or
that potent magi do not now exist, whose wondrous art can call spirits from the vasty deep. The Genii of the Ring and the Lamp, under the
more modern names of Wealth and Taste, can raise structures
equalling, in the richness of their architecture, the fairy palace of
Aladdin, and convert barren heaths to gardens of delight, rivalling in
beauty the oriental splendours of the happy valley. All that we read of
in eastern magnificence, all that we have imagined in the delicate
minuteness of Peri workmanship, is here, to dazzle and to charm.
Mephistopholas never exerted his skill with more effect, when his
object was to win a soul from Paradise, by creating an Elysium upon
earth. The king of the Gnomes has surrendered up the treasures of the
mine, and the elemental spirits have paid tribute to the mighty
enchanter. Here are translucent waters wherein a naiad might delight
to sport; the soft gush of fountains, mingling with the song of birds,
and the gently sighing of the air through exotic flowers of balmy
breath, form melody so sweet and witching, that the ear lists raptured,

deeming the soothing sound the unseen minstrelsy of fairy tongues, revelling amid the intricacies of fantastic rocks and bowery labyrinths: such is the 'silent lull of that voluptuous place'.

It is impossible, without the aid of language that may appear to border upon hyperbole, to do justice to the extraordinary beauty and splendor of Fonthill; so long jealously secluded from the world's gaze, it now bursts upon the public eye like a region of enchantment. We behold all the wonders of nature and of art, the richest and most precious materials, decorated with still more costly workmanship; wealth that would prove the ransom of an emperor, added to the laborious occupation of the longest span of life. The painter, the sculptor, and the architect, have exhausted the treasures of their genius; and the bodily strength of the mechanic, the sweat of the brow, and the waste of the limb, have been called forth to aid the designs of the most exquisite talent. We have here the work of ages past, and the touch of yesterday; and we require the recollection, that dust is all that is left of many of the sublime artists whose resplendent contributions form a miracle and a wonder, to prevent us from exalting human beings to a level with the gods, when we behold the perfection of beauty, the gorgeousness and the elegance which the hand of man has assembled at Fonthill. Mr. Beckford has judiciously chosen the Gothic style of architecture, which harmonizes delightfully with the surrounding scenery of rock, river, and wood; the severe beauty of the classic Greek models, or even the more redundant grandeur which characterized the Roman temple, would not so well accord with English landscapes as the Gothic Abbey; the wonderful creation of a barbarous age, which, to the romantic mind, is fraught with all that is most witching in the delusions of the imagination. The lofty hall is magnified in its proportions by the pointed and richly-wrought roof, where the eye seeks vainly for a termination mid the carved and sculptured ornaments. The gallery seems of illimitable dimensions, as clusters of pillars rise beyond each other, leading to an arch-way buried in the obscurity, which 'the dim religious light' shed from the painted windows can alone bestow; and the mind is transported back to ages long gone by, as, from amidst the embowering shelter of umbrageous trees, the Abbey rises to the view, or we gaze upon it from the smooth lawn, and fancy it the retreat of holy men, the asylum chosen for the scene of monastic solitude, so quiet, so silent, so sublime are the images that strike the eye, so exquisite are the associations, which no brilliant marble palace, spreading its wings and shining on the green earth in glaring contrast, could produce. Fonthill is inclosed in a magic circle, a wall of nine miles in circumference, which, by the spells of Genius, spans in its ring a labyrinthian maze of twenty-seven miles, so varied and romantic, that the wanderer has no idea that the space is so circumscribed, or that a fence divides him from the lovely prospects which greet his eye from the summit of every eminence. The approach to this terrestrial Paradise is through grounds wherein the perfection of landscape gardening is displayed: nature is never outraged, but art has planted and cleared, opened vistas, and concealed aught that is barren or unsightly, and formed a truly sylvan region, decked in the simple dress, the indigenous product of the soil. The meek daisy springs beneath the British oak, the primrose and the cowslip share the violet's lowly bed, and the earth is tapestried with wild flowers, and garlands of ivy hang from the graceful boughs of ash and elm. But, disregarding these comparatively minor beauties, we speed eagerly onwards to the grand magnet of attraction –

The gates are pass'd, and Heaven is won.

These delicious gardens bloom with the flowers of every clime, not scantily and delicately reared, but glowing with endless profusion: the broad-leaved giant plant of America, and the bright exotic from a fiercer sky, flourish like natives; the imperial amethyst crown of the rhododendron, and the rich creamy whiteness of the magnolia, the pink wreaths of the acacia, mix with

Anemones and seas of gold
And new blown lilies of the river.

*   *   *

Amaranths, such as crown the maids,
That wander through Zenara's shades.

The eye dwells enraptured on the luxuriant foliage, and the senses, steeped in the fragrance of the perfumed buds, are lapt in delicious dreams; sweet thoughts that have no stain of earth to mar their purity. From these flowery mazes we seek the borders of the broad lake, smiling in the summer sun, like a wide crystal mirror, yet to the autumnal gale heaving, from its fathomless depths, billows and sweeping waves, which finely contrast with the still calm beauty of its unruffled surface, when scarce a languid zephyr stirs his dainty plumes. Flocks of aquatic birds,

> With their rich restless wing, that gleam
> Variously in the crimson beam
> Of the warm west, as if inlaid
> With brilliants from the mine, or made
> Of tearless rainbows,

dip their pinions in the liquid diamond, float o'er the tideless waters, or skim through upper air, warm sheltered nooks, extensive amphitheatres, and lofty mounts. Grottoes, and woodland haunts, and terraces, invite the lingering footsteps by the boundless variety of their beauties, and we loiter long, unwilling to leave

> .... A wilderness of flowers,
> Which seem as though, from all the bowers
> And fairest fields of all the year,
> The mingled spoil was scattered ....

A stately avenue leads to the portal, and, swinging on eight brazen hinges, which weigh a ton, and appear to be the work of the Cyclops, forged in the centre of Mount Aetna, the massy door revolves, and we enter the superb and lofty structure with feelings wherein admiration is not unmixed with reverence. It is the feudal baronial residence of former days, enriched with all the improvements of modern art, the most noble designs executed on a scale of astonishing magnitude, and decorated with the most elaborate tracery, raised and embossed in endless complication. We gaze and wonder at this model of human industry, and, fancying the slow hand of man to be inadequate to the task, we deem it the fairy workmanship of sprites, who can 'put a girdle round about the earth in forty minutes'. Here is the

> Glittering saloon, boundless and bright as noon,
> All rich with arabesques of gold and flowers

the dark oak wainscotted gallery, blazing with achievements, and lofty hall beautifully softened by the warm crimson, the dark purple, and the deep green of the painted windows, which convert the yellow rays of the sun into rubies, amethysts, and emeralds, of 'colours that make dim the stones o' the Indian mine'; and though the princely magnificence of the fretted carved work must have cost sums equal to the dowry of a queen, not one amid the extensive suites of apartments, but is loaded with the treasures of eastern sultans; cabinets in which the least precious wood is rendered costly by the labours of years bestowed in the decoration, and triple caskets of amber, clouded with every shade, from the palest primrose to the deepest garnet, and wrought with cameos. Here is a cup which we may imagine to be the gift of Albaonfaris, scooped from a single gem, the largest topaz known to the world, and lavishly fraught with the rare workmanship of the Florentine wonder, Benvenuto Cellini. Another of sardonyx and 'vases to grace the halls of kings', of ivory, enamel, and crystal, set 'with pearls plucked from the gates of Paradise'; porcelain, fit for the richest temples of the Pagan gods, the choicest manufactory of japan, and ebony chairs, formerly belonging to the King-Cardinal, Wolsey; and when we add to these tables of precious marbles, agate, and lapis lazuli, jasper, and chrysolites, and calculate the value of the pictures and the books, we no longer look upon the Persian Tales as fictions, but see at once all that we have imagined in our childhood realized. It is with grief that we contemplate the near approach of the period which is destined to consign these treasures to the hammer. And we regret that the mine should ever fail that was devoted to the collection of works of such exquisite beauty; but though this prodigality of magnificence must vanish like the unsubstantial pageant of a dream, the tower of Fonthill will long remain one of England's finest monuments; raised upon a considerable eminence, it shoots so high

> That oft the sleeping albatross,
> Strikes the bright wonder with her wing,
> And from her cloud-rock'd slumbering,
> She starts, to find man's dwelling there,
> In her own silent fields of air.

EDITOR'S NOTE *The Gazette of Fashion and Magazine of Literature, the Fine Arts, and Belles Lettres*, August 31, 1822, pp. 65–7. The following note was appended to this essay, presumably by the editor: 'Those who have visited Fonthill, will admit that this picture is not overcharged; the cost has been estimated at a sum not less than fourteen hundred thousand pounds.' The author of this piece is unidentified and little is known about the publishing history of this weekly magazine. The proprietor (and editor?) was Charles Molloy Westmacott (1787–1868) who in 1825 became editor of the Tory weekly *Age*, where he became known as the 'blackmailing editor' for exacting money from individuals who wanted to avoid seeing their names in print in connection with scandalous activities.

A Visit to Fonthill Abbey

[ABBÉ ANGE DENIS MACQUIN]

The interest attached to the sale of effects announced at Fonthill Abbey, the grandeur of that structure, the magnificence of its furniture, and the distance at which public curiosity has hitherto been kept from its sealed precincts, induce us to hope that some account of a visit to it will be gratifying to those whom circumstances prevent from availing themselves of the new liberty to inspect its internal treasures, and perambulate its extensive demesne.

Fonthill Gifford, so called in contradistinction to the adjoining manor of Fonthill Bishop, was at the period of the Domesday survey, held by the ancient family of Gifford;[1] from whom passed into the possession of the Wests (Lords Delawar), and successively through other owners, including Bradshaw during the inter-regnum, and the Cottingtons before and after the restoration, till it was purchased by William Beckford, the ancestor of the present proprietor, and famous in the records of the City of London for a bold remonstrance which he is reported[2] to have delivered to the king in the year 1770.

Mr. Beckford possessed immense estates in Jamaica, and was twice

---

1 In 1285, Sir Orbert Gifford, knight (probably a descendant from Osbertus), was excommunicated by the Archbishop of Canterbury for stealing two nuns from the convent at Wilton, but was absolved on the following conditions: that he should not again enter into a nunnery or be in the company of nuns; that on three following Sundays he should be whipt in the parish church of Wilton, and as many times in the market and church of Shaftesbury: – that he should fast a certain number of months, and not take upon him the habit or title of a knight, or wear any apparel except of a russet colour, with lamb or sheep skins, or return into his military order; – and that he should restore the nuns to their convent to undergo the like conditions. All which he bound himself by oath to do; the bishop of Salisbury prescribing the mode of his fasting till he had served three years in the Holy Land. [This note and the (numbered) notes that follow appear to be by William Jerdan, the editor of the *Literary Gazette*. RJG]

2 We say reported because, if we are not misinformed, the speech was Wilkes's and not Beckford's, though inscribed on the monument of the latter in Guildhall.

Lord Mayor of London. At the time of his death, his son, the present proprietor of Fonthill, was a minor. Succeeding to almost boundless wealth,[3] endowed with an extraordinary mind, with an exquisite taste for the Arts, with literary talents of the highest order, in short, with genius perilled only by the measureless power of gratification which riches offered, the young owner of Fonthill commenced his career. Alderman Beckford, in the plenitude of his fortune, had, when the former mansion was destroyed by fire, built a noble house in the grounds to the right of what is now the entrance-gate on the London road, and fronting a fine bason of water, agreeably to the fashion of that time. But this noble residence fell far short of the ambition of his successor, who ordered it to be demolished, and, with a profusion probably unexampled in the history of a private individual, commenced the superb design which now receives, as it always attracted, the admiration of the country.

But we shall (at least for the present) lay aside the history of the building, which, according to loose calculation, cost four hundred thousand pounds,[4] and invite the readers of the *Literary Gazette* to accompany us in a survey of the place, as at present exposed to the rude gaze of the public at the admittance-rate of a guinea for a Catalogue and ticket, at first procuring entrance to one, now to two.

Passing through an arched Gateway, designed by Inigo Jones, in a classical yet rustic style, with a grotesque head in the centre of the arch, the visitor enters the old park, and, traversing that, the inner grounds, which are about seven miles in circumference. These are so ingeniously laid out, that a ride of twenty-seven miles may be enjoyed without retracing a single path or walk into which they are arranged each with characteristic differences of tree, shrub, and flower, from the hardiest British plant to the rarest exotic.

At the Gate into the Inner Grounds, which are encircled by a stone wall and *cheveaux de frise*, the tickets are *viséd*; and having already admired flocks of swans and *tame wild*-ducks, and other aquatic birds, the visitor begins to tread the *sanctum sanctorum* of the Abbey. The drive is a broad gravel road, with green alleys branching off in every direction between the dark firs of the plantation. This brings us to the

3 We have heard that when a young man in Italy, his income exceeded £90,000 per annum.

4 The same authority states that the four hinges of the great west door cost £1500 and weigh more than a ton!

southern front of the Mansion; but as there is no entrance on that side, the carriage sweeps round to the grand Western Door.

This is really a triumph of architecture – a glorious specimen of Mr. Wyatt's abilities and of modern Gothic.[5] There is no point of view in which its exquisite proportions do not please; and whether contemplated from under its pointed arch, or from any part of the fine rising avenue which extends from it for three quarters of a mile through the grounds, it is equally an object of delight and admiration.[6]

This is the entrance to a Hall (68 feet by 28), worthy of its style and beauty. The roof, nearly eighty feet high, is of oak, appropriately divided into panels, and adorned with shields in the old baronial manner. The light comes from three Gothic windows of painted glass on the right, of a cathedral character, and shedding a mellow lustre on the upper part of the superb flight of steps by which you ascend to the great Octagon. The lower steps are in broader day from the door-light and the *coup d'oeil* here is indescribably fine. The magnificent opening, by its Gothic associations rather than by its natural effect, seems to throw one shade upon the air-tint of the lawn; and the eye rests upon the gradually but slightly deepening tone of the ascent, till it rests upon the clustered shafts in the Octagon which support the principal tower. These are tinged with rose-colour from the hue of the windows, whose light is thrown upon them, and the whole resembles a magic palace more than any abode of luxury which we ever saw contrived by human art. Indeed this is one of the most peculiarly striking interior views of Fonthill; and visitors will do well to remember the old advice, and pause on the threshold. On the inside of the Hall, above the great door, is a Music Gallery, with an appropriate screen-work of stone, and over it a small Gothic window, with a Madonna and Child of stained glass. On the right and left of the landing, at the top of the stairs, are two arched recesses, in one of which is placed four paintings illustrative of the history of Tobit, by Stothard. This location, as it is a dim one for vision, was also, we presume, a temporary one, as the pictures seem arranged for a chimney-piece. They are charming compositions, not inferior to any by the Master, and were, we observed, lotted for sale. In the opposite recess is a gorgeous chest, but these sights are rather taken

5 It forms the frontispiece to Storer's description of Fonthill, 4to 1812, where it is accurately engraved. – Ed.

6 As we have directed an Engraving of Fonthill to be prepared for a future (we trust our next) Number, we shall not now dwell on the exterior details. – Ed.

on returning than on entering, for the attractions of the Octagon, into which a lofty arch (corresponding with the door below) admits the visitor, are such, that few can delay their footsteps from its contemplation. Of this glorious apartment we cannot do better than copy Mr. Storer's description:

> ... Between the piers of the octagon, which are composed of cloistered columns, bearing eight lofty arches, are four pointed windows of beautifully stained glass, copied from those of the celebrated monastery of Batalha, in Portugal; the other four arches that support the tower are the openings of the galleries, the entrance to the great hall, and another arch built up: this latter is reserved for the entrance to the chapel intended to be erected on the eastern side of the Abbey. The arches that have no place of egress, five in number, are hung with curtains, at least fifty feet high, which, concealing the termination of the building, give an idea of continued space: the light emitted through the painted windows of the octagon, presents a most enchanting play of colours, and the effect produced by the sombre hue of twilight, contrasted with the vivid appearance at different hours of the day, is indescribably pleasing and grand. Above the eight arches is an open gallery that communicates with the higher suit of apartments; from this springs a beautiful groining of fanwork, supporting a lanthorn, lighted by eight windows richly painted; the whole is finished by a vaulted roof, the height of which is one hundred and thirty-two feet from the ground. ...

Nothing more splendid than this chamber can be conceived, and whether viewed from its base or from the corridors above, it presents a noble impression. Standing in the centre, and looking east, we command a delicious view of the green walk already described; behind is the receding arch (surmounted by the Organ Gallery and corresponding with the Music Gallery at the entry), which leads into the Cabinet Room and a suite of other rooms; on the left is St. Michael's, and on the right King Edward the Third's Gallery, two of the most stately and interesting apartments that can be imagined; the former filled with the choicest books and a few articles of vertu, the latter also employed as a library, but enriched with a much greater number of choice and curious productions, and terminating in an Oratory, unique for its elegant proportions and characteristic consistency. It is at once

rich and luxurious as the temple of which it forms an appendage—
sombre and soothing as the religious feelings with which its designation
associates it require. Here

Retire, the world shut out;

it is but the drawing of a curtain, and not only all the glitter of the
adjoining splendour, but all the pomps and vanities of the world, seem
to the meditative mind to be excluded forever. Perhaps its pensive cast is
more deeply experienced from the immediate contrast: dazzled with
objects of useless show, fatigued with the examination of rare and
costly commodities and bewildered with the multitude of precious
devices which every where surround us, the soul retires with tenfold
delight within the narrow walls of the lttle Chapel,

Where heavenly-pensive Contemplation dwells,
And ever-musing Melancholy reigns.

This Oratory is approached by a short vaulted Gallery, a continuation of King Edward's, of which the descriptive publications correctly
say, it is

... wainscotted with oak and ribbed with deep mouldings, partly
gilt and partly coloured; the floor is entirely covered with a
Persian carpet of the most extraordinary size and beautiful
texture. This gallery receives a glimmering light through six perforated bronze doors, modelled after those of Henry the Fifth's
chantry in the Abbey of Westminster. These doors are hung with
crimson curtains, which increasing the solemn gloom, aid the
effect of the oratory. ...

The Oratory itself is formed of five sides of an octagon. The roof is
entirely gilt, in a grained pattern, which renders it wonderfully rich
without being unappropriately gaudy. A golden lamp was suspended
from the centre, and external light is sparingly admitted by two lancet
windows, of stained glass. The Altar, and a statue of St. Anthony, by
Rossi, are at this time removed, and several rich cabinets or chests
supersede the holy emblems.

From this Chapel to the southern end of the Gallery on the South,
the measurement is three hundred and thirty feet.

On Tuesday week, the number of visitors, from almost every part of
the kingdom, amounted to 150; but having described the larger features

of the scene, we shall at this convenient place break off, and resume in our next *Gazette* the details of what was presented to their view in the interior.

EDITOR'S NOTE *The Literary Gazette and Journal of Belles Lettres*, Saturday, August 17, 1822, pp. 520–1. Edited by William Jerdan (1782–1869). Author attribution for this essay, the following three papers, and a poem included in Appendix II, 'Contemporary Verse Inspired by Fonthill', is based on Jerdan who recorded that 'from Fonthill, in the autumn of 1822, he [Macquin] contributed … a series of papers giving an historical account of the Abbey, a biography of the family of Beckford, the author of 'Vathek,' and a fine description of the place and its contents previous to its sale. The second paper was illustrated by a drawing, of which I published a neat engraving. The fifth is in verse …'. See *The Autobiography of William Jerdan* (London, 1853), III, pp. 107–8. Jerdan identified himself as the author of notes 5 and 6. It is likely that he interpolated notes 1, 2, 3 and 4 as well. For example, it is highly unlikely that Macquin would have attributed the Lord Mayor's remonstrance to the king as the words of Wilkes.

Visit to Fonthill

[Second Paper]

[ABBÉ ANGE DENIS MACQUIN]

O n surveying the interior of Fonthill Abbey, where there is so much to strike the sight, the mind is distracted by the multiplicity of objects, by the minute beauties of some, by the curious nature of others, and by the splendour of all. Of these the catalogue contains *one thousand and four* items lotted for sale, and we confess that in our opinion, with the exception of a few of the articles, Fonthill will be a much more beautiful and desirable abode denuded of these ornaments, than if it continued to be enriched by them. We are not, under any circumstances, very ardent admirers of houses or palaces fitted up like goldsmiths' and jewellers' shops. A moderate collection of elegant and remarkable productions, serves to amuse visitors at vacant periods, when the contemplation of fine pictures, and even the works of immortal authors, may have palled upon the taste; but a whole Museum of trinkets, china, rarities, and precious *bijouterie,* can afford no satisfaction to the intelligent mind, and only for a brief space amuse even the weak and barren. If this be true generally, it is particularly applicable to such a place as Fonthill Abbey. In so noble, and we may say so affecting, a Gothic structure, the costly trifles of ingenuity, the oddities of Jad and Japan, the antiquities of Mosaics and porcelain, and the commingled fancies of all periods and nations, are more than any where else irrelevant and ill associated. Were we their owner, we should feel no pain at their dispersion. Let them go to give variety and pleasure to many mansions: Fonthill will be improved by their removal.[1] Its

---

1 The structure was begun sometime in 1796 after the plans and under the superintendence of the late Mr. Wyatt. Since the death of Mr. Wyatt (in 1813), his plans have been followed by the persons employed by Mr. Beckford without alteration; so that whatever of beauty belongs to the Abbey, it is entirely the result of that eminent architect's talent, and the poetical genius of its owner.

character is simplicity and grandeur, and to be appropriate, all its furniture should partake of these qualities. The noble library, the picture gallery of suitable subjects by excellent masters, and the general air of a magnificent repose, should belong to its exquisite proportions and imposing features

The conventual style, in which Fonthill Abbey is built, is not very favourable for the exhibition of what we would call finery, nor is it possible to display a very great number of excellent pictures to advantage in the lights afforded by its structure. The Grand Octagonal Tower suits nothing but the superb simplicity of its existing furniture; the noble arches, the beautifully clustered pillars, the softly stained glass, the rich sweep of curtain, and corresponding masses of sofa and Ottoman, the galleries circling above, and the exquisite fan-work and lantern which crown the whole, are all in the purest keeping and justest taste. The summit of the Tower remains in an unfinished condition and in ascending to enjoy the extensive view which it presents, you have to clamber up ladders and through rafters. The prospect is, however, a fine one, though the country round is not of a picturesque description. Salisbury Plain, ill named, offers few striking images to the eye; and with the exception of Salisbury Cathedral in one direction, and Stourhead, backed by Dorsetshire, in another, the immediate groves of Fonthill are the only pleasing features of the scene. On one occasion, when this lofty tower was pushing its crest towards heaven, an elevated part of it caught fire and was destroyed. The sight was sublime; and we have heard that it was a spectacle which the Owner of the Mansion enjoyed with as much composure as if the flames had not been devouring what it would cost a fortune to repair! And we can readily credit this report, for we are well assured that the building was carried on by him with an energy and enthusiasm of which duller minds can hardly form a conception. At one period, every cart and wagon in the district were pressed into the service, though all the agricultural labours of the country stood still. At another, even the royal works of St. George's Chapel, Windsor, were abandoned, that four hundred and sixty men might be employed night and day on Fonthill Abbey. These men were made to relieve each other by regular watches; and during the longest and darkest nights of the winter, the astonished traveller might see the tower rising under their hands, the trowel and torch being associated for that purpose. This must have had a very extraordinary appearance; and we are told that it was another of those exhibitions which Mr. Beckford was fond of contemplating. He is represented as surveying the work thus expedited, the busy levy of masons, the high and giddy dancing of the lights, and the strange effects produced upon the architecture and woods below, from one of those eminences in the walks which we have already described, and wasting the coldest hours of December darkness in feasting his sense with this display of almost superhuman power. These singular traits of character will not surprise those who have made mankind their study. It is the very course of nature, when satiated with all that inordinate wealth can purchase, to aim at higher, probably at extravagant sources of gratification. The soul, pampered with the easy attainment of almost every thing that is desirable in life, soon dis-relishes, despises, and finally loaths what others covet. The utmost bliss to the poor man is an object of apathy to the rich; and gaming, and other violent excitements, are rushed into with a mad avidity. The minds most nearly allied to genius are the most apt to plunge into these extremes: a Beckford builds a Babel by torchlight, a Byron writes a Cain with exultation; and an Eratastratus burns the Temple of Diana, to gain an immortal, though infamous celebrity

But we ask forgiveness for this digression, suggested by the Print accompanying this Sketch; and as that occupies much space shall, with our readers' kind consent, request them to defer their stroll with us among the curiosities of the interior, till our next week's *Gazette*.

EDITOR'S NOTE *The Literary Gazette and Journal of Belles Lettres*, 24 August 1822, pp. 527–8.

Visit to Fonthill
[Third Paper]
[ABBÉ ANGE DENIS MACQUIN]

The Sale at Fonthill Abbey has been postponed to the 1st of October, partly, we believe, in consequence of the number of visitors who continue to throng to that attractive spot from every quarter of the country. By one of those revolutions in learning which the world has sometimes witnessed, the diffusion of literature in Wiltshire is a result of this occasion. Perhaps it may not be immediately guessed how this happens; but such is the demand for certain publications, that there is not an innkeeper in the county who has not turned bookseller. Over the chimney of the very Alehouse we read, together with 'Soda-Water', 'Ginger-Beer', or 'Home-brewed Ale Sold Here', 'Catalogues of the Sale at Fonthill to be had here', or 'Rutter's Description of Fonthill Abbey'! Thus by a rare union letters and entertainment go hand in hand and the refreshment of mind and body are happily combined. With what delight, while picking the wing of a chicken at the White Hart, does a traveller enjoy the flights of the Muse! Thus with our coffee we had an opportunity of imbibing the following pretty little poem, by the author of the Grave of the last Saxon, and kindly given by him to Mr. Rutter aforesaid for his second edition. It is 'On the first View of the Abbey, Aug. 21, 1822.'... Similar feelings will fill every sentient bosom on approaching this magnificent pile; and Mr. Bowles has but impressed the common sentiment with his genius in the description. We have pleasure in accompanying it with a beautiful original epigram:

De Aede Fonthilliana

Splendida frondosis surgit de montibus Aedes,
   Tangit et augusta fronte superba polum:
Scilicet attonitus dubitat quid conspicit hospes,
   An coelum in terris, an super astra domos.

[249]

But we promised that this should be an interior visit, and here we are still outside. Enter! – Among the pictures, of which about a hundred and fifty are consigned to Mr. Christie's hammer, (115 in the 7th day's sale, others on different days) there are several very fine works. The Laughing Boy, by L. da Vinci, is perhaps more admirable as an undoubted specimen of that Master and a perfect example of his style, than as a production of Art. A study of two old Men's Heads by Quintin Matsys, is a valuable and characteristic piece by the Blacksmith. The Adoration of the Magi, by Franks, is the best grouped picture of many figures we ever saw from his pallet; and a Lady in a Red Corset, by Fragonard, the most highly-finished picture in the Dutch manner that could be adduced from a foreign pencil. Catherine Cornaro, by P. Veronese, and the Duke of Savoy, an oval, by Holbein, will also be looked at with attention by the amateur; and one of the most curious early works in any gallery will be found in 'Christ in the Garden', by A. Mantegna. In the sky there is an angel with a cup and the whole is a very odd display of the mechanical skill and the taste of the middle of the fifteenth centtury. A View of Ostend, by Peters, is a spirited piece; but in the class of landscape there is nothing to compare with two exquisite Berghems. No. 106, (7th day) is a small landscape by that painter, Cattle Feeding, two figures, a hilly distance, and a bright sky. Nothing in art can surpass this gem, which is, we think, perfect of its kind. The simplicity of the subject, and the truth of nature in its execution throughout, show of how much the art is capable on a very limited space. The Praslin Cabinet has also furnished another delicious piece, by the same hand, to the Fonthill collection: this is No. 113, the *Embarquement des Vivres*. It is a larger picture, and consists of a seaport in the gulf of Genoa, a ship at anchor, and persons employed in carrying provisions and dragging cattle on board. It is a superb production. The Regent Murray, by Jamieson, is a good historical portrait. F. Mieris, the elder, has contributed a Lady feeding a Parrot, in his most finished manner, and the famous Poulterer's Shop, by Gerard Dow, is so well known as a *chef-d'oeuvre* by that Master as to need no further notice than its name. A *Sybilla Lybica*, by L. Caracci, is highly spoken of, but did not strike us as a very superior performance. Indeed we were more forcibly struck, probably from the association of ideas, with a picture by Walckenberg, 'the building of the Tower of Babel, with a multitude of small figures'. This strange representation was in King Charles' collection! The modern Babel which sprung up in those days, dispersed the monuments of royal taste, and now this particular subject having rested long under its congenial Tower of Fonthill[1] is again about to find a refuge elsewhere. To use the common phrase, it should be bought in: no place will fit it so well, nor will it so well fit any other place. There is something remarkable in Mr. Beckford's predilection for towers. One might be induced to fancy that he set the example to Lord Byron of drawing from himself, and that Vathek was in this respect the prototype of Childe Harolde [sic]. The readers of that extraordinary tale may remember the following passages – (we quote it, though less finely expressed, from the more generally intelligible English version:).[2] ...

Next to the Paintings, and indeed in many cases before them, are the articles of Vertu with which Fonthill Abbey is literally crammed. Not only is every wall, every corner, every recess, filled with cabinets, laden shelves, commodes, jars, slabs, coffers, caskets, &c. &c. but the window seats are covered, little tables support curiosities, and the whole length of the Edward Gallery is filled up the middle as well as along the sides with rare and valuable productions of art and nature. There is china enough for the supreme head of the celestial empire; plate enough to challenge competition with Mr. Rundell or Mr. Hamlet;[3] and precious stones enow to make a Parisian belle or perhaps an English toast happy for nine entire months. Some of these household ornaments, Lares which as we have said we do not worship, are however not only extremely beautiful but extremely curious, from the workmanship bestowed upon them. Old Chelsea cups that have seen as much service as old Chelsea pensioners (for they belong to different services) are seen contiguous to egg-shell china of the most brittle and delicate form. Agates nearly as large and more charming than the agate of Upsala, (which is two spans long and a span and a half broad) mingle with jasper cups and Chalcedony vases. Visitors must view with wonder (No. 52 3d day) a Buhl Armoire, with figures and ornaments chased and gilt. This splendid piece of furniture, ten feet in height and five in breadth, was designed by Le Brun and belonged to the Duc d'Aumont. A Cabinet still more remarkable and worthy of minute examination is No. 43 5th day, composed of pear-tree and other woods, from

1 A Conflagration of Troy, by P. P. Breughel, seems also to deserve that it should retain its place.
2 Extended quote from Vathek and from the conclusion of the tale follows. RJG
3 London goldsmiths Rundell, Bridge & Rundell, 32 Ludgate Hill and Thomas Hamlet, 182 Princes Street, Leicester Square. RJG

the palace of Whitehall, and executed from designs by Holbein for Henry VIII. It is a singularly grotesque and curious performance, on which the moral inscriptions do not always agree with the freedom of the bas reliefs. But the spirit of that age was coarse sand licentious; Anne Bullen would probably have witnessed sights without a blush at which a servant girl of our *refined* period would cry shame and shut her eyes, at least cover them with her chinky fingers. No. 47, same day, is a most magnificent Cup, cover and stem of ivory, sculptured by Magnus Berg. The carving represents Diana and her Nymphs in a Forest scene; and is altogether as complete a specimen of what can be accomplished in this style of art as (perhaps) exists in the kingdom. It is equalled by No. 50. a Vase, from the largest known block of Hungarian topaz, also exquisitely sculptured and tastefully set on a tripod stand of gold, enamel, and diamonds. This is by Benvenuto Cellini, made as a marriage present to Catherine Cornaro, and is certainly one of the most superb gifts that could distract a lady's attention on such an occasion. We can vouch for its disturbing the minds of all the female visitors whom the spectacle draws to Fonthill and anticipate that Mr. Christie will have as much trouble in assigning it to an owner, as Paris had with the Apple of Discord.

EDITOR'S NOTE *The Literary Gazette and Journal of Belles Lettres,* Saturday, 31 August 1822, pp. 555–6.

Visit to Fonthill

[*Fourth Paper*]

[ABBÉ ANGE DENIS MACQUIN]

In our third notice of this sumptuous abode, we entered into some of its ornamental details, and left off deep in buhl, ebony, seve [quasi *sèvres*], crystal, Tazzas, Mandarins, quilts, and caskets. Nor can we yet tear ourselves from these fine things. No. 54, in the fifth day's sale, is justly styled 'a magnificent Table of Pietre Comesse:' It has an oval centre of mamillated oriental onyx, surrounded with jaspers and breccia, and the outer rim consisting of various marbles in a beautiful and bold arabesque. It was formerly in the Palace Borghese. Italy is the mart for such commodities; and it is worthy of remark, that among all our skilful mechanical processes, the art of cutting and polishing tables of this sort is not so perfectly practised here as in that country. The expense of forming a Mosaic of hard materials n England would be prodigious. An Onyx Cup (No. 41, 8th day,) exquisitely sculptured and richly jewelled, deserves a particular examination, for the beauty of its forms and the appropriateness of its tortoise feet. It is surmounted by a little golden figure, Minerva, whose shield is composed of a large ruby. Among the other elegancies of Fonthill are many superbly-mounted Nautilus Shells. One of these (No 52, 8th day,) is very large, and the surface it offered for the taste and ingenuity of art, has been exquisitely filled by an engraving by Hilliken, – the subject, the Triumph of Neptune and Amphitrite. The embossing, chasing, and minute finish of the whole of this design, render it one of the most precious curiosities of the place. N. 90, same day, is a fine group of Youth and Age, in ivory, by Fiamingo; the character of both periods well expressed. On the ensuing day (the 9th,) No. 56, is a Triple Jewel Cabinet of opaque amber, with transparent panels of the same material. This very uncommon work is stated to have been made for a Princess of Bavaria, in 1655. It is strangely carved, in sacred, legendary, and profane story, and the compartments are marked out or divided by cameos of white amber of which also are made a number of miniature figures of the Romish saints. These personages are, as in our old grotesque churches, inter-mingled with monkeys at the corners, lions with rings in their mouths, and other monsters. We have never read any good account of this species of ornament either in architecture or in articles of furniture. The intimate mixture of the most sacred and the most burlesque, not to say the most outrageously indecent representations, might afford much for an entertaining essay, which, if ably written, would not only throw a strong light upon the feelings and manners of bye-gone ages, but furnish an intelligent view of the operations of the human mind; of the conflict between barbarism and civilization, when their powers were equally balanced; of the grossnesses as well as refinements introduced by Christianity; and of that phenomenon of intellect which in acted mysteries in convents, in cathedrals, and in the business of life, united every thing that was holy and adorable, with every thing that was obscene and detestable.

Besides these considerations, suggested to us by the Holbein Cabi-net, the Amber Cabinet, the Hungarian Topaz Vase, and other rarities which we have described in our papers; many of the *valuables* at Fonthill acquire an additional *value,* from the enlarged view which they give of the state of the Fine Arts in the 15th, 16th, 17th, and 18th, and part of the 19th centuries. We here see how the talents of great Artists were often employed. In our times pictures and statues only are deemed deserving of the hand of Genius. A modern *Artist* would probably throw a teacup or a nautilus-shell at his patron's head, or at least let them fall (in astonishment) and break at his feet, if he were asked to exercise his ingenuity in painting them: in fact, such productions have been degraded from their station; and the successors of the famous chasers, designers, carvers, embossers, of former times, have sunk into a mechanical class. Under such a change, it is not a little striking to contemplate the minute and painful labours of those worthies whose fortunes flourished and whose immortality was achieved on the handles of vases and the embellishments of tankards. A multitude of their most remarkable performances are comprised in the collection at Fonthill, and may be very advantageously studied as works of fertile invention, high fancy, rich taste, and extraordinary execution.

From them the spectator turns to other articles of like curiosity, but contrasting forcibly with what has attracted attention in them. We allude to such specimens of Eastern manufactory as sea-green bottles, pink jars, Japan basons, &c. and especially a Chinese Sceptre, with the god Tongfongsok and the eight Tchin; a figure of the Japanese Idol Amida, above two feet in height, and not heavier than a small stick of sealing-wax; another Chinese Sceptre of jad, a present from Keen Long to George III.; and the mountings of the King of Candy's Sword !!

Among the interesting relics of note, from their being associated with celebrated persons or events, we may specify six Armed Chairs from Cardinal Wolsey's palace at Esher. They are of solid ebony, of a square shape, large, carved, and massive. They move on castors. A water-colour Miniature of Louis XII. at his devotions. A Bottle of pale sea-green Oriental China, which belonged to the Queen of Sicily, the friend of Petrarch, and the earliest known specimen of porcelain introduced from China into Europe. A silver gilt Cup and Cover, a most elaborate example of masterly chasing by Roemer, about the year 1580 (No. 48 5th day.) A Greek metal Shrine brought from Palestine by St. Louis, and part of the spoliation of the church at St. Denys during the French Revolution. An Ebony Cabinet of architectural design by Bernini the sculptor (No. 63, 9th day.) And among the plate, various dishes, &c. which have belonged to British monarchs.

These particulars will afford our distant readers some idea of the nature of the exhibition and splendid furniture at Fonthill Abbey. When the sale takes place, we shall probably resume the subject in another short notice; and in the meantime congratulate all those to whom we wish well, on not having to reside in superbly decorated palaces, on enjoying comfort without show, and being able to taste the elegant luxuries of life (if fortune has so blessed them) without the cumber of bawbles and toys. Fonthill Abbey possesses a library of more worth than all its wealth from gold and diamond mines; – the grounds are truly magnificent, (as a proof of their variety we may mention that the cultivated heaths alone amount to more than fifty species;) and when the Chapel is finished, the entire building will certainly be one of the most superb, if not one of the most convenient private mansions in the world.

EDITOR'S NOTE *The Literary Gazette and Journal of Belles Lettres*, Saturday, 14 September 1822, p. 585.

Fonthill Abbey

[CHARLES KNIGHT]

It is one of the characteristics of a class of Englishmen that the familiar and accessible possess little value in their eyes, whilst whatever is rare or remote becomes an object of intense interest. Upon this principle there are hundreds of Londoners who would consider it childish to pass an hour amongst the monuments of Westminster Abbey, but who would dwell with profound delight upon the architectural beauties of the Cathedral at Rheims. The British Museum, in their view, appears to co[u]nt in nothing very beautiful or rare, whilst the Gallery of the Louvre is alone worth a journey to Paris. The dome of St. Paul's is sometimes honoured with a passing glance by such observers, should they chance to look up to inquire the time of day from its unerring dials; but they leave to their children the pleasure of inspecting it, while they sigh for a voyage to gaze upon St. Peter's. It is thus that mail-coaches and steam-packets are in such requisition, and that the distance which divides us from other nations becomes an additional inducement to Englishmen to visit them.

We apprehend there has been a great deal of this feeling prevailing for many years in the world of fashion, and the world of taste, about Fonthill Abbey. Scarcely any human being had beheld this princely domain, though it stood within a small distance of a great road, was not a hundred miles removed from the metropolis, and its possessor was an English gentleman who exercised his right of enjoying his magnificence in ostentation or in privacy, as suited him best. It was indeed known in the circles of the gay, that a Prince of Orange and a Duke of Norfolk had been refused admission into this mysterious retreat; – and at length, therefore, it came to be thought of, and dreamt of, as something that might approach in extent and splendor, to the domes of Dom-daniel, the palace of Aladdin, or the tower of Vathek. It

[256]

was one of the wonders of the world, and happy would be the creature that should catch a glimpse of it.

We can hardly imagine any more sudden shock to the privileges of the great, than the announcement that Fonthill Abbey was to be stript of its rarities, and the refined and the vulgar might be equally admitted to feast upon its magnificence, at the cost of half a guinea. This was indeed a levelling system. Fonthill, we dare say, has lost a great deal of its ancient value in the eyes of a large class, in consequence of this proceeding. There are persons who will not buy a fine engraving because others may have a copy of it; – and there are some who will now stay away from Fonthill because a plebeian admirer of architectural grandeur might 'come between the wind and their nobility'. We rejoice in no man's misfortunes, but we are truly glad that a possession almost unequalled in its richness and beauty should have become, in some degree, the public property; – and that the splendor which here revels and luxuriates should be now the source of delight to thousands, instead of gratifying the solitary eye of the master-spirit who created it.

We are desirous to extend this pleasure as much as may be in our power; and we therefore think that a rapid description of this remarkable place may, in a small degree, amuse and inform our readers, and compensate us much more than any individual recollections for the trouble we have taken in viewing.

We established our quarters at Salisbury, to which fine city there has been a considerable accession of visitors since the opening of Fonthill for public inspection. The tickets for viewing the mansion and grounds are here, and at the neighbouring towns, obtained at one guinea each, admitting two persons; – a catalogue is included in this purchase. The tickets are delivered at the Abbey, and the names of the parties inscribed in a book, with a corresponding number which is marked on your catalogue. The admission extends to every day previous to the sale, without the purchase of another ticket.

The grounds at Fonthill are opened at ten o'clock. We proceeded at an early hour from Salisbury. The idea of anticipation was the mainspring of our minds, and we therefore passed almost unregardingly the elegant gate of Wilton Park, and did not stop for a moment to inquire into the prosperity of the carpet-manufactory. The country from hence to Hindon, the market-town next Fonthill, presents an agreeable contrast to the wildness of the downs with which Salisbury is almost surrounded. We had here thriving hedge-rows, orchards whose branches were bending with the ripening fruit, rivulets sparkling by the road-side, a mansion or so seated amidst beeches of a century's growth, and swelling hills planted with thickets of fir. But even this scenery could not engross our minds. We had the Catalogue of the Rarities of Fonthill as our travelling companion; and our mind became absorbed in dim visions of cabinets designed by Holbein, chairs in which Wolsey had sat, vases sculptured by Benvenuto Cellini, salvers that Kings of France had presented to their mistresses, coffers of Japan in which Mazarin had deposited his treasures and his secrets, – with all the unimaginable mysteries of Tezzas, and Linners, and Raphael-ware, and sea-green porcelain, and the King of Candy's sword. The genius of CHRISTIE was here in all its glory; and we swept along, regardless of the peaceful industry and the humble ambition of the villages on our route.

Our horses were ascending, at a slow pace, a hill called Chilmark, when we looked up, and beheld, at a distance of about five miles, the towers of Fonthill Abbey. This first view was one of exceeding beauty. Below us lay a richly-cultivated vale, stretching across to a bold hill, which was backed by a higher ridge, leading on the eye to the loftiest eminence of the distance, covered with trees, out of which rose a tower of prodigious height. By the help of a glass we could discern the octangular form of this immense building, with its lofty pinnacles; and just above the tops of the trees we could trace the heads of two other towers, and here and there descry some architectural forms mingling with the dark green woods. At our feet was the contrast of a modest, unassuming village-spire. The splendid abbey looked over an immense extent of earth with a giant-pride; – but the little church in the lowly fields pointed upwards to Heaven.

We drove happily on, and at length reached the entrance to the demesnes of Fonthill. We passed through a rusticated gateway of considerable elegance. On our left was a very beautiful lake, whose further bank rose to a great height, and whose steepest parts were clothed with a variety of the most graceful trees. The irregular outline of the banks, and the gradual expansion of the water, formed a landscape of considerable beauty. This, we were informed, is the Old Park. On the right, at no great distance from the entrance, stands a wing of the mansion erected by Alderman Beckford, the father of the present possessor. Judging from this remain, the house must have been of large dimensions, and of very respectable architecture. Its situation was, however, wretchedly flat; – and we are not, therefore, surprised that a man of taste, possessing almost unbounded resources, should have desired a happier spot for the employ of his riches and his genius.

We shall not weary our readers with an apology for half-a-dozen columns in 'an historical account of Fonthill'. There is a small description of the place just published, possessing all the tedious characteristics of local guides: and from this much edifying matter may be gathered – or be stolen. Some of our brother journalists have already been at it. It is enough for us to notice that the estate of Fonthill Gifford, as it is called, belonged to the Delawars, the Hungerfords, the Mervins, and the Cottingtons; – that riches, in the person of Alderman Beckford, thrust out the relics of nobility; – and that his son became possessed of the estate when a minor. The most remarkable facts of its ancient possessors are, that one was whipt and wore sheep-skins for stealing two nuns, and that another received the honour of knighthood by bathing. Those who are curious to know more may consult the proper authorities.

We drove about a mile th[r]ough the Old Park. We here passed a pretty little inn, round which visitors were crowding, and went on by a road of considerable steepness, till we reached a porter's lodge, where our tickets were inspected. We crossed the barriers of an immense wall, and a frowning fence, and were securely landed in the inner grounds of Fonthill Abbey. We had realized an object which a few months since could scarcely be obtained at any expence of riches or courtesy. Curiosity, we are told, has been so highly excited, that impudent connoisseurs have passed this boundary in the disguise of labourers; – but their clandestine ambition has been defeated, and they have been glad to escape with any punishment short of a duc[k]ing and a horse-whipping. We laughed at such woes; for time, which equalizes all things, had put us in possession of the high privilege, at the price of an opera-ticket.

Several winding walks brought us almost abruptly to the table ground on which the Abbey stands. It is nearly the highest hill in the country. Our attention was divided between the splendor of the building and the beauty of the scenery. There stood the Abbey, unlike any thing the imagination can conceive of a private gentleman's dwelling, covering as much space, and displaying as much architectural grandeur, as the most richly-endowed cathedral. The southern front, which we first approached, appeared like the nave of Canterbury or Ely, terminated at the eastern end by two towers of large dimensions, but upon which the great tower looked down, like an Atlas amongst pigmies.

Passing the west, we stood before the great entrance, superior in its height and the beauty of its proportions, to any specimen we have seen of conventual grandeur. On the right of the entrance is a cloister leading onwards to a regular gothic building, of itself splendid enough for the palace of the richest mitred Abbot; – on the left are a number of low-roofed elevations, leading up the eye by a series of ascending towers and pinnacles to the overpowering height of the great feature of Fonthill. We could no longer restrain our impatience to see the interior. ...

The great western entrance to Fonthill Abbey is, we think, arranged with the most refined judgment. The hall into which you at once step from the graceful lawn is in itself exceedingly splendid, but it excites an expectation of something even more magnificent. The lofty doors, swaying upon their 'harmonious hinges', at once call to mind

The gates of monarchs.

They are

Arch'd so high that giants may jet through,
And keep their impious turbands on.

The walls, in their beautiful simplicity, carry up the eye to the fine oak ceiling, – a perfect model of the purest specimens of baronial grandeur. But the mind does not rest satisfied in the apartment. There is a lofty flight of steps from the centre of the hall, and beyond these appear columns, whose arched terminations gradually display their extraordinary height, as we reach the landing place. We passed under a gallery on each side of which was an elegant recess – and we were in the Great Octagon.

It is impossible for the mind to conceive a scene of more imposing magnificence than is here presented. The octagon is formed of eight arches of the most overpowering height, but of the most graceful proportion. These carry the entire weight of the tower and lantern. Four of the arches are open, and four are closed with scarlet draperies. The arch immediately opposite the western entrance leads to the suite of apartments called the New Rooms. That on the left, to King Edward's gallery; that on the right, to Saint Michael's gallery. Referring the design of Fonthill Abbey to ecclesiastical architecture, we may be supposed, while in the great octagon, to be standing in the centre of a cathedral, with transepts.

We will ask our readers to repose a while with us, on one of the sumptuous Ottomans that fill the closed arches of the Octagon. How brilliant and yet how tender is the light that plays on the walls and pavement. It is produced by the judicious arrangement of stained glass, which transmits an ever-changing hue, as the sun proceeds on his splendid course. The first feeling that is produced as we look up to the height of the lantern is that of wonder – the next that of calm admiration at the elegance of its proportions, and the simplicity of its ornament. Here is nothing of ostentatious finery; – all is grandeur, simplicity and repose.

When the visitors of Fonthill are tired of gazing up at the height of the lantern, and of calling to mind Vathek, who 'having ascended the fifteen hundred stairs of his tower, cast his eyes below, and beheld men not larger than pismires', let them, without shifting their seats, look down either of the splendid galleries that present themselves. It is impossible to imagine more brilliant effects to be produced, as Mr. BECKFORD has himself expressed it, by a 'well managed perspective', or the 'magic of optics'. In the one, the light is admitted through scarlet draperies upon groined and gilded ceilings, heraldic achievements, splendid bookcases, and articles of taste, upon which the artists of Italy and France have lavished all their skill. This sumptuous vista is terminated by a window of plate glass, which lets in one of the most pleasing views of the Abbey grounds and the distant country. In the other gallery the eye wanders along the same vista of splendid furniture and books, portraits of the great of the heroic times, and models of the taste of the romantic ages; – but the light gradually becomes dim, and the eye at length rests upon the beautiful oratory which terminates this gallery, splendid in all the gorgeousness of tracery and gold, but so subdued by the hand of taste that we think of it as a place most fitting for retirement and devotion.

From this scene of splendor let us look back upon the entrance we have passed. We have again a vista, – but it is one which nature and art have united to render beautiful. Through the great doors of the hall we behold the soft green of a very long avenue, with its borders of flowering shrubs and lofty trees. The contrast with the internal decoration of the Abbey is the most delightful and refreshing imaginable.

Before we commence a minute account of the several apartments of Fonthill, we may relieve ourselves and our readers by a glance at *Vathek*, to trace the growth of those ideas of architectural grandeur, and ornamental gardening, which are displayed at Fonthill, from their first development in a work of fancy. The coincidence, if we remember rightly, is in some instances sufficiently curious: –

He surpassed in magnificence all his predecessors. The palace of Alkoremi, which his father, Motassem, had erected on the hill of Pied Horses, and which commanded the whole city of Samarah, was, in his idea, far too scanty: he added therefore, five wings, or rather other palaces, which he destined for the particular gratification of each of the senses.

The palace named 'The Delight of the Eyes, or The Support of Memory', was one entire enchantment. Rarities, collected from every corner of the earth, were there found in such profusion as to dazzle and confound, but for the order in which they were arranged. One gallery exhibited the pictures of the celebrated Mani, and statues, that seemed to be alive. Here a well-managed perspective attracted the sight; there the magic of optics deceived it: whilst the naturalist on his part, exhibited in their several classes the various gifts that Heaven had bestowed on our globe. In a word, Vathek omitted nothing in this palace, that might gratify the curiosity of those who resorted to it, although he was not abl[e] to gratify his own; for, of all men, he was the most curious.

At the distance of a few miles from Samarah stood a high mountain, whose sides were swarded with wild thyme and basil, and its summit overspread with so delightful a plain, that it might have been taken for the Paradise destined for the faithful. Upon it grew a hundred thickets of eglantine and other fragrant shrubs; a hundred arbours of roses, entwined with jessamine and honeysuckle; as many clumps of orange trees, cedar, and citron, whose branches, interwoven with the palm, the pomegranate, and the vine, presented every luxury that could regale the eye or the taste. The ground was strewed with violets, hare-bells, and pansies; in the midst of which numerous tufts of jonquils, hyacinths, and carnations perfumed the air.

… We purposely introduced … [these] passages from the celebrated work of Mr. BECKFORD, that those of our readers who may visit, or have visited, Fonthill, may have a subject for half an hour's reverie, when they see, or recollect, the most delightful place imaginable for contemplation. Fonthill Abbey is not to be regarded as a mere storehouse of curiosities. The extreme beauty, and the infinite variety, of its decorations and appendages, will abundantly gratify the most curious and exact research, even if it were prolonged for weeks. But the majority of those who avail themselves of the present opportunity of beholding this remarkable place are, necessarily, the visitors of a day. To such it is desirable that a strong impression should be produced upon their senses by the general character of the edifice; – and this can only be accomplished by a surrender of the imagination to the most obvious associations and impressions. Those will best remember the grandeur of Fonthill, who for the first hour or two of their visit wander about without any assistance from descriptions or catalogues. They will overlook many individual beauties, but they will be amply compensated by a vivid conception of the whole; – they will have all its poetry in their minds. The minor graces of Raphael-ware and Japan may be afterwards sought for, without any interruption of those splendid images which such a building must suggest.

With this view we will now accompany our friends up the staircase leading to the summit of the great tower. This staircase is circular. The ascent is very easy; – and without any great fatigue, we shall find ourselves on a landing, leading to four beautiful little apartments, called the Nunneries. These rooms are formed at the crown of the four open arches of the octagon. They are fitted up in a tasteful Gothic style, and furnish no inapt idea of those calm retreats from which they derive their name. They each open to the Octagon by the removal of flowing draperies. Going through these apartments, we pass completely round the Octagon, immediately under the fine windows of the lantern. The alternate arches, as we have before noticed, are closed; but a stone screen-work forms a gallery, completing the communication with the Nunneries. The visitor may well pause in either of these galleries to look down upon the brilliant scene beneath.

On the eastern side of the gallery, leading round the Octagon, we encounter something approaching to a painful contrast to the finished magnificence we have been viewing. We look through a window, and there behold a very large portion of the Abbey incomplete. The part which immediately presents itself to our observation is called the Basilica. It appears to be an immense room, whose sides, crowded with windows, run into a long perspective. But the windows are blocked with common boarding; the roof and floors present nothing but naked beams and rafters; we see the germ of a noble conception, which may probably never be perfected. We sigh over the comparative weakness, even of the most persevering intellects, and the most unbounded resources; and whilst we see around us much to soothe and satisfy the most extravagant pride, we can easily perceive that restlessness and disappointment must intrude themselves, in the bitter certainty of the limitations which time, and fortune, and the commonest accidents of humanity, present to the splendid visions of a tasteful and luxurious imagination.

But we must pursue our walk. The circuit of the Octagon brings us back to the part where we landed, and we continue to ascend, till we arrive at the roof of the staircase tower. We have here a very extensive view towards the West and North, and we may look down, without much sensation of fear, upon the elegant grounds at our feet. We are now at the part where the great tower springs from the roof; and we may here form a very impressive idea of its loftiness and large dimensions.

Entering the tower, we find ourselves with an obscure light, amidst the frame-work of the building. We ascend for some time, with little effort upon a rising passage without steps. But the common modes of ascent must be soon encountered; and we toil on, till we reach an outer gallery, where, with perfect safety, we may enjoy the extensive prospect we have earned. The unfinished part of the tower, through which we have passed, was intended for a complete suite of apartments, even to a kitchen at the top.

The height of this tower is two hundred and seventy-six feet. We have generally observed that the prospect from very great elevations, in a country distinguished for no very remarkable objects, rarely compensates us for our labour. In a large city nothing can be more interesting than the sensation produced by a commanding height. Who can look down from the dome of St. Paul's, upon the wilderness of houses, the broad river, the stately public buildings, and the immense crowds of busy mortals, without a strong feeling of the greatness and the littleness of human nature. But we have no associations of equal interest in a champaigne country. Hills, and plains, and woods stretching as far as the eye can reach, present no diversity, and excite no powerful emotions. Nature is to us very unlovely in a bird's eye view. And after all, at the greatest height we can attain, a feeling of our insignificance will intrude. What is the prospect presented from a tower of three hundred feet, compared with the range of vision which the eagle, and even the rook, have in their daily flight. There is nothing to be seen from the tower of Fonthill interesting enough to deaden this feeling. The most pleasing objects are the thickets and shaded walks of the Abbey. Beyond these a few bold hills present themselves, some of which are richly wooded. But the greater part of the prospect is formed of downs. The extent of the landscape does not compensate for its monotony. The only interesting object is Alfred's tower at Stourhead.

In our preceding notices of this remarkable mansion, we have very much confined ourselves to its general effects, as it would present itself to any tasteful and tolerably informed mind. Our own inclination would probably lead us to conclude this rapid description by an equally rapid walk through the beautiful grounds of the park. But our readers will not be so easily satisfied. We must afford a little time and space to the wonders of art which are collected at Fonthill; and we must describe, as well as we can, with a profound ignorance of many technical phrases, some of the most distinguished of those curiosities, whose dispersion will constitute an epoch in the history of many a virtuoso's collection. We will, therefore, at once lead our friends, from the prospect of russet downs, and green woods, and azure skies, into the heart of the Abbey; and descending once more into the octagon, we will pass through the eastern arch, under a door-way beneath the organ gallery, into the CABINET ROOM.

The *tout-ensemble* of this elegant apartment does not essentially differ from the general arrangement of superb rooms in the mansions of the great. It is an oblong shape, and of very correct proportions; – its hangings and furniture are of crimson damask; – it has two windows, looking into the court-yard. The paintings which it contains are chiefly portraits. Over the fire-place is a full length of the celebrated Alderman Beckford. There is much of vigour and decision in the countenance of this celebrated man; – and we can easily conceive that his memorable reply to the King was abundantly enforced by the calmness and courage of the speaker. We apprehend that the leaders of the Civic Senate are somewhat degenerated since the days of the great Alderman; – at any rate we cannot trace in his features any of those vulgar and repulsive qualities which belong to the full-blown demagogue of our own times. On the left of this portrait is that of a very remarkable personage, the grand-father of the present possessor of Fonthill; and on the right is that of his ancestor's lady. But the most interesting portrait is that of Mr. Beckford himself, when a young man. The features are full of spirit and intelligence. The eyes are bright and penetrating; but we looked in vain for that extraordinary power which common report assigns to those of Mr. Beckford. We neither saw 'the terrible eye' of *Vathek* – nor the eagle vision which can look upon the sun without shrinking. Either these reports are vulgar fables, or the artist was very unequal to the task of depicting that radiance which belongs to the display of a commanding intellect. In this room there is also a portrait of the present Duchess of Hamilton, the daughter of Mr. Beckford. A beautiful composition by WEST, 'Abraham and Isaac proceeding to the place of sacrifice', and 'a saloon of paintings', very elaborate and brilliant, by VAN OPSTAEL, complete the pictorial decorations of this apartment.

We are almost afraid to venture into the labyrinth that now presents itself, of Commodes and Armoires, full of massive plate and costly gems, less admirable for the rarity and value of their material, than for the beauty of their workmanship. We cannot affect to give any thing like a complete description of these curiosities; we made very few notes during our hasty visit; and our senses would be 'in wandering mazes lost', if we attempted to remember more than a few of the most remarkable objects to which their own splendour and Mr. CHRISTIE'S CAPITALS called our attention.

On each side of the fire-place is a cabinet, rich with tortoiseshell and gold. The catalogue informs us they are designed by LE BRUN. That on the left hand contains a most brilliant assemblage of plate. Those who have leisure may well devote some portion of it to an inspection of these brilliant specimens of antique luxury. On the east side of this room is an ebony cabinet, of considerable height, whose folding doors are of the most exquisite workmanship. This sumptuous piece of furniture contains some of the most remarkable specimens of the great Italian chasers. There is a vase of topaz, glittering with enamel and precious stones, and displaying the most exquisite and careful workmanship. It is the production of BENVENUTO CELLINI. It was with no common interest that we looked upon so beautiful of specimen of the art of this prince of jewellers. We thought of his bold and enterprising genius, his learning, his taste, his independence, his professional pride. CELLINI justly considered himself entitled to take rank with the sculptors and painters of the great age of art in which he lived; and he would never consent to be degraded into a mere mechanic. He was the companion of nobles and the friend of princes.

Before we quit this apartment, we recommend the visitors of Fonthill to look for, or recollect, a salver of enamel, representing a procession

nymphs – this was the present of Henry II, of France, to Diane de Poictiers; two or three beautiful vases of sculptured ivory; and two silver
cups, executed by ROEMER, a great rival of CELLINI.

The Cabinet Room leads into the New Room. Each of these apartments has been completed within a very short period. They are fitted
up in a sumptuous and tasteful style, but are more remarkable for the
works of art which are displayed in them than for any architectural
embellishments.

The NEW ROOM is an exquisite cabinet of very charming pictures; but
we could not look upon them till we had rested for a few minutes in one
of Cardinal Wolsey's chairs. These remarkable relics of that extraordinary man are of carved ebony, on silver castors; they formerly adorned
his palace at Esher. We should like to be able to trace their progress
from the palaces of the munificent cardinal to that of the no less sumptuous commoner; and figure to ourselves the vicissitudes which they
have undergone, and the changes of luxury in which they have participated. If Mr. BECKFORD pleased, he might make as entertaining a
history of Cardinal Wolsey's chairs, as the celebrated *Adventures of a
Guinea*. We must now glance at the pictures.

What an exquisite gem is that *Poulterer's Shop* of GERARD DOUW! It
was with difficulty we could obtain a satisfactory view of it. The tasteful and the merely curious, the informed and the ignorant, the artist and
the citizen, the elegant lady and the yeoman's wife, were all crowding
round it, equally wondering and delighted. The subject of this picture is
of the most ordinary kind, and in the hands of an inferior master the
arrangement of the figures would excite scarcely any interest. At the
opening of an arched window appears an old woman holding up a
hare, for which a girl is bargaining. On the sill of the window are –
some poultry, a blanket, and a metal pail; below is a cock in a basket; a
peasant and a woman are in the distance. Here are very common materials; but the force of the expression, the brilliant transparency of the
colouring, and the exquisite finish of the minutest part, were perhaps
never equalled. We could look for an hour upon the delicate wrinkles of
the old woman, and vie with the most enamoured housewife in her
praises of the how-natural skin of the plucked duck. GERARD DOUW has
succeeded beyond all masters in rendering the fineness of his touch
subservient to his general effects. His industry and his taste must have
been equally extraordinary.

We shall not have as many followers of 'the million' when we turn away to feast on two of the sweetest landscapes by BERGHEM that the most poetical imagination can conceive. The one is a very small *Cattle Piece*. A few cows are feeding and reposing on a rising ground, and near them are a shepherd and shepherdess piping. Under what a sky do they bask! The whole picture is full of gladness. It is as refreshing as the most beautiful landscape of reality; it tells at once a tale of innocence and joy. We see the glowing light, and hear the gentle music, and wish that life was one long summer's day of such happiness. No book can fill the mind with such images – hold! we forget thee, good ISAAC WALTON! thy pages, as much as this picture, belong to the beauty and freshness of creation, and happy is he that can relish their tenderness and simplicity. The other painting by BERGHEM is much larger and more elaborate, but it is scarcely so poetical. It represents a *Groupe of Figures and Cattle on the Shore of the Gulf of Genoa*. The buildings and shipping are in the most masterly style, and the a[e]rial perspective is quite a wonder in art.

On the same side as these beautiful paintings hangs a very remarkable production of LEONARD[O] DA VINCI. It is known by the name of *Laughing Boy*. A naked child (a half figure) holds in his hand a well-known toy. The figure is full of grace and animation, and the face expresses that joy and self-satisfaction which none but the most accurate observer of childhood could have adequately pourtrayed. This picture was formerly in the cabinet of the great Earl of ARUNDEL.

This room contains a very extraordinary picture by SALVATOR ROSA. It is essentially different from the general style of this painter, being a grand historical piece of which the figures constitute the principal interest. It represents *Job and his Friends*. The power of expression, and the general solemnity of the colouring, are evidences that SALVATOR was fitted for the sublimest walks of historical painting. The value of this picture is, we dare say, proportioned to the peculiarity of the subject. For ourselves, we would rather see this painter amidst his usual excellencies, and look upon his rocky landscapes and his fierce banditti, until our heads were as full of the terrific, as if we had submitted ourselves to the corresponding genius of ANNE RADCLIFFE.

Before our friends quit this room, we would recommend them to bestow some attention upon a glorious landscape by GASPAR POUSSIN; a grand historical picture, full of grace and freedom, by LUDOVICO CARACCI; and a pair of very beautiful TENIERS, painted with a most transparent effect.

We may pass out of the New Room into the China Closet; and here we fairly confess ourselves more than ever out of our element. It is a handsome room, whose walls are completely covered with as many vases, and jars, and dishes, and cups, and ewers, and tea-pots, as would furnish out the merely useful for five hundred tea-drinking establishments. But we shall not affect to laugh at what we do not understand. Mr. CHRISTIE has written a very elegant and classical work on the Worship of the Elements; and his proofs and illustrations are derived from such specimens as these of the arts of China. The collection before us is doubtless full of abundant interest to the scientific and curious.

A winding flight of steps will lead us to the Lancaster apartments. On the left of the door at which we enter is the Tribune Room. This beautiful little cabinet is in the Northern Octagon. It is adorned with several paintings by WEST, STEENWYCK, and MURILLO; and over the doors and windows are some beautiful specimens of modern stained glass.

We pass from this room into the Lancaster Gallery. This is a long and narrow apartment, with a beautiful vaulted roof. The recesses corresponding with the western windows, are fitted up with some very extraordinary pieces of ancient china; and the walls are covered with paintings and enamels, and illuminated drawings. The general effect of this gallery is extremely beautiful. It has not the imposing splendor of the magnificent rooms below, but it is equally elegant and tasteful, and equally different from the arrangement of ordinary mansions.

At the extremity of the Lancaster Gallery is the State Bedroom. We have no great relish for state beds; for the very idea of sleep seems to us alien from pomp and display: –

> Why rather, sleep, liest thou in smoky cribs,
> Upon uneasy pallets stretching thee,
> And hush'd with buzzing night-flies to thy slumber:
> Than in the perfum'd chambers of the great,
> Under the canopies of costly state,
> And lull'd with sounds of sweetest melody.

The ceiling of this room is particularly chaste and beautiful. It is a perfect specimen of the domestic architecture of the 16th century. Round the cornice is a carved and painted frieze, composed of the porte-cullis and the white and red rose. There are several paintings in this room, of which the most curious is a portrait by JAMIESON, of the *Regent Murray*.

We return, as we are sure every visitor to Fonthill must have returned, with the most eager pleasure, to a minute view of EDWARD IIId's GALLERY. It is impossible to imagine an apartment possessing more of the grace and richness of splendid architecture, or more sumptuously adorned with every ornament that can give delight to a cultivated taste. The room is illuminated by seven lofty windows on the western side, whose top compartments are of brilliant painted glass. The draperies are of scarlet and purple, and being generally closed, they shed the richest light over the gorgeousness of the gallery, and harmonize in one brilliant view the splendid objects which meet the eye on every side. The roof is of carved oak, and the frieze of the gallery is hung with seventy-two achievements, painted with the most exquisite minuteness. The chimney-piece on the eastern side is an arch of alabaster, supported by columns, with vine-leaf capitals of delicate sculpture. Above the fire-piece is a whole-length portrait of King Edward III, copied with great correctness and effect by Mr. Matthew Wyatt, from the celebrated picture in the Chapter-room of St. George's Windsor. On either side are very highly-finished portraits of John of Montford, Duke of Brittany, the Constable Montmorenci, Henry VII, Edward IV, and Alfonso, King of Naples.

The eastern side contains six recesses, corresponding with the opposite windows. These are filled with a part of Mr. Beckford's valuable library. It may be proper here to mention that St. Michael's Gallery and the adjoining YELLOW ROOMS are also the depositaries of these literary treasures. The books are not inclosed with glass, but their removal by the visitors is very judiciously prevented by a piece of brass wire longitudinally crossing each shelf. It was explained to us that this precaution was adopted in consequence of the larger portion of the volumes containing the most remarkable proofs of Mr. Beckford's industry. He is an indefatigable reader, and never studies without interspersing every book with his own observations. From a cursory inspection of the splendid exterior of these volumes, we should consider that few private libraries approach to the rarity and costliness of this collection.

Between the recesses of Edward IIId's Gallery, in which the books are contained, are placed six oak cabinets. These are of modern workmanship, and their rich carving at once displays the taste of their design, and the delicacy of their execution. They are surmounted by some very remarkable specimens of Oriental vases. It may be generally observed of this species of ornament, in which Fonthill is so rich, that the rarity and elegance of the porcelain is in many cases excelled by the singular beauty of the mountings. These display the utmost skill of the artist by whom they were modelled, whilst they add a richness and finish to the vases, which at once proclaims the taste of their possessor.

The middle of this apartment presents a feast for an almost inexhaustible curiosity. A number of tables, stands, and cabinets, are here arranged, crowded with the most rare and attractive objects. The eye is first charmed by the magnificence of a table of very large dimensions, whose top is formed of variegated marbles and precious stones disposed with the most symmetrical beauty. This was formerly in the Borghese Palace. There are several other tables of ebony, and some toilette tables whose burnished surfaces show like solid gold. Upon these are placed many of the gems of art which Mr. Beckford has collected during an industrious life. Here are drinking cups carved in ivory by the great artists of Rome and Florence; Nautilus shells, mounted upon the richest stands, and beautifully engraved with mythological subjects; cups of rock chrystal and agate; gold-japan basins and coffers; and a bottle of sea-green china, the earliest known specimen of porcelain introduced into Europe. We of course can only glance at the most remarkable of these rarities. They afford to the artist and connoisseur objects full of interest and instruction. We may be here allowed to express our satisfaction that the final disposal of the Abbey, with all its appurtenances, to an individual of immense fortune will prevent their dispersion. Two or three of them are enough to give value to any collection; – the possession of the whole, we think, imposes upon the gentleman, who has had the good fortune to secure them, the obligation to render them subservient to the progress of the arts in this country.

Folding doors of plate glass divide KING EDWARD'S GALLERY from the OCTAGON on one side, and from the VAULTED GALLERY on the other. This last mentioned apartment presents a singular and harmonious contrast to the splendour of that we have just quitted. It is without external windows, but a glimmering light is received through six perforated bronze doors, modelled after those in Henry the Seventh's Chapel, in Westminster Abbey. This gallery is wainscotted with oak, and ribbed with deep mouldings, partly gilt, and partly coloured. The sculptured frieze is hung with 36 achievements.

[271]

We ascend one step to the ORATORY. It is difficult to conceive, that so splendid an apartment can be intended for purposes of devotion. It is formed of five sides of an octagon. The ceiling is most beautifully groined and gilt; and its shape is determined by the elaborate fan-work springing from the columns of each compartment. A lancet window on each side, of the most elegant proportion, admits the light through painted glass. The place of the Altar is at present unoccupied; but under each window is a coffer of cedar, whose exterior is covered with the richest burnished gold. We have already noticed the enchanting effect of the view from the ORATORY.

We retrace our steps through these splendid apartments; and passing through the OCTAGON to the southern arch, enter ST. MICHAEL'S GALLERY. The visitor will be first struck with the richness of the vaulted ceiling. Its general arrangement is very like that of St. George's Chapel at Windsor, but as the work is smaller, it is also much richer. At the southern extremity of the gallery is an oriel window of the finest plate-glass. Nothing can be more beautiful than the view which it offers. The eye, satiated with the brilliant colouring of the interior, ranges with delight over the opposite glade, and rests upon the russet hills which bound the distance. The upper part of this south oriel is of stained glass, representing four of the fathers of the church. The two eastern windows are also ornamented with stained glass by Eginton. The western side also contains five gothic windows hung with scarlet draperies, which produce the same beautiful effect of light as in King Edward's gallery. This apartment contains several cabinets filled with articles of vertu.

Passing to the West of the building by a pair of glass folding-doors we enter the YELLOW ROOMS. These two apartments are so called from the yellow damask with which they are hung. They have a greater appearance of domestic comfort than any through which we have wandered; their ornaments being confined to the splendid library, and two or three cabinets of excellent workmanship. One of these is, perhaps, as great a curiosity as any which Fonthill contains. It is of carved pear-tree, of the time of Henry VIII and is said to be from a design of Holbein.

To the north of the yellow rooms in one of the octagon towers is a small CABINET ROOM, most exquisitely finished, and filled with remarkable specimens of antique jewelry.

There is nothing very singular in the BROWN PARLOUR below these rooms, except the unusual magnificence of the plate glass of the windows.

We have thus hurried our readers through a brief description of the principal apartments which have been lately shown at Fonthill. The hustle and anxiety which this remarkable exhibition created have now entirely ceased; and it is probable that the Abbey may still be destined to administer delight to the solitary pride of unbounded wealth. As the creation of one master-genius, this edifice and its surrounding scenery may be considered among the most remarkable objects in England. They have grown, as it were, out of a desert, by the magnificence and taste of one man. Whatever be his eccentricities, it is undeniable that, whilst he has gratified his own love of splendour, he has largely administered to the happiness of his numerous dependants. His taste has furnished active employ to an immense number of artizans; his riches have enabled him to be the most kind and considerate landlord to a large tenantry; and his singular benevolence has cherished, not only the poor of his immense domain, but has extended itself towards every living creature who there sought a shelter, for it is a remarkable fact, that Mr. Beckford never suffered a quadruped or a bird to be disturbed in his plantations, and that the very dogs which constantly followed him were so trained to obey their master's humanity, that a hare might cross their path without fear of molestation.

EDITOR'S NOTE *The Guardian* [London], 25 August, p. 269; 8 September, p. 287; 15 September, p. 294; 22 September, p. 301; 29 September, p. 309; 13 October 1822, p. 325. The identification of Knight as the author of this article is based on John Britton's note that 'in five succeeding numbers of '*The Guardian*' was a series of essays by its eloquent editor, who has since devoted his powerful talents to '*The Quarterly Magazine*'. See Britton, p. 16. Knight was editor and part-proprietor of *The Guardian*, a London weekly devoted to politics and literature, from 1820 to 1822. In 1823 he founded and edited *Knight's Quarterly Magazine*, which continued publication until 1824, and in which he authored, under a pseudonym, another original essay on Beckford and Fonthill. See Charles Pendragon, 'An Unpublished Episode of Vathek', *Knight's Quarterly Magazine*, I (July, 1823), pp. 294–301 and 309–14.

The Fonthill Fever

[THOMAS F. DIBDIN]

I AM just returned from the Abbey, Mr. Editor: in as high a state of FEVER as when I was pacing about its lantern and corridores. I perceive you have favored the public with one or two communications on the subject; but rather in the shape of an historical memoir, than of a journal from a spectator of its contents. Mr. Britton will doubtless, in his forthcoming work on this far-famed Abbey, give us all that we want to know respecting its architectural splendor; and, allow me to say, its architectural caprices and defects. On the present occasion, however, I will have nothing to do with snarling criticism. I hate it, although it be in many respects the fashion of the day. – I left town with two good fellows in the character of friends, on purpose to be gratified; and I have returned from the trip abundantly amused and delighted.

Our first object was *Salisbury Cathedral* which I saw for the first time; and which; is rather an unfortunate object to see as an introduction to Fonthill Abbey. The rule should be from little to big: from inferior to superior art: as what is the Shreckerhorn after Mont Blanc?– and what is St. Paul's after St. Peter's? But is not this *snarling?* I will go back to Salisbury where, on our arrival, every body seemed to be quite mad; perfectly, out of their senses. The FEVER raged without control. Bells ringing, landlady screaming, ostlers cursing, and ladies and gentlemen bewildered in their several movements. Chaises, carts, post-horses, cart-horses, gigs, and even light waggons, all put into a state of requisition. We go to Brodie and Dowding's, purchase our tickets, and a Guide as well as a Catalogue. All in confusion. Gentlemen talking, ladies laughing (exceedingly rude!) and little boys running their greasy little heads against you. 'This is our eighty-second ticket for to-morrow,' exclaims Mr. Dowding! 'So much the better for *certain folks*' replies Mrs.– 'Come, Madam, let us have no slander. ...'

We had now, in short, the most palpable and melancholy proofs of the ravages of the FONTHILL FEVER. Up hill and down hill, by cross roads and roads direct, every body was cutting and slashing, or posting, or pushing along on foot. A return from a review within 10 miles of London could scarcely have presented a more bustling scene. At length we near our head quarters: but it is growing dusk, yet not dusky enough to prevent a good view of the Abbey Tower – an octagon, of which the form is not the *most* correct, on Gothic principles, (though Ely Cathedral will be quoted against me) and of which the pinnacles are small and poor.

Crowds increase – dogs, horses, men, women, and children, present themselves in more rapid and thickening groups, as we draw up to the *Lamb Inn*. 'The name of your party, Gentlemen,' said a young lady habited in black silk, as our post-chaise stopt at the door – 'Bassanios, my fair one,' – exclaimed the gentleman, so called. ''Tis well (she replies): you will drive to the *Angel*, over the way where beds are prepared for you. We are here running over, even at the garret windows.' Away we drive to the Angel. ...

After a day of wind and rain, how bright and beautiful shines the sun of the morrow! So it was with us. We were stirring betimes; and had scarcely put our heads out of window when we saw all in motion for the Abbey. Carts, buggies, tilburies, post-chaises, carriages, and barouches: every thing was in requisition. All bespoke symptoms of THE FEVER, in a tenfold force. It was here, indeed, (*Hindon*) that it might be said to rage with nearly as much fury as within the Abbey. We call to the ostler to 'make ready!' and after swallowing our breakfast with a most imprudent voracity, at the hazard of a scalded mouth and an overcharged abdomen, we are 'off for the Abbey!' Whips crack, horses' hoofs rattle, wheels whiz round with increasing celerity, and villagers stand and stare with open-mouthed astonishment. It is all jollity, uproar, and *étourderie* of the very drollest description.

We approached the isolated outer gate – very ugly, though doctored by Inigo Jones – with all the pride and triumph of connoisseurship. The grounds opened on us, as we advanced; like a coy beauty, unwilling to show all her charms at the first gaze. The water is beautiful in form, and abundant in quantity. Above it are wooded heights – and I should say *expansiveness* was the chief character of the scenery as we continued to mount them; while, to the right, were luxuriantly wooded knolls, the summits of which were streaked with the warm and varying tints of autumn. Above them, rose the tower of the Abbey – grand, majestic, and imposing. The greensward is rich and well kept; while groups of boy-beggars, and eke of female beggars, stand, or run by the side of your carriage, intreating, your *petite charité*!

We now got pretty closely wedged among the thickest of the throng. The road became very precipitous: but 'mortalibus nil arduum est.' The poor horses of some poorer vehicles are flogged without intermission or mercy; while those visiters, whose coursers are of braver mettle, smile with a wicked triumph as they give them the 'go-by'. A red stage-coach (reminding us of those choice vehicles called Hammersmith and Turnham Green stages) is seen before us; stuck fast, or rather retro-grading, just where the road rises at an angle of 39 degrees and a half. 'Merciful heavens!' exclaimed Bassanio – 'a stage-coach in the grounds of Fonthill!' 'There have been more whimsical revolutions than this,' answered Vecelli, as we gained on it. The capital letters inscribed on the back, informed us that it was *The Salisbury Accommodation Coach.* Accommodation, with a vengeance! The passengers on the outside were dismounted; those within were screaming with apprehension – thrusting their heads out of the windows, with countenances indicative of the most deadly impending danger. 'Make way – we must pass' said the postboy of the carriage before us. No mercy, nor pity, nor sympathy. We treat these poor creatures as we did the little idle rogues and va-gabonds just mentioned, and like the obdurate lady Baussiere (as Sterne, or rather Burton, says) we 'ride on'. And now, not only the tower, but the body of the Abbey, bursts on our longing sight. As I have locked up all my critical memoranda on the style of the architecture in a small green morocco trunk, which has been unaccountably lost on the road, I cannot trust, either to my memory or unaided researches on this subject, to make you, Mr. Editor, acquainted with the same. Let them therefore pass.

Yet, before we enter the Abbey, allow me to say that the grounds on all sides presented a picture of rich, and bold, and varied scenery. Here, one would think that Charlemagne and his 'four sons' together with all his knights, pursuivants, and attendants, might have hunted the stricken deer from sun-rise to moon-rise: the valleys echoing to their shouts, and the hills thickly studded by the huntsmen! Even a good Roncesvalles battle might be fought within the *chevaux-de-frise* fence of Fonthill Park. But away with fiction. The *reality* of the sight could not have been improved. As we gallopped along the dressed greensward, within 50 yards of the mansion, we perceived (thus early!) at least three score of carriages drawn up in precise array, the horses being taken from them: while, behind, the train of carriages, of every description – including even the *red stage-coach* – seemed interminable. We alighted, showed our passports, in the shape of tickets, brandished our pink-covered catalogues, and moved *selon les règles* into the first show-room.

Sir, I beg leave to inform you, before I say another word on the subject, that we were all three downright angry, as well as disappointed, at the mode of entrance. 'Tis mean and impolitic. First impressions, whether in love or architecture, are three fourths of the thing! Judge therefore of our indignation, as well as surprise, on finding ourselves admitted to a mere common room – crowded with common china, and vestments, tunics, and draperies, of all manner of hues. The entrance of every visitor should doubtless be in front of the hall, where the huge folding doors, full 33 feet high, are made to open with almost the same ease and celerity as a certain great poet has described certain portals of Elysium to open. *This* should be the spot for the first grand *coup d'oeil*: and a *coup d'oeil* to be effective, should be instantly accessible – and not cut up by an artificial approach. But first, of these doors. 'Omne ignotum pro magnifico.' I had heard them described as being 60 feet high; and that each of the principal hinges, on which they turn, was not only 6 feet high, but had cost the owner of Fonthill £500! Nothing too silly and absurd for the credulity of *Master Johnny*!

Instead of the proposed entrance, you make one or two *détours*, and come to the bottom of a staircase, which occupies about a third of the hall – which is 78 feet high, 68 long, and 28 wide. It should have been 100 feet long, and 40 feet wide. The steps to the floor of the lantern, or great octagon, intrude too much, for the present dimensions: and I will further add, without offence (I hope) to the ghost of Mr. J. Wyatt, that the first lancet-shaped arch, seen from the folding doors of the entrance, is very much too lofty for its width. It is reduced to a *slit*. True it is, that there are arches of the same height within, as forming the sides of the octagon: but, as these arches are not *open* from top to bottom, and are relieved by a smaller arch, through which you pass to the respective portions of the Abbey, the effect is by no means bad. The lanky lancet arch, of which I speak, looks like a *fissure*. A truce now to architectural criticism; for, without having access to the aforesaid green morocco trunk (irreparably lost, I fear!) it would be impossible to anatomise with the dexterity necessary for the occasion. The height of this lantern is 128 feet from the ground.

We had no sooner entered, and looked on all sides – charmed by the novelty and splendor, and variety and bustle of the scene – figures gliding here, reposing there, intent on minute examination in a third place, and puzzled what to make of what they see, in a fourth place – when I observed a young man, abstracted from every thing around him, closely occupied in making a drawing of the hall looking westward, with an out-of-door prospect in the back-ground. 'Will you allow us Sir – for one minute only!' 'Readily, gentlemen; look as long as you please.' 'Very charming – and may we ask for what, or for whom, this drawing is made?' For Mr. Britton,[1] gentlemen.' 'Ah, that rogue of a Britton is always drawing the sovereigns out of my green silk purse: he *has* me again, I protest' – exclaimed Vecelli. The drawing was, without puff direct or indirect, very beautiful.

And now commenced the pleasurable toil of examination. Which way should we turn? On one side are cabinets filled with china, agates, onyxes, and cases of books – between which are gothic windows, veiled in part by scarlet and purple curtains; and through the former of which the sun-beams play along the splendid corridore: – on the other side are sculptures, ivory cups, verd-antique and mamillated onyx tables, japan boxes, cups and utensils, of a quality which sets all rivalry at defiance. In front appears the crimson lining of a room thickly studded with pictures. Which way, therefore, should we turn? To the right: where we see so much that is novel, and curious, and costly, to admire – in the way of china and agates, 'jasper and sardine stones', that even the tallest copies of the tallest and shortest books, though alternately coated in the vellum of Luchmans, and in the Morocco of Charles Lewis have no charms for our hungry eyes and appetites. To particularise would be to rewrite the contents of the pink-covered catalogue. In this corridore, after seeing the sweetest forms and qualities of china and agates, we are rivetted before the '*Bottle of pale sea-green Oriental China*—the earliest known specimen of Porcelain introduced from China into Europe.' The form is even elegant, and the ornaments singularly characteristic: and, as we were afterwards shown a delicately pencilled drawing of this vase, by the same accomplished artist whom we met on the floor of the octagon, I do, in all humility, recommend

1 Mr. Britton has already a RIVAL in the field: – a Mr. Rutter, of Shaftesbury; bred up in the school of George Fox: but is this flirtation with the fine arts according to the rules of his order? [George Cattermole did the sketch of this scene for Britton; Gastineau then worked up the final drawing; it was then engraved by R. Sands. RJG]

that gentleman, who takes so many sovereigns out of my friend's pocket, to introduce this vase as a sparkling vignette into his meditated work.

My friends are running away – almost to prostrate themselves before the *Japanese Idol Amida,* who has slouched ears, and encumbering drapery. I follow them instinctively; and we are all struck with amazement, not at the beauty, but at the quality, of this female. She is lighter than a feather, and about 2 feet high. You may put her into your breeches – or rather trunk hose – pocket, and scarcely fancy that you have an additional half-crown about you. The arabesque borders of the drapery of this figure merit the commendation they have received in the catalogue. This lady is made, indeed, 'of the most exquisite Japan lacquer, on wood of an olive color': I am not sure whether the two articles just mentioned be not among the most extraordinary UNIQUES in the collection. We turn to the right – pass through two comfortable and moderate sized rooms, lined with yellow satin, and fail not to notice *the Cabinet,* of which Hans Holbein is said to have furnished the designs for the carving: the whole as fresh as if it had just left the artist's hands. In such a cabinet, who would not wish to put their Greek and English coins? Your Timoleons, Othos, Edward III's, Elizabeths, Oliver Cromwells, and Queen Annes – how doubly brilliant would they look, when drawn out of such receptacles!

A boudoir terminates this suite of apartments: and here is a delicious unaffected, yet brilliant little Persian cabinet; while above are some very old ivory diptychs! Sundry other singularities grace this highly-decorated retreat. We emerge again into the warm glow of the yellow rooms – where THE BOOKS make the chief display, and where I saw enough to keep a Roxburgher capering, in the most *tantalised* manner, for a good 20 minutes: for not a book can be taken down. They are barricadoed by brass rods and wires. The most sly and subtle thief could not dispossess a shelf of one volume. Yet it was *some* comfort to observe, from their *letterings,* what these books *were about*; and we saw sufficient to convince us that Grolier, Maioli, Diane de Poictiers, and De Thou, had taken up pretty snug quarters in this retreat. At any rate, it was a delightful reverse of the barbarous spectacle seen at Wilton. In retracing our steps, fresh beauties seemed to beam on us, and a series of hitherto unobserved curiosities to demand our closest attention. One of my friends (it was Julius) on a sudden was missing, – but on looking downwards, we saw him absorbed in silent extacy before two beautiful little silver-tipped china bottles, or vases. 'Look ye here' – said he – 'how modest, how sweet and interesting, appear these little jars, of the most perfect quality and color, in the midst of all the gorgeous and obtrusive objects by which they are surrounded! –

So shines a good deed in a naughty world!'

But... a sudden chill, or rather sadness approaching to melancholy, has shot through my heart. All this fairy palace is consigned over to ... There is to be NO SALE! The land is not to be enriched with the fructifying streams which were about to issue from this long locked-up reservoir. Is it so, Mr. Editor? ... And wherefore have the rich men and the wise men come from the east and the west, and the north and the south – to gaze on treasures, which they had fondly and perhaps rightly, conceived might be shortly their own? Wherefore was the kingdom agitated with the throes and throbs of VIRTU, from one extremity to the other? For my part, I am half heart-broken; having been locking up, for these last 4 months, all the little spare treasure I could muster, for the possession of that 'Idol' of my heart, *'Amida!'* For her, I have traversed deserts, and picked my way through bogs – while my friend Julius declares that he shall live and die inconsolable, unless he quaffs tokay out of the afore-mentioned 'silver-tipp'd China bottles'. Yet we live in a free country; and the reported *new* proprietor of the *Fonthill domain* may act as it seemeth best to him, in the retention, or disposal, of his recently acquired property. It seems to me, Mr. Editor, that some of the Morning Papers have most rudely and ungenerously described his figure and habits. Let him be old or young, tall or short, rich or poor, I contend that he has shown *game*; and I do not yet despair of embracing Amida, and finding her consigned to me from the courteous arms of Mr. Christie: who, I think, between ourselves, was BORN for the dispersion of the Fonthill effects, beneath magic of his well-managed sceptre.

When a man finds himself in the midst of all sorts of marvellous works of art – curious, precious, costly, uncommon, and of exquisite finish – he naturally rubs his eyes, and looks about him again and again, to see and be convinced whether the objects before him be real or imaginary? Whether this kind of 'day-dream' be like a 'night-dream'? Whether he be living in the land of his fathers, or in that of giants, and fairies, and knights of romaunt lore? Something of this kind is attachable to the first view of the interior of Fonthill Abbey; but as I have already described a material portion of it, I need not dwell on generals, but on particulars. Let us turn to the left or, in other words, to that corridore, in the centre of which is the *famous mamillated onyx table* – reflecting all hues from its surface – studded with the stars of night – replete with rare and precious specimens of lapis lazuli, onyx, agate, jasper, and breccia – and once the chief ornament of the Borghese Palace! The stand, the work of a living, ingenious, and modest artist, is of oak, well carved, but it is too homely, too simple, and too solid. A stand to such a piece of furniture, fit only for Cardinals and Queens to eat pine-apples and to loll on, should be made of ebony, richly orna-mented with gold. Solid oak, with such unobtrusive decoration, belongs to King Arthur's Round Table.

Near this blazing sun of furniture stands an exquisite *Cup, Cover, and Stem of Ivory,* curiously carved all over by *Magnus Berg.* Well may the artist be called *Magnus!* Here are dogs, nymphs, Diana, and wild boars; now in chase, now reposing, and now banqueting. A master-piece of art. I love it because it is not choked with innumerable unmeaning little pieces of ornament, which show more skill and perse-verance than sense or taste. Yonder tall ostrich-like looking jars, of a pale greenish hue, and mounted each on a cabinet, please my eye prodi-giously. They should stand centinels at the entrance of a green-house, cased in crystal, where nought but the fragrance of otto of roses, mingled with that of jessamine and mignonette, of perennial blossom, strikes the enraptured visitant. One can hardly conceive *too* profuse and luxuriant a *nature* to accompany such *art. As* to *potpourri* – whoever stuffs them with *this* ingredient should himself be stuffed with garlic for the remainder of his days!

In this apartment, or corridor, or gallery – call it what you please – are deposited the most precious specimens of JAPAN. I know not how it is, but I like not Japan. It has a dingy, black-a-moor, an uninteresting appearance to my eyes; and I hardly know one department of Virtù that requires so much, and such a peculiar training, or discipline, to compre-hend its merits. But here is a magnificent gold Japan Bason and Cover, spotted with golden pins, which if I admire not, I suppose I must be anathematised by old worshippers of sooty furniture. Be it so, then. And yet I have a sort of fancy for a large square box of this species of furni-ture, which is described as having 'raised flowers and rocks on a ground sprinkled with gold'; and if I were to enact the part of *Iachimo, I* should like to pop out of such a box to gaze on the slumbering *Imogen.*

One is really 'cloyed with sweets', in the shape of all manner of splendid and out-of-the-way productions of china, crystal, ebony, ivory, and japan; and, like a surfeited child, I move on to the extremity, which is called a chapel. Wherefore, I could not discover. There was scarcely light enough to read the largest print in the largest prayer-book; while something like stained glass, a suspended lamp, and a marble pavement, tell you that it is, at any rate, a very *queer* place. Here poor Lady Hamilton is said to have played off many of her *freaks,* (among them, that of Agrippina carrying the ashes of her husband,) when Lord Nelson's heroic spirit lighted up this gloomy recess some 20 years ago.

At the risk of breaking your nose by not seeing a step, you retreat; and my friends were as glad to retreat as myself. We now moved slowly on, with an increased rush of visitors, towards the drawing-room which contains the PICTURES; and here indeed we were most exceedingly delighted. My friend Julius rushed to the armoire, about 8 feet high, which faces you on entrance; for here sparkled the HUNGARIAN TOPAZ – the largest known – set in precious stones of all the colors of the rainbow and moulded in its present graceful form by the unrivalled hand of Benvenuto Cellini. No hand *now* dares touch it, but that of the showman; who is very civil and very pains-taking. Of its worth, I will not pretend to form a notion, or venture a guess: but, be it what it may, and if dissolved pearls – more precious than that of Egypt's voluptuous Queen – have been quaffed out of it ... no matter for me! A sweeter object meets my eye, and calls forth my exclamations of rapture. 'A little on one side, Sir, if you please; only let me have an unobstructed view of yon *Salver of Limosin Enamel,* once the property of Diane de Poictiers, as a present from her royal lover. Thank you; I see it now perfectly.' Yet I doubt whether the central gilt piece, and the gilt border, be genuine. At least they have a very modern air. Oh, how I should covet the delightful occupation of carrying six melting peaches on this salver, to be accepted and eaten by * * * ! But the days of chivalry are gone.

Well, what would you have, Mr. Editor, in the description of a drawing-room filled with PICTURES? The same objects, and the same strain of remark, belong to most drawing-rooms of a similar character. I look about, and admire much. The Leonardo da Vinci pleases me not. It is the subject of a boy, half length, with a toy in his hand. They call it *The Laughing Boy;* but the expression of pleasure is that of the vacant grin of a little idiot.[2] Again, I say, I like not this silly-looking child, but

2 *De Gustibus non,* &c. We know our friend's excellent taste; yet here we presume to differ from him – EDR.

prefer much *the Infant Savior,* by the same hand. I choose, however, to be sceptical on both subjects – as to their being by the pencil of Da Vinci; though I would not have avowed this scepticism on the top of the Tower, for fear of being precipitated below. Yet I may be wrong in the indulgence of it. There is a fine head of a young man, said to be by *Velasquez.* By whomsoever painted, 'tis a really fine, animated, vigorous, and intelligent countenance. I shall certainly leave a commission of three score sovereigns for this picture... if it be ever to be sold. See, what crowds rush in and rush out: there is no room for contemplation. But I am now before the *Berghem* – the larger picture by this master: and shall I whisper in your ear, Mr. Editor, that, although the learned (among whom, of course is my friend Vecelli) say the *smaller* picture is the more exquisite performance, yet give me this fine composition of men, women, cattle, water, shipping, castles, and forts – all beneath a sky of delicious tone and transparency. 'Tis the *Hungarian topaz,* in its way! The small Berghem has perhaps more admirers. It is fresh, brilliant, and even peculiar; for the cows are *dotted* over the green bank in meditating solos, and not grouped. However, the whole is as fresh as if Berghem had put the finishing touch to it only the day preceding the throwing open of the Abbey doors to the public.

Above is a fine *Ecce Homo,* by *Salario;* a little hard and Gothic, but a finely colored and impassioned picture. I must endeavor to secure this for my inner library, where are chiefly placed my theological tomes; nor shall 100 guineas take it from its *prospective* place of destination. Two small upright *Bassans* delight me much – very much; there is a thorough Titianic tone of coloring about them. The *Salvator Rosa* disappointed me; but the light is not favorable for it. Now I dare say there will be more hands and voices lifted up against me, if I venture to throw – even the smallest pebble – at the far-famed *Poulterer's Shop of Gerard Dow,* than if I had pocketed one of the pieces of family plate which blazes in an armoire to the left on entrance. My objection is to the features of the women, which, for Gerard Dow, are, I submit, somewhat hardly and coarsely executed. All the accessories are in the usual exquisite style of the master, and as the best part of 1000 guineas will, I confidently guess, be devoted to the purchase of this picture, I pass on – perhaps bewailing my poverty – and feast my eye on two precious 'little bits' (as they are called) of *Teniers.* The subjects are *Skittle Players.* I will have them for my boudoir, and peradventure 100 guineas a-piece will *fetch* them?

But what is yonder silvery little *morceau,* which, like the waning moon peeping over the tranquil waves of the Adriatic, catches and comforts my wearied eyes? 'Tis a specimen of the elder Mieris – *a Lady in a satin and fur cloak, feeding a parrot.* Well may it be called in the catalogue, 'a very rare and precious gem'. 'Look at this love of a picture,' exclaimed Julius - still, however, occasionally sighing, as he bethinks him of the silver-tipped china jars – 'I learn it cost its owner 400 guineas.' I sigh in turn, as I pass on – hopeless and desolate – for it is beyond the powers of my purse to obtain. Here are two *Vernets;* one, a storm, very vigorously and skilfully painted. *Bellini* here holds a powerful sway. Two portraits of Doges – that of Loredano very fine – convince us that the artist was one on whom Titian, in his earlier life, fixed a steady eye. He may be considered as the father of the Venetian school of painting. Now my eye wanders upwards and is fixed on *a Lady reading a Missal,* by *Lucas Van Leyden.* The [masses] do not vouchsafe it a look; but it touches my heart. So pure a specimen of this early and able master must be obtained, if possible; and an unoccupied Gothic niche, by the side of some stained glass, in my inner library, must surely become its resting-place – if a score and half of sovereigns can win the Lady over to me. But of early masters, there are few gems more perfect than *the Virgin,* by *Cima di Conegliano;* a most beautiful and scarce specimen of the master.

In different parts of the Abbey are several specimens of *Breughel* and *Rotenhaemer* (united) and *Van Balen:* the best of these, in my humble estimation, is that of the *Four Elements,* in the corridor leading to a bed-chamber, up stairs. The figures floating in the air are perfectly marvellous in execution. Our *West* has a brilliant sketch or study, of *A Grand Mass in the Interior of St. George's Chapel, at Windsor.* N. B. His small pictures are always the best. Nor let *Phillips* be passed over in silence, his *Ancient Kings of England,* in the mamillated onyx gallery, are executed in a soft and characteristic manner – so as to have the appearance of old paintings – after the best models in oil or stone of the originals: while in the drawing-room, his portrait of Mr. Beckford's daughter, the present Duchess of Hamilton, has nothing to fear – even from the Sir Joshua which faces it. The picture is rich, warm, and lady-like.

I hope the foregoing, Mr. Editor, will satisfy any reasonable reader of your Journal, respecting the *Pictures at Fonthill:* it being frankly observed, at the same time, that scarcely half of them have been noticed. To return, for the last time, to the Abbey. We now breathed the air at the top of one of the towers, about mid-way up the central tower; and saw groups of visiters pacing the lawn below, or visiting the marquees for refreshment. The sun was well out, and every thing around wore the aspect of luxuriance and cheerfulness. The view of the grounds was necessarily grand and uninterrupted. On descending, we all instinctively confessed our fatigue; and on gaining a couch, I had well nigh closed my eyes, and dreamt of what had passed before me as a vision – but the exclamation of Julius over his silver-tipped little china jars – of which he was taking a fond and final leave – roused me from my sleepy fit. I started up, descended the flight of steps by which we had entered, found the post-chaise at the door – and, on stepping in, we gave the word for 'Stourhead'. In 15 minutes we were beyond the boundaries of the Park, having returned by a different route. Let me breathe a little, Mr. Editor, before I give you a sketch of the beauties of this latter place; and consider me, in the interim, yours &c. C. T.

P. S. 'Fiat justitia ruat coelum.' Methinks I have wronged Mr. Rutter. Let him go on with his intended work on the Abbey, in spite of the statutes of *George Fox*. His Guide is a spirited little earnest of his future efforts: and the plate prefixed to it, as well as the book itself, 'has sold like lightning'. If the vendition of 5000 copies be not *something* 'like lightning', I know not what is. And besides rivalry is a good thing in the fine arts. What has a *Briton* to fear?

As we turned our backs on Fonthill, in the way to STOURHEAD, we began to reason about the propriety of calling a domestic residence an ABBEY. Surely, unless all the pages of Dugdale, Du Fresne, and Wachter are incorrect, an abbey is a building exclusively appropriated to religious uses. The Abbot, if you please, has a mansion hard by; as the parsonage house is close to the church; but you may as well call the parsonage house a church, as a residence like Mr. Beckford's an Abbey. To be sure, we have, mixed up in this building, a suite of apartments called the *Abbot's-house;* but, did ever Abbot's house contain such furniture as we see in the *Abbotry* at Fonthill? The Abbots of old would have been anathematised and excommunicated, 'by bell, book, and candle', had they ventured to introduce such gay and comical things as we notice at Fonthill.

I am afraid, Mr. Editor, you will think that we started for Stourhead in a very crusty mood, and by no means sensible of, or thankful for, the wonders we had seen in the edifice then at our backs: but no – very much otherwise, I assure you. Only it is fair and even fitting, that when a man has expended the best part of half a million in the erection of a building on which he must, in his heart, challenge the critical observations of every person of taste, real or pretended, every such person should exercise his opinions with freedom and integrity. And seriously speaking, I should call the whole structure a *solecism,* from beginning to end – as to its present object: for who would like to sleep 100 feet aloft, in a tower rocking to the wind, or, at any rate, apart from immediate domestic attendance in case of illness? The best, or most natural inhabitants of a tower, are a good peal of bells; and I own that I should like to have heard the sounds of this tintinnabulous music, increasing, or dying, in the gale, as we receded from the Abbey... .

I should ... observe, Mr. Editor, that the live long day, Sir Richard [Colt Hoare]'s house exhibited symptoms of the FONTHILL FEVER – as parties, coming from thence, were in constant succession of arrival and retreat. The whole country seemed to feel, in a *social* degree, what the earth would, in a *physical* degree, if a slight shock of an earthquake had agitated it. Across the country, in all directions, for some 50 miles, parties were in a perpetual state of locomotion. ...

My story, or rather history, of the FONTHILL FEVER is now at an end. We reached Bath the same evening ... every horse engaged for the Abbey – and at six the next morning we started for the metropolis; where, thanks to the incomparable travelling in this country, we arrived at the same hour in the evening, in time to sit down to a Maintenon cutlet at Jacquier's in Bond St. The Marquis and Sir Richard were our first toasts. But I have done.

Your servant, CUTHBERT TONSTALL

EDITOR'S NOTE Published in a series of six articles in *The Museum, or Record of Literature, Fine Arts, Science, Antiquities, the Drama, etc.,* 5 October 1822, pp. 379–80; 12 October, pp. 393–5; 19 October, pp. 410–12; 26 October, pp. 428–30; 2 November, pp. 441–2; 9 November, pp. 455–6. Author attribution based on Britton, p. 15 ('written by the lively and versatile pen of the learned author of several volumes on bibliography and bibliomania; and who, by his writings on the latter subject, has contributed more to increase than to cure the disease'). Furthermore a piece on Stourhead extracted from this extended review appeared under the pseudonym Cuthbert Tonstall in *The Gentleman's*

Magazine, XCII, pt. 2, (1822), pp. 388–91. The Nichols file indicates that Tonstall was Dibdin. See Kuist, p. 56. Thomas Frognall Dibdin (1776–1847), prominent bibliographer of this period and original member of the Roxburghe Club, paid little attention to Beckford as a collector in his published works except for this series of articles. Beckford himself, was critical of Dibdin, viewed him as an antagonist at London book sales and frequently referred to him derisively as 'Puppy Dibdin'.

Candid Critique on the Architecture
of Fonthill Abbey

W[ILLIAM] G[ARBETT]

The curiosity so long and so ardently excited by the unexampled exclusion, not only of strangers, but of almost every individual (not employed in its construction) from inspecting the edifice called Fonthill Abbey is at length in part satisfied.

Amongst the multitude of persons so suddenly admitted to gaze upon this novel and extensive structure, with its precious contents and surrounding beauties, it is natural to expect that by far the greater number will view the varied scene with enthusiastic delight, while others will express a more qualified degree of approbation, and some an affectation of indifference. We are accordingly prepared to hear many 'applaud with fashion pomp of phrase'; but when we find panegyric heightened into bombast, and *'a descriptive Guide'* spun into a political disquisition, we are involuntarily led to suspect that even Books may be *'made to sell'*.

It is truly curious to observe expression of different opinions and different feelings upon this subject, which is now become a public theme; some who consider the design and its accomplishment as the *acme* of perfection, are disposed to divide the merit between the taste of the proprietor and the skill of the architect; some are anxious to impress the idea that the whole design was digested and arranged before the unfortunate decease of the late Mr. Wyatt, and that the execution of the whole has since been conducted by his original plans; while others not entertaining so exalted an opinion of this extraordinary effort of munificence, taste, and skill, are disposed to believe that a more perfect specimen of what is called 'Gothic Architecture' would have been produced if the late Mr. Wyatt had been allowed to form the design upon his own judgment. But however this may be, and without noticing in this place the hackneyed observation, that the styles of various periods are indiscriminately blended together, it may be proper to observe, that the legitimate object of criticism, is to improve the future, rather than to cast ill-natured censure upon the past; and that the venial errors of taste should not be visited with the severity necessarily tolerated in the reprehension of immorality or vice. If we view the edifice in question under the guidance of this principle, although we may find some essential errors, we may also find some real beauties, even in parts which pseudo-critics may condemn, as deviations from their abstract notions of correct and congruous style. To elucidate this observation, we may refer to the lofty Western Portal, which, whether viewed from without, or from the floor of the Hall, may with some propriety be considered disproportionately high; but view it from the floor of the Octagon, and it will be found that any diminution of its height would destroy one of the finest effects produced on this stately edifice, and it will then be acknowledged that the ease with which the ponderous doors are said to turn on their hinges is not the only merit to be ascribed to them. It may also be said that the arches of the Octagon are too acutely pointed for the style proposed to be adopted in the edifice; but here I may be answered, that the piers supporting the Tower, being evidently elevated to the utmost admissible proportion, the acute shape of the arches rising from them will, in the eyes of those who prefer pleasing forms to fancied rules, appear a beauty rather than a defect. Another charge of mixture of style may probably be founded upon the absence of mullions and tracery in the windows of the Octagon; here the *cavilling* critic may be told, that the introduction of those members would not only have diminished the quantity of light necessary for that spacious apartment but would have prevented the simple arrangement of the stained glass, to which it owes so much of its serenely splendid effect; and here the judicious critic will be inclined to admit, that the architect was not insensible of 'a grace surpassing rule and order'. It has been fashionable to accuse the late Mr. Wyatt of disregard of uniform style in the several buildings erected by him, in imitation of those of the middle ages, an accusation which would not be so flippantly made, if many who assume the office of censors had the penetration to discover or the candour to acknowledge, that most of the edifices remaining as models of the ancient style exhibit in themselves the very varieties of which they complain. They may also recollect that the revival ancient art has in every former instance been accomplished by progressive

steps: the characteristic elegancies of the Grecian style were not transferred to imperial Rome in their native perfection, nor was the revival
of classical architecture in Europe, after ages of desolation, suddenly
effected; for we have seen in our own time structures denominated
Doric, bedecked with Corinthian foliage, without producing the
squeamish sensations now effected upon seeing combinations far less
anomalous.

The impartial observer must, however, admit that the architecture of
Fonthill Abbey is not without its faults, though some of them are
evidently attributable to expansion of ideas after the formation of the
original design, which was probably intended to consist of little more
than the octagonal Tower; for, if the erection of the Hall or Western
limb of the edifice had been originally contemplated, it is difficult to
conceive that the plan of the Octagon would have been so confined at
the base, that the extent of its side should be less than the span of the
Hall, which latter member being in this instance no more than a
spacious porch, should, by every rule of symmetry in architectural
composition and natural reason, appear inferior to the principal structure. A proportionate increase of the lower stories of the Octagon, or
rather of the thickness of its walls, would have given to the general
mass the ostensible and real solidity which at present it seems to
require; and in the spaces thus obtained, staircases might have been
contrived without resorting to so many turrets for those purposes,
which, however they may add to picturesque effect, may be questionable as objects of intrinsic beauty in design. Such an arrangement
would also have afforded space for a more commodious gallery and
useful apartments, on the level of the rooms called 'the Nunneries', as
well as have formed the foundation of flying buttresses, to give elegant
and useful support to the Tower, which might then have been rendered
capable of supporting a spire elevated to the 'cloud-capt' height once
contemplated by the munificent Founder. Another sacrifice of rational
symmetry to picturesque effect is to be regretted in the want of height
and width in the North and South limbs, or Galleries, more particularly
in the upper spaces within their roofs, and in the diminutive upper
windows. The gigantic part of the structure somewhat ambiguously
attached to the Eastern side of the Octagon is rather calculated to
diminish the effect of the other members than to give consistent dignity
to the whole; and in this point of view the want of magnitude in the
base of the Octagon is most sensibly felt as a defect. The three South

windows of this Eastern limb are of dimensions and character so imposing, that if those features should not be recognized in a suitable apartment within the edifice, disappointment must ensue; and those who have duly observed the manner in which Hawksmoor contrived at All Souls College, Oxford, to unite with the spacious and decided outline of his windows the indication of internal arrangement, will regret that an example so judicious has not been followed in the instance now under consideration. But methinks I hear some fastidious critics exclaim, 'Hawksmoor's is mongrel Gothic!' Such persons may be told that although their great archetype Lord Orford has accused Hawksmoor of blundering into beauty in his design for All Souls, yet the expedient here alluded to is to be seen in a building of a period so pure that its adoption may be justified in the present discriminating age; or if (as perchance might have been the case) that example had not met the eye of Hawksmoor, then his use of it must be considered as a proof of his taste and ingenuity, rather than the effect of a blundering career.

But the design would have been still more complete if an apartment had been provided similar to an ancient Hall, appropriated to the hospitable purposes of the banquet; in such a room the windows might have been in reality what is promised by their exterior appearance.

It must also be regretted that members so characteristic as buttresses should be omitted both to the Western and Eastern limbs of the Edifice; to the former, which in reality, as well as in appearance, consists of one lofty room only, they should been considered as truly appropriate. When we view the extreme Eastern end, flanked as it is by turrets richly ornamented, we are unable to account for the absence of every species of ornament in the vast space between them; and when we elevate our eyes from this naked space, to the perforated parapets by which this and other parts of the edifice are surmounted, we cannot but consider those parapets as too light and undecided in their character to harmonize with the general tenor of the design.

If, without noticing some minor defects of details, we proceed to examine the interior of the principal apartments, we shall find that the arches terminating the Hall at either end are intersected by the timber arches of the roof in a manner not the most pleasing; and that the ribs of the corbels, or fans, supporting the lantern of the Octagon, have not the elegance of form or gracefulness of proportion by which many other parts of the interior are distinguished. It may, however, be observed, generally, that in this edifice, as in many of those erected in the middle ages, there may be traced a progression of improvement in style, with varied excellence of workmanship; and it appears highly probable that in this instance, the improvement of style was uniform, from the commencement of the vast and novel undertaking up to the period of the decease of the Architect who originally conducted it; and it is equally probable that, if the professional career of that ingenious individual had not been so suddenly and unfortunately terminated, this extensive work would not have been liable to some of the foregoing strictures.

In tracing this progression we shall find, that the interior of the Brown Parlour (which was probably the first apartment finished) partakes but little of the style professed to be adopted, and that the Westernmost of the two Yellow Rooms over it exhibit but little improvement; but when we come to the Hall, the Octagon, and the South and East Oriels, we find the style approximate much nearer to ancient models; the Lobbies to the Brown Parlour, the Green Cabinet Room, and the West and South Arcades, approach still nearer to perfection; and finally, the Galleries forming the library, combined with the Sanctuary and Oratory, merit the highest commendation, as well for general effect as for elegance of details.

In forming a candid opinion upon the whole, it should not be forgotten that the erection of this edifice was an effort to revive a style of architecture which there are strong reasons to believe was never practised under definite rules: commenced at a period when little progress had been made in producing correct graphic representations of buildings and ornamental details in the style called Gothic. The admirers of this style are, however, since that period, much indebted to the enthusiastic and indefatigable exertions of Mr. Britton, who has selected and presented to the public eye, in his 'Architectural' and 'Cathedral Antiquities', very many elegant specimens of the ingenuity and taste of our ancestors, which for correctness of drawing and effect of engraving, far surpass any preceding works of the same description, and have excited a degree of emulation that must lead to the development of data calculated to correct the taste of the Architectural Student.

It should also be recollected, that actual practice is much more necessary for the acquirement of a complete knowledge of this intricate subject than the mere study of doubtful theories.

There are probably architects of the present day who could erect a Gothic structure, of equal magnitude, with less faults than are to be found at Fonthill; if it were not so, the benefit of that experience, which might have been acquired in thirty years, would be lost; for within that period much more has been done towards the restoration of our ancient Ecclesiastical Edifices, than in the whole century preceding, and a disposition to cultivate a correct taste has been evinced.

It is, however, too frequently forgotten, that the improved conveniencies of modern times prevent in a great degree the adoption of ancient models, without incurring the charge of innovation. This was felt by Lord Orford himself at Strawberry Hill, of which he found it necessary to observe, that he did not wish to make his house so Gothic as to be unfit to live in; and this, it must be presumed, was felt by Mr. Beckford: it must therefore be pretty obvious, that the most fastidious architectural critic of the present age would be as little pleased to inhabit a mansion built after the exact model of one of the fourteenth century, as the most discontented political reformer would be with the precise constitution of the same period. When all these circumstances are duly considered, it must remain forever questionable, whether any other person would have conducted the same undertaking with greater success than the deceased Architect of Fonthill.

EDITOR'S NOTE *The Gentleman's Magazine*, XCII, pt. 2 (December, 1822), pp. 491–4. Author attribution comes from a clue left behind by John Britton. In his Preface to *Graphical and Literary Illustrations of Fonthill Abbey*, p. 16, he referred to a paper on the architecture of the Abbey that appeared in *The Gentleman's Magazine* as by 'the skilful architect attached to Winchester Cathedral'. William Garbett (c. 1770–1834) was surveyor to the Dean and Chapter of Winchester for twenty-five years and superintended the architectural repairs of Winchester Cathedral during the years 1812–28. He also wrote the account of the city of Winchester for Britton's *Picturesque Antiquities of English Cities* (1828–30). Britton, who was a friend of Garbett, shared this article in manuscript form with Beckford shortly before it was published: 'I enclose a few remarks on the Abbey written by my friend Garbett, an Architect of Winchester, & intended by him for Gents. Mag.' Copy of a letter to Beckford, 23 October 1822, Beinecke Library, Beckford Collection, GEN MSS. 102, Box 8, f. 181.

An Unpublished Episode of Vathek

[CHARLES KNIGHT]

The taste for tower-building, of which Vathek had set the example, became infectious in the country about Samarah. This monarch was at first indignant that his subjects should presume to copy his extravagances; but his vanity was stronger than his pride, and he left them in the quiet possession of their follies. His most ambitious rival was the merchant Bekfudi. The riches of this superb person were enormous. His caravans every year brought him silks and jewels that would have rivalled a princess's dowry, and the slaves that cultivated his groves of cinnamon might have formed the rear-guard of a sultan's army. He became dizzy with his wealth, and fancied that he was descended from the Assyrian kings; – though his grandfather had carried a basket in the streets of Bagdad.

Bekfudi had a handsome palace and extensive grounds; the hills and the valleys of a little province were his; a broad lake lingered in his groves of citrons and palms; and the apricots of his garden almost rivalled those which Vathek so prized from the isle of Kirmith. The ladies of his seraglio were as numerous and as beautiful as the harem of the grand vizier, and the other furniture of his palace was equally rare and costly. But Bekfudi began to be satiated with the pleasures and the magnificence of ordinary mortals: in an evil hour he pulled down his palace and sold his women. He built an impenetrable wall round his extensive gardens, and vowed to raise, upon the highest hill which this barrier enclosed, a palace upon a new fashion. Bekfudi had no violent reverence for the religion of his country; and he therefore considered it a sinless profanation to make his dwelling-place like a mosque, and his tower resembling a minaret, though he modestly proposed it to be only ten times higher than the minarets of Bagdad. It was the extravagance of his ambition which prompted him to shut out all the world till he should have finished his mosque; and when his tower rose above the highest pines of the neighbouring hills, he solaced himself with the hope that the peasants who gazed at an awful distance would believe that within its walls dwelt one of the sons of men, as powerful as the Genii, and as mysterious as the Dives.

Bekfudi possessed abundance of taste. His command of wealth enabled him to engross the rare productions of art which were sometimes too costly even for emirs to acquire; and he lavished his gold upon those who could best apply their talents to the excitement of his self-admiration. All the ornaments of his palace had reference to his ancestors; but though the artists, who recorded in fit emblems the mighty deeds of his progenitors, had an especial regard to truth, they sedulously avoided all allusion to the basket-bearer. In a word, the mosque was a very magnificent place. It was the handsomest monument that taste ever reared to pride; and though Bekfudi in his arrogance had tried to make his tower rival the dome of the great mosque at Damascus, and had only been stopped in his presumptuous aspirings by the equally insolent hurricane, which twice blew it down, – and though in his profaneness he had built his dormitories like the cells of the most pious santons, and had constructed studies and refectories after the models of sanctuaries and shrines, – still the palace was gorgeous and elegant, and such as no subject ever before raised in the dominions of the Commander of the Faithful.

Bekfudi went on for many moons building and embellishing his mosque, – heaping stones upon his tower till the uncivil blasts gave him hints where to stop, and hanging up new draperies of Persian silks till the limited art of the dyer forbade any further change. The superb merchant lived away in a round of selfish enjoyment; his slaves racked their inventions to prepare him viands of the most costly materials; and as his health would not allow him always to drink the red wine of Shiraz, he took care, under the fatal necessity of resorting to so common a beverage as water, to render it palatable by sending caravans and escorts to bring it from a fountain at a hundred leagues' distance.

The great Mahomet, who had commissioned the Genii to mature and then pull down the presumptuous darings of the caliph Vathek, also resolved to crush the ambition of the merchant Bekfudi. But as the pride and power of the mosque-builder were bounded by natural limits, it was unnecessary to work any miracles for his instruction. He lived on in his round of luxuries; and as his caravans came duly over the desert, and his ships were seldom lost upon the sea, he thought that the spices and the fruits of his fertile isles would last for ever. But there was a sudden change in the fashions of Samarah. The cooks began to make their comfits without cinnamon, and the green dates of their native plains came into request, to the exclusion of the dried fruits of our wealthy merchant. His spices and his figs lay rotting in his warehouses, and, for the first time in his life, he began to think that his mine of wealth was not inexhaustible.

Thirty moons had passed before Bekfudi ceased to pull down and build up the apartments of his mosque, or to send a hundred leagues for his water. The pastry-cooks were inexorable, and his own household even could not endure the flavour of cinnamon. He at length discharged his masons and his carpenters, and, as a great effort of economy, abridged his table of one of the fifty-two dishes with which it was daily covered. But all these privations were unavailing; Bekfudi was in debt, and his creditors would not wait for a change in the taste for spices. He resolved to invite all Samarah to see his mosque, and to purchase his curiosities. For three moons all Samarah went mad. Away ran the idle and the busy, to scramble up Bekfudi's tower, – to wander about his long galleries upon carpets from Cairo, – to touch his gold censors, or to pore upon his curious pictures. As to his books, Bekfudi carefully locked them up. He was a great commentator, and his relish for theological speculations led him to fear that his performances might introduce him to too close an acquaintance with the mufti and the cadi.

Amongst the mob who had been to see Bekfudi's tower, was a clever little Persian Jew, who had the reputation of being one of the most discreet dealers in Samarah. Did a courtier require a thousand piastres to bribe a judge, our little Jew would raise the sum in a moment, upon the pledge of the courtier's carbuncle; or did a lady of the seraglio desire a pound of gold dust to see an eunuch, our little Jew would furnish it upon the most moderate interest. His warehouses were full of the moveable treasures of all the great men of the palace, from the grand vizier to the principal mute; and everybody vowed that he was the honestest Jew in the world, and it was a great pity so useful and so clever a trader should be a dog of an infidel.

Bekfudi had a hatred of all Jews; but, nevertheless, our little factor contrived to approach him. 'He had come to proffer his services to the great merchant; he humbly proposed to purchase his matchless curiosities, and his magnificent furniture.' 'What! he, the giaour from Persia? he presume to offer a price for rarities that monarchs might covet?'

'Yes: and moreover, he would purchase his books and his paintings, his vessels of gold and of silver, his wine, his —.' The merchant was in a rage, and drove the Jew from his presence; but he quickly recalled him. 'Slave,' cried Bekfudi, 'I will hold a moment's parley with thee. How much wilt thou give for my topaz cup, and my goblet set with emeralds?' 'I will not purchase these alone,' said the Jew, 'but I will purchase thy lands, and thy mosque, and thy silken draperies, and thy woven carpets, and thy golden vessels, and thy jewels, and thy books, and thy pictures, and all that thy palace contains; and here, without, I have twenty dromedaries laden with four hundred thousand sequins, which shall be thine.' Bekfudi was in a rage, but the eloquence of the dromedaries prevailed; and that night the little Jew locked up the mosque with the airs of a master.

The mob from Samarah was soon dispersed; and Bekfudi prepared with many a sigh to leave a palace of which he had so long been the uncontrolled lord. The little Jew haunted him from gallery to gallery, and from the gloom of the sanctuary to the sunlight of the great lantern. With the most provoking malice he dwelt upon the beautiful proportions of this pavilion, and the magnificent furniture of that saloon; and swore that none of the monarchs of the world could rival the great merchant in taste and splendour. 'And what will you do with this unequalled palace?' said Bekfudi. 'I have bought it for a dealer in sulphur,' replied the Jew. The pride of Bekfudi was ground into the dust; but he was curious to see the rival of his wealth and the inheritor of his possessions. It was agreed that they should meet at dinner.

The hour came, and Bekfudi appeared in the grand saloon, attired in a splendid vest; the aigrette of his turban was composed of the largest diamonds, and the plume that it bore was from the wing of a bird of paradise. His delicate hands were washed with the choicest essences, and the perfumes of his garments plunged the senses into a languor which nothing but the excitements of the most exquisite viands could dissipate. He expected to have met, in the dealer in sulphur, a personage whose riches would have procured for him some of the refinements which belonged to the dealer in spices; but how was he humiliated when a miserable old man presented himself, as ugly as a *faquir* that had been doing penance for fifty years, wrapped round with a wretched robe of dirty cotton, and his head surmounted with a beastly turban, that all the waters of Rocnabad could never purify. The forehead of this captivating personage was covered with knots and wrinkles, his blear eyes twinkled in their little pursed-up sockets, his enormous mouth exhibited three teeth of the most delicious blackness, and his rheum was freely bestowed upon those whom the flavour of his breath did not keep at a respectful distance. Bekfudi shrieked, and shouted for his dwarf; but the obsequious Jew called in a loud voice for dinner, and the unhappy merchant was constrained by his politeness to take his seat at the board. The new possessor of the mosque was equally attractive in his diet; a ragout of garlic was served up for his especial pleasure; and as he dipped his grimy hands into the golden dish, Bekfudi would have fainted at the odour of the savoury steams, had not his faithful dwarf thrown the reviving attar over his forehead and forced a cup of sherbet down his throat. The mouth of the dealer in sulphur distended into an audible grin, and he pledged the dainty merchant in execrable brandy. Their conversation at length became interesting. The man of sulphur had a most agreeable collection of oaths; and as he swore by Solomon and Eblis, by the sacred camel and the dog of the seven sleepers, the man of spice perceived that he had a high reverence for the mysteries of theology; and a wonderful sympathy in this particular grew up between them. They embraced and parted; but Bekfudi never forgot the garlic.

The little Jew soon applied his master's purchase to good account. Within a week the superb merchant began to indulge a wish for the possession of some of his former most splendid baubles; he bethought him that his free habit of expressing his thoughts in the broad margins of his beautiful manuscripts might one day cause some awkward inquiries; and he was desirous of securing some pictures, of which he thought none but himself knew the peculiar value. He of the dirty hands was as ready to comply with these reasonable wishes, and Bekfudi began to think that his turban and his garlic might in time be endurable. The articles were selected, but the little Jew had yet to name the price. Bekfudi raved and tore his hair when a fourth of his four hundred thousand sequins were demanded for what had cost even him not a tenth of the sum. He raved and tore his hair; but the Jew and the sulphur-merchant were calm. Bekfudi had not yet learned to subject his desires to his circumstances; and two dromedaries marched off with their costly load.

The Jew and his merchant passed the winter very industriously. From his warehouses in Samarah, this active dealer brought all the glittering pledges which the misfortunes of his clients had left unredeemed; and he decorated the mosque, like a grand bazaar, with a great many new curiosities, and a great many rare commodities with fine names from the east and the west, which the artists of Samarah could manufacture as well as those of Persia or China. The little Jew knew where to find expert limners, who could imitate the paintings even of the celebrated Mani, so as to deceive the most critical eyes; clever copyists, that would transcribe the tales and poems of Arabia with a correctness that would enchant the most exquisite connoisseurs; and acute chemists, that would give to the secretly pressed grape-juice of the gardens of Bekfudi himself, the inimitable flavour of the wines of Shiraz or Kismische. The little Jew had, however, not quite so complete a judgment as the builder of the mosque, and he therefore committed a few mistakes with a very enterprising spirit. Amidst the solemn and subdued splendour of the sanctuary, upon which Bekfudi most prided himself, he hung up an enormous mirror which brought all the varied colours of the neighbouring galleries, and all the garishness of day, into the heart of its former deep and impressive gloom; and in the hall which the spice-merchant had dedicated to the worthies of his country, he stuck up the statue of one of the rebellious princes who had presumed to contend against the justice of the great Haroun al Raschid.

But the little Jew was yet a most deserving factor. All Samarah again flocked to the mosque with the great minaret; and all Samarah came this time with money in their vests, to purchase some relic of the magnificent Bekfudi. Every one was pleased, except the unhappy builder of the palace, for every one was agreeably relieved of his sequins at his own free-will. He alone writhed under the mortifications of his pride, and the outrages upon his taste. He stalked one day into the palace of his splendour, now metamorphosed into one large bazaar, and with a yell of fury he overthrew the statue of the foe of the caliph, and shivered into a thousand pieces the mirror which deformed the sanctuary. He then coolly paid the price which the Jew demanded, and retired to a humble dwelling without a minaret, to pass the remainder of his days in composing treatises on temperance and humility.

EDITOR'S NOTE *Knight's Quarterly Magazine*, I (July 1823), pp. 309–14. Knight (1791–1873), author and publisher, published this piece under the pseudonym Charles Pendragon. For Beckford's favourable reaction to this satire, see *The Consummate Collector*, ed.

R. J. Gemmett (Norwich: Michael Russell, 2000), p. 209. Knight was
the publisher of John Rutter's *Delineations of Fonthill and Its Abbey*
(1823) and had the occasion to visit the Abbey at Rutter's request. He
was accompanied by the artist Stedman Whitwell, who did some of the
drawings for the volume. Another contributor, the artist George Cattermole, was also in residence at the Abbey during the same time. Their
experience, as Knight described later, was somewhat unsettling: 'The
first night I was led by him [Harry Phillips] through a long corridor
apart from the saloons and galleries of this architectural marvel, and
was installed in a chamber of state, where the hangings of the bed were
of velvet, and the chairs were of ebony reputed to have belonged to
Wolsey. I sat in a reverie, moralizing upon the probable dispersion of
these splendid things, when I heard a whirr – my wax candle was
suddenly extinguished – the bat that had dwelt in the gorgeous
draperies was hovering about me. I was glad to creep into my downy
bed. But I could not sleep. ... There were others to whom sleep was that
night more difficult to be secured than to myself. Two or three adventurous artists – I think George Cattermole was of the number – elected
to lodge in the dormitories of the great tower, some hundred and fifty
feet above the floor from which it sprang. The wind rose; the storm
grew louder and louder; the frail structure rocked, as Gulliver's cage
rocked in the eagle's beak. The terrified guests rushed down the broad
stairs, and sat directly in the dark saloon till the daybreak gave them
assurance of safety.' Phillips also introduced Knight to the Fonthill
Library and invited Knight to transcribe any of Beckford's notes that he
left behind in the fly leaves, indicating that he had also extended a similar invitation to William Hazlitt. 'Something was whispered', Knight
wrote, 'about a new book, to be called 'Fly Leaves from Fonthill'. My
curiosity was roused, though I shrank from making profit by book or
article out of my notes. In truth, as far as I could trace, there was little in
these volumes to alarm their annotator or interest the public.' *Passages
of a Working Life During Half a Century* (London, 1864), I, pp.
309–12.

Knight republished 'An Episode of Vathek' in *Once Upon a Time*
(London, 1865), with the following interesting head note: 'In the Year
1822, the world went mad about Fonthill. Salisbury Plain became
populous, with May Fair and Cheapside travelling to see Mr. Beckford's wonders. No profane eyes had ever looked upon his towers and
pinnacles – his domes and galleries. There was mystery, then, to

combine with what was really worth seeing at Fonthill. Its exhibition and its auction produced as much excitement as a Crystal Palace upon a small scale. The towers of Fonthill are in the dust with its magnificent builder. They might have fallen, without a revival of my old recollections, had I not considered that the public curiosity to see their works of art was an anticipation of the feeling of a better period. The people saw nothing of Art in those days but the dingy Angerstein Gallery in Pall Mall; and the state-rooms of Hampton Court and Windsor, at a shilling a head for the showman. The nobility kept their pictures locked up; and Poets' Corner was inaccessible except to sixpences. Other days have come. Fonthill belongs to the Past.' (p. 506)

A Second Visit to Fonthill Abbey

ARTHUR M. TEMPLETON, JUN.

Here burst at once
Upon the astonish'd sight, the rarest spoils
Of Eastern mines, and of Peruvian ores;
The gold which Tagus in his waters rolls,
The shining sands of famed Pactolus, and
All precious metals, with more precious gems
Adorn'd; a world of wealth, a radiant heaven
Of matchless beauties!

Southampton, August 11th, 1823

YOU enquire, my dear PERCIVAL, if I yet remember last year's excursion to Fonthill? Most assuredly do I; and but, that your office may fairly employ half of the elves of Argus, and full two thirds of Briareus' hands, – that you are juvenile, – a bachelor, – and over head and ears in love, much should I marvel how the idea of my possibly forgetting it, could, by any chance, have impressed itself upon your mind. Why, my dear fellow, each minutest circumstance, each kind and particular companion, every little drawing out of friendship, and out-pouring of spirit, the speculations of fancy, the smiles of satisfaction from the lips and upon the cheeks of unaffected, unspoiled beauty, all, – even the very four quadrupeds which dragged our chariot wheels included, – that shared in and improved that delightful and satisfactory pilgrimage to the shrine of wonder and curiosity, are in my 'heart of hearts' remembered, and preserved. –

Imperishable; all enduring as the rock
Which morn and evening tides do beat against,
Lashing but not destroying. –

Thus satisfying you, Somerset, of the hold which the past still has and will maintain, upon me, I proceed, *currente calamo*, to advise you as briefly as I may, of my *this* year's visit to the same Temple of Enchantment, just previous to its being again thrown open to the inspection of that portion of the public who could, and would, part with their guineas for the favour. Of course I mean since it has been under the rule of a Farquhar, and the ministry of a Phillips: Christie having gone out of office when its former possessor, he, who was to the 'manner born', was compelled to quit that palace, and those domains, which, with such anxious and persevering solicitude, such acquired and natural taste, such gigantic and peculiar efforts, he had after so many years' tireless toil, reared, fashioned, and embellished; – it, alas! – only to witness the disorganization and dispersion of its wonders, and glories, into a thousand channels, and all its mighty congregation of curiosities and riches, scattered and parcelled out at the fall of the salesman's hammer. Fonthill, as connected with Mr. Beckford, is no more! and the great rival of Wiltshire's other wonder, Stonehenge, will hereafter lose half of its interest and its glory since it can no longer be associated in name with the author of '*Vathek*'.

In the observations which I was enabled to make at my late visit to the Abbey, and which for your delectation, – as you positively assure me, you cannot come down, I now repeat, – I shall, – except for sake of reference, – solely confine myself to the alterations which have been made, and the regulations adopted, since last September. For after the very spirited and correct account which you then gave in the NEW EUROPEAN, and which well merits a second perusal, it would be indeed a work of supererogation to attempt more.[1]

My visit to the Abbey being undertaken a little previous to doors being thrown open to general visitors, it may, therefore, be possible that my *Précis* may not tally to the very letter with the appearance it at this moment presents, as some changes and removals were subsequently made. Indeed, up to the very eve of exhibition, the whole of its embellishments were not entirely completed. One advantage, however, I then enjoyed, which later visitors could not so luxuriously revel in; I mean the perfect beauty and fragrance of the Abbey's gardens and grounds; which, we, last year, Perc[i]val, only saw in their season's dotage, for

1 Refers to the editor's article published the previous year: 'The Editor's Excursion to Fonthill Abbey', *New European Magazine*, I (October 1822), pp. 362–70. RJG

they had then scattered their foliage, and the colours at the shrine of Autumn, and the yellow leaves of decay were fast usurping the fresh hues of their vernal days of glory. At *my* visit, however, the bowers, as if culled from various Edens, were indeed

> perfumed with shrubs
> Of foreign growth, all speckled with bright flowers
> Of passing odorous scent. –

The giant oaks, and the stately firs, interspersed and variegated with the clustering laburnum and its beauteous rivals, were now indeed striking in array; and the glorious great Western Avenue, which you must well remember extends, for nearly a mile, in a line towards the Beacon, wore its most magnificent and gorgeous appearance, as if Nature had embroidered her green mantle with the choicest of her splendour to regale us, as in ecstasy we contemplated it from the great doors of the Abbey. The American Plantation, which, as well as all the other grounds, appears not to have pined for lack of care and attention, now displayed its multitude of transatlantic wonders, in such dazzling profusion, that the senses almost ached to gaze and feed upon its sweets and odours; while the contrast which its gay colours formed to the less gaudy, but more stately features of nature and art, that its neighbourhood contains, increased the effect and attraction of the whole. It seemed, indeed, as though we were occasionally called away from contemplating the grandeur and wildness of a Salvator Rosa, to the warmth and exquisite tenderness of a Claude or a Wilson. The Dwarf's Garden too, wore a better and more flowery appearance, than when M. Pero,[2] its consequential little Swiss master, did us the honour of tasting our Champagne, and accepting our l'Argent, within its narrow precincts. He also has, as I heard, departed, thinking it, no doubt, wiser not to hazard the experiment of a new master, when he is well off with an old one.

As connected with the exterior, the first alteration which struck me, was the arrangement of a number of rare exotics and green-house plants, on either side of the approach to the unparalleled Octagon; and which by their diversity and freshness formed a pleasant relief to the deeper shadows of the place, without, as might at first be supposed, at all injuring the solemn character of the surrounding magnificence. This

2 Pierre de Grailly, called Piero or Perro, a dwarf servant employed by Beckford. RJG

addition, unlike your handful of saw-dust in a currant pie, I conceive to be a great improvement; not so, however, is the substitution of a huge Mirror for the splendid and far-famed Cabinet in the *Great Drawing Room*, immediately fronting the entrance by the great gates of the Abbey. From the drive, this mirror is clearly discernible, and has a most singular and indescribable effect; which is not by any means realized as we approach nearer, by the reflection it gives of the Hall and the door-way, and the long green avenue I have mentioned. Its deception distracts, rather than rivets attention; and we are busied in observing, unseen by them, the antics and the physiognomies of other visitors, an employ as ludicrous in idea as it is perfectly ridiculous in fact, and altogether incompatible with the seriousness and solemnity of the scene. As before, the authorities for admission are still shown at the southern Entrance-Hall, and the company thence pass to the *Tapestry Dining Parlour*, still redolent of cups, covers, bowls, and *Dresden Porcelain*. A door, – till now closed against curiosity, – in the south-western corner of this room, leads to another novelty, called *Nelson's Turret*; so designated from the Hero of the Nile and Trafalgar having paid a visit to the Abbey in 1801: and a bust of that chief of Britain warriors appropriately ornaments its summit. The *Oak Library*, so called from its panels, and bookcases being formed of that hardy material, is chiefly valuable and interesting, from the number of rare and useful publications it possesses, principally on the Polite Arts; and which, to the credit of its gifted possessor, were intended for the use of the artists who were employed upon the works of his palace. There is here also placed a marble Figure of *Cleopatra reclining*, – 'which was not so before', and I really think it quite a gem in its way, and an imitation of nature so admirable, that *Anthony* may almost be pardoned for suffering his 'world to be well lost' in pursuit of the voluptuous original. There are here too some very highly finished Bacchanalian subjects by Poussin, which do not ill assort with the company of Egypt's luxury-loving Queen. The *Cedar Boudoir* and the *Gallery Cabinet*, are the adjoining newly opened apartments, and are in themselves, and as repositories of additional riches, extremely interesting. In the first, Mr. Beckford was accustomed to read; and the latter room he appropriated as his own summer chamber. The articles of Art and *Vertu*, more particularly striking, are Girard Douw's *Dropsical Woman*, with the usual attendants of a sick-bed Physician, Nurse, and the Daughter of the sufferer; a very elaborate painting, by Vanderwerf, of *Boreas carrying off Orethea*; a beautiful pair of *Landscapes* by Teniers; some very curious old prints, by Hollar, and two or three paintings of former Fonthills, of the dates of 1566 and 1755. A fine antique bronze of *Bacchus with the infant Hercules*, and another small figure, also a new importation, should be, also 'aye remembered in the Calendar'. The order of the march, as laid out, brings me next to notice the *Chintz Boudoir*, in which is again placed a handsome Mirror; – by the bye, Perc[i]val, our friend Phillips has a wonderful *penchant* for these modern ornaments, so much so one may almost exclaim, with jolly old Bacchus, and without making the verb subservient to a pun, '*Quem bis terque, bonum cum risu miror.*' This Mirror is so placed as to reflect the lengthened vista of the Galleries, terminating with the lovely landscape of Nature's own pencil, as seen through the opposite windows. This apartment's fitting up, consists principally of oak book-cases, well stored with ancient and modern lore. Its other furniture and embellishments have nothing of novelty. Passing through the vestibule of *St. Michael's Gallery*, *Grand Saloon*, or *Octagon*, and thence through the *Western Vestibule*, I don't know that one could really do better, than implicitly follow our friend Rutter's advice, as laid down in his systematic guide, – which, the honour of a man and a gentleman, Somerset, I am not paid for puffing – 'and descend the flight of stone steps, and enjoy a few refreshing turns upon the lawn', previously to again encountering blaze and brightness of the new array of glories, that like sunbeams are to glow upon and dazzle you within.

'Sed Ibimus O Socii comitesque,' – my pen is mended, my notes in order, you must be refreshed, and thus I proceed to the *Laocoon*, on the ground floor of the *Great Hall*. This is not, however, the veritable *Laocoon*, by Carbonneau, but an inimitable cast from it, and one too that, at the first gaze, raises the '*age of Bronze*', in our estimation top-mast high from the dread abyss of Bathos, to which his Lordship of Byron has recently precipitated it by his doggrel [*sic*]. The suite of rooms we now enter, commencing with the *Great Dining-Room*, are those which you must so well remember, and have so admirably described; therefore, *hey Presto*! to the *Grand Drawing-Room*, which is the principal new wonder of the Abbey, and adjoins, or nearly so, the *Crimson Drawing-Room*, in which you *Cardinalled* so well in *Wolsey's Chairs*. This apartment is hung throughout with blue Damask satin which, in addition to its elegance and lightness, I should suppose to be a colour well calculated to give effect to the numerous paintings. The surbase and ceiling are of oak; the latter supported by carved brackets, picked out with gold. Its just proportions, being nearly a cube of thirty-five feet, are extremely striking. A magnificent chased gilt Chandelier is suspended from the ceiling, and the floor is covered with a tapestry carpet, expressly manufactured for no less a personage than he who *was* the Emperor Napoleon! There is also a splendid saloon Table brought from Egypt by the same extraordinary man, and which he presented to the Empress Josephine, little dreaming its imperial keeping was so soon to be exchanged for the custody of a Wiltshire gentleman. It is formed of a circular slab of *breeche universelle*, considered extremely rare, and of extraordinary size; the diameter being four feet, 'on a grand and massive standard, formed of three Bronze Dolphins, sumptuously gilt, in or-mat, on a corresponding plynth, and ebony pedestal'. Several pictures, also, which ornamented other rooms in 1822, are now removed to this apartment, in addition to which, hang several new efforts of the pallet and the pencil; not at all derogatory to the situation they hold, and the company they keep. Of these, Rubens' *Le Jardin D'Amour*, containing portraits of himself, his Wife, Vandyke, Snyders, &c. and in which is introduced the celebrated *Chapeau de Paille* portrait; and a picture of *Himself by candlelight*, by Schalken, the famous Dutch Painter, are worthy of particular, and individual, notice. *Becket's Passage*, and the *Octagon Cabinet*, possess some good specimens of the Dutch and Flemish Schools of which, my old favourite, Teniers, has supplied two excellent specimens, as has Schalken also an excellent one of *A Lady holding a candle, in a rich dress trimmed with Ermine*. The effect produced by the artificial light on the face and drapery of the female is really wonderfully effective. The apartment in which this hangs – the *Cabinet*, – is, I assure you, quite a cosy and liveable one enough, and if we could but cut the exclamation of regret, and say 'sic omnia,' your sentence upon Fonthill Abbey – 'that it is not a comfortable residence,' – must be rescinded, and a contrary verdict recorded.

A fine bronze statue of the *Venus de Medicis* ornaments the *Northern Passage*, which leads to *The Crimson Breakfast Parlour*; also an habitable and pleasing apartment. It occupies, as I was informed, the site of the intended new grand staircase. The walls are hung with crimson Damask, decorated with many paintings by Dominichino, Wouvermans, Ruysdael, and others, who give a name and character to art, and whose fame needs not the emblazonment of my panegyric. We will, therefore, 'an it please you, good my lord,' ascend to the only new show-room in the Lancaster department, the *Picture-Room*; in which a handsome Billiard Table occupies a considerable space, and the Paintings, which are all its other ornaments, have been of 'old time' recorded, with the exception of two or three. Of these, one by De Cort, of *Fonthill Mansion, as erected by the late Alderman Beckford*, I must crave leave to mention. To me, who so well remember that beautiful, and comfortable, aye, and hospitable abode, this reminiscence of what it *was*, gave a gratification superior even to that felt by others, engaged in the examination of more laboured subjects: yet; it was a gratification that brought its regrets in the contemplation, invariably forced upon me, of what it now *is*. Scarcely could I forbear addressing its ruins,

> A heap of dust alone remains of thee,
> 'Tis all thou art, and all the proud shall be;

for little better is left to mark the spot where once, on the borders of that beautiful lake in the outer park, stood this model of a mansion; – and yet *enough* remains to memorialize the folly and fickleness of that taste which could consent to its downfall and dilapidation. Its few inconveniences were more than compensated by its many comforts, and are very far from being redeemed by the mere splendours of the 'tall' fragile 'bully,' for which it was made the sacrifice. But how few of us, Somerset, even in deeper things than towers and turrets, are content to 'bear those ills we have', rather than 'fly to others which we know not of'. But, good gracious! here am I, like Othello's lieutenant, moralizing 'half seas over'; and sermonizing upon the past, instead of attending to the improvement of the present.

Now therefore, King of Magazine men! and President of our Council! pass by, without playing *Tom of Coventry*, 'my Lady's chamber', and brace your sinews, summon up your blood, and let us enter those 'cabinned, cribbed, confined,' rooms, – Heaven defend the devoted sisterhood that are to inhabit them! - yclept *Nunneries*. Often, since together we gazed from this giddy and insecure height, upon the *Octagon* below, have I, in my dreams, and o' restless nights, conjured up phantoms of their startled votaresses rising from their wind-serenaded slumber – lifting, in their insensibility, the thin veil of curtain that divides them from the grand Saloon, and then, surmounting the low fret work of masonry that alone stands in the gap between them and destruction, – with one frenzied leap, falling, mutilated and destroyed

upon the broad pavement below; the only reply to the scarcely
conscious shriek of death, the echo of vaulted galleries; the only light
upon the victim's changing features, the pale and chilly moonbeam! –
From this picture, and these reflections, which have indeed often
impressed themselves on my 'curtained sleep', let me now breathe you
upward, till immediately beneath the pinnacles, the topmost point all
this wondrous display, we are lodged in the *Gazebo,* or *Star Chamber*,
of the Tower, and there, after the fatiguing, and from its very incomplete character, appalling ascent, let us recline, satisfied to have won the
point at any hazard, upon the comfortable and well arrayed couches
around. The light is admitted through windows of stained glass, of
which *Christ crowned with thorns,* – *the last Supper*, – and *the
Emperor Napoleon on Horseback*, are amongst the finest of the specimens. Descending down to level earth again, we next come – passing
over the intermediate old ones, – to the last of the newly opened apartments, the *Eastern Drawing Room*, which in every respect corresponds
in character with its *fac simile* the *Western*; Rembrandt's *Head of an
Angel*, Morrillo's *Ecce Homo* and Hayter's *Portrait of Cardinal Wolsey*,
are its chief pictorial embellishments: but Cabinets of ebony, Canteens
of gold japan, from the Duc de Bouillon's collection, Toilette Boxes,
Rosewood Tables, all well set out 'to make up a show', are in such
profusion, and so overwhelm and perplex one's memory, that mine is
too brittle individually to describe them. Take them, therefore, all *en
masse*.

I am fully sensible, my good fellow, that I have suffered many rare
morceaux to escape my record, and on recurring to what I have written, find I have omitted mentioning a fine *Portrait of Charles I.* by Van
dyke, and *the taking down from the Cross*, by Rembrandt, both highly
valuable pictures. Many embellishments and articles of *vertu* have also,
without doubt, shared the same fate, and gone unmentioned, but I
must stand excused for not now endeavouring to recollect them.
Amidst all his curiosity, under all circumstances, and in every situation,
John Bull is ever particularly assiduous in keeping upon the best possible terms with himself; and it would be highly discourteous therefore,
and withholding the palm from those who have deserved it, did I not,
after detailing all that Fonthill has accumulated to delight the eye and
gratify the mind, say a few words explanatory and laudatory of what
it also has to bestow on, and to maintain the grosser portion of man,
his body; and to exhil[a]rate the lighter, his spirits. A thing that is

worth while doing at all, it is worth while to do well, and on this principle have the Fonthill Commissariat department acted. For instance
the Fountain Court is fitted up very elegantly as a refectory, and clev-
erly tapestried, where refreshments substantial or dainty, Wines of
every description from 'humble Port to Imperial Tokay', are in abundance, and not exorbitantly, to be obtained. A *programme* of the
procurables enables every one, as *Old Rapid* would say, to 'cut their
coats according to their cloth'; and *Mon bon camarade* and *gourmand*,
of the Albion, and the Freemasons', and Drapers' Hall, and the
Mansion House, &c. &c. &c. my excellent wise judge of Champagne
and Turtle! I do indeed – assure thee, that friend Dore, of the White
Lion, Bath, – no bribe received in this case either, – does not keep the
word of promise to the ear only, but that the appetite also feels, and
owns, the 'soft-impeachment'. For those, however, who yet prefer,
what you learnedly call the *rusticatory* plan, tents are still pitched
about the grounds; cooled by the breezes, and shadowed by the green
trees, and flower shrubs. Guides are also provided, habited in a kind
of undress livery, to conduct strangers over the exterior wonders of this
Wiltshire Paradise; and I ought to have earlier mentioned, that there
are persons stationed in every room, for the purpose of accommodat-
ing the visitors' curiosity in the examination of its contents. The regulations now adopted as to tickets differ much from those of last year,
as they now admit but twice to the view, and the method used to prevent imposition is ingenious. At the bottom of the ticket, which in itself
is more in character, – being a view of the Abbey, and otherwise ornamented in gothic compartments, than was Mr. Christie's imitation of
the Plate of the Poole Bank Notes, – are two ornamented pieces of
card, each bearing Mr. Phillips' signature, one of which is cut away
after the visitor has paid his first visit, and the second upon its repetition: after which except as a memento, it is worthless, as an M. P.'s
over-run frank, or a protested bill of exchange. The advantages so
unjustifiably taken in 1822, and of which you and I were witnesses,
perfectly, in my view of the thing, warrants this very prudent precaution. The sort of Guard House at the Barrier Gate, which you will recollect from the confusion there caused by the congregation of
carriages, and the examination of tickets, has now also given place to
a pretty 'moss clad shed,' of which the Vignette in Rutter's *New Guide*
gives a very correct idea. And thus my task is finished; and I have now,
as far as memory and my note book would carry me, assisted and

refreshed by the observations of friends, replied to your enquiries as to the state of Fonthill 'at this present writing.' Rumour,

> Which doth outstrip the panting wind,
> And shame the boisterous ocean wig its roar;

has spoken pretty peremptorily of the almost boundless wealth of Mr. Farquhar. His desire and attempts to become possessed of every inch of land money can purchase, within the reach of this Wiltshire Palace, bespeak Rumour, in this instance at least, to be a veracious gossip. Is it not then deeply to be lamented that the filthy 'lucre of gain', or the mere spirit of change, – an evil spirit it must be, – should, whilst the casket remains unflawed and perfect, permit its precious contents to be rifled and dispersed, like the goods and chattels of a bankrupt pedlar, or the remaining gewgaws of the prodigal and the spendthrift unredeemable, and never to be replaced? —

> Can such things be,
> And overcome us like a Summer's cloud,
> Without our special wonder ? —

Percival, my dear fellow, at the bottom of my third sheet of foolscap, I must say farewell! Fail not to remember me very kindly to the Council, who in our flowing cups, and we have plenty here, are never forgotten; and make all the excuses you can for me that I have not earlier since our last Court proclaimed my allegiance. If Longbow does not consume all the columns set apart for his threatened thirty pages, – Prodigious! – and you are short of Balaam, you may show me up in lieu of the Lions, and less honourable beasts! – I shall be in London at the usual quarterly muster, and will endeavour to smooth my passage to your throne, and obviate frowns, and a vote of censure for my protracted absence, by a Michaelmas Goose or a Forest Haunch. – Regards, and 'all that sort of thing, and every thing in the world', that is polite and pretty, to Emily, and the ladies, and believe me,

Thine always, and most truly,

A. M. TEMPLETON, JUN

P.S. I mentioned that the *The Cabinet* was removed from its old situation, but forgot to add that it is still in the Abbey, and exhibited with all its blushing honours think about it. The Chroniclers of Fonthill declare, – but it was when the fatal *'t'other bottle'* was before us, – that Mr.

Beckford was once tempted to give 100 guineas for a *mere sight* of its greatest wonder, the Hungarian Topaz!' 'How this world is given to – *mais n'importe.*' 'The world is still deceived by ornament!'

P. S. *secundus.* My respects to friends T. T. Trumpet, and *Maestro Nicolo.* It glads me much to see that you have such champions. You should really give them an invite to our next jollification, and make much of them. [Greek letters] is down here, and sends his compliments but can't 'come to time' this round; and once more, and for the last time Adieu!

To PERCIVAL G. SOMERSET, ESQ. N. E. M. Office, London

EDITOR'S NOTE *New European Magazine*, III (August 1823), pp. 135–42. This magazine was published under this title by John Letts, Jr., 32 Cornhill, London, from July 1822 to June 1824. The editor and most of the contributors remain unknown. Arthur M. Templeton, Jun. is a pseudonym. Percival G. Somerset is the editor's pseudonym. See *British Literary Magazines The Romantic Age, 1789–1836*, ed. Alvin Sullivan (Westport, Conn., Greenwood Press [1983]), pp. 327–30.

Notices of Curious and Highly Finished Cabinet Pictures at Fonthill Abbey

[WILLIAM HAZLITT]

A Riding House by KAREL DU JARDIN No. 333, is one of the most complete and captivating works we have ever seen of that capital artist. It is the very truth of nature where the highest finishing is combined with a feeling of the effect and general look of external objects. KAREL DU JARDIN painted indeed what happened to be before him, but not 'as it happened'. The trees in the back-ground (if *back-ground* it can be called, where the objects are seen close upon the eye) are exquisitely touched, with every leaf almost detailed, and yet the masses are finely rounded off. You might fancy the air to have stirred their branches just before, but that they had stopped while the artist was painting them – so accurately is every thing expressed, at the same time with 'such happiness and pains', that you hold in your breath while looking at it, as if you could hardly examine with sufficient care, nor admire long enough. Under the trees and between their stems there is indeed a bit of blue distance (a precious bit), a pure streak of *lapis lazuli!* How well it is brought in! How it sets off, and, as it were, draws together the *home* scene before us. The man riding forward with black mustachios is so naturally done that you might swear, from the expression alone, it was the face of a person in the action of riding on horse-back, and in the open air. The black horse near has the air and stiffness of a *manage* horse; the boy with the red-tasselled cap, stooping down and holding him, is admirably painted. Another horse, at some distance, that is practising at a leaping-bar, seems fairly in the act of clearing it. As we *must* point out a fault, the white horse on the right hand, galloping forward, appears to us clumsy and not very well drawn. Again, the slight branches of the trees in front, that are sprinkled against the more massy foliage behind, look flat and *in a little manner*; but we have seen nature with this look sometimes, and have said to ourselves, 'If that were painted, it would be found fault with.' In fine, this is a picture for the cabinet of a Prince, for it is nearly perfect!

There is another small Landscape, by the same artist, in No. 62, with Cattle and Figures equally good. The Ass is so exactly like an Ass – the Cow is so like a Cow; the Sheep have such meek, innocent, ruminating faces; and then that bit of misty green on the mountain's brow is so like the green moss with the dull, dank mist upon it, that nothing can be better. This painter somewhat resembles BERGHEM in his subjects and grouping, but he is less *mannered*, and his colour is more true and simple.

The *Sea-port* by BERGHEM (No. 260) has not that general *japanned* and varnished look that has been attributed to his pictures. It is painted with a light and free pencil, and seems to have a sparkling haze spread over it. The accidents are well chosen and capitally executed – the men in the barge smoking, the Ass braying near them, the boys plaguing a goat, are evidently done after nature; and the whole has the busy, idle, straggling appearance which characterizes that scene of bustle and confusion – a Sea-port.

We cannot bestow too high commendation on No.182, A *Group of Children, with their Attendants*, by WATTEAU. The artist has in this picture (it hangs in one corner, near a window) surpassed his usual excellence. There is no flimsiness, no fritter. He has given to the playful subjects of his pencil all the innocent archness and fresh colour of children in the height of enjoyment, together with the mimic airs and graces of future courtiers and fine ladies. Whether considered as a representation of nature, or a piece of comic invention and manners, this charming composition reflects the highest credit on the genius of WATTEAU. It strikes us, in looking at the production here mentioned, and some of the Dutch pieces, which are its near neighbours, that they exhibit much the same difference in the Art, that there is between the butterfly in its grub state, and the chrysalis.

No. 168. *The Elements*, by BREUGHEL and ROTTENHAMER, has been much admired; and it is a work of infinite brilliancy of effect and delicacy of execution. We have no words, fine, evanescent enough to describe it – the colours are so dazzling, the forms so elegant! The flowers are like butterflies; the Cupids are just ready to take wing; the Nymphs are like *pixies*, or little fairy-creatures of the very size and shape that they are here drawn, and that could never become, by any stretch of fancy, great RUBENS-like women! Nature seems coarse and clumsy compared to ROTTENHAMER's ethereal creations – and dull, compared to BREUGHEL's ever-living ground of green!

A *Judgment of Paris* (No. 76) by the same Artists, displays great beauty of form, taste in the grouping, and exact finishing.

Perhaps two of the most valuable and masterly pictures in this Collection are *The Temptation of St. Anthony*, No. 147, and the companion to it, *Boors dancing at the door of a Cabaret*, by TENIERS. The last is of a larger size than the artist usually painted such subjects; and the expression seems to come out bolder and freer on that account, instead of becoming flat and insipid. His noses, lips, chins, as they enlarge, appear fuller of 'no meaning' – never were there faces of such living wood – there is a glimmering of cunning in the twinkle of an eye, a roguish anticipation of enjoyment at the corners of a mouth – all the rest is mechanical, and is just thawing into sense and motion. Nothing can be better done than the woman dancing, who stares and lifts up her feet like an automaton put into action or coming to life. The two women looking on to the right, and near the gate which has just been closed on a drunken fellow reluctantly led off by his companions, are also admirable. They really look like *potsherds* set on their feet to laugh and twist their hard features into a jest. The bagpipe-player looking down upon the dancers has the prim, pedantic air of a person who is paid for other people's folly. The two pair of rustic lovers, and the man with a broken pipe snapping his fingers with delight, are in perfect truth and keeping. We know no picture of this master which more exactly and pleasantly hits that nice point between *still-life* and animation, in giving which with good-humour and facility his chief excellence lay. – *The Temptation of St. Anthony* is out of his usual walk of art; but it is as strikingly and as happily grotesque as his general mode of painting is literally true. – The odd jerks of imagination, and wild, terrific combinations of form, are such as we should not at all expect from Teniers, and certainly not in the perfection in which they are here seen. The Devil blowing the trumpet through his nose, which partly resembles the jaws of a monkey and partly the beak of an owl, those riding in the air on huge lizards with tin tunnels for skull-caps, the tea-pot with its broken spout, the attendant on the Lady who is bringing in the charmed cup, half-baboon, half-demon, all display a strength of tragi-comic fancy which is not surpassed in Pope's description of the Cave of Spleen, nor in Burns's Witches Dance in *Tam o'Shanter*. For the painting of this picture, we never saw anything so like Paper as the blue and brown covers of the books of magic in front of the Saint. There are several very clever small pictures by the same unerring hand; one with a rainbow, as gay and airy as landscape can be; another, of a Merry Making, in which (for a wonder) the trees in the back-ground are *green*; and a third, of an *Incantation*, with the same spirit and a repetition of many of the same details as in the *Temptation of St. Anthony*.

No. 280, *The interior of a Chamber with a Lady bathing her hands in a Font of Limoge ware, held by a Page characteristically dressed, etc.*, by EGLON VANDERNEER. If Teniers made his men and women of common clay, Eglon Vanderneer made them of the finest china. The faces, the necks, of the women, the pillars, the carpet, everything in this picture has a look of the most beautiful porcelain; even the Lady's satin gown has a tenacity of appearance, and the figures seem as if they would break, were they to fall. Yet under this extreme and artificial uniformity of texture, there is nature, character, and some share of beauty. The cup held by the Page being identified in the Catalogue as a 'Font of *Limoge* Ware' shews at once the accuracy of the painter and the knowledge of the critic. Indeed, nobody could be a better judge of such matters than Mr. Beckford. It may be questioned, however, whether the comparison of Vanderneer's masterpiece to Gerard Dow is just. *The Poulterer's Shop*, by the last, No. 248, is highly finished and glazed, but it has no *manner* in it: it is a pure, transparent representation of nature, minute and common, but not in any degree sophisticated. The touches of his pencil put you in mind only of the objects he intends to represent. This is still more strikingly the case with this artist's *Portrait of his own Wife* (220), which is a breathing effusion of nature, full of freedom, truth, and spirit. GERARD DOW and OSTADE belonged to one class of art in this respect, NETSCHER and EGLON VANDERNEER to another. TERBURG held perhaps a middle place between them. No. 81, *A Lady drinking a Glass of Wine, and a Cavalier Asleep*, may illustrate what we mean. The part of the Lady's face which is seen through the glass, is nicely distinguished from the rest, and her complexion is heightened probably from the infusion of the juice of the grape, while there is a *dormant* humour in the man's being asleep while the Lady is taking off her heel taps. All this is very clever and natural; but still there is a look, a *conventional* style about this artist as if he had gone on finishing his picture after his models had done sitting.

133, *A Female with a Porringer*, by SLINGELAND is not liable to this objection. The young woman, you may be sure, sat to the last moment. It has all the freshness of truth and nature about it.

In the same room are two admirable portraits by HOLBEIN, one of A *Jew Rabbi with a green ground*, which is delightful from the venerable simplicity of character it displays.

No. 56, *The Interior of a Cathedral*, by STEENWICK, is a masterpiece of architectural perspective and finished drawing in the figures introduced.

47. *The Dance under the Oak*, by CALLOT, displays a great variety of small figures, accurately drawn, and in lively groups and action, but they have too much the appearance of figures cut out of paste board and stuck on the canvas. *Christ Mocked*, 132, by the same artist, has the same desultory, detached character, and is not at all pleasing.

270, A *Landscape and Figures*, by KAREL DU JARDIN, is a curiosity in art. It appears painted on slate, from its smoothness and dimness. It has a faint brilliancy about it, which it is difficult to describe or account for. At a short distance you can distinguish nothing; advance a step nearer to it and you distinguish everything, made out with the pencil's finest point, and in the most delicate tone of colouring. – Here is a number of hair-line distinctions, which, in their sum total amount to nothing. One would suppose that the artist had painted the landscape with great clearness and precision, but on some kind of leaden or absorbent ground, so that the colours sink in, and lose their effect at a very small distance. It is one of the prettiest playthings, the most pleasing toys we ever saw; and has the utmost neatness to commend it to the *virtuoso*, combined with that kind of beauty, which arises from the absence of everything coarse or disagreeable. Still there is a finical simplicity in the execution, and in this respect, it differs from a beautiful and highly finished specimen of *Ruins*, by POELEMBOURG (No. 310), in which everything is of an artificial and equally refined character. The red stone-walls are of amber, and their rough edges are softened into air. In his Landscapes POELEMBOURG was the Gentleman all over: he touched nothing that he did not give the last polish to it. We cannot say so much of his figures – they 'do somewhat smack'!

There are two small Domenichinos in this Collection, well worthy the attention of the Artist and the Connoisseur. A *St. Barbara* (Number 137), 'painted' (as the Catalogue expresses it) 'with great sweetness and delicacy', and *The Raising of the Cross* (Number 207). What is it that constitutes this strange difference between the spirit that breathes from

Dutch and from Italian art? It may be said with respect to the former picture, that the figure and face of St. Barbara are full of grace and beauty, and that it has 'a look commercing with the skies'; but this is not the case with the latter production, which is (like a picture of the Dutch school) small, high-finished, meagre in the outlines, and painful in the subject and expressions. Still it is Italian. How so? Because it has masses, a choice of effect, because nature in it is seen with a certain feeling, and from a commanding point of view. One part is connected with another, the whole is worked up to a given standard, and there is a soul of passion pervading it. The works of the Dutch artists represent objects, as seen through a medium of perfect indifference. It is no matter what is the subject of their pencil, or how it is viewed – The Italian masters select their subject, go round it, combine it with an *ideal* purpose, and inform it with a sense either of pleasure or of power. This, at least, generally happens; and it is the case with the two pictures before us.

We would also notice a *Holy Family*, by GAROFALO, No. 189 as an admirable specimen of early Italian art. The Virgin and Child are deficient, perhaps, in beauty and simplicity; but the head of the Elizabeth is as full of fine sense as her figure is of dignity and grace: the two Saints near her are spirited studies of thoughtful monkish expression (the style of the hair in one of them is a little too Frenchified) and the St. Joseph is a fine Rabbinical accompaniment. The style of the drawing and execution of this composition cannot be too much praised for firmness and vigour; it is at the same time chargeable with the harshness and rigidity of that early period.

We have only room for a bare enumeration of the following curious and valuable specimens of the infancy of the Art.

No. 34, *A Crucifixion painted on a gold ground*, by ANDRA ORCAGNA; very curious indeed.

No. 77, *Christ in the Garden*, by A. MANTEGNA.

No. 84, *The Adoration of the Magi*, OLD FRANKS, with a crowd of figures, remarkably picturesque and well drawn.

No. 80, *The Entombment of a Cardinal*, by VAN EYCK, very elaborate and expressive.

177, *The Marriage of St. Catherine*, G. BELLINI.

178, *The Woman taken in Adultery*, MAZZOLINO DI FERRARA, with strongly marked expression, and a striking architectural composition; and

236, The *Virgin supporting the Infant on a Table*, by ALBERT DURER, with great finish and character, but timid and flat.

The last in this list of antiquarian works of art was presented by Philip V. to a Convent of Nuns at Saragossa; and they must all be looked at, by the genuine student, with a mingled feeling of curiosity and awe.

In taking a farewell view of the pictures here, we met with a number of *gems* which in the multiplicity and variety of works of art, we had either overlooked or omitted to mention. With a brief indication of a few of these, for the benefit of such of our readers as may visit this attractive resort of taste and fashion, we shall take leave of the subject for the present.

The first we shall notice is No. 200, *A Lady with a Parrot*, by F. MIERIS the elder. In its kind nothing better was ever painted. It is a fine mixture of the natural and the genteel. The Lady, it must be confessed, is a Dutch Lady – observing a certain decorum of attitude and manner, with a fresh ruddy complexion (a little like *rouge)*, a look of fixed and pleased attention, simple yet significant, and with a satin and fur dress finished up to the exact point of perfection, – that is, so as to look just like satin and fur, and not like anything else in the world. The parrot is above all praise and all price. He holds his head down, and you almost expect to hear him speak. He is bridling, and seems equally proud of the attention of his mistress, and of his perch, which is made of wicker wood, new, well-scoured and shining. The spectator is unwilling to leave this charming little picture; comes back to look at it again, and feels a strong desire to touch it, to see if the objects are not real.

In the same room (a small cabinet, looking out upon the lawn, and commanding a delicious prospect), with one or two other exquisite specimens of the Dutch school, is a portrait by SCALKEN of a *Lady holding a Candle*, No. 78, which has great airiness of manner, brilliancy, and effect.

No. 15, A *Lady, playing a Harpsichord*, by NETSCHER, has a fine, homely, healthy look of nature; but the expression is as hard and as little sensible to the effect of the music, as the keys of the instrument she is playing on.

103, *The Presentation in the Temple*, by BASSAN, is a small but exquisite performance. One does not know which to admire most, the skill of the grouping, the elegance of many of the figures, or the beauty and pleasing effect of the turtle doves, which are brought in numbers as offerings to the Temple.

107, *A Woody Scene, with Cattle and Figures*, by BOTH, is one of the most transparent and highly finished efforts of this master.

114, *A Landscape, with Cattle going to Water*, by CLAUDE, is a small, circular picture, of great polish and elegance.

116, *Portrait of the Duke of Savoy*, by HOLBEIN, is in his *liny*, worn manner, but possesses wonderful spirit and high character, with a some-what saturnine look of defiance.

148, *The Three Marys at the Tomb of Christ*, VANDERWERF. To those who are fond of delicate pencilling and the enamelled look of flesh, this picture, must be a treasure. We cannot say a word more in its praise. The same remark would apply to 184, *The Judgment of Solomon*, by W. MIERIS, which is a work of exceedingly elaborate execution.

There is a fine *Portrait of the young St. Louis Gonzaga*, by BRONZINO, which has much of the commanding air and spirit of TITIAN, but without the colouring.

173, *The Annunciation*, by POELEMBURG, is elegant and affecting in the mode of telling the story. It has the excellencies without the faults of this accomplished but somewhat effeminate artist.

179, *The Wise Men's Offerings*, by RUBENS, is as bold, as rich, and as masterly a sketch as we ever saw from the pencil of this great painter. Can we say more in commendation of it? It is almost superfluous to point out the noble head of the Negro, where all is fine, and breathes the true spirit of the subject.

275. *A Landscape with a distant Camp, Soldiers playing at Cards, &c.*, is one of CUYP's most glowing and delicately pencilled scenes.

A Boy with a Parrot, 213, and *Susannah and the Elders*, 300, by VANDERWERF, are perfect specimens of that Master's power over elegance of outline and polish of surface.

Among the pictures which have been added this year are two noble Gallery Pictures – *The Martyrdom of a Saint*, by PALMA, and a *Holy Family*, by ANDREA DEL SARTO. The *Sybilla Libya*, by LUDOVICO CARACCI, still however retains its precedence in the historical depart-ment –We shall only mention one more picture of a very different stamp – 357, *Monkies Feasting*, by TENIERS, which, if the amateur can over-look the unpleasantness of the *Dramatis Personae*, he will find full of comic humour, spirit and satire.

EDITOR'S NOTE Published in serial form in four issues of the *Morning*

Chronicle in 1823: 20 August, p. 3; 22 August, p. 3; 25 August, p. 3; 1 September, p. 2. Professor Stanley Jones, University of Glasgow, has attributed, based convincingly on internal and external evidence, the authorship of this essay as well as a dramatic skit involving the Fonthill collection (published on 30 September) to Hazlitt. See 'The Fonthill Abbey Pictures: Two Additions to the Hazlitt Canon', *Journal of the Warburg and Courtauld Institutes*, XLI (1978), pp. 278–96. In serious financial straits, Hazlitt accepted a commission from auctioneer Harry Phillips to puff the Fonthill pictures. Professor Jones argues that Hazlitt, after having sacked the Fonthill collection the previous year in the *London Magazine*, managed to be true to his artistic 'conscience' by being subtly ironic throughout this piece. Troubled by the bad canvases he had to endure in the process, he then proceeded to 'distil his exasperation' into a more direct satire on false taste entitled 'The Science of a Connoisseur', the text of which follows.

The Science of a Connoisseur

[WILLIAM HAZLITT]

'But the Metzu! Have you seen the Metzu?' said a little old man in black to a man in a green hat. 'Not seen the Metzu? Let me have the pleasure of showing it to you.' I followed, thinking to pick up some crumbs of knowledge; for my genius was rebuked at the sight of the admirer of Metzu, as Anthony's was by Caesar. This striking little personage was the quintessence and perfection of the science of a Connoisseur – a very mummy and petrifaction of criticism. I have called him old; but he was withered with *virtù*, not palsied old. 'His bones were marrowless, his blood was cold,' it is true; but it was with study, his face was pale with the shadows and reflection of a thousand works of art. His nose was sharpened into the utmost acuteness of objection, or to what Shakespeare calls 'the fine point of seldom pleasure': his eyes, half shut, seemed to disdain their office – his coat was buttoned over his breast, as if to guard the chill air of criticism, and his person appeared to contract and shrivel up within itself from a fear of too hasty admiration. His whole aspect and manner was a foil to grace; and he crawled and wriggled up to the Metzu like a crab, sideways, as if reluctant to approach the object of his admiration, yet unwilling not to be the first to point it out. 'There, Sir – a perfect specimen of the art and of the master. They talk of their Ostades, their Mieris's, and their Gerard Dows, give me the ease and nature of Metzu. The *pensive Selima* – the expression is in Gray – look at that kitten on the top of the brass pan, watching the operation of scraping the fish – demure, devout, cautious, expressing the very soul of the feline tribe, and looking as if a turn of the brass pan on which she has perched herself might suddenly upset all her speculations – and then the pencilling is actually of fur.'

FRIEND – I don't think it at all like a cat.

CONNOISSEUR – (*doucement*) – You are fastidious! But what do you say to the face of the woman? Is it not charming? Such an easy air, such an arch expression, such clearness of tone, such freedom of touch; and then the fish seem absolutely alive! I confess this picture is my favourite in the collection. – I think I shall bid for it. If you observe, all is done here that can be done by the art of man, and it is done without any appearance of labour. Facility of execution is what charms me most in a picture.

FRIEND – Was it here in Mr. Beckford's time?

CONNOISSEUR – No, it is one of those lately added; and alone establishes Mr. Phillips's claims as a judge of art.

FRIEND – Pray what do you think of that Claude; is it not a little stiff and hard?

CONNOISSEUR – Claude was often so. It may be a Claude. Claude, like other men must have painted at different periods of his life, and not always equally well. I cannot pretend to say exactly. The subject is classical; and the composition is in the usual style of Claude, with trees, water, and distance.

FRIEND – Give me your opinion of the Cuyp. Is it not crowded with too many groups of figures?

CONNOISSEUR – Perhaps it wants simplicity; but the clearness, the sunny effect seems to prove it to be Albert Cuyp's. It is a very glowing brilliant picture.

FRIEND – What do you think it will fetch?

CONNOISSEUR – I cannot speak to that point precisely, but I should think it would go high – or else I had some thoughts of it myself.

FRIEND – You like the Netscher and the Mieris yonder. I have heard it objected that the flesh in the one looks like parchment, and in the other like china. Does not the child in the *Judgment of Solomon,* for instance, look as if it would break, if the executioner were to let it fall on the glazed pavement?

CONNOISSEUR – We must not attend to all the nonsense we hear; and we may sometimes hear nonsense talked on the subject of the Fine Arts, as well as every other. *Allons.* These pictures undoubtedly rank among some of the choicest in the collection; and Mr. Beckford must be allowed to have been a judge in this style of art.

FRIEND – But did not his taste run too much on merely high-finished and furniture pictures? There are, I grant, a number of capital and indeed first-rate specimens of minute and elaborate workmanship; but are not the productions of the grand historical style of art a very indifferent description – heavy, lumbering, coarse, and uninteresting?

CONNOISSEUR (*drawing himself up, and the numberless little lifeless wrinkles, into which his face was puckered, expanding into a genial warmth, and smiling expression of candour*) – Softly, my friend, pause and reflect a little – it is well sometimes to lay aside our prejudices – HAS it not occurred to you as a mere possibility that the disproportionate effect you complain of is not owing so much to the inferiority of the specimens of the higher works of art, as to the superior elegance, delicacy, brilliancy, and fine preservation of these so much despised imitations of common nature, which, after all, in ninety-nine instances out of a hundred, are perhaps the only ones that attain their object, and are not mere *waste canvas*? There is a large and very much admired picture by the late President, of the *Sacrifice of Isaac*, but (*absit invidia* – I know this is tender ground) my charming little Metzu cuts it up. What want is there of historical *chef d'oeuvres*? Is there not the *Sybilla Lybica* of Ludovico Caracci, the interview between *Job and his Friends* by Salvator Rosa? Are there not the Paul Veronese, the Andrea del Sarto, and the old Palma? What fault can be found with these names or with these works, in reference to the high style of art? Yet it must be confessed, few look at them, for the spectator has been dazzled by the dear little Mieris's, Netschers and G. Dows, those minions of the fancy, and darlings of the eye, till history becomes cold, barren and repulsive. May we not say that the Italian is to the Dutch style of art what a black mountainous tract of country is to richly cultivated inclosures, and delicious plots of garden ground? I myself should like to be lord of large acres, but I have no ambition to be owner of acres of canvas. What is the use of encumbering one's house with huge sprawling limbs, dingy backgrounds, damaged faces, and disagreeable tragic stories? How many interesting little works of art, how many excellent gems, how many lively incidents, how many rare touches, might enrich and sparkle in a space that is now occupied by an unsightly blot! Besides, as representations of the passions, how seldom is it that history is anything but a gross failure, and a mockery of the very name? One half of these vaunted specimens of the Italian school one cannot see – the other half one cannot understand. I am no friend to the *Black Masters*. This is an opinion, however, which I wish to remain *entre nous*. Come this way – there is someone listening to what we say. Did you ever read the CATALOGUE RAISONNÉ of the British Institution?

FRIEND – No.

Here the little old man in black drew him of the green hat on one side, and whispered in his ear – 'I WROTE IT.' On this his face puckered up again into a thousand little wrinkles, like a bowl of milk that is set in a window to cool before it is skimmed; he pulled his hat over his brows, hobbled out of the room, and his friend followed him with round shining face, quite satisfied never to have heard of the work, and with having no opinion on the subject!

EDITOR'S NOTE *Morning Chronicle*, 30 September 1823, p. 2. See previous essay for attribution information.

A Day at Fonthill Abbey

FROM *THE NEW MONTHLY MAGAZINE*

The world may just at present be divided into two classes of persons; those who have seen Fonthill Abbey, and those who have not: and it is the somewhat monopolizing and ambitious desire of this paper to make itself agreeable to both these classes. For the former, it would endeavour to retrace the scenes which they have lately visited, but which the cursory glance they were compelled to take at them can scarcely have permanently fixed on their memory, and which a second view of this kind may perhaps effect; and to the latter it would present the best, because the only substitute they will be able to compass, by the time they are reading this. But to each it can only hope to offer a sketch, an outline, a mere pen-and-ink drawing of the scene in question; – leaving the fillings-up, the colouring, and the light and shade, to be supplied by the memory of the one and the imagination of the other.

The domain of Fonthill is so extensive, and the attractions it offers to the spectator are so numerous and various, that, in order to apply our limited time and resources in the most advantageous manner, we shall adopt the arrangement laid down for the casual visitors to this singular spot; for we can afford but a day to what cannot be duly examined and explored in less than a month; – unless, indeed, the readers of the *New Monthly Magazine* are disposed to meet in a body, and sign a *Round Robin* to the Editor, insisting on *our* being allowed to exercise 'sole sovereign sway and mastery' in these pages during the next or any given month. In which case, on receiving due notice and double pay, we will engage to supply the usual number and variety of articles, including the usual quantity of entertainment, and of course written with the usual, or rather the unusual portion of talent, – the subject-matter being all drawn from this fertile source. In the mean time, we must proceed in the routine above-named.

Placing the reader at once before the outer gateway of what is called the Old Park, we will first invite him to admire the grand character of this almost triumphal arch, and then, passing through its noble portal, enter the outward inclosure of the grounds immediately attached to the mansion. On passing this gate we find ourselves on the borders of a noble lake, the banks of which rise majestically on the opposite side, and are clothed with a rich grove of forest trees, of an immense height. The first sight that we have to point out, as not exactly consistent with the true taste that we had expected to find reigning and ruling throughout this spot, is a whole *flock* of swans, congregating together on the lake. There is a saying, that 'some people's geese are all swans'; but it is quite as great and as common a mistake, to make all our swans into geese. There is nothing enhances the value of a thing like its rarity; – or rather its value chiefly *consists* in its rarity, if it is an object of mere ornament. Even if it be ever so beautiful to the sight, its beauty loses its effect in proportion as it becomes multiplied. The swan that

    .... on still St. Mary's lake
    Floats double, swan and shadow,

is a lovely and highly poetical object; but multiply it to a whole flock, and the charm is broken at once. A swan is an object which depends, for its effects, purely and entirely on the beauty of its form and motion; its appearance as an ornament to natural scenery should therefore be, like those of angels, 'few, and far between'. The effect, of a whole company of *moons* floating through the sky together, would border on the ludicrous; and a whole flock of swans are, upon the same principle, no better than so many geese!

'But how is this?' we hear our companion exclaim; 'a Cicerone turned critic, will never do. We came all this way to see beauties, not defects; and unless we *look for* them, we never *can* see them. Away, then, with the critical spirit, shew us nothing but what is worth seeing – or rather, worth coming to see; which faults and defects can in no case be, though they were the finest that were ever committed.' The reproof is merited, and we bow before it, and stand corrected. Once for all, then, this spot does include many points well worthy of discommendation; and let those who like the task, undertake to supply this desideratum.

This, then, is the portal, behind which has been rising, year by year for a quarter of a century, – 'rising like an exhalation' – a scene which was said to surpass the fictions of eastern fancy, and which was created apparently only that it might *not* be seen! And what is the 'Open

Sesame!' which is at last to dissolve the charm, and lay bare these mysterious inclosures to the rude and vulgar gaze of all comers? Alas ! a little bit of gold! – Gold – the only universal picklock – the only ve-ritable *aqua mirabilis*, which can dissolve all things – the only true Talisman of Oromanes, – which no force nor art can withstand, and which sooner or later, all things must and will give way before – from the *most* accessible and yielding, to the least so – from the conscience of a politician to the pride of a misanthrope – from the impalpable echoes of Saint Stephen's Chapel, to the massive portals of Fonthill Abbey! That which would not hitherto have moved at the mandate of all the Sovereigns of Europe, the Holy Alliance included, now flies open of itself a hundred times a day, at the mere sight of a *half-sovereign*, presented by the, perchance, soiled fingers of a London cockney or a country boor!

Proceeding along the carriage-way through the old park, with the fine lake before mentioned lying all along the view on the left, backed by a lofty grove of trees, and embowered lawns rising and falling on the right, we presently arrive at an elevated spot, where this part of the domain terminates; and passing on for a short distance to the west-ward, along a public lane, we reach a rusticated lodge, beside a gate-way cut in the wall which surrounds the whole inner portion of the grounds.

There is a pleasant story connected with this wall, which may amuse us while we are waiting our turn to be admitted through its mysterious gateway. Two young gentlemen, one of whom has since turned out an enterprising traveller, and whose success may probably be traced to the spirit excited by the romantic termination of this first adventure, contrived to scale this barrier, and make their way into the grounds – attracted by the rumoured wonders of the place. But it so happened, that they were almost immediately met by the owner, who, instead of directing his servants to shew them the gate, received them with a haughty politeness, and, after leading them through the splendours of his solitary dwelling, set them down to a princely entertainment. When night arrived, however, and they proposed to take their leave (doubt-less overjoyed with the success of their adventure, and anticipating the curiosity and envy they should excite among their friends, by the tale they had to tell), they were conducted to the spot where they had been first met, and informed, that, as they had found their way *in*, they might now find their way *out* again as well as they could! And they were left to themselves! What became of them, it is difficult to guess, and they themselves have probably never disclosed: for the place is a perfect labyrinth even in the day-time, and there is a single pathway through it which measured above twenty miles, without once crossing or retreading a footstep of the same ground. This capital piece of practical wit was not unworthy the author of Vathek, and is in fact not unlike some of those bitter ones which Vathek himself used occasionally to indulge in.

The avenue we enter on passing through the above-named gate, consists of a narrow carriage-way, with a greensward path on each side of it, bounded and shut in by a thick plantation, chiefly consisting of firs, larches, and pines, the spaces between the pillar-like stems of which are filled by a variety of flowering shrubs, and wild underwoods so that you cannot judge of its extent, except by the almost impenetrable darkness which pervades it wherever you attempt to look through; with the exception, however, of one point, where a magnificent view of the adjacent country suddenly breaks upon you at an unexpected opening on the left, near the termination of the road. This road is above a mile in length, and winds about perpetually, so that you can never see for a hundred yards before you; and you get no glimpse of any object but the road itself and the bordering plantation, except at the opening I have just noticed.

Before we reach the summit of this road, which ascends nearly the whole length of it, let us examine this delightful carpet on which we are treading: it is worth the trouble; for it is rarer than that which proceeds from the rarest looms of Persia. Nothing but the absolute solitude which has reigned in this spot during so many years, could have completed the formation of such a one. You observe, as your feet cease to press upon it, it springs up from under them, as if it were not made or accustomed to be trod upon. It is composed of a thick elastic body of various kinds of evergreen moss, low ground-fern that is almost like moss, wild thyme, and numerous sweet-smelling ground-flowers; the whole matted and interlaced together by a network of wild strawberries; their innocent little flowers peeping out here and there, as if it were afraid, yet anxious to be seen. Smile not contemptuously, *gentle* reader, if we now ask you to step off this sweet border, and not to make a common footpath of it. It was made for the eye and the mind, not for the feet; and if we do nothing better than induce you to keep on this gravel road instead, we shall not have accompanied you here in vain, either as it regards ourselves or you. If Mr. Wordsworth's poetry had done nothing better than teach a few lovers of Nature never to tread upon a daisy, the consciousness of this alone might repay him for all the ignorant and heartless vituperation it has called forth!

Having arrived within a few paces of the summit of the above road, now, for the first time, the extraordinary building, which we have chiefly come to see, bursts upon us – first its majestic tower, clothed, as it frequently is, in obscuring mists, which almost give it the appearance of descending from the clouds, instead of ascending to them; then the crowd of *subject* towers, turrets, and spires, which cluster round about it; and lastly, that gigantic wing which projects from the eastern side, and forms the exterior of the great baronial hall – not yet completed. It is not part of our plan to pause here, and examine the details of this unique building, which, on a slight turn of the road, we now stand in the august presence of. Whether viewed from this point, or from any of the numerous others which the grounds afford, we shall find that the general impression derived from it is of a complicated nature, but in every respect commensurate with the means which have been lavished to produce it.

Before we proceed farther in our examination of this stupendous building and the external objects connected with it, we had, perhaps, better at once take a cursory glance at its interior; for, otherwise we may chance to get so imbued with the impressions of its external grandeur, as to be disposed to look at its internal and merely ornamental riches in too critical a taste.

The view which we have now seen of the Abbey must be considered as the back part of it; and it is here that, following the routine laid down for the casual visitors, we will enter, – at a little low portal, latticed, and opening to a small narrow passage. Those who are disposed to exclaim against this unimposing entrance, (and this number includes nearly all that come), should remember that it belongs to the *offices* alone; and is under the usual circumstances intended merely for the servants: the principal entrance itself, looking to the West, being incomparably the grandest portion of the building.

On passing through the Eastern entrance just named the first room we enter is one which gives a good foretaste of the splendours we are to expect in the rest of the internal arrangements. It is called the Oak Dining-parlour; and though sadly disfigured at present by tables set out with ugly Dresden china, and execrable modern-looking silver *plateaus*, *epergnes*, and the '*un*like', it is a noble apartment, enriched with elaborate oak carvings covering every part of it, except the large pannels, which are filled with tapestry. The rich massive gothic window-frames of this apartment, glazed with immense sheets of plate-glass, and finished at top by small compartments of painted glass, are in admirable taste; and that portion of them which bows out on the South, forming the lower part of the oriel which is thrown out here produces a fine effect. These windows are hung with curtains of purple damask satin, without draperies, but depending straight down from brass rods. It may here be noticed that this is the fashion of all the curtains throughout the mansion: there is not a single drapery to be seen, or any substitute for it; but merely the curtains themselves running on plain brass rods. If it were not for the extraneous objects which at present disfigure this room, it would be the richest and most characteristic that we shall see among them all. Quitting this room which is numbered 3,[1] we pass through a passage (4), and ascend a small confined turret (5) and, continuing on through a narrow corridor (6), we reach the Oak Library (7). Here we find a vast variety of splendid works on Art, such as the Florence, Dresden, anal Orleans Galleries, &c., and a charming little sculpture of a reclining Nymph. The room itself calls for no particular remark. 'Leaving it, we pass on to a little boudoir (8) pannelled entirely with cedar-wood, in which we find the finest work in bronze which this collection contains. It is a reduced copy of the antique statue of a Faun and Child now at the Louvre. Passing on through two small antechambers, and another corridor looking to the East (9, 10, and 11), we arrive at the Gallery Cabinet (12); a sweet little room hung with crimson and gold, and presenting a splendid look-out from its high narrow windows, each consisting of one piece of plate-glass. It is not uncommon, in passing through these rooms in company with casual visitors, to hear them complain of the want of *comfort* which exists throughout the place. There is no accounting for people's tastes; but they must have strange and most exclusive notions of comfort indeed, who cannot find it in some one or other of the different classes of apartments that they will meet with here. To our thinking (and we are unluckily somewhat fastidious in such matters) this little apartment that we are now in is the very ideal of snugness and comfort; and there are many such.

1 The Arabic figures in this paper refer to the numbers in the descriptive catalogue of the building. [Rutter's *A New Descriptive Guide of Fonthill Abbey and Its Demesne* (Shaftesbury, 1823). RJG]

In order to preserve the routine on which we set out, we will now return through 11 and 10, to the Vaulted Library (13). Admiring, as we pass through it, the sweet and sombre stillness of this little low-roofed gallery (for such it is), and contrasting it with the lively richness of the little Chintz Boudoir (14) in which it terminates, we now descend another turret staircase (15), and passing through a small but lofty vestibule (16), we suddenly find ourselves in a place perfectly unique in its kind, and magical in its effect on the senses as well as the imagination. This is the Grand Saloon or Octagon (17). The centre portion of Fonthill Abbey consists of an octangular tower, springing up from amidst the surrounding portions of the building, to a height of more than two hundred and sixty feet; and it is within this tower that we now stand. We will place ourselves in the centre, and for a while contemplate the detail around us; for the general impression which this unrivalled apartment produces, it would be idle to attempt to *describe*, because in every spectator it must vary in a thousand different degrees, according to the different associations he may connect with it, and even the mood of mind in which he may visit it. For ourselves, we have experienced its effects under every variety of circumstance; in the stillness of the fresh morning, when the sun was visiting it with his first rays – in the glare of mid-day, when gazing crowds were pacing it, looking upward and around in empty admiration, and not daring to speak, lest they should put to flight the superb silence that seems to be the presiding Genius of the place – in the gloaming of evening, when the receding light seems reluctantly to leave its gorgeous windows, majestic arches, and mysterious recesses – and finally, in the still darkness of midnight, by the guiding ray of one glimmering lamp, we have wandered through its 'visible darkness', and explored the dim vestibules and vaulted corridors, and winding turrets, that adjoin to it, till the spirit of old Romance young again within us, and we have yearned to act over again. The Mysteries of Udolpho! – We shall, however, not attempt to describe the general impression received from the sight of this superb saloon; but its individual features may be glanced at with advantage. Standing in the centre, then, and looking first on a level with our sight, we see before us, supposing our back to be turned towards the great Western entrance, a lofty arched vestibule and portal (20 and 21) opening into a grand state apartment (22), all that we can discover of which is an immense mirror reflecting the external scenery presented to it through the opposite entrance from the grounds. Turning to the right, through a similar vestibule (16) we look down a superb oak gallery (74) with a rich stone ceiling covered with fan-shaped tracery, and terminating in a gothic oriel window of three compartments. On the left again, through a corresponding arch and vestibule, (31) we discover, first a long gallery (32) somewhat similar to the last named, except that the ceiling is flat, and of brown oak richly carved and ornamented: in continuation of this, ascending one step, is a vaulted corridor (33) dimly lighted by rich painted windows and the ribs of the vaulting richly gilded; in continuation, a smaller apartment called the sanctuary (34), rising another step, hung with crimson satin damask, with a superb fan-shaped and gilded ceiling, and dimly lighted by pierced gothic doors lined with crimson cloth; and last of all, rising another step, the perspective is terminated by a still smaller apartment called the Oratory (35), hung also with crimson satin damask, the mouldings richly gilded, and the ceiling being still more superbly worked than either of the preceding. This apartment consists of five sides of an octagon, and is finished, in the centre compartment, by a large mirror, which repeats the whole opposing scene as far as the oriel window which terminates the other long gallery.[2]

From the centre of the Saloon, where we are now standing, the detail of these apartments cannot be distinguished quite so plainly as would appear by this description: but they have been brought a little forward here, and just looked into, in order that we may avoid passing through them again in performing our regular routine. We have now seen three points of this view. The fourth and last, which presents itself on turning to the West, is infinitely finer than either of the preceding, and is perhaps quite unrivalled by any thing else of the kind that can be seen. Instead of looking along a level, as in the preceding views, the eye, immediately on reaching the extremity of the octagon, or saloon, descends down a spacious staircase, which terminates in a grand entrance-hall, built in the old baronial style (19); which hall opens on the great western Avenue, or lawn, by a pair of arched gothic doors, more than thirty feet in height. Immediately over this great arched doorway is an organ-gallery; over that a high narrow painted window; and then the pointed roof shoots upward to a height of eighty feet, at once supported and ornamented by massive beams of dark brown oak,

2 As part of the transfer of property arrangement for the sale of Fonthill, Beckford kept the statue of St Anthony that occupied the Oratory. Farquhar filled the empty space with a full-length mirror. RJG

richly carved and fretted. The effect of the view through this door, up what is called the Great Western Avenue, is highly characteristic and impressive; and it is imagined in fine taste – blending together, as it does, the outer domain with the inner, and forming them into one stately and magnificent whole. This avenue consists of a smooth-cut lawn, extending about half a mile, and about the width of the great saloon itself – bounded on either side by low shrubs, which jut into it somewhat irregularly, so as to take away any stiffness and formality, yet of sufficient uniformity to preserve the general unity of effect. Immediately behind, or rather out of these shrubs, rises a plantation, consisting chiefly of firs and larches, which have not yet attained a sufficient height to give them a character of grandeur; but, from the spot we are now situated on, they produce all the required effect.

Having gazed our fill at the magnificent *coup-d'oeil* which presents itself from the centre of this saloon, we must now proceed in our routine. We quitted it at number 17; or rather we have been remaining there all this while, and only making excursions, with our eye, into the adjoining apartments. Passing on, then, through the eastern vestibule and portal (leaving 18 and 19 behind us – as we have looked down them in our last *coup-d'oeil*), we enter the Great Dining-room (22), the first of the grand state-apartments. This is of great height, and is hung and carpeted with crimson; and the ceiling is of solid square oak beams, finished with gilded carving at the extremity of each beam. And it is here that we first find ourselves among the ornamental riches of this extraordinary place. Pictures, cabinets, vases, candelabras, and curious objects of various kinds, here crowd upon us in a profusion which so entirely distracts the attention, that we will not pretend to concern ourselves with them at all; for, however rare and valuable many of them may be, they are unquestionably much too numerous to produce any distinct and satisfactory effect; and they are, in fact, altogether unadapted to the situation in which we find them. Once for all, then, we will here take leave of the mere *curiosities* of Fonthill Abbey, as in no way connected with that permanent and characteristic part of it, which it is alone worth while for us to endeavour to *fix* on the visitor's memory: confessing our belief, however, before we finally dismiss them, that they offer to the taste (or want of taste – whichever it may be) which hungers after such matters, the most gorgeous and costly assemblage of the kind that was ever collected together under one roof, in this portion of the globe at least; and that they go near to give one a glimmering and indistinct notion of the treasures of the pre-adamite sultans themselves![3] The pictures, however, we would not willingly pass over so lightly, as there are many in this collection which deserve the utmost attention and admiration that can be bestowed upon them. But we must restrain ourselves altogether on this point for the present; or the resolution we had formed, of not encroaching on more than double our allotted limits, will be of no avail; to say nothing of such encroachment including another, which we are still less disposed to make, on the department of our coadjutor, the author of 'British Galleries of Art.'[4]

From the great dining-room we pass into the Crimson Drawing-room (23) – another noble apartment – square, lofty, with a ceiling of solid beams, and a 'great gazing window', occupying nearly the whole side on which it is placed. This is followed by another drawing-room (24), of similar character, but still larger in its dimensions, and more rich in its architectural decorations, as well as those appertaining to art and virtù. This apartment is hung with blue satin damask, and is probably the first time this kind of hanging has been used as a ground for the exhibition of pictures. The effect, however, is extremely good. The unrivalled cabinets, tables, chandeliers, &c. which enrich this and the last room, may be glanced at as we pass on, but must not be attended to in detail.

Passing out of this grand suite of rooms, through what is called Becket's Passage (from the great painted window at the extremity of it representing Thomas à Becket), we again find ourselves among the small *cabinet* apartments; and here, to say the truth, we feel ourselves more at home, and would more willingly pause and reflect, than in the more imposing and gorgeous portions of this vast labyrinth – for such the visitor will suppose that it has the air of being, when we tell him that he has not yet passed through one-third of the different parts enumerated in the routine which we are following. But he need not be alarmed at this information; as we will contrive to hurry him through what remains, in a manner that shall not fatigue him, in order that we may have a little time left, before our 'day' closes, to look at the external objects which appertain to this spot.

Pausing, then, for a moment, in the little octagon cabinet (26), – is another of those exquisite little apartments that we have noticed before,

3 *Vide Vathek.*
4 Peter Patmore, who published his essay on Fonthill in the *New Monthly Magazine* as part of his series 'British Galleries of Art'. See pp. 343–50. RJG

– it is impossible to avoid looking at a few of the gems of art which it contains – for we shall find nothing like them in any other part of our search. But we must *only* look at, not describe them; for if we once begin to do that, adieu to all hope at completing our circle *to-day*.

Quitting this lovely little retreat, we pass on through the Northern Passage (27), which contains a fine bronze statue of the Venus de Medici, the size of life; and, peeping into the Crimson Breakfast Parlour (28) as we pass by, continue our route through (29) the Porcelain Room – which is only another name for a mere china-shop. This room is in by far the worst taste of any in the Abbey, and deserves all the censure that the most carping critic can bestow upon it – as being altogether out of keeping with any other part of the building. Passing through, and forgetting it as quickly as we can, we find ourselves again in the long grand gallery noticed in our *coup-d'oeil* from the centre of the octagon. Passing over, then, this noble suite of apartments, from number 30, to number 35, we continue our route, by turning up a narrow staircase (36), which passes out of the sanctuary on the left, and leads to the upper Lancaster room (37). This is a billiard-room, and is hung with many pictures. It is followed by the State Bedroom (38) – a fine and characteristic apartment, containing a superb bed of crimson damask, with solid ebony pillars and framework, covered with a quilt of the richest Brussels lace. As our fair companions take an interest in these matters, it may be well to let them know, that if rarity alone deserves their admiration, they cannot bestow too much upon this same coverlid; for they may search all the royal palaces in Europe, and not find another of the kind. There are various other articles in the economy of this rich apartment which will attract and deserve their attention; but we must leave it hastily, and pass on through the ante-room (39), and the little vaulted gallery adjoining (40), into what is called the Tribune Room (41). Here we must stop a moment to admire the stupendous and truly impressive view from this room, which opens on to the great saloon, in the form of a parapet or tribune. The view is, above, to the top of the great tower; around, to the galleries and vestibules that occupy this part in correspondence with the room in which we are standing, and between each compartment of which is an immense painted window; and below, to the great Saloon itself, where the gorgeous shadows from those windows are falling; and, across these, down the stairs of the Great Hall, and through the lofty arched door-way, on to the great western avenue and lawn. In the above we may confidently reckon on looking upon a view altogether unique in its way; and not only so, but conceived in admirable taste, and executed in a manner as nearly as possible faultless, and producing an effect on the spectator which cannot be experienced without emotions of the most rare and valuable kind.

We will now pass on again, and, taking but a glance, as we go, at the series of apartments, &c. from number 41 to number 47 - descend the winding staircase of the Lancaster turret, and passing across the grand saloon, arrive at a lobby (48) which leads us to the great staircase of the tower (49). This, though it is rather tiresome work, and will scarcely repay us for our trouble, we must hastily ascend, or we shall be accused of not having seen the chief *lion* of the place. Mounting, then, a tedious number of stairs – which are a little relieved by the looks-out that we now and then get through the loop-hole windows that give them light – we arrive, at last, at a sort of gallery, or arcade, which runs round the upper part at the great tower, and communicates with four small apartments, called Nunneries, which fill as many of its sides. These occupy the numbers from 50 to 57. Having passed through these, in which there is little to admire except the view on to the great saloon below, we again ascend the great staircase, till we reach an open platform (58). As we have mounted thus far, we may as well complete our ascension, from this platform, up through the interior of the central tower (59) and the Gazebo, or star-chamber, (60) to the Tower Gallery itself – which is the highest point to which there is any regular means of ascent. Here we stand, then, on the summit of this far-famed tower, overlooking a spot which, even within the memory of most of us, was a barren heath – an interminable extent of bare *down,* with scarcely a tree upon it; and which now, by the means of one man, and under the inspection of one superintending assistant, has become what we now see it – a magnificent domain, including nearly all the natural beauties that can belong to a spot of the kind, and crowned by a building of unrivalled extent and grandeur.

But it is not for Ciceroni to indulge (themselves) in reflections upon what they see; otherwise here would be a fine opportunity for so doing. Leaving this, then, till we have cast off our present character – (which we must be allowed to do so soon as we have shewn our company fairly through the labyrinthine mazes of this extraordinary building) – we will pass on again, – first commending to their attention the view that presents itself from this tower; chiefly on account of its enabling them to glance, as on a map, at the *plan* which has been pursued in arranging the grounds within the inner circle of the domain: for the surrounding country presents nothing peculiarly entitled to notice, or that may not be equalled, if not surpassed, by most other views taken from an equal height.

Descending now the Grand Staircase (which, by the way, is any thing rather than grand, except as compared with the exceedingly confined ones which lead to every other department of the building, with the undernamed exception) we reach, at the foot of it, the great hall, and again descending the staircase of *that*, which really *is* a fine one, and correspondent with its situation, we turn to the left at the foot; and crossing the western cloisters (62), – leaving on the left a little court-yard with a small and insignificant fountain in the centre, – we once more, by passing up a narrow staircase leading from the oak dining-parlour, find ourselves entering upon a new suite of internal apartments, as richly arrayed as those which we have already passed through, and as gorgeously ornamented in the way of pictures, cabinets, curiosities, and costly articles of virtù of every denomination. The first of these is called the Western Yellow Drawing-room (72), which is hung with yellow damask, and gilt mouldings; and fitted up in parts with gothic oak bookcases, carved and arranged in admirable taste. This room also contains the grand *show-piece* of the place, in the shape of an enormous ebony cabinet, occupying nearly the whole side of the apartment, and reaching to the ceiling; and which is filled with a nondescript and nameless variety of what, for lack of a better generic title, we are obliged to call, in the language of catalogue-makers, 'articles of virtù', but which are, generally speaking, in as vicious a (want of) taste as any thing can well be; being costly merely in virtue of their rarity and remoteness from all pretensions to either beauty or utility: using the term 'beauty' to signify a quality founded in some natural principle of taste; and 'utility', as that which is, or may be made, in some way or other, subservient to our mental wants and propensities; – in which sense, indeed, the one quality may be said in some degree to merge in the other; since beauty is, in this view of it, the most *useful* thing in the world.

Passing out of this gorgeous apartment, through a little ante-room (64), we find ourselves in another of those sweet little retreats which are the exclusive boast of this spot, and which in some sort redeem the splendours by which they are surrounded, by permitting the latter to be used as contrasts to *them*. But there is no feeling the rich repose and still sweetness of this and similar apartments, unless we could visit them alone; so, glancing round for a moment at the really beautiful works of art which this little cell contains, and looking out upon the flower-crowned terrace on which it opens (71), and, through the loop hole windows which light it, upon the rich prospect below, we will pass through another yellow drawing-room (73) nearly similar to the one above-named, and across the gallery noticed in our first *coup-d'oeil*, and finally close our peregrination by resting our somewhat wearied forms – for there is no denying that, by this time they *are* so – on one of the couches which stand before the mysterious curtains that fill the recesses of the great Saloon.

Thus, gentle reader, – for 'gentle' we will evermore proclaim you, if you have borne with us, pleased and patiently, all through this long, and (which is not our fault) somewhat monotonous range of splendours – thus have we led you through every open apartment of a building which is, with all its faults, calculated to excite a deeper interest in the spectator than any other of the kind that we could any where point out: and we have endeavoured to indicate to you chiefly the merits of what we have met with. The defects (as we hinted in the outset of our examination) we are ready to expatiate on at equal length, on the conditions there named; which we have little hope (or rather, fear) of being complied with, since the world is more than sufficiently supplied with persons whose chief talent lies in finding fault, and who are so conscious of the superiority of their claim on this score, and so desirous that others should be equally convinced of that superiority, that, if they cannot get paid for calling it into action, they are generous enough to perform the task gratis.

Here, then, beneath this great western arch of the saloon, we slip off our character of Cicerone, and having rested a moment to get rid of the feeling of it, descend the stairs of the Great Hall, and sally forth, alone, into the scene which has been all along beckoning us to its company from every window that we have passed; and which invitation we have had much ado to say nay to: for, after all, it is the external part of Fonthill Abbey, and the natural objects appertaining to it, that are alone worth serious and particular attention; and it is only when the spectator is alone, that this attention can be bestowed upon them.

It is, of course, not our intention to give any thing in the shape of a detailed description of grounds, the inner circle of which extends above seven miles. All our already transgressed limits will permit us to attempt is, to notice the general impression they are calculated to produce, in connexion with the magnificent building which crowns and overlooks them. And first of the building itself. There are various points of view from which it may be seen; but none towards which it presents an aspect of more imposing and majestic beauty than that which is situated at the top of the great avenue on which the western doors abut. Standing on this spot, it rises before us with a look of solemn and stately grandeur, the effect of which has probably never been surpassed; and which effect, if we mistake not, arises in a considerable degree from the peculiar character of the building, coupled with the situation in which we meet with it. It has all the individual as well as general character of one of those stupendous religious temples which have come down to us from Gothic times; but, unlike any one of those, it stands detached from all other of the works of man, on the summit of an immense fir-clad hill, which it crowns as with a diadem. Hitherto the idea of a great cathedral has come to us accompanied by all sorts of associations connected with cities, societies, and population; but here we meet with it, utterly silent and solitary: reigning, it is true, but reigning over the still realm of Nature alone, – like a queen on a desert island, without a people.

There is still another accidental feeling which contributes to the effect produced by this building. It is, as far as the memory of a general impression of mere size will enable us to judge, of greater extent than any other building of a similar character in Europe; and we come to enquire into the history of these latter, we find, when they are finished at all, that *such* a portion was completed under the direction of *such* an abbot, in the year so and so; that this wing was added a century or two after, by such a bishop, by the aid of funds collected in such and such a manner; and so of the rest: that all, in fact, have demanded the united means, talents, and spirit of several individuals, or public bodies and the lives of several architects, to bring them to the state in which we now see them: – but that *here* is one, equal to, if not all of them in extent, grandeur, and beauty, which has sprung up at the command of *one* private individual and under the direction of *one* architect.

In threading the interminable mazes of the grounds surrounding this majestic mass of architecture, it is probable that something like the same complex and imaginative impression is received. Speaking for ourselves, we are sure that this is the case. The late owner of this place was at once the inventor, the creator, and the *sole* possessor of it. This, however, would have been nothing, if he had been like the usual possessors of such spots. But the author of Vathek is no common person; and the paths which he, and *he alone*, has trodden – where he has pondered his bitter thoughts, and dreamed his fantastic dreams, and mused his lofty imaginations; and whence he is now exiled for ever, only that they may be made a common thoroughfare for all the idle and curious – all the high and low vulgar of the land; – *these* paths cannot be paced (at least by those who have a jot of sympathy with either the strengths or the weaknesses of our human nature) without feelings and associations which are perhaps the more, rather than the less active, because they are not easily to be communicated or explained – in fact, they cannot be paced without what was, and must long continue, the *genius loci*, being ever present in imagination, under such form or image as the mood or recollection of the moment may invest it with. For our parts (who are, it is true, somewhat addicted to the romantic in such matters), we have seldom wandered alone through the mazes of this spot without fancying by the side of us an inhabitant of the Halls of Eblis, permitted for awhile to visit these Elysian fields; but still condemned to wear its right hand upon its left breast; or only allowed to lift it up now and then, to shew beneath, through the transparent flesh, the red heart burning like a flame of fire.[5]

We must now positively take leave of Fonthill at once, by saying, of the grounds generally, that as far as the mere planning and arrangement of them goes, they strike us as being nearer to the perfection of this sort of spot than any thing else we are acquainted with, or had previously formed a conception of. The *spirit* of them, be it understood, is that of pure Nature; not unassisted indeed, but entirely unadorned, and almost uncontrolled. Every thing she is capable of producing, that will live under our skies, is here collected together; but scattered about with so artful a hand, that the art of it is entirely concealed. The usual natives of the forest, the heath, and the garden, here meet together in one spot, and form one beautiful and happy family; and all flourish and bloom together, by mutual consent. Roses blush from out the bosom of the heath furze; rhododendrons fling their gorgeous flowers at random among ferns and forest shrubs; the frail woodbine hangs its dependent clusters upon the everlasting laurel; and on the ground all sorts of rich

5 See the conclusion of *Vathek*.

[341]

(so called) *garden* flowers group themselves with those gentle families of the earth which we (happening to be 'drest in a little brief authority' over them) have chosen to banish from our presence into the fields and hedges, and denominate *weeds*.

The above refers to particular spots that present themselves occasionally as you wander about. But the general character of the place, as a whole, is that of one vast solitude, half wild, half cultivated, spreading itself over a plot of earth which includes every variety of natural beauty; here opening into rich lawns studded with lofty forest, trees or low clumps of evergreens and underwood – there stretching away into interminable vistas through lines of larches and pines – now descending abruptly, and shewing, from between the topmost branches of the trees beneath, lovely lakes basking in the still light, and reflecting all the beauty about them; and now opening suddenly at a turn of the green path, and permitting a rich expanse of distant country to burst upon the eye for a moment, only to be lost again, as you pass on, in the dark shadows of some deep fir-grove: a solitude; but – (and this is one of its greatest charms) 'a populous solitude': – for here, all the animal tribe, save their would-be lord alone, have had permission to wander, unmolested, and uncontrolled, but by their own wills; and for *them* at least it has been, until lately, a new Paradise. Even now, when the idle crowds that at present haunt and disturb this peace-hallowed spot have quitted it for a few hours, and in the sweet mornings before they have broken in upon it, we have seen the hares sporting about within a few yards of our feet like kittens, and heard the birds sing to each other upon the bough above our head, as if the place were all their own. For this alone, if for nothing else, we shall never cease to regret that any cause, but the inevitable one of death, should have laid bare the secret beauties of Fonthill Abbey, and divorced them from the only possessor who could be said to have a *natural* right in them, in virtue of their having been purely the work of his own hand.

EDITOR'S NOTE *The New Monthly Magazine and Literary Journal*, VIII (1823), pp. 368–80. The poet Thomas Campbell (1777–1844) was the editor at this time. Cyrus Redding was serving as the sub-editor. This essay was republished in New York in December 1823 by D. A. Borrenstein. See R. H. Schoemaker, *Evans Checklist of American Imprints for 1823* (Metuchen, N. J., 1972), #12341, p. 65.

Fonthill

[PETER G. PATMORE]

A work of high art deserves to be traced and followed to whitherso-
ever the chances and changes of time may carry it – its *biography* is
worthy of being recorded and read, even when itself, from the perish-
able nature of the materials which form it, may have passed away from
among existing things. We have few volumes more interesting than that
would be which should duly trace the history of what once formed the
treasures of the Louvre, – hinting, in its progress, at the causes and
consequences of the events referred to; and its value and interest would
be greater rather than less, now that the principal objects of its notice
are again scattered abroad over the face of Europe. It is on this account
that I have thought it worth while to give a short notice of the Fonthill
Gallery, – although, by the time this paper is before the public, it will no
longer exist as such. But the few, the very few works which compose its
principal ornaments, will exist, and will even (in imagination) keep
their places on the walls where they have once hung, when nothing else
belonging to the spot is cared for or remembered. I, for one, could walk
up to the bare walls which the objects I am about to notice lately
covered, and mark out with a pencil the identical space which each of
them occupied. In fact, for me, and for those who have seen and duly
appreciated them, *there* they will continue to hang, till we shall chance
to see them in some other place; as the image of a lost friend for ever
occupies the spot where we *last* saw him.

It has been said that the works now forming the Fonthill Gallery are
not the same of which it consisted before this singular spot area opened
to public inspection. It may, or it may not be so. With this I shall not
concern myself. The true lover of art cares not to whom a fine picture
may *belong*; he, and he alone, is the *possessor* of it, who is sufficiently
impressed with its beauties to be able to enjoy the memory of them; and
he sees no difference in those beauties, whether they look upon him

from the walls of a palace or of a picture-dealer's shop; – nay, he scarcely thinks the worse of them for having an auctioneer's lot-mark in the corner –since this does not oblige him to read the *description* appertaining to it!

A paper which appeared in the last number of this work has superseded any thing that I might have to say on the place which contains the Gallery I am now to notice.[1] I shall, therefore, proceed at once to the pictures themselves; – arranging them without any reference to their relative situation, but merely in the order in which they may happen to present themselves to my recollection; which will probably be nearly correspondent with what I conceive to be their respective merits. In pursuance of this plan, the first that returns to me, in all the freshness of its beauty, and as if it were actually before me while I write, is one of almost miniature size, but for rich purity of colouring, severe sweetness of expression, and inimitable truth and delicacy of finishing, equal to any thing of the kind I am acquainted with. It is by Albert Durer, and represents the Virgin and Child, in an interior, with a distant landscape seen through a window on the right. The infant Jesus is eagerly looking out of the picture, and straining forward towards the point to which his eyes are directed; while the Virgin-mother is tenderly restraining him with one hand, which encircles his body, and presses into the soft flesh in front. This hand of the Virgin, and indeed the whole picture, may be offered as a perfect specimen of what *finishing* ought to be – of how far it ought to be carried, and at what point it should stop. We have here all the details of the actual object, in their most delicate minutiae, producing all the force and spirit of general effect which is so usually frittered array, or diluted into mawkishness, in attempts of this kind. But the chief charm, in the detail of this rich little gem, is the expression of the Virgin: it is the perfection of a divine humanity; blending together, into one lovely whole, all the attributes with which the imagination invests this most interesting of historical characters.

The next picture that I shall notice, is one of corresponding and perhaps equal merit with the above, but in altogether a different class of art; the first being, notwithstanding its truth, all ideal, and the second being a piece of actual unmingled nature. But I place them thus side by side, because they seem to have been dictated by the same spirit, and to

1 'A Day at Fonthill Abbey', *New Monthly Magazine and Literary Journal*, VIII (1823), 368–80. RJG

proceed on the same principles: each being actually *true* in every particular; but the one being true to the imagination, and the other to actual
knowledge and observation. The exquisite work to which I now allude
is by Metzu, and represents a woman scraping fish on a table, before
the door of a cottage; on the table are placed some parsnips, and a brass
kettle, with a kitten seated on the top of it. Among all the specimens
that I have seen of the Flemish school of finishing, this is without exception the very best, with reference to the ostensible *object* of all finishing
– viz. to produce natural impressions. Any thing which proceeds
beyond this – (which much of the Flemish finishing frequently does –
that of Vanderwerf, W. Mieris, and G. Dow, for example) – is distinct
from the purpose of *painting* – which was and is as 'twere 'to hold the
mirror up to nature'. The reader will, perhaps, pardon me, if I direct his
attention in a particular manner to this last illustration, because it
precisely explains what I mean, with reference to pictures of the class
now in question. Their perfection, in fact, consists in representing
objects, not as they actually appear when presented directly to the eye,
but as they would appear if *reflected from a concave mirror*. Looked at
in this point of view, the little work before us is the most purely *natural*
effort of the pencil that I have ever seen; so much so, as to have required
nothing less than *genius* to produce it – which is more than I should be
disposed to say of any other similar work, that I am acquainted with, of
the Flemish school.

As an illustrative contrast to these two charming works, I would
have pointed out, had the collection remained entire, an execrable
picture by W. Mieris, which was (strange to say) considered as among
the chief boasts of the gallery. The subject is the Judgment of Solomon;
and the whole scene (with the exception of the real mother) is the ideal
of what a work of art should *not* be – whether regarded as a composition, a piece of colouring, or an effect of high finish. To convey a notion
of the spirit in which the work is composed, I will mention that the false
mother is standing, with a smile on her countenance, holding out her
apron to receive *her share* of the infant!

As a fine contrast to the above, in point of style, I will here notice a
noble gallery picture, by Ludovico Carracci, – the only one in the
collection, of this class, which is worthy of particular mention. It is a
long low picture – the figures larger than life –representing the Libyan
Sibyl, seated on the ground, and giving forth her oracles; while youths
are attending her on either side, with tablets, taking down what she

delivers. The figure, attitude, and whole expression of the Sibyl, are grand in the highest degree; but grand from the pure and severe simplicity of their conception and execution; for any thing like the adventitious aid of art or refinement is totally abandoned. She is sitting on the ground, – self-collected, as it regards her attitude, and involved in a noble drapery, which seems to wrap itself about her like a solemn thought; but her eyes are gazing forth into the void space before her, as if searching for inspiration from the elements or the clouds. The youths who are holding the tablets on which her words are to be recorded, are no less fine, but in a different way. As specimens of anatomical design, they are admirable; one in particular – that on the right of the Sibyl, holding the pen and looking round towards her – includes an astonishing union of power and truth. The colouring of this picture is correspondent with the conception and design; and it is altogether a noble specimen of what truly merits to be called the grand style in Art.

In as highly imaginative a class of Art as the above, though at the very opposite extremity of the scale in point of style and subject, is the Temptation of Saint Anthony, by D. Teniers. This is one of those grotesques in which Teniers had no rival, and, indeed, no imitator; and in which he displayed a force of conception, a vividness of imagination, and a truth and facility of hand, that have never been united in any other person, either before or since. The Saint, with a fine solemn, self-possessed, but anxious countenance, is seated in his cell, looking towards a seeming lady who is *gliding* onwards to offer him a cup of wine which she holds in her hand; while all around him are seen nondescript creatures, composed 'of every creature's worst' making the most hideous mops and mows, to 'fright him from his propriety'. It is in the expressions thrown into the faces of these creatures that the wonderful power of the picture consists. Though any thing but *human*, yet unquestionably their effect arises from some recondite resemblance that they bear to something that we have either seen or dreamt of in human faces. Teniers must, I think, have been an opium-eater, or he never could even have imagined, much less embodied, such expressions as we find in this and some other of his pictures on the same subject; for 'such tricks hath strong Imagination' only when she is under the influence of some adventitious circumstances. That these expressions do owe their power upon us to some resemblance they bear to what we have previously seen with the mind's eye, I am convinced from the fact, that upon general spectators they have no effect at all – except that of

mere strangeness. To be affected by them, and consequently to appreciate the astonishing skill displayed in them, demands an imagination
akin at least to that from whence they have sprung. Not that I am
disposed to rank the value of this skill higher in consequence of its
effects not being generally intelligible; on the contrary: but I merely
refer to the fact as explanatory. – To shew the variety of his power, the
artist has depicted the seeming lady, who forms the principal object in
the picture, with a grace and dignity of deportment which cannot be
surpassed, and which could little be expected to proceed from *his*
pencil, by those who do not know that, whatever he could see, *that* he
could depict – any one thing as well as any other; and that he adopted
one particular line of Art, not because be excelled in it, but because he
preferred it.

There is another picture in this collection on the same subject with
the above, and of almost equal merit, but on a much smaller scale. –
There is also one which deserves to rank with the very finest he ever
painted, in his own peculiar class, – a Village scene. It is of a large size,
and yet includes but few figures; but for skilful composition, truth and
harmony of colouring, and rich touches of nature and character, it
merits to be called a noble production. It represents a bagpiper standing
on a tub before an alehouse door, and playing to three or four couples
who are amusing themselves about him. I adopt the following passage
from a Catalogue Raisonné of this collection, which has been printed
but (I believe) not published; as I could not vary the description with
any advantage. 'The most conspicuous parts in the detail of this fine
work are – first, the couple who are dancing in the centre. There is an
indescribable expression of half shame-faced, half chuckling delight in
the woman, which is peculiarly rich and striking; but so far from
moving on "the *light* fantastic toe", she lifts up her feet as if weights
were tied to them. The "tipsy dance and revelry" that looks out from
the face of her partner, is equally rich and fine. The figure next in merit,
on account of the truth as well as imagination which its expressions
combine, is that of the old man who is watching the young couples
romping, and rejoicing over them as if the sight renewed the very spirit
of youth within him, and made him able to "fight his (love) battles o'er
again". The bagpiper elevated on the tub, and at once playing his tune
and partaking in the game that is going forward below him, is also
wonderful.'

The next picture that I shall notice is perhaps, upon the whole, the most perfect in this collection, and, to my mind, the very best that I have ever met with of the master. Indeed it has raised my opinion of his talents to a height that it had never approached before. It is a picture by Berghem, which was formerly in the gallery of the Duke de Praslin, and known there by the name of *L'embarquement des Vivres*. The scene is the Gulf of Genoa, with various figures and cattle on the shore in front, about to embark in a passage-boat; and buildings and shipping occupying different points of the distance. The manner in which these latter are steeped in air, and as it were blended with it, is truly admirable, and in no degree inferior to some of Claude's best efforts in the same class; and the objects in the foreground are equally effective in a different way. There is a man seated at the head of the passage-boat, whose whole character might be written from his face and air. He cares no more about his customers than if he was to get nothing by them, because he knows that they *must* come to him; and instead of dancing attendance upon them, there he sits as if they were coming to his levee. In the centre is a woman counting her money, with a prospective eye to the amount of its increase by her marketing expedition. On the left are two men spelling the contents of a posting-bill; and near the boat are two boys, one pushing and the other dragging a goat that they want to embark, but that seems to feel an instinctive horror of its fate, and will not stir a step. The boys are urging it with an expression made up of half fun half anger. But the general effect of this picture is its great charm; and this seems to arise chiefly from the extreme lightness and elegance of the handling, and the exquisite harmony and sweetness of tone that is preserved through the different gradations of the perspective and the colouring. This charming picture, if it does not evince so high and rare a degree of power as some others that I have noticed, is, I repeat, the most faultless work in the whole collection.

If I do not pass over Leonardo da Vinci's 'Laughing Boy', it will be more in respect to its celebrity than in conformity with my own opinion of its merits – which strike me as being very limited indeed. It is a small upright picture, representing a very young child amusing itself with a toy; and the expression of infantine simplicity which beams from the happy countenance is extremely pleasing and appropriate. But to hold the picture up as a distinguished effort of high art, is to betray an ignorance or an indifference as to the true import of the phrase. It is a pleasing specimen of a natural expression most naturally depicted; and nothing more.

As it was not my intention to notice in detail any objects of the Fonthill Gallery but those of surpassing merit, I shall conclude this notice by merely naming a few others which remain upon my memory, and adding a few words on the general character of the whole collection.

Of the Flemish school of finishing there are several most exquisite specimens, and one or two that are perhaps unrivalled. Of these latter, a lady in a satin and fur cloak, feeding a grey parrot, by F. Mieris, is the best. There is another on the same subject, by the same master, which is extremely beautiful in its way. G. Dow's 'Poulterer's Shop' is also inimitably rich and elaborate; and its expressions are more natural and characteristic than this master usually took the trouble of making them: for his care was chiefly applied to tangible things. Among the gallery pictures is an Adoration of the Shepherds, by Philip de Champagne, which possesses extraordinary merit in the design and the chiaro-scuro; among the portraits there is an admirable one by Bronzino, and two by Sir Anthony More which are little inferior to Titian; and finally, there is a charming set of pictures by Watteau, representing the Four Ages of Man, and two others by the same artist in his usual courtly style.

In taking leave of the Fonthill Gallery, I should not give a fair impression of its character to those who have not seen it, if I did not add, generally, that it is (or, by this time, *was*) more miscellaneous in point of merit than any other great collection that I could point out. It contains (as I have shewn) a few fine works – but those, with one or two exceptions, not of the finest class; many that do not reach to mediocrity; and some that are totally bad. Whether this argues a want of taste, or only a want of means is more than I shall determine. It must be confessed, however, that it might be difficult to say where four hundred fine pictures are to be found. In fact, the mistake of picture-buyers is to limit themselves in price rather than in number. Oh, for the two best rooms in Fonthill Abbey, and a hundred thousand pounds to furnish them with! With this space and this sum alone one might, even in the present day, collect together a finer private gallery than any one now in existence; – bartering his paltry gold for the 'riches fineless' of truth and beauty; and (if *that* were his appetite) acquiring a lasting fame at the same time. The late Mr. Angerstein was known all over Europe, and will not soon be forgotten, for no other reason than that he possessed ten of the finest pictures in the world!

EDITOR'S NOTE Published as no. IX of the series 'British Galleries of Art' in the *New Monthly Magazine*, VIII (1823), pp. 403–8. Patmore (1786–1855) published this series in book form anonymously in 1824. Eventually he became known as the author during his lifetime. See *The Gentleman's Magazine*, XLV, New Series, pt. 1 (1856), p. 206. He was also the author of *Imitations of Celebrated Authors, or Imaginary Rejected Articles* (London, 1826) and ultimately became editor of the *New Monthly* in 1841, serving in this capacity until 1853.

Fonthill Abbey

FROM *THE LEEDS INTELLIGENCER*

We took the liberty a few weeks ago at the hazard of provoking the displeasure of a Nabob, and the frown of an auctioneer (persons both of them very formidable in their way), to offer a few remarks on the sale now in course at Fonthill Abbey; in some sort as a set-off to the gross puffs with which the more venal part of the metropolitan daily journals have been induced to cajole and mislead the public on the subject. In stating that a large and valuable portion of the Beckford library had been withdrawn and sold by private contract, we spoke the truth; although not the whole truth, as we neglected to mention how the *hiatus* has been supplied. It is a well-known and admitted fact, that the late proprietor of Fonthill, in making his arrangements with its present possessor, secured to himself the privilege of retaining one-third of the original library, to be selected as his good taste should dictate, from the entire collection. Subsequently to the completion of the transfer of Fonthill and its appendages, he is understood to have purchased another third of the library, with a similar portion of the pictures originally offered for sale by Mr. Christie. As the choice was to rest with Mr. Beckford, and he happens to be an individual of the finest possible taste both in matter of literature and *virtu*, it is not unreasonable in us to infer that he had withdrawn the 'flower of the library', and some of the most valuable of the paintings. Now, had these circumstances been fairly and candidly stated to the public, accompanied by an assurance from the proper quarter, that, with the exception of what had been retained by Mr. Beckford, the property would be submitted for sale precisely in the condition in which it was originally transferred (without the addition of one single item, whether in the shape of a book, a picture, or a looking-glass), all chance of misrepresentation would have been obviated, and all imputations of trickery and imposition entirely removed. What, however, has been the fact? Not a whisper of the arrangement with Mr. Beckford was suffered to transpire publicly until something like a confession was extorted from the auctioneer a few days ago by the statement published in this paper. On Tuesday week, Mr. Phillips informed his company from the rostrum at Fonthill, that 'not a single book had been removed but according to the terms of agreement between Mr. Beckford and Mr. Farquhar'. This announcement, it will be remarked, was the first official mention of the 'agreement' which the parties had thought proper to make; although we think it will be sufficiently clear that the circumstance ought to have been announced in all the advertisements of the sale. The suppression of this information, really of so much importance, coupled with the fact that the present library is more extensive and the pictures nearly three times as numerous as they were when originally offered for sale by Mr. Christie, has given rise, as might have been expected, to many disagreeable reports and surmises. In consequence of the imputations which have naturally enough grown out of these several circumstances, the auctioneer, Mr. Phillips, has thought it incumbent upon him to circulate the following notice: –

Mr. Phillips feels it due to the public, as well as to the protection of his employer's property, to pledge himself, that every report and insinuation which has fallen within his knowledge, evidently to prejudice the sale, are erroneous. That, as far as relates to the intended sale, Mr. Phillips also pledges himself, that a more honourable exposition of property has never occurred than will characterize the approaching sale at Fonthill Abbey.

That the public should presume to question the fallacy of these reports after they have been contradicted on such authority, can only be accounted for by the indefinite character of the denial. It is quite impossible for people to know how many of the reports in question have 'fallen within Mr. Phillip's knowledge', or what he considers 'an honourable exposition of property'. The explanation is therefore less than it might have been. A few additional lines, intimating that no part of the effects originally announced for sale had been withdrawn, nor any item added (whether to the books, paintings, or household furniture), would have been far more conclusive, and would have reduced the question to a tangible shape. We need not inform our readers that such a declaration could not be made without a gross violation of truth.

That a considerable portion of the property now selling at Fonthill Abbey never was in the possession of Mr. Beckford at all, begins now, we believe, to be pretty generally understood. It would indeed be a cruel libel on the taste of that gentleman, to suppose for a single moment that he could have admitted into his library such books as are now selling under the sanction of his name at his late magnificent residence. We should deserve to be scorched to a cinder by the terrible eye of the Caliph Vathek, if we could bring ourselves to believe for a single moment that Mr. Beckford, of Fonthill, who spared neither pains nor expense in the collection of his books, could ever have been prevailed upon to admit within the precincts of his splendid library, 'A Dictionary of Painters, bound in sheep, to imitate morocco'! or triplicate copies of such publications as the following, which we notice among a vast many more of the same quality in Mr. Phillips' Catalogue: –

Watt's Views of the Seats of the Nobility and Gentry, 3 copies!
Angus's Views of the Seats of the Nobility, 3 copies!
Rogers's Imitations of the Old Masters, 3 copies!

These copies, the triplicates of which are, as may be supposed, introduced at respectable distances from each other, are all of precisely the same quality and appearance. Of the last book each copy is differently designated – a system which is pursued in numerous other instances throughout the catalogue. The object of thus varying the titles 'cannot be mistaken'. That the *genuine* Fonthill library should have comprised three sets, none of them proofs, of such common trashy Auction Mart works as the above, is perfectly incredible; and almost equally so, that it should ever have contained duplicate and triplicate copies of such rubbish as

Beaumont's Travels through the Leopontine Alps.
Smith's London and its Environs, folio.
Deuchais' Etchings, folio.
Marchant's Gems (one of the sets *framed* and *glazed*).

There are a vast many other items hardly more worthy of preservation, which it would be an insult to common sense to consider as a part of the collection of Mr. Beckford. In many cases, where the citation of the date of the publication of the book would proclaim it a surreptitious edition, a blank is judiciously substituted in its stead, as, for instance.

1419. The British Essayists, 45 vols., half bound, London. –

Some of our readers may require to be informed that there are two editions of the British Classics; one edited by Chalmers, and another spurious and ill-printed vamp, generally to be had at a fourth of the price usually given for the former. If the copy here mentioned had been one of the best edition, we may fairly presume that the date would not have been omitted. But it would be endless to particularize similar instances of finesse. We will therefore take our leave of the library, and adjourn to the picture-gallery. The first thing that is likely to arrest the attention of even the casual observer, on comparing the catalogue of Mr. Beckford's paintings, in 1822, as described by Mr. Christie, with that purporting to be of the same collection by Mr. Phillips in 1823, is the extraordinary discrepancy in their numbers. In the former publication, we have in all only 115 pictures mentioned, about a fourth of which (comprising, with one or two exceptions, of course the 'choicest and the best') are not mentioned in Mr. Phillips's catalogue, having probably been disposed of to Mr. Beckford; and yet this identical catalogue, in spite of these deductions, is now made to contain the names of no less than four hundred and fifteen pictures! Our acquaintance with Cocker has been limited, but some of our readers can perhaps inform us, by whose system of arithmetic a man can subtract one from four and make an obvious residue of sixteen. The following tabular view – the result of a casual comparison of the two catalogues – may not prove entirely destitute of interest: –

Mr. Christie's Catalogue.		Mr. Phillips's Catalogue	
Carlo Dolcis	o	Carlo Dolcis	4
Carraccis	o	Carraccis	6
Lod. Caraccis	1	Lod. Caraccis	3
Cuyps	1	Cuyps	4
Domenichinos	1	Domenichinos	4
Gerard Dows	1	Gerard Dows	4
Backhuysens	o	Backhuysens	6
Guercinos	1	Guercinos	6
Guidos	o	Guidos	4
Holbeins	3	Holbeins	6
Jan Steens	o	Jan Steens	7
Michaus	o	Michaus	4

Mieris	1	Mieris	6
Rembrandts	0	Rembrandts	4
Ruysdaels	0	Ruysdaels	6
Wouvermans	1	Wouvermans	7
Vanderveldes	0	Vanderveldes	4
Rubens	1	Rubens	5
Paul Veroneses	1	Paul Veroneses	4
Watteaux	0	Watteaux	4
Ostades	0	Ostades	10
Teniers	1	Teniers	22

It would be a reflection on the understanding of our readers to suppose that they needed any further proofs of the 'honourable' character of the Fonthill 'Exposition of Property'. But the following extract from the conditions of sale is worthy of quotation, harmonizing as it does so completely with the whole tone of the proceeding: –

The lots to be absolutely cleared away, with all faults and errors of description, at the purchaser's expense, without any reference to the identity of subject of Master, within three days after the sale.

Among the household furniture of Fonthill, we have a profusion of looking-glasses, pier commodes, and the like; most of which we do not observe in the catalogue, although they are doubtless intended for sale with the other effects. Unfortunately, however, Mr. Beckford is known to have had a singular antipathy to looking-glasses of all sorts and sizes – an aversion almost as decisive as that of Pennant's to a wig. The looking-glasses, which are now to be met with in almost every room in Fonthill Abbey, recall to our recollection a laughable anecdote of the auctioneer who had the disposal of the celebrated Dean Milner's effects at Carlisle. Among other anomalies produced during the sale in question, as the undoubted property of the estimable Dr. Milner, was a brace of duelling pistols; but finding the sense of the company greatly against this experiment on their credulity, the auctioneer had the modesty to pass the lot: it would be well if all auctioneers were similarly endowed!

EDITOR'S NOTE From the *Leed's Intelligencer*, as quoted by *The Times*,

30 September 1823, p. 3. Alaric Watts (1797–1864) was the editor of the *Leeds Intelligencer* at this time, serving in this capacity from 1822 to 1825. There is no evidence that Watts wrote it, but he was sufficiently interested in the subject to have published a lengthy poem on the Fonthill sale in the November issue of the *Literary Museum and Register of Belles Lettres* (pp. 701–2) in which he devoted part to the controversy outlined here. This poem and some additional notes are provided in Appendix II on contemporary verse inspired by Fonthill (pp. 398–403).

Fonthill Campaign
A Slight Sketch

[THOMAS F. DIBDIN]

A Book campaign is at all times an object of attraction; but at Fonthill, irresistible. That magic name spirited me up; and, braving the boisterous gales and weeping waters, I found myself once more at Fonthill Abbey.

As I entered the grand Court Yard, an unsightly excrescence protruding from the eastern limb of the building presented itself: the frowning dark towers above the newly erected platform – the narrow opening leading to the dark barrier within recalled to my imagination the melancholy fate of the Marys, the Greys, and the Staffords, of former days. But a truce now with sadness.

I ascended the elevated *stage*, and threading a dark, narrow passage, a few paces farther brought me into the *Atrium Auction*. An elevated *position* on the right enabled me to view the skirmishing in the arena below.

Asmod, with truncheon in hand, took *his* position in the rostrum at the upper end; the recruits had failed to attend by sound of trumpet; and confidence in their valour seemed ebbing fast, when Drum-major Lexfordius gave signal of their approach. Asmod then essayed to give tongue, in glibly measured tones, with apparent self-complacency. Previous to the commencement of the action, two or three brace of feathered beauties planted themselves in the opposite alcove, to observe the manoeuvres; impatient of delay, and shivering with cold, they soon took flight. Their starved, moping, winged relatives in the Court Yard below, had cause to rejoice; they were regaled with crumbs of comfort by these kind, good creatures from the tables of the Fountain Court.

On a cross bench, near the rostrum, sat the Scriptores Minores Rerum Fonthillianarum, Tabellarius, Chronon, Molli-gloss, and

Prelum, all stanch men and true, issuing their daily laudatory bulletins to the honour and glory of the little Buonaparte in his way – the mighty Asmod.

The renowned Atticus, in restless strides, fidgeted about the rostrum: single-handed, he was almost powerless; the sturdy Bipoles slackened his fire in an instant, captured his war-helmet and baggage: a brawny Milesian took in hand the sabre of Atticus, and furiously parrying his opponents, a desperate struggle ensued; Rodius, by a well-timed thrust, snapped in twain the sabre of the Milesian, and gained the victory.

Fossa and Clerus, of the Bipole Legion, also kept up a brisk fire; this was answered from *behind* the ranks by the Drum-major Lexfordius. The tactics of the said Drum-major, not according with strict military discipline, would not have been allowed *en face*: being an inexperienced marksman, and unacquainted with the attenuating properties of Farkar powder, the spent balls, from a misdirection of his piece, instinctively dropped into the lap of Asmod, producing contortions that indicated great bodily pain.

The Asmodaeans finding themselves worsted, were compelled, as a last resource, to call to their aid the Cavaliere Ronzino, a prancing old stager and experienced tactician. His strategems, however, not succeeding, he vapoured about a considerable time; at last, becoming skittish, and almost overpowered by the foetid odour of Farkar powder, he rapidly scampered off the field of action.

The regiment 'Praestigiae' – rogues in buckram, headed by *Drum*-major Lexfordius, and drawn from the metropolitan sinks and alleys, were *drummed* out of the ranks, one by one, by Clerus, Quarter-master-general.

P.S. – The Cavaliere Ronzino is gone over to the enemy, and brings intelligence that the discomfited Asmodaeans, disappointed of the expected plunder, are in a state of mutiny. Drum-major Lexfordius has orders from head-quarters to collect the remnants of the baggage; the wooden *tirailleurs*, and all their frippery trappings, to be sold for the benefit of the starving recruits. Through the kind offices of the Cavaliere, who has secret communications with his late comrades, I hope in my next to send you an account of the portions allotted to each man.

September 25, 1823   I am, Sir, yours,
                                     Isaac Littlebury

EDITOR'S NOTE *The Literary Gazette and Journal of Belles Lettres, Arts, Sciences &c.*, 4 October 1823, pp. 634–5. This attribution is based on Beckford's identification of Littlebury as Dibdin, or 'P. D.,' for 'Puppy Dibdin,' as he commonly referred to him. The occasion was Dibin's second visit. The account of his first visit in 1822 appeared in five succeeding numbers of *The London Museum* under the pseudonym of Cuthbert Tonstall. Beckford's identification appears in a note with another article by 'Isaac Littlebury' that appeared in the *Morning Chronicle* of 26 August 1823, p. 3, dealing with a complaint about the books in the Abbey being behind wire mesh and inaccessible. Dibdin wrote: 'During the autumn of last year I visited Fonthill Abbey; *my compagnon de voyage*, a learned Orientalist, entertained me on the journey with some extraordinary anecdotes respecting the owner, connected with his splendid library. My imagination revelled in graphic and typographic luxury; and curiosity was at the highest pitch, by the expected perusal of the numerous manuscript criticisms, and remarks, with which the collection is said to have enriched almost every volume in his library: these are of so piquant a nature, that the dullest tomes sparkle with intelligence – the plastic hand of the master "maketh the foul stone precious". Judge of the mortification we endured, on our arrival, at beholding the magnificent volumes *within imprisoned bars*. Sad and sickened to the heart to be constrained to confine our adoration to their exterior, we had recourse to our tablets, in order to be gratified when the happy period of their thraldom should cease.' Beckford reacted: 'Poor P. D. treated with very little ceremony. Woeful disappointments – probably an effusion of P. D. himself under the signature of Isaac Littlebury.' MS. Beckford, Bodleian Library, b. 6, ff. 65–6. See a second letter on Fonthill by Dibdin, again using the pseudonym 'Isaac Littlebury', in the *Morning Chronicle* of 30 August 1823, p. 3.

The Carvings in Ivory at Fonthill

FROM 'APOLLO' MAGAZINE

... The carvings in ivory at Fonthill are among the most splendid ornaments of that splendid place, and may rank as some of the most curious
in the world. Those by Benvenuto Cellini, by Strous, by Magnus Berg,
and Fiamingo, are the finest. The first we shall mention is by Cellini,
and is made use of as the stand of a cup, framed by a Nautilus' shell. It
represents a group of cupids, playing with an eagle and a goat. Nothing
can be conceived more true to nature than their childish forms; the
ivory is moulded into all the softness of flesh: – (Titian's pencil would
not give more yielding flexibility) – and the expression is full of innocent serious grace. The size of the work appears to have been no impediment to the freedom of the sculptor's chissel. There is a total and
delightful absence of littleness of manner, of timidity, and restraint; so
that the figures look of the size of life. This rare performance answers
fully to the reputation of the artist, of whose works we have heard so
much and seen so little. Who has not read the life of Benvenuto Cellini,
and who would not give something for a glimpse at one of those matchless productions, about which he himself makes such a rout? We find
no traces of his bold and licentious life in the classic purity of his style;
and his fiery spirit seems to have been tamed into a sort of playful ease
and tenderness by the difficult materials in which he worked.

There is a very fine Marine Venus with Tritons, by Strous, carved on
an ivory vase. The figures are not perfectly proportioned, but they have
a grace and spirit, and the faces a voluptuous, passionate expression,
which redeems every mechanical defect, and is wonderful in so small a
compass. – The celebrated Hunting Piece, by Magnus Berg, has not this
capital excellence; but is a most curious and elaborate piece of workmanship. The pains taken, the finishing, the spirit, the resemblance to
life in the figures, the animals, the landscape, are admirable, but they, at
the same time, excite a feeling of regret, that where so much was done

and attempted, there should be a want of any thing to crown the success of the artist, and that he should be so near touching the highest point of art, and yet come short of it. The figures reposing in the forest of ivory are asleep, but they are not nymphs or goddesses asleep: the figure of Diana on the top of the lid is executed with great dexterity and knowledge, but it is not the figure of the goddess of the chase, of the moon, or of hell: the Hercules that supports the cup (the Atlas of this little world) is old. Magnus Berg had not the ideal faculty. He was a German and medallist to the Emperor! Infinite were the pains he took with this, the chef-d'oeuvre of his hand. Infinite were his hopes and fears in the progress of the work. Much was there that he succeeded in, much that he failed in, to his own thinking. How different the interest the artisan feels in a task of this kind in his workshop, and that which it afterwards excites in the mind of the spectator or possessor! It occupied his mind for years, and every thing depended on its success. Let it succeed, which is a million to one, and it forms an article in a catalogue of curiosities, is placed in a gallery, is one among a thousand other trifles, is looked at for a moment, and forgotten!

There are several small ivory sculptures of the hand of Fiamingo in the Fonthill Gallery. The little allegory of Youth and Age is the best. The figures of the old man, and of the children, are finely understood, and executed with much taste and feeling; and considering the dimensions, are almost a miracle of accuracy. These, together with the topaz Cup, carved by Cellini, and presented to Catharine Cornaro – (the materials stamp its solid worth, the historic names shed a glory round it) form a collection of themselves.

EDITOR'S NOTE 'Fonthill Abbey', *Apollo Magazine*, I (1823), pp. 204–6. Little is known about this monthly publication except that the proprietor was Thomas Hughes, bookseller and publisher, 35 Ludgate Street, St Paul's and it was printed by William Lewis, 21 Finch Lane, Cornhill. The first issue appeared in May 1823 and the last in December 1828. The title and the paragraphing were supplied by the editor.

Fonthill as a Landscape Garden

J. C. LOUDON

A UG. 28.[1835] – *Hindon* – The occasional glimpses caught of
Fonthill from the high parts of the open downs, surrounded by
woods, and without a single human habitation, a fence, or a made road
appearing in the landscape, convey to a stranger a correct impression
of the character of the place; viz., that of a monastic building in a wild,
hilly, and thinly inhabited country, such as we may imagine to have
existed three or four centuries ago. On arriving, at the miserable little
town of Hindon, its appearance serves rather to heighten than to lessen
this impression; without trade or manufacture and with no main road
passing through it, it contains only a few houses, the largest of which
assume the character of inns; but of these inns the best does not even
take in a newspaper. Till the passing of the Reform Bill, Hindon derived
its support chiefly from the return of members to parliament; but this
resource being gone, the inhabitants are now in the greatest misery.
Before Mr. Beckford sold Fonthill, he generously gave 20 acres to the
poorest inhabitants for ever as garden ground; observing, as it is said,
that they had need of a friend.

Fonthill Abbey; H. Bennett, Esq. – This place, independently of the
historical associations connected with the name of Beckford, well
deserves to be visited by every person who takes an interest respecting,
or is desirous of improving himself in, landscape-gardening; because it
is the only one in England, in which he will find the most perfect unity
of character preserved throughout the grounds, and that character one
belonging to an age long since past in this country, and only now to be
found in certain mountainous regions of Catholic countries on the
Continent. The chief object of Mr. Beckford seems to have been to
impress this character on all the great leading features of Fonthill, and
only to have modern artificial scenes, as occasional episodes. Hence
there is not a single gravel walk or made road about the place; nor in

the immediate vicinity of the house is there an exotic tree, shrub, or flower, save an apricot and a fig tree planted against the south side of the grand entrance, as we may suppose by some monk who had brought the seeds of these fruits from some Italian or Swiss monastery.

To receive the full impression which the abbey and the scenery immediately around it are calculated to make, it is necessary to enter by what is called the Stone gate, which is situated at the end of a straight avenue, nearly a mile long, while the front of the abbey is at the opposite end. The elevated region in which the spectator finds himself, and the solemn solitary grandeur of this scene, recall the associations which we have formed of monasteries in alpine countries. The avenue forms the top of a high wooded ridge, which declines on the right and left to deep valleys, the sides of which appear to be covered with natural wood, through which are occasionally seen glimpses of water forming lakes. The trees, for the greater part, are of the spiry topped kind, which adds to the prevailing, expression of alpine scenery. This avenue is naturally of that fine close turf peculiar to elevated regions and chalky soils; and, in Mr. Beckford's time, it was kept smoothly shaven: the work being always performed during the night, in order that the prevailing character of solitariness might not be interrupted during the day. The breadth of the greater part of the avenue is about 100 ft. from tree to tree. There is a depression in it about half way from the gate to the abbey, which adds much to its effect, by giving a natural air, as compared with the broad stately avenues on level ground, which led to ancient baronial mansions; but that which completes this natural effect, and prevents us from thinking for a moment that it is a planted avenue, is, that its sides are bounded by trees and undergrowths of different sorts, not at regular distances, but just as we may suppose they would have been if the avenue had been cut out of a natural wood. The presence of undergrowth among these trees decides this question at once in the eye of the stranger. A planted avenue, with trees of the same sort at regular distances, would have spoiled the character of Fonthill. The depression in the surface of the ground adds greatly to the dignity of the abbey, by elevating its site, while it adds variety to the avenue, and preserves its natural appearance, by varying the direction of its perspective lines. Near the abbey the avenue widens so as to leave a broad area in front; and this area is so admirably broken by scattered native trees and wild bushes, as to leave no doubt in the mind of the spectator, of its having been cleared by the founders of the abbey from the native forest. In one angle, formed by two projections of the building, there was a small flower-garden, with a sun-dial and fountain; but exterior to this there was nothing exotic. At the distance of a few yards, there was a range of humble sheds, in which workmen of different kinds were employed, hewing and carving for continuous additions of improvements; and this was quite in character with the scene, as such was often the case with ancients monastic establishments. A little farther there were sheds for carts, a room for Mr. Beckford's carriage, and stables for ponies. There never were any regular stable offices, as post-horses were always employed when the carriage was made use of. The ponies were used, not only by Mr. Beckford, but by his principal servants and attendants. It may be proper here to state for the information of those who are unacquainted with the history of Mr. Beckford and of Fonthill, that, while these improvements were going on, from 1800 to 1820, Mr. Beckford resided almost constantly on the spot, saw scarcely any company, and seldom went from home.

The appearance of the abbey character being complete, in the general expression, the next point to be studied is the extent and the manner in which Mr. Beckford introduced modern improvements in the grounds: this was exceedingly simple. He confined himself entirely to the introduction of exotic trees and shrubs in secluded places only; and these he disposed in what may be called by-scenes in the woods, in such a manner as that a person who knew nothing of trees could never suspect that they were not natives. There was an American ground in the place, consisting of many of the trees and shrubs of that country, disposed in groups and thickets, as if they had sprung up naturally, with glades of turf kept smoothly mown to admit of walking through among them, and examining their separate beauties. There was a rose-ground, a thornery, and a pinetum treated in the same manner; but, along the numerous walks and drives, the common trees and shrubs of the country were those principally introduced. The next point of study is the manner of conducting the walks and drives. There was, first, from the end of the grand avenue, a broad carriage drive of several miles in length, which made a circuit of the whole place, and displayed the finest views of the abbey and the surrounding country. The greater part of this country is sufficiently naked to keep up the idea of a past age; and the tower at Stourhead, and the woods of Wardour Castle, are sufficiently distinct not to counteract this impression. Within this outer drive there is a park wall that encloses nearly 600 acres, the greater part of which is covered with wood, but with innumerable grassy glades, and some small lakes. Through this scenery, subordinate drives have been formed, to the extent, as it is said in the *Guide-Book,* of 27 miles. Two small garden episodes may be mentioned: one an herb garden, containing such plants as we may suppose the monks might have cultivated to use in medicine; and the other a garden (which, when we saw it in 1807, had a small hot-house in it, not much bigger than a cucumber frame) for a favourite dwarf. The kitchen-garden was in the outer park, about a mile and a half from the abbey, and was only seen from one part of the grand drive. There remains only one point which we think particularly worthy of study; viz., the very natural manner in which masses of trees of one kind are introduced into the woods. Even in summer, when the difference in the foliage of trees consists merely in shades of green, the good effect of this disposition is obvious. The deep dark foliage of the Scotch pine, and the green of the oak, form the conspicuous masses around the abbey, contrasted by the light tints and graceful forms of a few larches and birches, and with hazel, holly, thorn, and furze as undergrowth. On some of the very steep sides of hills, the Scotch pine and larch are almost the only trees, with birches and alders in the bottoms. The silver fir prevails in some places, and attains a noble size, and the beech is also prevalent in others in very large masses. All this is done on so large a scale, and in such a free and natural manner, as never once to excite the idea of art or formality.

We have spoken thus far of Fonthill as it was, or as it may be supposed to have been, during its occupation by Mr. Beckford; and we have done so partly from our recollections of what it was when we first saw it, in 1807, through the kindness of Mr. Milne, the gardener at that time, and partly from its present state; but the reader will recollect that the greater part of the abbey is now in ruins, and all the interesting parts of the grounds (unless we except the grand avenue and drive, and the American grounds) are in such a state of neglect, as hardly to be recognised for what they were in 1807. To preserve the abbey from falling was impossible, from the nature of its construction; but it is deeply to be regretted that the grounds have fallen into hands which, from some cause or other, could suffer the ruin to extend to them. The expense would have been very trifling of thinning out the native trees and shrubs in those places where they crowded upon the exotics in such a manner as to injure many of them, and to destroy a still greater number. In addition to this expense, there would have been little more than that of mowing the walks and drives; for the thinning and pruning of the plantations generally, we may reasonably suppose would pay itself. It is a fact worthy of notice, that scarcely any place of the same extent was ever formed that could be kept up at so little expense as Fonthill. The saving by having no gravel walks is very great; and, we are persuaded, the expense of mowing grass and sweeping up leaves might be greatly lessened, by the use of such machines for this purpose as might be dragged by horses. At all events, by letting all the mowing and sweeping up of the leaves, by the year, to one man or party of men, the cost would be nothing to what it generally is on gentlemen's grounds where these operations are performed by labourers of all work by the day. From what we have seen of the rides or drives at Fonthill, Stourhead, Bryanstone House, and Wardour Castle, we are persuaded that there are many situations on dry soils, in which gravel walks, not only in pleasure-grounds, but even in kitchen-gardens, might be dispensed with altogether, as in former times. We should then be saved from the harsh lines and sunk ditch-like excavations, bottomed with loose sand or coarse gravel, which now disfigure so many pleasure-grounds; not from their own nature, but because they are so very seldom properly formed, and kept in complete repair.

We spent the greater part of two days in looking over this place, even to the cottages and cottage-gardens in the village; and, having met with some of the old men who had worked on the grounds during the whole of Mr. Beckford's time, we indulged ourselves in asking questions, and procured much curious information respecting the building of the abbey, the mode of life of Mr. Beckford while he resided in it, the falling down of the tower in Mr. Farquhar's time, and the general effect of Mr. Beckford's immense expenditure on the surrounding population.

It appears that Mr. Beckford pursued the objects of his wishes, whatever they were, not coolly and considerately like most other men, but with all the enthusiasm of passion. No sooner did he decide upon any point, than he had it carried into immediate execution, whatever might be the cost. After the abbey was commenced, he was so impatient to get it finished, that he kept regular relays of men at work night and day, including Sundays; supplying them liberally with ale and spirits while they were at work, and when any thing was completed, which gave him particular pleasure, adding an extra £5 or £10 to be spent in drink. The first tower, the height of which from the ground was 400 ft., was built of wood, in order to see its effect: this was then taken down, and the

same form put up in wood covered with cement. This fell down, and
the tower was built a third time, on the same foundation, with brick
and stone. The foundation of the tower was originally that of a small
summer-house, to which Mr. Beckford was making additions when the
idea of the abbey occurred to him; and this idea he was so impatient to
realise, that he could not wait to remove the summer-house, to make a
proper foundation for the tower, but carried it up on the walls already
standing. The kinds of masonry, brickwork, and carpentry which were
used may easily be ascertained from the parts remaining. Nothing can
be worse: the walls are carried up in some parts of brick, in others of
stone, and in others of studwork, sometimes enclosed in stone or brick
casing, but always of the very worst description of workmanship. The
mortar seems to have been particularly bad, and never to have united
either with the stone or with the brick; since, even in the most solid
parts of the wall which remain, it may be picked out with the fingers in
a state of powder. The appearance of the ruins, as they now stand,
produces an impression of meanness mixed with grandeur that it is
impossible to describe. The greatness of the dimensions of the parts
which still exist, and which, from being covered with cement, have the
appearance of stone; and the shattered remains of lath and plaster,
studwork, and bricks, and bond timber; and, above all, the long strings
of tarred pack-thread hanging from the nails and other remains of what
were once mouldings worked in Roman cement, have a tattered
appearance, the very opposite of the grandeur produced by durability
of execution. We feel as if we had discovered that what, at a distance,
we had supposed to be a marble statue, was, in reality, a mere bundle of
rags and straw, whited over to produce effect. To those who are
acquainted with the details of building, and especially with the practices of the worst London builders, the exhibition here is most amusing
in a scientific point of view; and one may easily conceive that the work
has been chiefly carried on by men in a state of intoxication. The
manner in which the tower fell may be mentioned as something
remarkable. It had given indications of falling for some time, and the
more valuable parts of the windows and other articles had been
removed. Mr. Farquhar, however, who then resided in one angle of the
building, and who was in a very infirm state of health, could not be
brought to believe that there was any danger. He was wheeled out in
his chair on the lawn in front, about half an hour before it fell; and
though he saw the cracks, and the deviation of the central tower from

the perpendicular, he treated the idea of its coming down as ridiculous. He was carried back to his room, however, and the tower fell almost immediately. From the manner in which it fell, from the lightness of the materials of which it was constructed, and partly also from a number of workmen having been for some days making a noise in taking down articles, which it was supposed by Mr. Farquhar's nephew the tower would injure if it fell, neither Mr. Farquhar nor the servants, who were in the kitchen preparing dinner, knew that it had fallen; though the immense collection of dust which rose into the atmosphere had assembled almost all the inhabitants of the village, and had given the alarm even as far as Wardour Castle. Only one man (who died in 1833) saw it fall. He is said to have described its manner of falling as very beautiful; it first sank perpendicularly and slowly, and then burst and spread over the roofs of the adjoining wings on every side, but rather more on the southwest than on the others. The cloud of dust which arose was enormous, and such as completely to darken the air for a considerable distance around for several minutes. Such was the concussion in the interior of the building, that one man was forced along a passage, as if he had been in an air-gun, to the distance of 30 ft., among dust so thick as to be felt. Another, on the outside, was in the like manner carried to some distance. Fortunately, no one was seriously injured. With all this, it is almost incredible that neither Mr. Farquhar nor the servants in the kitchen should have heard the tower fall, or known that it had fallen, till they saw through the windows the people of the village who had assembled to see the ruins. Still, we were assured by different persons that this was the fact. We can hardly account for it by the lightness of the materials and the distance of the tower from the kitchen, and the room inhabited by Mr. Farquhar, though this was very considerable, since the dust must surely have penetrated everywhere to such an extent as to excite suspicion. We were informed, however, that the dust occasioned by taking out the windows, &c., was so considerable, that, when Mr. Farquhar's table was covered with dust from the falling of the tower, he thought it arose from the same cause. Mr. Farquhar, it is said, could scarcely be convinced that the tower was down; and when he was so, he said he was glad of it, for that now the house would not be too large for him to live in. Mr. Beckford, when told at Bath, by his servant, that the tower had fallen, merely observed, that it had then made an obeisance to Mr. Farquhar, which it had never done to him.

In confirmation of our idea that Mr. Beckford's enjoyments consisted of a succession of violent impulses, we may mention that, when he wished a new walk to be cut in the woods, or any work of that kind to be done, he used to say nothing about it in the way of preparation, but merely give orders, perhaps late in the afternoon, that it should be cleared out and in a perfect state by the following morning at the time he came out to take his ride. The whole strength of the village was then put in requisition, and employed during the night; and the next day, when Mr. Beckford came to inspect what was done, if he was pleased with it, he used to give £5 or a £10 note to the men who had been employed to drink, besides, of course, paying their wages, which were always liberal. Even his charities were performed in the same manner. Suddenly he has been known to order a hundred pairs of blankets to be purchased and given away; or all the firs to be cut out of an extensive plantation, and all the poor who chose to take them away to be permitted to do so, provided it were done in one night. He has also been known suddenly to order all the waggons and carts that could be procured to be sent off for coal to be distributed among the poor. Mr. Beckford seldom rode out beyond his gates, but when he did he was generally asked for charity by the poor people. Sometimes he used to throw a £1 note or a guinea to them, and sometimes he used to turn round and give the suppliants a severe horsewhipping. When the last was the case, soon after he had ridden away, he generally sent back a guinea or two to the party who had been beaten. In his mode of life Mr. Beckford had many singularities; though he never had any society, yet he had his table covered every day in the most splendid style. He has been known to give orders for a dinner for twelve persons, and to sit done alone to it attended by twelve servants in full dress, eat of one dish, and send all the rest away. There were no bells in the house, with the exception, we believe, of one room, occupied occasionally by his daughter, the Duchess of Hamilton. The servants used to wait by turns in the ante-rooms to the rooms which Mr. Beckford might occupy at the time. The rooms in which he lived in general were exceedingly small, and even low in the ceiling. In short, according to our ideas of a well-proportioned room, there never was one in the building. The finest were cubes of 22 ft. on the side.

One of the last things which Mr. Beckford did, after having sold Fonthill, and ordered horses to be put to his carriage to leave the place for ever, was to mount his pony, and ride round with his gardener, to give directions for various alterations and improvements which he wished to have executed. On returning to the house, his carriage being ready, he stepped into it, and has never visited Fonthill since. Though Mr. Beckford spent immense sums of money at Fonthill (we were informed, on what we consider good authority, that the place in all cost him £1,600,000), it does not appear that he has at all elevated the character of the labouring classes in the neighbourhood; on the contrary, we were informed by Mr. Joy, the manager for the present proprietor, that the effect was directly the reverse. The men, in Mr. Beckford's time, were sunk past recovery in habits of drunkenness; and the consequence is, that there are now only two or three of the village labourers alive who were then employed. The labourers, however, generally, in this part of the country, are deeply degraded by the system of making up their wages from the poor's rates; so much so, indeed, that many of the married men drink every shilling that they earn, and leave their wives and children to be supported entirely by the parish; declaring, what, indeed, appears to be their belief, that there is a law obliging the parish to provide for their families, and that they are only bound to take care of themselves.

These are but a few of the numerous tales which were told us by different persons about Fonthill; and it must be recollected that we do not vouch for the truth of any of them, though we think the whole of them are very likely to be true. We admire in Mr. Beckford his vivid imagination and cultivated mind, and that good taste in landscape-gardening which produced the perfect unity of character which pervades the grounds at Fonthill. We also give him full credit for his good sense in having quitted the place when he could no longer afford to keep it up, and the honourable principle he showed in never getting into debt, but paying liberal prices and ready money to the last. We must, however, enter our protest against the recklessness with which he employed his wealth to gratify his wishes, without regard to its demoralising effects on the labouring population of his neighbourhood, effects so serious that it will take a generation to remove them. Far happier will it always be for a country gentleman to cultivate feelings of kindness and sympathy for all those that are about him, and to encourage similar feelings in them towards him, than merely to lavish money upon them. Still, it is as impossible not to admire Mr. Beckford, as it is not to admire Lord Byron, from the native grandeur of his mind, its superior cultivation, and the high aristocratic feeling which he possessed, unmixed with the slightest shade of meanness. His faults and eccentricities appear to have been chiefly caused by an ardent temperament, stimulated by the early possession of almost unbounded wealth, and unchecked by the restraints of reason, prudence, and human sympathy.

EDITOR'S NOTE 'Notes on Gardens and Country Seats', *The Gardener's Magazine*, XI (September 1835), pp. 441–49. John Claudius Loudon (1783–1843), horticultural writer and a foremost authority on landscape gardening, authored the *Encyclopedia of Gardening* (1822), among other books in the field.

The Gem and the Wonder of Earth

HENRY VENN LANSDOWN

On the 28th of October, 1844, we left Bath determined to examine the once far-famed Abbey of Fonthill, and to see if its scenery was really as fine as report had represented. The morning was cold and inauspicious, but when we reached Warminster the sun burst out through the mists that had obscured him, and the remainder of the day was as genial and mild as if it had been May. We procured the aid of a clownish bumpkin to carry our carpet bag, and left Warminster on foot. About four miles from that town those barren and interminable downs are reached which seem to cover the greater part of Wiltshire. The country is as wild as the mountain scenery of Wales, and the contrast between it and the polished city we had left in the morning was truly singular. We took the road to *Hindon,* but a worthy old man, of whom we asked particulars, pointed out a pathway, which cut off at least a mile and a half. We followed his direction, and left the high road. Mounting the hill by a steep and chalky road we reached a considerable elevation; before us extended a succession of downs, and in the extreme distance a blue hill of singular form, at least nine miles off, was crowned by buildings of very unusual appearance. Curiosity as to the place was at its utmost stretch, but our ignorant bumpkin could tell nothing about it. It surely cannot be Fonthill was the instant suggestion? Impossible. Can we see the remains at this distance? We continued our walk for about two miles, without losing sight of this interesting edifice, and at length all doubts were cleared in the certainty that the long wished-for object was absolutely before us. It is impossible to describe the feelings of interest experienced by the sight of these gigantic remains. The eastern transept still rises above the woods, a point, pinnacle, and round tower. Descending the hill towards Hindon we lost sight of the Abbey. A most singular specimen of country life was presented by an old shepherd, of whom we inquired the way.

'How far is it to Hindon?' 'About four miles.' 'Is this the right road?' 'Yes, you cannot miss it, but I haven't been there these forty years. Naa, this is forty years agone save two that I went to Hindon: 'twas in 1807.'

This place, which once sent members to Parliament, and which the author of 'Vathek' himself represented for many years, is not so large as the village of Batheaston! There are neither lamps nor pavement, but it possesses a most picturesque little church. It was one of the rotten boroughs swept away, and properly enough, by the Reform Bill. Here our rustic relinquished his burden to a Hindon lad, who acted as our future cicerone, and undertook to show us the way to the inn called the Beckford Arms. Soon after leaving Hindon the woods of Fonthill were reached. We mounted a somewhat steep hill, and here met with a specimen of the gigantic nature of the buildings. A tunnel about 100 feet long passed under the noble terrace, reaching from Knoyle to Fonthill Bishop, at least three miles in length; the tunnel was formed to keep the grounds private. The beech trees, now arrayed in gaudy autumnal tints, seen through this archway have a lovely effect. Emerging from the tunnel, the famous wall, seven miles long, was just in front. To the left you trace the terrace, on a charming elevation, leading to Fonthill Gardens, and here and there you have glimpses of the great lake. The ground is broken and varied in the most picturesque fashion. You pass some cottages that remind you of Ryswick, and soon come to the church of Fonthlll Gifford. This church is perfectly unique in form, its architecture purely Italian; one would think it was designed by Palladio. There is a pretty portico supported by four tall Doric columns, and its belfry is a regular cupola. We at last gained the inn, and were shown into a lovely parlour that savoured of the refined taste that once reigned in this happy solitude. It is lofty, spacious, and surrounded by oak panels; it has a charming bow window, where are elegantly represented, in stained glass on distinct shields, the arms of Alderman Beckford, his wife, and the eccentric son.

The evening was most lovely. A soft haze had prevailed the whole afternoon, and as there was still an hour's daylight I determined on instantly visiting the ruins. Just without the sacred enclosure that once prevented all intrusion to this mysterious solitude is the lovely little village of Fonthill Gifford; its charming cottages, with their neat gardens and roses, are a perfect epitome of English rusticity. A padlocked gate admits the visitor within the barrier; a steep road, but gently winding so as to make access easy, leads you to the hill, where once stood 'the gem and the wonder of earth'.

The road is broad and entirely arched by trees. Emerging suddenly from their covert an astonishing assemblage of ruins comes into view. Before you stands the magnificent eastern transept with its two beautiful octangular towers, still rising to the height of 120 feet, but roofless and desolate; the three stately windows, 60 feet high, as open to the sky as Glastonbury Abbey; in the rooms once adorned with choicest paintings and rarities trees are growing. Oh what a scene of desolation! What the noble poet said of 'Vathek's' residence in Portugal we may now literally say of Fonthill.[1]

> Here grown weeds a passage scarce allow
> To halls deserted, portals gaping wide.
> Fresh lessons, ye thinking bosoms, how
> Vain are the pleasures by earth supplied,
> Swept into wrecks anon by Time's ungentle tide.

Of all desolate scenes there are none so desolate as those which we now see as ruins, and which were lately the abode of splendour and magnificence. Ruins that have been such for ages, whose tenants have long since been swept away, recall ideas of persons and times so far back that we have no sympathy with them at all; but if you wish for a sight of all that is melancholy, all that is desolate, visit a modern ruin. We passed through briars and brambles into the great octagon. Straight before us stands the western doorway of the noble entrance hall; but where is its oaken roof, with its proud heraldic emblazonments, where its lofty painted windows, where its ponderous doors, more than 30 feet high? The cross still remains above, as if symbolical that religion triumphs over all, and St. Anthony still holds out his right hand as if to protect the sylvan and mute inhabitants of these groves that here once found secure shelter from the cruel gun and still more cruel dog. But he is tottering in his niche, and when the wind is high is seen to rock, as if hi[s] reign were drawing to a close.

Of the noble octagon but two sides remain. Looking up, but at such an amazing elevation that it makes one's neck ache, still are seen two windows of the four nunneries that adorned its unique and unrivalled circuit. And what is more wonderful than all, the noble organ screen,

1 From canto I, st. XXIII of Byron's 'Childe Harold's Pilgrimage'. RJG

[374]

designed by 'Vathek' himself, has still survived; its gilded lattices, though exposed for twenty years to the 'pelting of the pitiless storm', yet glitter in the last rays of the setting sun. We entered the doorway of the southern entrance hall, that door which once admitted thousands of the curious when Fonthill was in its glory. This wing, though not yet in ruins, not yet entirely dismantled, bears evident signs of decay. Standing on the marble floor you look up through holes in the ceiling, and discover the once beautifully fretted roof of St. Michael's Gallery. We entered the brown parlour. This is a really noble room, 52 feet long, with eight windows, painted at the top in the most glorious manner. This room has survived the surrounding desolation, and gives you a slight idea of the former glories of the place. Each window consists of four gigantic pieces of plate-glass, and in the midst of red, purple, lilac, and yellow ornaments are painted four elegant figures, designed by the artist, Hamilton, of kings and knights, from whom Mr. Beckford was descended. As there are eight windows there are thirty-two figures, drawn most correctly. What reflections crowd the mind on beholding this once gorgeous room! There stood the sideboard once groaning beneath the weight of solid gold salvers. In this very room dined frequently the magnificent 'Vathek' on solid gold, and there, where stood his table, covered with every delicacy to tempt the palate, is now a pool of water, for the roof is insecure, and the rain streams through in torrents. On the right hand is the famous cedar boudoir, whose odoriferous perfume is smelt even here. We entered the Fountain Court, but sought in vain the stream that was once forced up, at vast expense, from the vale below and trickled over its marble bason.

> For the stream has shrunk from its marble bed,
> Where the weeds and desolate dust are spread.

One would almost imagine Byron had written his lines in the 'Giaour' describing Hassan's residence amidst the ruins of Fonthill, so striking, so tangible, is the resemblance. He says of the fountains –

> 'Twas sweet of yore to hear it play
> And chase the sultriness of day,
> As springing high the silver dew
> In whirls fantastically flew
> And flung luxurious coolness round
> The air, and verdure o'er the ground.

[375]

'Twas sweet, when cloudless stars were bright,
To view the wave of watery light
And hear its melody by night.

But the shades of evening, now rapidly advancing, warned us to depart
while there was yet light enough to trace our path through the gloomy
wood. We entered its thick and umbragious covert, and were near
losing our road before we reached the barrier gate. The road was
strewed with dry leaves, which reminded me of the earthly hopes of
man.

He builds too low who builds beneath the skies,

and he who wishes for solid happiness must rest on a broader base than
that afforded by momentary enjoyment, tempting and blooming as the
foliage of summer, but evanescent as its withered leaves.

The next morning was finer than our most sanguine wishes could
have anticipated. We were not long dispatching our comfortable breakfast, and hastened to the barrier gate. We here met a venerable woman,
whose noble features and picturesque dress could have served as a
splendid model for Gainsborough or Ben Barker. Stopping to inquire a
nearer road to the Abbey, as she seemed indigenous to the place, I was
tempted to ask if she know Mr. Beckford. 'I have seen him, sir, many,
many times; but he is gone, and I trust – I do trust – to rest. He was a
good man to the poor, never was there a better.' 'You astonish me; I had
heard that he never gave away anything.' 'Good gracious, sir, who
could have invented such lies? There never was a kinder friend to the
poor, and when he left they lost a friend indeed. Not give away
anything! Why, sir, in the winter, when snow was on the ground and
firing dear, he used to send wagons and wagons for coal to Warminster,
and make them cut through the snow to fetch it, and gave the poor
souls plenty of firing, besides money, blankets, and clothing, too, and as
for me I can answer for three half-sovereigns he gave me himself at
different times with his own hand.' 'You surprise me.' 'I saw him
coming once with his servants. I had my baby in my arms – that's she
that lives in that cottage yonder, she's grown a woman now – and I was
shuffling along to get out of his way, when he called out, "what a
beautiful little babe, let me look at it," and then he smiled and made as
though he would shake hands with the child and, bless you, he slipped
half-a-sovereign into my hand.' I confess I was delighted at the little

anecdote, and I am sure the good woman's praise was perfectly disinterested. Those who know anything of the poor are convinced they never flatter those from whom they can never again derive any benefit. I had almost expected to hear curses, if not loud at least deep.

A bailiff resides in the Abbey stables, who has charge of the place, but the 'steeds are vanished from the stalls'. We inquired if we could see the remaining apartments, but found the bailiff was gone to Hindon, and had taken the keys with him. Here was a difficulty indeed. 'Perhaps,' said his daughter, 'you can get into the great tower staircase; I think the door is open.' We proceeded thither, but alas! a ponderous door and locked most unequivocally denied all entrance. 'Perhaps father has left the key in his old coat; I will run and see' said our interesting young cicerone. She scuttled off, and we waited in anxiety, till in five minutes she returned with a large bunch of keys, the passport to the extraordinary apartments still remaining. My joy was as great at hearing the lock turn as was ever 'Vathek's' when he discovered the Indian at the gate of the Hall of Eblis with his *clef d'or*. The great circular staircase survived the shock of the falling tower. The stairs wind round a massive centre, or newel, three feet in diameter; the ascent is gentle, the stairs at least six feet broad. They form an approach light, elegant, and so lofty that you cannot touch with the hand the stairs above your head. Numerous small windows make the staircase perfectly light, and the inside is so clean that it is difficult to believe it is not continually scoured and whitened, but this I was assured was not the case. Two hundred and ten steps lead to a leaden roof, the view from which beggars description. You have here a bird's eye view of the lovely estate. Majestic trees, hanging woods, and luxuriant plantations cover the ground for two or three miles round, whilst beyond this begin those immense and interminable downs for which Wiltshire fair is so noted; they are dreary and barren enough in themselves, but at such a point as this, where the foreground and middle distance are as verdant and richly clad with trees as can possibly be desired, their effect is very beautiful. The absence of enclosures produces breadth and repose, and the local colour melts gradually into the grey distance in the most charming manner. Looking westward the great avenue, a mile in length, presents itself; to the south the Beacon-terrace, a green road more than two miles long, leads to a high hill, where the Alderman commenced, but never finished, a triangular tower. This road, or rather avenue, has a most charming effect; the trees that bound its sides are planted in a zigzag direction, so as to destroy the appearance of formality, whilst in reality it is a straight road, and you walk at once in a direct line, without losing the time you would if the road were more tortuous. On the south side the view is most fascinating. In a deep hollow not half-a-mile off, enbosomed, nay almost buried amidst groves of pine and beech, are discovered the dark waters of the bittern lake. The immense plantations of dark pines give it this sombre hue, but in reality the waters are clear as crystal. Beyond these groves, still looking south, you discover the woods about Wardour Castle, and amongst them the silvery gleam of another sheet of water. To the southwest is the giant spire of Salisbury, which since the fall of Fonthill Tower now reigns in solitary stateliness over these vast regions of down and desert. Stourton Tower presents itself to the north, whilst to the west, in the extreme distance, several high hills are traced which have quite a mountainous character –

> Naveled in the woody hills,
> And calm as cherished hate, its surface wears
> A deep, cold, settled aspect nought can shake.

The north wing of the Abbey, containing the oratory, does not seem to have suffered from the fall of the Tower, and we next proceeded to inspect it. A winding staircase from the kitchen court leads you at once to that portion of the gallery called the vaulted corridors. The ceilings of four consecutive rooms are beautiful beyond all expectation. Prepared as I was by the engravings in Rutter and Britton to admire these ceilings, I confess that the real thing was finer than I could possibly have imagined. King Edward's ceiling of dark oak (and its ornaments in strong relief) is as fresh as if just painted, and the beautiful cornice round the four walls of this stately gallery is still preserved, with its three gilded mouldings, but the seventy-two emblazoned shields that formed an integral part of the frieze have been ruthlessly torn off. The roof of the vaulted corridor with its gilded belts is the most perfect of the series of rooms, and that of the sanctum is beautifully rich; it is fretted in the most elegant way with long drops, pendants, or hangings like icicles, at least nine inches deep. Here alas! the hands of vandals have knocked off the gilded roses and ornaments that were suspended. These three apartments are painted in oak, and gold is most judiciously introduced on prominent parts. But the ceiling of the last compartment is beyond all praise; it gleams as freshly with purple, scarlet, and gold as if painted yesterday. Five slender columns expand into and support a gilded reticulation on a dark crimson ground. In the centre of the ceiling is still hanging the dark crimson cord which formerly supported the elegant golden lamp I had formerly admired in Lansdown-crescent; it seemed to have been hastily cut down, and its height from the floor and its deep colour, the same as the ceiling, has probably prevented its observation and removal. The southern end of the gallery has been stripped of its floor, and it was with difficulty, and not without danger, I got across a beam; and, standing with my back against the brick wall that has been built up at the end, where were once noble glazed doors opening into the grand octagon, I surveyed the whole lovely perspective; the length from this spot is 120 feet. The beautiful reddish alabaster chimney-piece still remains, but it is split in the centre, whether from the weight of wall or a fruitless attempt to tear it out I know not. The recesses, once adorned with the choicest and rarest books, still retain their sliding shelves, but the whole framework of the windows has been removed, and they are open to the inclemency of the weather, or roughly boarded up. The stove, once of polished steel, is now brown and encrusted with rust as if the iron were 500 years old. It is impossible for an architect or artist to survey the ruthless and wanton destruction of this noble wing, unscathed and uninjured but by the hands of barbarous man, without feelings of the deepest regret and sorrow. How forcibly do the lines of the noble bard recur to the mind on surveying these apartments, still magnificent, yet neglected, and slowly and surely falling into ruin –

> For many a gilded chamber's here,
> Which solitude might well forbear,
> Within this dome, ere yet decay
> Hath slowly worked her cankering way.

I ran up the circular staircase, and entered the noble estate bedroom. The enormous plate glasses still remain; the ceiling is of carved oak relieved by gold ornaments. With what emotion did I turn through the narrow gallery, leading to the state room, to the tribune, which looked into the great octagon. A lofty door was at the extremity. I attempted to open it; it yielded to the pressure, and I stood on the very balcony that looked into the octagon.

Here the whole scene of desolation is surveyed at a glance. How deep were my feelings of regret at the destruction of the loftiest domestic apartment in the world. Twenty years ago this glorious place was in all its splendour. High in the air are still seen two round windows that once lighted the highest bedrooms in the world. What an extraordinary idea! On this lofty hill, 120 feet from the ground, were four bedrooms. Below these round windows are the windows of two of the chambers called nunneries. Landing on this balcony I quickly conjured up a vision of former glory. There were the lofty windows gleaming with purple and gold, producing an atmosphere of harmonious light peculiar to this place, the brilliant sunshine covering everything within its influence with yellow quatrefoils. From that pointed arch once descended draperies 50 feet long! The very framework of these vast windows was covered with gold. There was the lovely gallery opening to the nunneries, through whose arches ceilings were discovered glittering with gold, and walls covered with pictures. Exactly opposite was another tribune similar to this; below it the immense doors of St. Michael's Gallery, whose crimson carpet, thickly strewed with white roses; was seen from this place, whilst far, far above, at an elevation of 130 feet, was seen the lofty dome, its walls pierced with eight tall windows, and even these were painted and their frames gilded. The crimson list to exclude draught still remained on these folding doors, but the lock was torn off! I closed the doors, not without a feeling of sadness, and returning to the small gallery again ran up the Lancaster Gallery to another noble bedroom. Finding the stairs still intact I mounted them, and found a door, which opened on to the roof. We were now on the top of the Lancaster Tower. Though not so extensive as the view from the platform of the great staircase, there is a peep here that is most fascinating; it is the extreme distance seen through the ruined window of the opposite nunnery.

The glimpse I had of the bittern lake having sharpened my appetite to see it, I descended the staircase of the Lancaster turret, and marching off in a southerly direction hastened towards its shores. But it is so buried in wood that it was not without some difficulty we found it. Never in happy England did I see a spot that so forcibly reminded me of Switzerland. Though formed by Art, so happily is it concealed that Nature alone appears, and this lovely lake seems to occupy the crater of an extinct volcano. It is much larger than I anticipated. A walk runs all round it; I followed its circuit, and soon had a glorious view of the Abbey, standing in solitary stateliness on its wooded hill on the opposite side. The waters were smooth as a mirror, and reflected the ruined building; its lofty towers trembled on the crystal wave, as if they were really rocking and about to share the fate of the giant tower that was once here reflected. We followed the banks of the lake. Passing some noble oaks that were dipping their extended boughs in the water, we soon gained the opposite side. Here is a labyrinth of exotic plants, a maze of rhododendrons, azaleas, and the productions of warmer climes, growing as if indigenous to the soil. We passed between great walls of rhododendrons, in some places 15 foot high, and reached a seat, from whence you see the whole extent of this lovely sheet of water. What I had seen and admired so much on Lansdown was here carried to its utmost perfection; I mean the representation of a southern wilderness. In this spot the formality of gardening is absolutely lost. These enormous exotic plants mingle with the oak, the beech, and the pine, so naturally that they would delight a landscape painter. These dark and solemn groves of fir, contrasting so strikingly with the beech woods, now arrayed in their last gaudiest it dress, remind me forcibly of Switzerland and the Jura Mountains, which I saw at this very season. Nature at this period is so gaudily clad that we may admire her for her excessive variety of tints, but cannot dare to copy her absolutely. In this sheltered and sequestered spot the oaks, though brown and leafless elsewhere, are still verdant as July. Every varied shade of the luxuriant groves – yellow, red, dark, and light green – every shade is reflected in these clear waters. Three tall trees on the opposite shore have, however, quite lost their leaves, and their reflection in the wave is so exactly like Gothic buildings, that one is apt to imagine you see beneath the waters the fairy palace of the Naiads, the guardians of this terrestrial Paradise.

EDITOR'S NOTE Charlotte Lansdown, *Recollections of the Late William Beckford of Fonthill, Wilts and Lansdown, Bath* (Bath, 1893), pp. 38–48. H. V. Lansdown, a Bath artist, had intended to publish these recollections at the time of Beckford's death but delayed doing so. They were then published by his daughter in a limited edition of one hundred copies. Lansdown was one of the select few to gain access to Beckford in Bath. As Charlotte wrote in her preface to the letters: 'Mr. Beckford and my Father were kindred spirits, conversant with the same authors, had visited the same countries, and both were gifted with extraordinary memories.'

Contemporary Verse
Inspired by Fonthill
1800–1829

Written in an Arbour of the Alpine Garden Fronting the Lake

[JOHN LETTICE]

In every Season, every Day, each Hour,
    Save when rude Wind, or rougher Tempest blows,
    Yon Scene is character'd by pure Repose.
    But on this favour'd Eve, as from this Bow'r,
I view the Lake's Expanse, what heavnly Pow'r,
    While golden Sunset on its Bosom glows,
    While Tuft or Spiry Tree, or Shrub or Flow'r,
    Reflected, each, within its Mirror Shows,
Does to this Vale yet more than Stillness lend,
    Repose more hush'd, a softer, deeper Calm.
    Well, with Reluctance, listless may I bend
My Footsteps hence; for sure the sacred Balm,
    Sweet Influence on my Heart of Heav'n's own Peace,
    To sooth me, ling'ring here, can never cease.

Fonthill Aug 4 1800

EDITOR'S NOTE MS. Beckford, Bodleian Library, c. 33, f. 73. Revd John Lettice served as Beckford's principal tutor in the 1770s. At the time of the writing of this and the following poem, Lettice was the tutor to Beckford's daughters.

Written in the Grotto

J[OHN] L[ETTICE]

Hither, while Noontide Heats of August fall
   Full on the Pilgrim's or the Reaper's Head,
   As this his Sickle, that, with toilsome Tread,
   Scarce plies his dusty Staff, the Naid's Call
Me to her favourite Grot allures; no Thrall
   To Gloom or Toil! And here at Fountain Head,
   I breathe the Freshness of her pebbled Hall
   And humid Caves, by genial Zephyrs led.
Cool Umbrage hail! of Rock or Sparry Roof:
   Hail! liquid Lapse of many a tinkling Rill,
   Re-echoed all around, below, aloof,
And fan'd by mural Foliage, waving Still.
   Of Grace, if more She deign her Vot'ry Proof,
   Here may light Day-Dreams aye my Fancy fill.

Aug. 6, 1800   J.L.

EDITOR'S NOTE MS. Beckford, Bodleian Library, c. 33, f. 72.

Lines on a First View of Fonthill Abbey

WILLIAM LISLE BOWLES

The mighty master wav'd his wand, and lo!
On the astonish'd eye the glorious show
Bursts, like a vision; SPIRIT OF THE PLACE,
Has the Arabian wizard, with his mace
Smitten the barren downs far onward spread,
And bade th' enchanted Palace tower instead?
Bade the dark woods their solemn shades extend?
High to the clouds yon spiry tow'r ascend?
And, starting from th' umbrageous avenue,
Spread the rich pile magnificent to view?
Enter – from this arch'd portal, look again,
Back, on the lessening woods and distant plain.
Ascend the steps – the high and fretted roof
Is woven by some Elfin hand aloof,
Whilst from the painted windows' long array,
A mellow'd light is shed, as not of day.
How gorgeous all! Oh never may the spell
Be broken, that array'd those radiant forms so well.

EDITOR'S NOTE Dated 21 August 1822. 'Written for the Second Edition of J. Rutter's Description of the Abbey.' *The Gentleman's Magazine*, XCII, pt. 2 (August, 1822), p. 102. William Lisle Bowles (1762–1850), divine, poet and antiquary, served as vicar of Bremhill, Wiltshire from 1804 to 1850. He published poems, an edition of Alexander Pope and various ecclesiastical and antiquarian works.

Fonthill: A Sonnet

M. J.

Upraised as by a wizard's powerful spell,
Or like the fitful scenery of a dream,
Far on the eye the towers of Fonthill gleam,
While memory wakes the ancient minstrel's shell.
Borne on the breeze now choral anthems swell,
Now fancy scenes of long past years will frame,
Scenes swept away by Time's devouring stream,
Which crush'd the monkish fane and hermit's cell.
Yes, they have vanish'd; but this gothic pile,
With magic power, the mental eye inspires
To trace long trains, amid the vaulted aisle,
Of holy monks and red-cross knights and friars;
To raise the spirit of those days of yore
When steel-clad warriors strove on Judah's shore.

EDITOR'S NOTE *The Literary Chronicle and Weekly Review*, 24 August 1822, p. 540.

De Aede Fonthilliana

[ABBÉ ANGE DENIS MACQUIN?]

Splendida frondosis surgit de montibus Aedes,
Tangit et augusta fronte superba polum:
Scilicet attonitus dubitat quid conspicit hospes,
An coelum in terris, an super astra domos.

On Fonthill Abbey

A magnificent building rises from the forest-clad hills,
With a majestic and superb façade, towering to touch the celestial
    vault:
Naturally astonished the visitor doubts what he sees,
A heaven on earth, or a mansion above the stars.

EDITOR'S NOTE This poem appeared in Macquin's third essay on
Fonthill in the *Literary Gazette*, 31 August 1822, p. 555. Macquin was
a Latin scholar and as the author of the essay he could also be the
author of this epigram. (The translation supplied by RJG.) However,
the way he introduced the poem in the essay by saying 'We have pleasure in accompanying it with a beautiful original epigram' suggests that
it might have been written by someone else, possibly Beckford himself,
who enjoyed writing verse from time to time and could have permitted
Macquin to have included it in the essay. Rutter incoporated this poem
on the title page of the later editions of his guidebook on Fonthill in
1822 and 1823.

Fonthill Abbey

[ABBÉ ANGE DENIS MACQUIN]

Mr. Editor, – Most of the following lines were pencilled *extempore* on the solitary bench facing the southern aspect of Fonthill Abbey, and near the border of the lake, upon the unrippled surface of which I enjoyed the pleasure of seeing this magnificent edifice invertedly repeated and enlightened by the crimson glow of a beautiful afternoon. An insertion of them in your interesting publication will oblige, Mr. Editor, yours &c.

A VISITOR

From verdant scenes of groves and woody hills
Of lofty eminence, where stately firs
And giant oaks, and aspens gray, defy
The patting anger of the blast, and wave
Their dewy foliage in the breath of morn,
When first the spiry boast of Sarum's pile
Cradles the infant ray of light –
   Or when
They swing their leafy branches in the breeze.
What time the fiery orb descends apace,
And shoots his glory through the checkered pines
That crest the Beacon-cliff – a sacred spot
Of deep and silent sorrow, for it looks
As if some dear, departed friend slept there –
   And from th' unruffled crystal of the lake
Below, the deep, mysterious, old remain
Of silenced craters, of volcanoes dire
That once disturbed the soil, and shock around
The feverish land – but now a watery plain,

Pellucid and so smooth! with sedgy banks
Of lively green or pebbly margins, where,
Happy and conscious of their freedom, play
The water-fowls, and mix their clamorous notes
With the deep groanings of the labouring wheel
That robs the Naiads in the lonely glen
Of the clear treasure of their silver urns,
To heave and send it upwards to the hill
That swells aloft –
   And from the bowers
Of various Edens, all perfumed with shrubs
Of foreign growth, all speckled with bright flowers
Of passing odorous scent – above the clouds –
Solemn in gothic majesty – the ABBEY starts
In full display upon the sapphire vault
Of purest air! –
   Thus, so they feign, sublime,
'Twixt heaven and earth, by magic art, arose
The mountain-son of Japhet, huge and bold,
To prop the Spheres.
No Gorgon's direful face,
   No secret talisman, nor fairy wand,
These wonders wrought; – but Genius, Taste, and Power
Combined, conceived the whole, and bade it rise
Magnificent – its bosom to contain
What plastic Nature and what skilful Art
Could e'er achieve.
   Here burst at once
Upon th' astonished sight, the rarest spoils
Of Eastern mines and of Peruvian ores –
The gold which Tagus in his waters rolls –
The shining sands of famed Pactolus – and
All precious metals with more precious gems
Adorned – a world of wealth – a radiant heaven
Of matchless beauties! –
   Here the spotless vase
Of icy crystal vies with agate, stained
By Nature's fancy-hands; the ruby bright,
In crimson lightnings, flashes on the eye

Its living fires – the faint, the lovely amethyst
That looks so like the swooning virgin's lips –
The sanguine stone, that spills the poisonous draught –
Celestial sapphires, verdant emeralds – all
Meet here.
    The Pallet too, on lofty walls,
Her tributary stores displays – the works
Of hands now clasped in the cold grasp of death,
Inimitable. –
    Through the blazoned halls,
The storied galleries and princely rooms,
A bright galaxy of heraldic stars,
Long lines of noblest ancestry, declare
Who planned, who raised the splendid mansion, where
Above the puny jarrings of the world,
Above the strife for glory and for power,
Wrapt in his cloak of learning and of wit, –
A mind of fire, a deeply feeling heart, –
The founder stands aloft – a stranger to our sphere!

Notes. The Abbey stands nearly due west of *Sarum's* Spire, which can be distinctly seen with the naked eye over a most beautiful and Arcadian vale, checkered with arable grounds of dark brown hue, and green pastures well studded with cottages and cattle; the distance, as the bird flies, may be about fifteen miles. On the west of the Abbey, another object of no mean consideration is 'Alfred Tower', a triangular building erected on the loftiest ridge of hills, forming part of the estate belonging to that classical lover and promoter of the Fine Arts, Sir Richard Colt Hoare, Bart., whose seat at Stourhead presents to the observer what art can do when aided by Nature and *vice versa*. The giant features of Fonthill are not there, we must confess; but if pastoral gods haunt, and skip about, the immense forests of the one, we must allow that the nymphs of the waters and of the groves are not likely ever to desert the other. The distance from the Abbey is about fourteen or fifteen miles, and the sister towers of Fonthill and Stourhead, with the Spire of Sarum, rise up in the sky as land-marks for travellers.

    'The Beacon-cliff' – This spot is the highest peak in Mr. Beckford's extensive demesnes; – it is really a cliff produced by the throes of pregnant Nature at some very ancient period of time. It commands a nearly unlimited view over Dorset and a great part of Devonshire; and through the intricate interweavings of hills and vales, the eye, with the help of a common telescope, can reach some rising grounds above the towers of Exeter. But the possessor of the place sees it plainly with his naked eye, and what is much more extraordinary, like the bird of Jove (I state it as a fact), he can stare at the sun when in the most splendid radiancy of meridian pride, without being hurt in the least by so daring an experiment.

'The labouring wheel' – The simple and yet powerful mechanism of this wheel, which is set to work by the overplus of the lake below, supplies the Abbey with plentiful streams of water. It is situated in a most romantic *ravine*; and, as I was determined to get a peep at it, I dashed through worlds of nettles and brambles, scattered stones, decayed trunks of trees, bullrushes, and furze; and after much trouble, many stumbles and scratches, I alighted, at last, on the very spot. The melancholy sound of the ever-returning clack of the main arm of the pump lulled me into such a meditating mood when I sat down upon the fern-strewed ground, under a lovely canopy of elms and larches, that I might have passed there the whole night, lost to myself and to my friends, who were waiting for me at a neat cottage behind the Beckford Arms. However, I roused my spirits, and groping along the American Garden, a most delightful paradise of exotics in full blossoms, I hardly know how I found my way back to the gate, and hurried, through a delightful lane planted with luxuriant laurels and lofty firs, to my place of repose.

'The mountain-son of Japhet' – Atlas metamorphosed into a mountain at the sight of Medusa's head shown to him by Perseus. – Lucan. IX. 657 – *in cantes Atlanta dedit.*

'A world of wealth' – These superb objects were pointed out to us and accurately described by a Portuguese gentleman (Chevalier Franchi), with so much vivacity and politeness, kindness and knowledge, that we might have styled him a most useful and entertaining 'Catalogue ambulant et raisonné' of the immense collection of beautiful works of art which surrounded us in the various apartments of the Abbey.

'The Pallet too' – It is generally understood that the pictures exposed for sale have already excited such an emulation among the numerous competitors for the finest works of the pencil, that each painting is looked upon as a most interesting subject for auctioneering contest.

'Wrapt in his cloak,' &c. – To the possessor of these riches we may apply the words of Horace – Carm. III. 29. 54. –

$$— — — — \text{ mea}$$
$$\text{Virtute me involvo.} —$$

'A stranger to our sphere' – See what Pope says of Lord Bolingbroke – Spence, 295 – 'He has so great a memory as well as judgment, that if he is alone and without books, he can sit down and write as fully on any subject as another man would with all his books about him. He sits like an intelligence, and recollects all the question within himself.' And again: 'He (Bolingbroke) looks as if he was placed here by mistake.' To which Pope answers, 'It is so; and when the comet appeared to us a month or two ago, I had sometimes an imagination that it might possibly be come to our world to carry him home, as a coach comes to one's door for other visitors.' – Spence, 316. Whoever knows Mr. Beckford personally, will find these passages fully applicable to him.

EDITOR'S NOTE *The Literary Gazette and Journal of Belles Lettres*, 21 September 1822, pp. 602–3. Abbé Ange Denis Macquin (1756–1823), miscellaneous writer and professor of rhetoric and belles-lettres at Meaux. He came to England in 1792 and was appointed heraldic draughtsman to the College of Arms a year later. Macquin was part of Beckford's circle at this time, providing assistance with the Fonthill library and conducting genealogical studies of the various coats of Beckford's ancestors.

On the Alienation of Fonthill Abbey

The Magnificent Seat of Mr. Beckford, near Bath, England

[HENRY PICKERING]

Sic transit gloria mundi

O BECKFORD! no more shall these hills and
these vales
Stretch around their lov'd lord, to delight
him again:
Nor these groves wave their tops to the soft
sighing gales,
But to murmur adieus, or thy absence to
plain.

And no more shall these turrets ascend to the
sky,
To catch the first rays of the sun at his
rise;
Nor be wrapt in soft light when the moon rides
on high,
Thy fancy to charm, or enrapture thine
eyes.

And those fair princely halls thou wast wont to
adorn,
Where Art and where Wealth every means
had essay'd
Thy regard to attract – now, alas! are
forlorn,
And will echo no more to thy voice or thy
tread.

Ah Beckford! when youth and when vigour
were thine,
And when fortune her treasures display'd to
thy sight –
When the world to thy fancy seem'd all to
combine
To fulfil every wish and to yield thee
delight –

Didst thou dream that ere long the gay vision
should cease,
And that riches might not e'en with thee long
abide ?
That that world should desert thee? that,
robb'd of thy peace,
Thou should'st soon be expell'd from the
halls of thy pride ?

How it pains me, the thought! ah, could wishes
restore
Thy mansion august, and thy splendid
domain –
Thou should'st not, as now, their desertion
deplore,
But should'st hie thee to this lov'd seclusion
again.

Alas! when I think of the changes which
here
Oft to each unexpected bring joy or bring
wo[e];
I may sigh for his fate, and to him yield a
tear,
Who, in grandeur's lap nurs'd, is by fortune
laid low.

O Beckford! methinks I can see thee e'en
now,
In the dawn of thy youth, and when all was
thus fair,

Exploring the regions where fancy and
thou
Had fondly erected your structures in
air!

And not there alone: those bright visions once
past,
See! as if by enchantment, thy palace
arise!
In dimensions as grand as thy mind itself
vast,
And boldly aspiring, like that, to the
skies.

And, lo! at thy call, see the land and the
main
To thee unreluctant their treasures
confide;
While the arts eager throng thy attention to
gain,
And thy groves wave around thee in beauty
and pride.

Thou mansion superb! and ye scenes of
delight!
How long will ye ravish the heart and the
eye? –
Hah! the spell is dissolv'd – and to thee all
is night,
And a dream, which must end in a heart-
rending sigh.

EDITOR'S NOTE *Ruins of Paestum: and other Compositions in Verse*
(Salem, Mass., 1822), pp. 53–5. Henry Pickering (1781–1838) was the
author of *Elegiac Stanzas* (1822?) and *Athens; and other poems* (1824).

Fonthill Sale

A Parody

A[LARIC] A. W[ATTS]

Who has not heard of the Sale at Fonthill,*
With its *bijoux* the brightest that earth ever gave;
Its pictures and books – and its knights of the quill,
Who of all its 'attractions' so ceaselessly rave.

Oh! to see it at mid-day, when warm o'er the HALL
Its full gathered splendour an autumn sun throws;
Ere the smug auctioneer to his seat in his stall
'Like a bride full of blushes' so smilingly goes;
And punctual to Time, without stoppage or stammer,
Reads his List of 'Conditions' and raises his hammer.

---

*The chief part of this Fragment is an imitation, or rather Parody, of the celebrated description of the Vale of Cashmere, in *Moore's Light of the Harem*, beginning:

> Who has not heard of the vale of Cashmere,
> With its roses the brightest that earth ever gave;
> Its temples and grottoes, and fountains as clear
> As the love-lighted eyes that look over its wave.
> Oh! To see it at sunset – when warm o'er the Lake;
> Its splendour at parting a summer eve throws;
> Like a bride full of blushes, when lingering to take
> A last look at her mirror to bed ere she goes.
> Here the music of Prayer from a minaret swells,
> Here the Magian his urn full of perfume is swinging,
> And here at the altar a zone of sweet bells,
> Round the waist of some fair Indian dancer is ringing,
> &c. &c. &c.

When gems, bronzes and paintings, are gleaming half shewn,
(Mr. Beckford's we mean – t'other half would not please Sir)
From tables of ebony – rosewood – and one
Which they tell us belonged to the Prince de Borghese, Sir;
But *geese* we should be all we hear thus to hug,
Since we know many come from the Prince of HUMBUG!

Then to see all the China from Nankin and Dresden,
The 'rare Oriental' and 'famed Japanese',
Mixed with all kinds of trumpery, but recently pressed in,
Our judgements to dupe and our pockets to ease!
With bronzes and boxes – *chef d'oeuvres* of skill, –
Made 'to order' they say, for the sale at Fonthill!

Here the music of bidding grows loud and more loud; –
Here the *sweetener* is conning his hints for the day;
And here by the rostrum, apart from the crowd,
Billy Tims and his brethren are scribbling away
(Striving who shall bedaub Mr. Phillips the most)
Their puffs for the *Chronicle, Herald* and *Post*!
Let us pause ere we blame, for 'tis well understood,
Though some things are so so, Harry's dinners are good;
And since paying and feeding the piper's no jest,
Sure they ought to play for him the tune he likes best.

Here a black-letter hero, with rat-smelling air,
Tipping winks full of meaning, squats down in his chair,
The veteran of many a Book-auction is he,
And he'll not be bamboozled, we think, Mr. P.!
If the item is genuine, away goes his nod,
And if cheap, is knocked down with ''tis yours, Mr. Rodd.'
If a *'foist'* and his glance of contempt is enough,
Why, he dives for his snuff-box and only takes snuff!

Here the man who is neighbour to famed Mr. Squib,
(He may call us *obscure* and perhaps tell us we fib)
The 'spirited bidder', for whom we sha'n't say,
Is beginning as usual his work of the day,
And before the great clock of the Abbey strikes four,
Will have made some two hundred bold biddings or more.
Till Clarke justly incensed at the fellow's assurance

Lets him in with a look of affected endurance,
Saying, 'Sir, 'tis your own – give you joy of the lot, it
Has long been contested and now you have got it.'
Oh to see how he changes from yellow to blue,
As he answers, 'I'm ready to yield it to you;
I have *run* up the thing, but if called on to *pay*,
Why I think I must finish by *running* away!'
But a smile from his Patron sets all matters right,
And he boldly bids on 'in his pocket's despite'!

Here the famous Count *Buff* – with his eye-glass and seals,
His rings on his fingers and spurs on his heels,
His straw-coloured wig and magniloquent air,
And his hat cocked aside like a clown's at a fair –
Strutting up to some daub – with his hand o'er his brow,
And wiping the canvas, cries 'RUBENS I vow! –
His colouring – relief – light and shadow are there –
His expression – his grouping – his breadth to a hair!
Then that CUYP there beside it's as pearly and clear,
As the first break of day at the spring of the year;
Tho' it can't be compared with yon dewy METZU,
So melting and mellow, so tasteful and true:
They've a charm above all, that must make them divine,'
(Speaking under his breath) '*entre nous*, Sir, they're mine.
Yes, you're doubtless surprised that a man of my air,
Should thus chaffer in pictures, but list while I swear,
'Twas my love for the Arts – and I'm master of some –
That first made me a DEALER, and led me to roam.
As for money, my friend, I would have you to know,
I care nothing about a few thousands or so;
There's my own private income – a mere bagatelle –
Just five thousand a year, which you know's pretty well, –
A trifle admitted, but surely enough
To buy a few baubles – and pay for one's snuff;
Then my wife, besides beauty, of which we'll be mum,
Has, 'fore God I declare it, two-thirds of a PLUM;
To say naught of an Uncle who lives in the Indies,
(By the bye, can you tell me, my friend, how the wind is),
Who has promised – and sure he can do it with ease,

To send us, ere long, a few lacks of rupees!
Then my private "collection" is worth – so they say,
Just a cool hundred thousand (not much by the way),
And my house and its trappings – (pray speak if I bore)
Has been valued by some at a good hundred more!
As you guess, in "my own hackney coach" I came down,
To see how matters go, and look after my own –
And thanks to yon pliable knights of the quill
I shall do pretty well by the sale at Fonthill.'

Here the white-trousered Dandy and black-whiskered Swell,
The lean sprig of fashion – the beau and the belle –
The Lord and the Lady – but few of the latter –
Have all journeyed, post-haste, not to buy but to chatter, –
To lounge, look about them, and prate at their ease,
Of Mieri, Correggio, and Paul Veronese!
But vainly the vender directs his keen glance
To many a gay groupe as the biddings advance;
Inattentive are they to the beam of his eye,
And he turns to Clarke, Lawford, and Rodd, with a sigh, –
Mid sunshine and storm, mid report good and ill;
The heroes and props of the sale at Fonthill!

Here Colnaghi, Thorpe, Phillips and Farquahar, good men,
We could sketch to the life with four strokes of our pen;
But we think we had better not touch off a verse on all
Lest some ill-natured booby should say we've grown personal!
However to prove that no evil we mean them,
We'll give them a sweet-tempered couplet between them.
The two first are good fellows, we own with good will,
The two last are as good – as the sale at Fonthill!

There are auctions for ever unchangingly dull,*
Like a long winter night ere the moon's at its full,

*There are beauties for ever unchangingly bright,
Like the long sunny lapse of a summer-day's light;
Shining on – shining on – by no shadow made tender,
Till Love falls asleep on its sameness of splendour.
This was not the beauty, 'twas nothing like this
That to young Nourmahal gave such magic of bliss.
&c. &c. &c. – *Vide Lalla Rookh.*

Selling on – selling on, but in bidders so slender,
That ere buyers are caught, half asleep is the vender;
Where excepting for brokers, booksellers, and one
Like the spirited Lawford, no sale could go on.
Where Report, like a spectre call'd up from the tomb,
Whispers 'Humbug', and 'Trick', and bids bidders be dumb!
These are not the Auctions, – 'tis nothing like these
That has taught Jemmy Christie all parties to please,
That has given him a power he can wield at his will,
With the flower of west-enders his sale-room to fill:
And *sans* sweeteners, and spoonies, to kick up a pother,
To get biddings in plenty of one sort or other!
'Tis plain honesty lifts him so far o'er his peers,
And has crowned him the Emperor of Town Auctioneers; –
With that sprightliness ever in motion which plays
On the eye and the pocket, and charms us both ways;
Now here and now there, wiling cash as it flies,
From the eyes to the purse, from the purse to the eyes!
If in pictures he deals, – such his elegant ease,
You would swear he was born to sell nothing but these;
And his passing mistakes do but serve to awaken
New mirth, while his credit stands firm and unshaken.
If on Books he dilates – he's as deftly at home,
Be they Novels from Paris or Classics from Rome;
If on Music – he knows the deep art to unriddle,
When from far-famed Cremona he sells you a fiddle;
In short, such the power of his spells, I've been told,
He can turn what he touches, like Croesus, to gold:
And dull before him, you may say what you will,
Is the keen Auctioneer of the Sale at Fonthill.

EDITOR'S NOTE First published in *The Literary Museum and Register of Belle Lettres*, 1 November 1823, pp. 701–2, under the title 'The Sale at Fonthill – A Fragment'. This periodical is extremely rare. Fortunately, Beckford, as was his habit, saved a clipping of the poem, which I found among his papers at the Bodleian Library. This poem was also issued separately as a broadside under the title 'Fonthill Sale – A Parody' and signed with the initials 'A. A. W.', which stands for Alaric A. Watts

(1797–1864), author of *Poetical Sketches* (1822) and editor of the *Leeds Intelligencer*, the newspaper that launched the attack on Harry Phillips for including books and works of art in the sale that were not considered to be genuine Fonthill items. I have used the broadside here since Watts revised the first printing with textual variations and punctuation. He also added notes in the broadside that did not appear with the first printing in *The Literary Museum*. Author attribution derives from Watts's own admission in a copy of the broadside on file in the Beinecke Library, Yale University. Watts sent the broadside to John Britton, noting on the verso that there were errors in the first printing that were corrected in the broadside. The broadside also contains a date handwritten at the top as '19 Jan 1824'. Beinecke Library, Beckford Collection, GEN MSS 102, Box 4, f. 100. Lewis Melville reproduced the broadside for the first time, but without author identification, in *The Life and Letters of William Beckford of Fonthill* (New York, 1910), pp. 315–19.

Fonthill: A Poem

JOHN JEFFERSON

STUPENDOUS ART! whose mighty remnants gild
Those Climes and Scenes, once with thy glories fill'd;
Those Climes, alas! where now Barbarians stray,
Or Despots rule, and trembling Slaves obey;
But still, where struggling, panting to be free,
Man strives to burst the bonds of tyranny;
Stupendous Art! I hail thee on thy throne,
The proud Acropolis, thy favor'd zone;
Where rear'd in all thy grace, magnificence,
Unrivall'd soars, and awes the lab'ring sense:
Yes, Architecture, there thy crown is hung,
There thy chief witchery, there thy beauties flung;
Revolving ages thence have sung thy praise,
And o'er thy forehead shook the victor bays;
Announc'd thy triumphs, from all rivals won,
While Fame's wide trump resounds the Parthenon.

What, tho' the grandeur of hill-planted Rome,
In arch, in column, and the spheric dome,
Bespeaks celestial genius, hov'ring round,
That nurse of arms and arts, that magic ground,
Where every glance reveals some deathless name,
Bright in the Temple's grace, or Statue's flame:
Yet, to thee, chief, fam'd Parthenon is giv'n,
More than to aught of mortal under heav'n; –
The attribute divine, to quench all thought,
When seen, save what, thy power sublime has wrought.

Yes, let us wander o'er old Pestum's scite,
Whose ruins tell of desolation's might;

Or let us rove colossal Balbec through,
Or search Persepolis, for aught like thou,
Or tax Egyptian monuments, or seek
Those wilds where roams the fierce barbarian Shiek;
Or, easier toil, those older beauties scan,
When nature taught plain unadult'rate man;
Those older beauties, which yon classic shore
Still vaunts, tho' pass'd ten thousand whirlwinds roar,
Since first the Chief* by fam'd Oenope's grove
Rear'd his high fane to Panthellenic Jove:
And then, pure Taste, unfold thy eagle eye,
Expand thy judgement, lift thy soul on high;
Draw from the stores of Science all her springs,
View wide creation, mount proportion's wings;
Considerate, now, poise with minutest skill,
Their charms with those that deck the Athenian hill,
And straight decide – 'tis done, – the fiat's gone,
And farthest space gives back the Parthenon.

When Greece, at length, by faction worn and war,
Fell from her sphere, like some erratic star,
That loosen'd from its circling axis, rolls
In meteor flashes, 'twixt opposing poles,
And shakes mankind with dark portentous fear,
Who in the omen view some Kingdom's bier;
When SHE beneath the 'eternal City' lay,
Subdued her prowess, quench'd her burning day,
Still even as now her Architecture shone,
Like some tall Pharos, in the ocean lone,
To guide advent'rers in the mighty art,
To awe, to dazzle, and improve the heart.

Hail mighty science, hail thou art divine!
An pow'rful still, or in the pagan shrine,
Or Goth's proud Temple, where a Saviour reigns,
Where penance weeps, and praise pours forth her strains;
Behold that structure, see those arches grace,
With beauteous order, yon vast sacred place;

*Aeacus.

[405]

The clustering columns mark, that rais'd on high
The soul enthral, and chain the raptur'd eye,
Forming a pillar'd vista; – Hark! what sound
Breaks on the ear, where silence reign'd profound;
'Tis hush'd! – again, the solemn tones arise
In pealing triumph; – now their cadence sighs,
In sweetest murm'rings, down the quiv'ring aisle,
Now bursts majestic thro' the tow'ring pile;
Each light poised arch with strains harmonic breathes,
Each sculptur'd column shakes thro' all its wreaths,
And, as the concave dome gives back the sound,
Re-echoing loud the trembling walls around,
Imagination sees, the crowd among,
Some list'ning angels catch the lofty song,
By Architecture's magic, now endow'd
With voice sublime, like that which fills the cloud
Before the heavenly throne – beneath whose ray
The thrilling Cherubim, their pinions lay,
With music vibrate, drawn from mortal lyre,
But made immortal, thro' arch, dome, and spire.

    Thus Music own'd and felt thy potent rod,
Thou highest emanation of the God; –
That great first Architect, whose mighty plan
Frowns in the Andes, smiles in Tinian;
In Caverns darkens, thro' the Valley beams,
Builds up the Rock, and frets with ice the Streams,
Sustains the Firmament, the Ocean awes,
Measures all space, and gives to Chaos laws,
Wields the huge Earth, the balanc'd Air suspends,
The Comet bridles, Orb with Orbit blends
In wond'rous concord, while each radiant sphere
Runs its fix'd course, nor yet too wide nor near,
And so shall run, 'till his behests complete,
Each flaming world shall hiss beneath his feet.

    To him I bend; and now due homage given
To his eternal power in earth and heaven,
Renew the verse, in trembling strains, to say
When Rome, imperial, fell beneath the sway

Of Hun and Vandal, Goth and Visigoth,
Wild as the tempest, as the lightning wroth,
(Who, led by ATTILA, the 'Scourge of God,'
On slaughter'd Kings, and welt'ring Cities trod;
And tow'ring ALARIC, from the bleak domains
Of frozen Boreas, pour'd on Europe's plains;)
While with Briarean arms, destruction rode
High on their banners, and colossal strode
With reckless triumph, and blood-dripping spear,
O'er crouching Nations with untam'd career; –
How desolation then unbar'd her arm,
Steep'd it in gore, and fir'd the locust swarm
That spread o'er Kingdoms, misery's dread wings,
Crush'd Art's exertions, shut up Learning's springs,
Led Science chain'd, and with demoniac blast
The breathing Statute from its basis cast;
Threw down the temple, in her fury wild,
The Column broke, the Catacomb defil'd ;
The Arch defac'd, the Aqueduct made void,
The Dome, the Spire, the Pinnacle destroy'd;
Yes, thus she triumph'd; Night cimmerian fell
O'er Europe's plain, her mountain, and her dell,
Her people felt the bolt, by Heav'n shot forth,
And scorch'd, and mangled, grovell'd in the earth.
Slaves of the barb'rous Victors, there they laid,
And toil'd and trembled, as the Tyrants bade.

At length some sparks of buoyant Science rose,
In minds as barren as the torpid snows,
Which annual clothe in frozen mantle drear,
Those climes, from whence deriv'd their Sire's career;
Thus heaven, inscrutable, from darkness draws
Its ends unfathom'd, and propounds its laws.

Then Architecture first her light began
To spread unconscious, thro' awakening man;
The warlike Chief his lofty Beacon rear'd,
And liv'd the Despot of the Cerfs he fear'd;
Gradual advancing, soon the feudal hall
Show'd its proud turrets and embattled wall;

The Village then in op'ning order shone,
The City thicken'd with the chisel'd stone;
While Man gregarious sought his fellow nigh,
And trade and commerce bless'd the social tye.

But chief, RELIGION, drew from hence her pow'r,
Religion, soothress of misfortune's hour;
Here the rich Abbey lifts its crested head,
And fills beholders or with hope or dread,
As conscience speaks to this in peaceful terms,
Or tortures that with all her gnawing worms;
The vast Cathedral now attracts the eye,
With Spires that seem to reach the midway sky;
While there the historic Cross its moulding shows,
And with the grace of gothic order glows;
The curious arch, the soaring column tell
The mighty pow'r with which her vot'ries swell;
Each Christian Kingdom by that pow'r imbued
Built Fanes to heaven as vaunting Babel proud;
(Tho' not alike to brave eternal might,
But bend the Soul to seek Devotion's rite;)
BATALHA from the holy impulse sprung,
And NOTRE DAME her tow'ring spires flung,
High up to Heaven; whilst all ITALIA fir'd
By ancient splendor, thro' the world admir'd,
Unnumber'd temples rear'd within her clime,
Chaste yet majestic, gorgeous yet sublime; –
At length, great BU'NAROTTI, wondrous name,
Threw midst her brightness his unequall'd flame,
As Vesta's pure; magnificent as now,
Etherealized, it beams creation through.

Unrivall'd mortal, whose elastic soul
Alike dispos'd the Chisel and the Trow'l;
Whose plastic hand the shapeless block array'd
With intellectual seeming, or display'd
The pencil's wonders to the dazzled sight,
Or rear'd the Palace, or the Temple's height, –
Thy name, thy works, shall still examples live,
And to thy mem'ry unbought plaudits give,

Until succumbing at the Doomsday roar,
Rome, and her grandeur, Earth and Sea, no more
Exist, but back to primal Chaos cast,
Void space shall reign illimitably vast.

One feeling thus thro' wakened Europe ran,
Tho' still enslav'd, Man crouch'd to tyrant Man;
Where e'er the Cross its holy influence spread,
Where e'er Religion rais'd her hallow'd head;
And Ah! where e'er some petty Despot reign'd,
In sad pre-eminence, o'er man enchain'd,
Or where ambition will'd extended power,
Or bandit Chiefs their plunder to secure;
Bright Architecture! still was sought thy aid,
In grandeur there, in rudeness here array'd,
But hush the theme; and Oh! Uranian Muse,
Thro' these cold veins thy noblest heat diffuse;
Let me at once the ESCURIAL's wonders view,
Eye SEVILLE's beauties, search GRANADA through;
Rich in her gothic and her moorish tow'rs,
Her wide ALHAMBRA, with its walks and bow'rs;
Where now alone in Christian climes are seen
The fallen glories of the Crescent's mien,
Which, like 'Archangel ruin'd', awe inspire
And force the soul to bend, and deep admire.

But tho' these wonders of a foreign strand
High notice claim let not OUR PARENT LAND
Remain unsung; whose Gothic beauties shine,
E'en now resplendent, deck'd with art divine;
Tho' sour fanatics, and a bandit crew,
Her Abbeys plundered, and her fanes o'erthrew,
Yet still their ruins (like some mountain riven,
From its deep base, by God's resistless levin,
Which once with nature's chiefest beauties cloth'd,
All eyes attracted, and all feelings sooth'd),
Speak to the heart, and with unerring tongue
Those glories tell, which ign'rant Zealots flung,
With impious hand, on earth's deep wounded face,
Where yet they lie, in many a sacred place; –

Yet, let not these, unsung, unknown, remain, –
The task is needless, and the labor vain –
For every soil, where Architecture's light,
Lends its clear flame to scientific sight,
Of TINTERN speaks, on WINTON's grandeur glows,
O'er WIMBORNE ponders, sighs where NETLEY rose,
Unrivall'd once; now mould'ring to the gale,
But, 'points a moral, or adorns a Tale'.

    These prove the Genius of our parent Clime,
Majestic, beauteous, tow'ring, chaste, sublime;
That genius which, for her, a deathless name
Has won triumphant, thro' the Battle's flame;
Or still more glorious, intellectual bays
Has gain'd in fields, of Lore's intensest blaze;
Or brighter still, when with tear-streaming eyes
The wretched, of all Nations, claim her sighs,
Her splendor beams magnificent afar,
Despair's sole anchor, mis'ry's guardian star.

    Thus, thro' all Christendom, the Gothic style
Diffus'd its beauties in each lofty pile;
And long pre-eminent, each Kingdom own'd
Its ruling sway, by gen'ral suff'rance crown'd;
'Till time, destroyer of all earthly things,
That soon or late shall sap Creation's springs,
And his own power, last Suicide! destroy,
Nor longer tempt, with agony or joy,
'Till HE decreed that Taste and Art should change,
And give anom'lous fancies uncheck'd range;
Fancies, which broke thro' Order's purest laws,
Scorn'd fair proportion, yet obtain'd applause;
Mix'd Grecian, Roman, Gothic, Arabesque,
All stiles, all orders, in their plans grotesque;
Thus, that vast Hydra, which 'the Mob' we call,
Despotic monster, rules this giddy ball,
Makes light seem darkness, darkness turns to day,
As changeful passion points the rainbow way;
Then chas'd one trifle from the rapid breast,

Some newer toy lifts up its tinsel crest;
Sheer dullness tramples, prostrate wisdom bleeds,
And science droops, and quackery proceeds.

So went the world – the once far beaming light
Of Gothic architecture, gloom'd in night;
'Till led by Taste, by soaring genius driven,
One mighty spirit rais'd a Pile to heaven,
A Pile, where grandeur mix'd with beauty reigns,
And tow'ring lordly, rules extended plains;
Whose height, aspiring, seems the clouds to brook,
And whence the advent'rous mortal fears to look,
Who, toiling, gains its battlemented stage,
Fit seat for some calm astronomic sage,
When, gath'ring courage, lo! he casts around
His wond'ring vision o'er the scene profound;
Till dim with light, the faint and wearied eye,
Stretching o'er Wood and Mount, to meet the sky,
Whose horizontal sweep at many a league
Checks the vast prospects, which the sight fatigue,
Sinks dazzled, blinded, underneath the rays
Of Nature's glory, which the view displays.

Thou spark, celestial, whose bright ray inspir'd
Old Homer's Song, which every Age has fir'd;
Whose beam, divine, led sacred Virgil's pen,
When Aeneas sang, and 'Arms and Men';
And Tasso taught, as with description's powers,
He drew Armida's Palaces and Bow'rs;
Oh! grant that now one gleam of chasten'd light,
From thy pure seat, may radiate my sight,
And lift the soul far from the Earth below,
With 'thoughts that breathe', and 'words that fiercely glow';
That so enwrapt, the high and splendid theme,
Sink not dishonored down Oblivion's stream;
Yet still let Judgment lend her cooler aid,
And ripen all by her strict balance weigh'd.

Hail, Tower of Grandeur; Fonthill's glory, hail!
Bend thy proud head which scorns the peaceful vale,

[411]

That trembling not upon thy fearful verge,
My soul composed may more serenely urge
The task she dreads – but no – perch'd on thy brow,
Where Oracles might catch prophetic dew,
And Inspiration more inspir'dly breathe,
Let it be mine, to throw the Poet's wreath
Around thy Crest, yet undisplayed in song
Tho' Albion's genius in her favored throng
Of Souls congenial to the lofty strain
Has viewed thy majesty, yet view'd in vain.

Rear'd on a mountain's brow, superb in all,
That gothic art conceiv'd before her fall,
Beneath the barb'rous hands of zeal perverse,
When dark Enthusiasts prov'd a Nation's curse,
The wond'rous pile looks forth – now Fancy soar,
And boldly seize description's proudest oar.
Try all thy skill on that unrivall'd Tow'r,
A princely appanage, or Queen-like dow'r,
Which 'twixt four columns, lifts its form on high,
'Till its proud summit leaves the wearied eye,
And toise, on toise, exalted from the earth,
Gives as it rises deep emotion birth;
(For tho' the sight corporeal, fainting, droops,
Imagination like the Eagle swoops
Athwart each spiral turret with her wings,
And there, remote from dull terrestrial things,
Soars uncontrolled, invisible, unknown,
And holds command, in regions all her own.)
Mark its proportions – note the fairy grace,
Which plays amidst the grandeur of its face;
Behold the pow'r of Architecture, shine,
In all its stages – thro' the whole design;
'Till from its magic height, the structure seems
To give conviction to Arabia's dreams;
Whilst all around, in well group'd beauty rise
Arch, column, battlement, to meet the skies,
But far beneath the master pile they stand,
And pay their homage to its high command.

Thus 'Ammon's Son' look'd from his lofty throne,
When prostrate Nations own'd his pow'r alone;
His mighty Chiefs in princely state surround
The God-like Hero in his glory crown'd;
But tho' each Warrior's firm decided eye
Beam'd sway imperial, yet the Victor nigh
Chain'd every look upon his regal brow,
With conquest radiant, and triumphant hue.

Renew the theme to each dim window soar,
Rich in the wealth of legendary lore,
Where saints and sinners, fools and sages join,
In beauteous colours but grotesque design,
Maintaining true the quaint peculiar style
That still pervaded each conventual pile,
And made religion bear upon her face
A mixture strange of reverence and grimace.

Yes, this proud Tower, inferior roofs among,
More mighty seems; tho' all the splendid throng
Of cloisters, gall'ries, parapets and halls,
Of columns, oriels, and embattled walls,
Gigantic lift their beauties to the sight,
Eclips'd alone by its unrivall'd height.

Now, round the pile, the ling'ring vision send,
And thoughtful o'er each part component bend;
Here, on the North, two massive buildings stand,
There, on the South, the Artist's potent hand
A variegated line of grace displays,
With grandeur mix'd to each astonish'd gaze;
While Science true, with deep admiring soul,
Views in contrasted parts one perfect whole.

In vain description strives, some wizard spell
Her power enfeebles, and locks up her shell;
The Wizard of the place – whose lyre alone
Could aptly sing his Mansion, and his Throne,
Yet tho' appalled, again the task we urge,
Dare cynic censure, and the critic's scourge.

See yon rich Cloisters rear their fretted points,
On shafts supported, where unseemly joints
No blot display, to mar the Master's aim,
But soar as proudly, as some hero's fame,
Aerial firm; with sculpture's power emboss'd,
And with her various witchery beauteous cross'd;
In fluting, moulding, ornament profuse,
Which leave fastidiousness, no theme to chuse,
Whereon to vent her never-dying spleen,
Or turn the scowlings of her sullen mien.

Next, view that Oriel, whose projecting Arch
Stays in its course some Gall'rys lengthen'd march;
Or soft recess, by purest Taste design'd,
To charm the eye, and recreate the mind;
Where paintings dazzle, and where books improve,
And where the swelling Statue seems to move.

Again, we turn to hail the mighty Tow'r,
Gigantic proof of Architecture's pow'r;
Behold those Gates – What Sage of eastern clime,
Who lock'd in cavern deep, achiev'd the time,
A long, long Century, pass'd in studious toil,
Chastened from sense, beneath the sick'ning oil,*
Which to his labours proud dominion gave,
O'er Spirits of Earth, of Aether, and of Wave;
Ere found his ductile Genii bring to light
A loftier entrance to the human sight!
These mighty doors, whose bulk colossal seems
To mock the judgment, like dissolving dreams,
And in their strength appear the arm to scorn,
That dares aspire their massive weight to turn;
When touch'd, revolve upon each brazen hinge,
With noiseless motion, and elastic springe;
The wond'rous vision chains the awe struck soul,

---

*It was an opinion among the followers of the Eastern Magic, that perfection in the Science was unattainable, unless a hundred years were dedicated to the pursuit, in solitude, abstinence, and privation of daylight.

As gradual on their pivots back they roll,
Like Giants retreating from some pigmy band,
'Till staid their course, by Art's repellent hand;
When from their height, like some tall mountain pine
By Nature nurs'd, on storm-clad Appenine,
Their forms majestic spurn the crowd below,
But fancy fire, with grandeur's highest glow.

Now pass'd those Rhodian Monuments, unique,
Behold the Hall in Gothic glory speak;
View the tall Roof, where Warrior Arms preside,
In all the splendor of baronial pride;
Emblazon'd Quarterings grace the polish'd wood,
And fill the sight with one chivalric flood
Of 'Scutcheons, Tinctures, Ornaments, and Flags,
Of Lions, Eagles, Martlets, Crowns, and Stags,
Of Owls, and Satyrs mix'd – the gorgeous field
Of each commemorative ample Shield,
Flames with the produce of heraldic fire,
With 'Hydras, Gorgons, and Chimeras dire';
Here shines with Or, there glows with Gules, red,
And there in Sable marks some Warrior dead;
Thus the high heaving of each ancient breast,
In mute solemnity, stands proud confest.

Three lofty Windows, rich in painted glass,
Admit the light with varied rays to pass,
High on the dexter hand – the left contains
Three niches deep, wrought with elaborate pains;
A crimson drap'ry each recess imbues
With broader splendor, or with milder hues,
As Phoebus pours abroad meridian day,
Or sinking seaward, sheds a fainter ray;
Or breaking dimly, thro' some watery veil,
Throws glist'ning radiance o'er each object pale.

Yet, ere we quit the lordly feudal hall,
Yon central niche attention seems to call;
Approach and view, within its sacred verge,

The CIVIC GLORY,* England's welfare urge;
Beneath a Monarch's frown, undaunted see
The patriot stand, firm, dignified, and free;
The gen'rous emblem of a British soul,
Prepar'd to start for Honor's proudest goal,
His COUNTRY'S CAUSE – should venal Courtiers dare
To press still further vile Corruption's snare,
Around that Country's weal; – its guardian laws
Then almost crush'd beneath their harpy claws.

Thus, Jove all-pow'rful, hid from human gaze,
Casts, at long intervals, some splendid blaze
Of mortal worth, across his mystic plan,
To show the World 'just semblance of a Man'.

Now from the top of yon gigantic grades,
An Arch superb its graceful segment spreads,
In massy clustering, see those Columns eight
Support eight Circles, which the enormous weight,
Of that proud Tower upon their shoulders bear,
And lift its splendors to the midway air,
And prove at once vast Architecture's skill,
Which to achieve, sole needs express the will.

Here, once again, prismatic beauties play,
And changed and tinctur'd by the varying day,
Illumine the Octagon† with every hue,
That tends the mind reflective to subdue
With those deep feelings, melancholy, mild,
Which give to Man the meekness of a Child.

O'er those eight lofty Arches, now behold
A Gallery spring, magnificent and bold,

---

*In this niche is a statue of the late William Beckford, Esq. – The celebrated remonstrance presented by him in the name of his fellow Citizens, while in his second Mayoralty of the City of London, and the manner in which it was received by his late Majesty, with the spirited reply made in consequence, fully entitle that Gentleman to the appellation here given him. The circumstances must be within the knowledge of every Reader, and therefore unnecesary to be repeated. The Statue of Mr. B. represents him in the act of replying to his Majesty.
†The great Tower, which rises 276 in height, between four Pediments.

From whence innum'rous tasteful branches rise,
In fan like grace, before the raptur'd eyes;
And on their points a beauteous frame aspires,
Of lantern shape, lit by refractive fires,
Which thro' eight painted casements dart in streams,
And shed around their glittering iris-beams;
While far above, the lofty roof looks down,
The mighty whole with kingly state to crown.

As here the soul in fond amazement strays,
Profoundly fix'd her deep admiring gaze,
Loud Music speaks; – quick starting from her trance
Again, around, she sends her wakened glance;
Attentive then, she hears the 'Vocal frame',
With voice sublime, record CECILIA's name;
And underneath the Gall'ry's rich design,
(Where rests the pageant like some beauteous Shrine)
A Portal arch'd new scenes of glory shows,
Within its verge, where e'er her sight she throws,
In countless splendors art and affluence join
To deck that seat, of luxury and wine.

Sacred recess! had fam'd LUCULLUS seen
Thy Sideboard loaded, he had died with spleen,
Or had APICIUS COELIUS view'd thy Cates,
His hand had sooner doom'd him to the fates,
When mighty NELSON with his prescence grac'd
The gorgeous banquet on thy tables plac'd;
When pomp and wealth, and luxury and pride,
Rode high enthron'd, and o'er each other vied,
In reign alternate; – yet why thus seduc'd
To tell one feast; revolving hours produc'd,
Day after day, all that the Earth can claim,
Or Aether holds, or Seas bring forth by name,
To form the sumptuous fare – while plates of gold
Bore the rich viands in their dazzling mould;
A host of Menials in attendance wait,
Superbly cloth'd, and aid the lordly state,
Then feast luxuriant in some spacious hall,
On food which Monarchs might delicious call.

Thus, FONTHILL, thus, thy later Owner far'd,
And princely, thus, his untold riches shar'd;
But here the Muse casts off her grosser Zone,
And mounts again description's higher throne; –
What themes of wonder and delight appear
Within this seat of epicurean cheer;
Armoires, and Cabinets, in order shine,
Rich with elab'rate carving's work divine;
Tazzas, Calcedonys, Candelabra, glow,
Dishes emboss'd, and Ewers aid the show;
Vases and Salvers, wrought with curious skill,
(In rock, in flood, in forest, and in hill)
Wrap up each sense in admiration's pause,
And call from taste the guerdon of applause,
'Till with MOUETTE, or BENVENUTO, tired,
The soul reverts, and then again is fired
With Topaz, Buhl, Mosaic florentine,
With Sardonyx, and ground avanturine,
Marble and Ebony, and Or-moulu,
Em'ralds and Gems of every varied hue;
While Masks and Mouldings bold and graceful raise,
Each rich material in the scale of praise.

But now, from gen'rals call the Muses wing,
Some proud Armoire in fitting strains to sing,
Where Art scarce equalled holds divided reign
With every stone that owns a precious stain;
Of ebon wood is form'd the beauteous case,
Two fluted columns bear the centres' grace,
Whose tops with mimic gold resplendent beam,
While rich mosaic fills the space between;
Above, the tints of Flora's kingdom glow
In all the beauty of her cultur'd row,
And fill a sumptuous Vase – the splendid sight,
Compos'd of gems dug from Golconda, bright,
And from what soil soe'er within its womb
Contains the treasures of the watchful Gnome,
Competes the work of every ancient hand,
And stands unrivall'd in each modern land;

While higher still, a small recess we view,
Whose polish'd mouldings, form'd of Or-moulu,
The wand'ring eye restrain, with magic curb,
And fix attention on the whole superb.

Within, to match the outboard gorgeous mien,
Turquoises, Rubies, Amethysts are seen,
With Bloodstones and Vermilions; while in turn
The lacquer'd Coffer, and the antique Urn,
Have each their charms – here man's discursive soul
Knows no disgust, for judgment plann'd the whole.

On either hand what glorious forms arise,
Illum'd or darken'd with the pallet's dies,
As o'er the lifeless Canvass genius threw
Her final tints to radiate or subdue; –
Genius in WEST, and REYNOLDS mighty seen,
In REMBRANDT, HOLBEIN, and the fam'd POUSSIN.

But while the limits of the devious muse
Scarce leave selection freedom where to chuse,
Amid those glories of the pencil's power,
Which dazzling fill each Gall'ry and Boudoir,
Where RAFAEL, RUBENS, and DA VINCI breathe,
And GUIDO claims the Arts' immortal wreath;
Where CLAUDE, and GASPAR in the Landscape glow,
She gives one tribute to her GERARD DOUW.

Soft Nature's artist, thou, whose lynx-ey'd sight
The smallest touches fill'd with life and light,
Who caught from her that rich and wond'rous mine
Of vivid truth, which marks thy every line,
And warms and freshens all thy fancy plann'd,
And gives perfection to thy master hand;
Receive this homage, unadult'rate paid,
In rev'rent feeling to thy honor'd shade.

But mid' these splendors, faint, the mind aspires
To catch the ray that lit up Eblis' fires,
Then might she follow, thro' the endless train
Of Gall'ries, Cloisters, Oriels; – now in vain: –

[419]

Each lofty room, each gorgeous chamber shows
One mass of radiance, and with Vertu glows;
There tyrian wealth, embodied, richly gleams,
In gold, in purple, and in crimson streams;
Where e'er the astonish'd eye its orbit turns,
The raptur'd Soul with fancy's light'ning burns,
Or all entranc'd, forgets life's dull career,
And wings her plumes to some immortal sphere,
Till human sounds destroy the vision's might,
And bring her, sighing, from her aerial flight.

Yes, had some Vet'ran in poetic wars,
Some tow'ring leader, in that host of stars,
That intellectual galaxy of soul,
Rich Britain boasts within her proud controul,
Assum'd his armour, pass'd the high barrier,
Brac'd on his shield, and fixed his mighty spear,
Then seized the theme – his frenzied eye on fire,
To catch the glittt'rings of Apollo's lyre;
FONTHILL, a tenfold radiance thus had own'd,
And been immortal, with the laurel crown'd.

Where one continued scene of grandeur glows,
Where deepest wonder no cessation knows;
Where wealth, where taste, where judgment each displays
Its sep'rate power in some peculiar blaze;
Where countless beauties of the Artist's hand,
In what, immortal genius, yet hath plann'd;
And Books, innum'rous, cull'd with choicest care,
Present a mental feast of all that's rare,
Amusing, or instructive in the fields
Of Literature, whose crown imperial wields
High domination o'er the human mind,
And science-beaming, luminates the blind;
When these, condens'd, in each apartment, rear
Their variegated forms, tier pois'd on tier;
Or, with judicious hand, effective plac'd
Extort applause from strict intu'tive taste:
Say, shall description then uncheck'd remain

Till dull monot'ny flags the creeping strain?
No – prudence speaks, and whispers soft and sure,
'Leave all that rests to fancy's vivid hour;
Whose magic wand, o'er many a gorgeous sight,
Shall raise her vot'ry fill d with deep delight,
In realms where reigns personified and true
All that Aladdin's lamp e'er brought to view.'

Now, from this vast Elysium, once again,
We reach the Octagon; – A beauteous plain
Of softest Verdure draws each wand'rer nigh,
Flank'd on each side in tow'ring majesty,
With every Chieftain of the lofty wood,
To raise the palace, or to stem the flood,
Most amply fit; while each interstice pours
Delightful fragrance from its shrubs and flowers,
Whose tints innum'rous, and whose varied rays
Seem nature's own mosaic wrought by fays.

At length, this all attractive Vista ends,
And back his eye the wond'ring stranger sends;
What burst of glory then astounds his sight
In Architecture's grace and soaring height,
As once again the pile stupendous breaks
Athwart his vision, in those beauteous streaks
Of yellow radiance, which adorn the stone
Like sonic Chrysanth[e]mum scarce fully blown;
Or with more sombre hues affect his mind,
And throw each worldly feeling far behind.

Ye ever changing, ever charming Glades,
Ye Lawns, ye Terraces, ye deep'ning shades,
Where Contemplation's God might chuse to dwell,
Or on each high ascent, or sloping dell,
I tread again, thro' recollection's will,
Your magic scenes, and gain the Beacon hill;
Lo! what an orb of Landscape rolls around,
With Art superb, and Nature gorgeous bound!
But chiefly rests the eye where gay WARDOUR,
In princely beauty, sits mid many a bow'r,

Where Knights of old, and Dames of stately show,
Held high carouse, or shook the graceful toe;
And still where Honor holds her lordly throne,
And mild Benevolence girds on her Zone,
While Hospitality her bounteous horn
All-social shakes, of Wine and Oil and Corn.

Now wand'ring rapt, at length the Tourist gains
That spot where each Columbian Flora reigns,
In all the glory of her native Clime,
Bright, fragrant, graceful, stately, rich, sublime;
Magnolias, Rhododendrons, Cloethras, fill
The laughing space, or line the joyous rill,
Which murm'ring soft its gen'rous course along
Throws health and vigour to the exotic throng,
Imbues their tints, and thro' the enchanting whole
Diffuses life, and gives to each a Soul.

O'er verdant Mounts, mid' Cliffs, and Lakes, and Groves,
Still deep admiring, on the stranger roves;
Contrasted Scenery all its witch'ry lends,
And Sky, and Wood, and Earth, and Water blends;
While 'cross his path, flee whirring partridge glides,
Or screams the wild-fowl from the placid tides;
The timid hare, encouraged, views his face,
Unscar'd, unscath'd, by Man's inhuman chace;
The Pheasant, beauteous, surges thro' the trees,
And waves his plumage to the am'rous breeze;
His burnish'd corslet, sparkling to the day,
Sheds gorgeous lustre round his floating way;
The 'native Burghers' of the forest shade,
In antler'd majesty, stalk thro' the glade;
Thus unmolested, Beast and Bird obtain
Repose, mid' Fonthill's wood, and stream, and plain.

Farewell ye Walks, farewell each tangled brake,
Farewell ye Rills, farewell thou peaceful Lake;
And you, ye mighty Oaks, may no rude blow
Assail your stems, and lay your branches low:

Ye laughing Flowers, may Spring's returning gales,
Balsamic, open still your beauteous veils,
Unharm'd by frost, from bitter snow storms freed,
And from the crush of man's destructive tread;
And may those streams which wind your roots among,
Still flow luxuriant as the Poet's song,
Who told your loves, your sex, in verse imbued,
With Nature's language and her power endued.

    Hail! WILTSHIRE, Hail! thou heart awak'ning Seat
Of patriot Interest, join'd with feeling sweet,
As mem'ry turns her recollective eye,
And tells inspir'd of Times and Deeds gone by;
Where once the BRITON held his druid rites,
Mutter'd his spells, and called his Pagan sprites;
Where once the conqu'ring ROMAN lov'd to bide,
And choose his grave along some mountain side,
Or raise the barrow on the smoothe green sward,
Or sing the strains of some Augustan Bard;
Where next the ruthless SAXONS rear'd their crests,
Who called to save, within the hapless breasts
Of unarm'd Nobles plung'd the murd'rous brand,
Where STONEHENGE lifts her monumental band
Of Stones colossal; rear'd as Poets say,
To mark the crime, 'till Doom's avenging day:
Where DANES and NORMANS all were fond to dwell,
Charm'd by thy Soil's rich undulating swell,
And still, where Wealth and Rank their Mansions raise
To deck thy plains, and vouch thy ancient praise;
Where LONGLEAT soars magnificent, sublime,
And BOWOOD smiles, to grace thy favor'd clime;
Where SARUM boasts her beauteous TEMPLE's height,
And older SARUM her entrenchment's might;
Where Manufacture strains her toil-mark'd hands,
And show'rs her produce o'er far distant Strands;
Where Agriculture shakes her teeming fields;
Where the ripe fruit its luscious nectar yields;
And where, to crown the whole, FONTHILL aspires,
In all her pride of Battlements and Spires.

Yes, FONTHILL, yes; pre-eminent, unvied,
Thy splendors beam, all rival works to chide;
Alone, unequall'd, to a wond'ring World,
Thy endless glories all have been unfurled;
Thy view, like some giant-ensign, high array'd,
Throws Tow'rs, Cathedrals, Castles, into shade,
And, save the remnants of old GREECE or ROME,
Or BU'NAROTTI's boast, or WREN's high dome,
No age, no land, no genius e'er brought forth
A nobler fane to gild the breathing Earth.

FINIS

NOTICE

THE AUTHOR feels it necessary to apologize to those individuals who favored him with their patronage in an early stage of this work, for the delay in the publication – It has arisen, partly from those circumstances which will always occur to disarrange the pursuits of every man connected with business, when those pursuits are directed to a foreign object; – and partly from the nature of the task itself, which the more it became developed, presented the greater obstacles to its execution; – so great indeed, that the original intention of describing each part of the Edifice, in succession, was necessarily abandoned, and the general plan, as now adopted, introduced in its stead: – In fact, the former arrangement must have occasioned an eternal repetition of the same terms, and, though perfectly consistent with the nature of a prose Vade-mecum, have infallibly subjected the Author to a classification with those, who,

Sleepless themselves, to make their Readers sleep,

have been transfixed with the arrows of criticism.

The same fate probably awaits him – He has nothing to urge in extenuation of such a judgment; – His own act has placed him before the Bar of the Public, and he is therefore fully and submissively amenable to its decision. May that decision prove favorable!

Blandford, February 4, 1824.

EDITOR'S NOTE Published by T. Oakley in 1824. Jefferson was also the author of *Salamanca* and *Vision of Fame*. Excessive punctuation throughout the original text necessitated adjustments to facilitate the reading of this poem.

Fonthill Abbey, Wilts, Seat of W. Beckford, Esq.

IN JULY 1827

Softly we tread these tangled slopes;
Sad wild shrubs sigh o'er blasted hopes,
And perfumes from neglected flowers
Breathe of these once Elysian bowers.
So Beauty fades – so flit the brightest hours.

All that unbounded wealth could claim –
High genius and an honour'd name –
Were here enshrined. Rich works of Art
To thrill and warm the coldest heart,
All gathered here – like shadows to depart!

Thou Vathek in thy vast enchanted Hall
Didst Monarch sit o'er slaves in abject thrall.
The Nobles of the land, its plumed Head,[1]
Bow'd with an awful superstitious dread.
Such talismanic power was in thy sway,
That the whole world would deepest homage pay:
The Arbiter of all that gives a zest
To this life's pleasures on thy throne confest!

Why on this cold and lonely waste
Was this his gorgeous Abbey placed?
To frown with scorn upon the towers
Of Wardour – Arundel's fair bowers,[2]

1 He once, it is said, refused the Prince Regent admittance to the Abbey.
2 Wardour Castle, in the vale below.

Here friendship flourish'd and sweet peace;
Yon Hermit little knew of these.
The proud Plebeian could not brook
The high-soul'd Noble's open look,
And sought at length in life drear wane
To fly his sated fancy's pain.
His air-built Castle sank to nought,
When gold its transient treasures bought.[3]
His Dwarf and grooms in gothic state
No longer tend that Abbey gate.

Dim had become the far-West gold;
    The slaves he once had own'd
Burst from their chains' despotic hold,
    Wherein they long had groan'd.[4]

Broken the spell! A motley crowd
    Flock from all countries round:
Where silence reign'd, now voices loud
    Profane this fairy ground.

The lofty Tower and gilded halls
    Are throng'd from morn till eve;
Art's glorious works that grace those walls
    All doom'd each niche to leave.[5]

The master-mind is working still –
    The Painter's, Sculptor's eye
Has deftly with consummate skill
    The choicest gems laid by

To deck some lowlier hermitage,[6]
    Where long the rill of life
Flow'd murmuring on. The Sacred Page
    Quell'd not his spirit's strife.

3 Purchased by Mr. Farquhar in 1822.
4 The failure of his estates in the West Indies.
5 Alluding to the sale of his property.
6 Two houses in Lansdown Crescent, Bath, united by a corridor over an archway.

Man's bright creations soon must fade,
Soon sink in dark oblivion's shade.
A crash was heard at midnight hour –
Low in the dust that lofty Tower![7]

Broken the spell! Behold that mass!
So swift away earth's glories pass!
Two turrets, all that now remain,
In sadness o'erlook the plain!

Oh, Beckford! could no inward conscious shame
Prevail - still wouldst thou to the world proclaim
The scene of all thy gloomy selfish days,
And on a distant hill a watch-tower raise,[8]
To view those turrets crumbling in decay,
Mocking thy gaze at evening's parting ray?
Thou too art fall'n – thy tinsel glory set,
We pay thy name at least a willing debt;
Would that thy honour'd Sire's[9] well-earn'd renown
Had shone thy life to grace – thy death to crown!
O'er hours this gifted Anchorite had pass'd
Let Charity her kindly mantle cast,
The Judge will on his awful Day decide
Our brother's state; 'tis ours his faults to hide.
A Beacon still for wealth and genius to behold:
The Haven is not gain'd by talent or by gold!

E.K.

Jaulnah. Bombay, July 1856

EDITOR'S NOTE Found in the Scrapbook of Ezra Hunt (1809–76), ff. 170–1, Bath Public Library.

7 The Tower was weakened by the great concourse of people entering it during the sale.
8 On Lansdown, near Bath. The turrets of the Abbey just visible on the horizon from the top of the Tower.
9 Alderman W. Beckford.

Fonthill

Man and his works! The meteor's gleam,
The sun-flash on a winter stream,
A vision seen in sleep, that gives
Of gladness more than aught which lives,
A palace from a splendid cloud
Formed, while the wind is rising loud,
A bubble on the lake, a cry
Heard sad from sea when storms are high,
Ways made through air by wild birds' wings,
Are sure and well established things;
Man and his works! words writ on snow
Are emblem of them both below:
Stars dropt from heaven to darkness thrown,
A moment light – and all is gone.

See, Art has cast her spell to check
Man's greatness ere it goes to wreck;
Here, Turner, with a wizard's power,
Has fixed in splendour tree and tower;
And bravely from oblivion won,
A landscape steeped in dew and sun.
A grove, a shepherd, sheep, a rill,
Towers seen o'er all – behold Fonthill!
Where, like a saint embalmed and shrined,
Long worshiped Beckford dozed and dined;
Strayed through that wood, strolled by that brook
Ate much – thought little – wrote a book;
Tattled with titled dames and sighed
In state like any prince, and died.
And that's Fonthill! things of high fame
Less lovely are in look than name –

Spots bright in song and fair in story
Glow far less lustrous than their glory:
Historians' heroes, poets' lasses,
Shine glorious through Fame's magic glasses,
Who in rude war, or rapture's hour,
Had no such heart-inspiring power.

So fares it with Fonthill, which proud
Shoots there in lustre to the cloud;
Give fame its portion, art its share,
And all the rest is empty air.
No longer, through the lighted hall,
Its lord at midnight leads the ball;
Nor, dancing 'mid its dazzling rooms,
Young jewelled beauty shakes her plumes;
Nor bards are there, glad to rehearse
A rich man's praise in trembling verse;
Nor shrewder souls who breathe rich wines
In laughter when their landlord shines:
All, all are gone – the green grass sward,
On jewelled belle and beau and bard
And man of rank, grows long and green,
Nor seems to know that such have been.
The tower that rose so proud and fair,
Hath left its station in mid air;
While in its place the sunbeam flings
Its glory down – the skylark sings:
O'er the wide space usurped by vain
Man, Nature hath resumed her reign.

So, hath it been, and will be still
With all, as well as proud Fonthill.
Where's Cicero's villa, Caesar's hall?
Attila's hut, Alaric's pall?
The throne of iron whence late flew forth
Napoleon's words which shook the earth?
Men, glorious men, where are they gone,
Who ruled and fooled and sinned and shone?
And women who, like babes in strings,
Led mighty earls and conquering kings?

They lie beneath our feet – we tread,
Regardless, o'er the illustrious dead!
The dust which we shake from our shoe,
Once breathed and lived and loved. Adieu!
Dames with their charms, bards with their laurel –
Read ye who run, and sigh the moral.

EDITOR'S NOTE Allan Cunningham, ed. *The Anniversary; or, Poetry and Prose for MDCCCXXIX* (London: John Sharpe, 1829), pp. 214–16. A plate of one of Turner's views of Fonthill, engraved by T. Crostick, appeared opposite p. 214. Cunningham (1784–1842), miscellaneous writer, secretary to Francis Chantrey from 1814 to 1841, published *Lives of the Most Eminent British Painters, Sculptors and Architects* (1829–33) and an edition of Robert Burns (1834), among others.

A Fonthill Bibliography

THE MAJOR ARCHIVAL COLLECTIONS OF FONTHILL ABBEY

ADDITIONAL COLLECTIONS RELATING TO FONTHILL ABBEY

BOOKS, GUIDE BOOKS, CATALOGUES

ARTICLES ON FONTHILL

POEMS ON FONTHILL

SECONDARY SOURCES

A Fonthill Bibliography

I THE MAJOR ARCHIVAL COLLECTIONS OF FONTHILL ABBEY

A. **Beinecke Rare Book and Manuscript Library, Yale University.** Based on the description compiled by William K. Finley, December 1997 and personal examination of material:

Gen MSS 102

Box 1, ff. 7–8, WB to John Britton, 1823

Box 3, f. 44,   WB to Lord Nelson, 1801

Box 4, f. 67,   John Britton to WB, 1837
  f. 71,   Thomas Adams to John Britton, 1823
  f. 85,   John Britton to Thomas Adams, 1823
  f. 87,   John Britton to George Cattermole, 1822
  f. 90,   George Cattermole to John Britton, 1822
  f. 100, Alaric Watts to John Britton, 1824

Box 6, f. 109, Statement of expenses for work at Fonthill by John Soane, 1787–88
  f. 110, Lists of plate belonging to William Beckford, 1818
  f. 111, Watercolour sketch of bridge and roadway by James Wyatt, [1781]

Box 8, ff. 162–74; 177–8, Articles and newspaper clippings on Fonthill, 1801–1957
  ff. 175–6, Contemporary notes and articles on Fonthill kept by John Britton
  f. 180, Holograph description of Fonthill Abbey (unidentified author), n. d.
  f. 181, List of subscribers to Fonthill; letters copied by John Britton, [1822]
  f. 182, Plan and survey of the estate of WB, [1800?]
  f. 183, Price list for books at Fonthill Sale, 1780; prints and photographs

Box 9, ff.184–8, Collection of sketches and descriptions; prints and photographs

    f. 189, Tribute dinners [for] Fonthill, 1823–4

    f. 200, Slides of Fonthill remains

Box 12, ff. 272–4, Articles and clippings on Fonthill, 1822–3

Box 13, ff. 277–80, Articles and clippings on Fonthill, 1822–3

B. Bodleian Library, Oxford University. Based on the description compiled by T. D. Rogers in 1987 and personal examination:

MS Eng. Lett. d. 222, Papers of John Britton relating to Fonthill Abbey

MS. Beckford b. 6, ff. 1–173, Newspaper cuttings relating to Fonthill, 1822–38

MS. Beckford b. 8, ff. 1–2; 7; 10–11; 19–20, Design for the state bed at Fonthill by John Soane, 1788; Description by Robert Baldock of a Cellini vase; Genealogical material prepared by Isaac Heard, 1797; Memorandum of agreement for the sale of Fonthill, 1822

MS. Beckford c. 14, ff. 28; 55; 81–2, Draft to unidentified artist regarding Fonthill, 1802; Draft to John Farquhar, 1823; Draft regarding visit to Fonthill in 1835

MS. Beckford c. 15, ff. 11–12, Copy of letter to Thomas Wildman regarding plants for Fonthill, 1787

MS. Beckford c. 16, ff. 4; 15–16; 18–20; 21–2, Copies of letters on Fonthill: to John Lettice, 1796; to Mrs Nevill Walker, 1798; to Isaac Heard, 1798; to Robert Bowyer, 1798

MS. Beckford c. 19, Letters from G. F. Beltz to Beckford regarding pedigrees, 1800–41

MS. Beckford c. 21, f. 46, Sketch by Beckford of part of Fonthill, 1814

MS. Beckford c. 22, f. 58, Sketch by Robert Hume of a gallery from the state bedroom at Fonthill, 1825

MS. Beckford c. 27, ff. 8–43, John Britton correspondence, 1822–43

MS. Beckford c. 28, ff. 78–9, Letter from William Clarke on the Fonthill sale, 1823

MS. Beckford c. 30, ff. 70–1; 115; 122–3; 175–6, Draft letter on Fonthill [c. 1793]; Copy of a bill for work by Eginton, 1799; Copy of a letter to Fownes [?] regarding the contract for the sale of Fonthill, 1822; Agreement between

Beckford and Edward Foxhall about the sale of Fonthill Splendens and its contents, 1807

MS. Beckford c. 32, ff. 161–3, ALS Henry Hope requesting a visit to Fonthill and Beckford's response, 1809

MS. Beckford c. 33, ff. 72–3, John Lettice sonnets on Fonthill, 1800

MS. Beckford c. 37, ff. 48; 52; 69–99;100–1, Copy of letters to James Wyatt, 1791, 1801; Price lists of Japan items bought at the Duc de Bouillon sale, 1801, and other antiques, items purchased later; Portraits in the windows of the brown parlour of Fonthill Abbey

MS. Beckford c. 39, ff. 125–8, Correspondence with Fownes & White, mainly about the sale of Fonthill, 1821–2

MS. Beckford c. 84, ff. 63–7; 110; 117 Cuttings from the *Sunday Times*, 1823, attacking Beckford, and drafts of a note by Beckford, 1839; James Wyatt's drawing of a landscape plan for Fonthill Splendens, n. d.; Drawing entitled 'Scheme of the Board of Works', Fonthill Abbey, n. d.

MS. Beckford c. 85–6, Draft of 'Memoirs of William Beckford, Esq.' by Cyrus Redding, published in 1859

MS. Beckford c. 88, An abstract by Isaac Heard of deeds at Fonthill, 1798, relating to Witham Priory and the manor of Fonthill, with extracts from the Fonthill parish register

MS. Beckford d. 10, Draft of an essay entitled by Boyd Alexander 'Fonthill Foreshadowed' [c. 1777–8]. Text is available as an edited manuscript on the internet by Dick Claésson with a different title, 'The Transport of Pleasure' (1996). See http://www.hum.gu.se/~litwww/TransportOfPleasure.pdf

MS. Beckford d. 27, Printed Phillips auction catalogue of furniture and furnishings belonging to Beckford, 1801

MS. Beckford e. 4, 'Journal & dates of my life', by Lady Anne Hamilton, 1788–1835, containing notes and sketches of Fonthill Splendens and Fonthill Abbey

II ADDITIONAL COLLECTIONS RELATING TO FONTHILL ABBEY

A *Public Collections*

1 **Art Gallery of Ontario**

    a. 'South-west View of a Gothic Abbey (Morning), now Building at Fonthill, the seat of W. Beckford, Esq.', watercolour and gum Arabic on wove paper by J. M. W. Turner, 69.4 x 102.9 cm, 1799. Exhibited at the Royal Academy in 1800, no. 341, accession no. 51/39.

2 **Bath Public Library**

   a. The Scrapbook of Ezra Hunt (1809–76), containing engravings, notes etc. on Fonthill, Beckford's Lansdown Crescent residence and Lansdown Tower, 171 ff..

3 **Beckford Tower Trust, Bath**

   a. Model of Fonthill Abbey, reinforced cardboard, by Michael Bishop, 25⅛ x 31½ in., c. 1981.

4 **Bolton Museum and Art Gallery**

   a. 'Perspective View of Fonthill Abbey from the South West', watercolour by J. M. W. Turner," 50.2 x 77.5 cm, c. 1799, accession no. BOLMG: 1963. P.2.

5 **British Museum, Department of Prints and Drawings**

   a. 'South-west View of Fonthill Abbey, Wiltshire, the Seat of William Beckford; the Abbey Seen at a Little Distance, Trees and Bushes in the Foreground', brush drawing in grey wash by John Buckler (1770–1851), 351 x 457 mm, 1821, accession no. PRN: PDB5784.

6 **Brodick Castle, The National Trust for Scotland**

   a. 'East View of the Gothic Abbey (Noon), now Building at Fonthill for W. Beckford, Esq.', watercolour by J. M. W. Turner, 685 x 1035 mm, c. 1799. Exhibited at the Royal Academy in 1800, no. 663.

7 **City Art Gallery, Leeds**

   a. 'View of Fonthill from a Stone Quarry', watercolour by J. M. W. Turner, 298 x 442 mm, 1799, smaller version of II, A, 6, a, accession no. 13.224.53.

8 **Library of the Wiltshire Archaeological & Natural History Society, Devizes Museum**

   a. John B. Nichols's subscription copy of John Britton's *Graphical and Literary Illustrations of Fonthill Abbey* with an ALS from John Rutter, newspaper cuttings, and ms. notes relating to Nichols's book on Fonthill and to various owners of Fonthill following the sale to John Farquhar in 1822. Also pasted in are two reports on the trial involving George Mortimer's financial liability to Farquhar's estate.
   b. John Britton's personal copy of *Graphical and Literary Illustrations of*

Fonthill Abbey, extra illustrated with additional plates from Storer and Rutter. Also bound in are Britton's ink tracings of James Wyatt's drawings of Fonthill Abbey; pencil and ink drawings of the Abbey grounds and interior scenes and contents of the Abbey by Britton, Cattermole, and other artists; Beckford's drawing of an early conception of Fonthill as a mausoleum and his drawing of a part of the central tower. Bound in are various ALS to Britton from Chevalier Franchi, Harry Phillips, Joseph Taylor, Benjamin Hobhouse, Thomas Adams, Richard Colt Hoare, John Broadley, George Beltz, William Lisle Bowles relating to Fonthill and to Britton's anxiety about Rutter's book on Fonthill.

c. Collection of over 90 engravings relating to Fonthill.

d. Collection of watercolours of Fonthill Splendens and Fonthill Abbey by John Buckler and George Cattermole.

9 **Montreal Museum of Fine Arts**

a. 'South View of the Gothic Abbey (Evening), now Building at Fonthill for W. Beckford, Esq.', watercolour by J. M. W. Turner, 70.5 x 104.4 cm, 1799. Exhibited at the Royal Academy in 1800, no. 566 and engraved by T. Crostick, 1828, for *The Anniversary*, 1829, accession no. 1963.1385.

10 **Royal Institute of British Architects**

a. Sketch of west end and details of Fonthill Abbey by David Mocatta (1806–82). Drawings Collection, C 4.

b. Topographical drawing of Fonthill Abbey, 1822 by an unidentified 19th century English draughtsman. Drawings Collection, G8/27.

c. James Wyatt's preliminary designs for Fonthill Abbey. Drawings Collection, K 8. See also Derek Linstrum. *Catalogue of the Drawings Collection of the Royal Institute of British Architects: The Wyatt Family*. Westmead: Gregg International, [1974].

11 **Salisbury and South Wiltshire Museum**

a. 'View of Fonthill Abbey from the South West', watercolour by William Turner (1789–1862), 10 x 14½ in., c. 1820, cat. no. PD3751, accession no. 13/1996.

b. 'The Ruins of Old Wardour Castle with Fonthill Abbey in the Distance', watercolour by J. B. Knight, 7¼ x 12 in., c. 1820-30, cat. no. PD1029, accession no. 109/1952.

c. 'Fonthill Abbey with Figures Strolling and Riding in the Grounds', watercolour, artist unknown, 9¼ x 14½ in., c. 1823, cat. no. PD1030, accession no. 144/1984.

d. 'Fonthill Abbey in the Distance Across Fields and Woodlands with

Two Boys Playing a Game in the Foreground', pencil drawing, artist unknown, 8½ x 11 in., c. 1820, cat. no. PD2058, accession no. 303/1933.

e. 'Distant Views of Fonthill Abbey', two pencil drawings by Harriet Byard Sheppard (wife of Revd William Dalby, Prebendary of Salisbury Cathedral 1833–61), 4¼ x 6¾ x 2 in.(sketch book), c. 1817-20, cat. no. PD3808, accession no. 120/1956.

12 Tate Britain

a. J. M. W. Turner's 'Fonthill Sketchbook', containing various sketches and views of the Abbey under construction in1799, A. J. Finberg inventory, T. B. XLVII:

- i. 'Men Asleep Under a Fallen Tree, Near Water, with Swans Fighting', pencil, 13¼ x 18½ in., (20), f. 5.
- ii. 'Trees on the Edge of a Lake, with Swans, and Two Men Lying on the Grass' [probably at Fonthill], black chalk, 13½ x 18½ in., (14), f. 6.
- iii. 'Rocks in a Stream, with Foliage, and Trees Beyond', black chalk and pencil, 13⅜ x 18½ in., (15), f. 7.
- iv. 'Woods by a Lake, with a Fallen Tree', pencil and watercolour with stopping-out, 12⅞ x 18⅜ in., (48), f. 8.
- v. 'Distant View of Fonthill Abbey, from the South', pencil, 13⅜ x 18⅜ in., (16), f. 9.
- vi. 'Farm Buildings Near Fonthill, with the Towers of the Abbey Visible Behind Hill to the Right', black chalk, 13$\frac{5}{16}$ x 18½ in., (17), f. 10.
- vii. 'A Wooden Shelter in the Grounds of Fonthill with a Flock of Sheep and Shepherd' [shows Abbey in the distance], pencil and watercolour, 13⅛ x 18$\frac{7}{16}$ in., (47), f. 11.
- viii. 'View Across a Valley Towards the Unfinished Tower of Fonthill Abbey, from the North-East', pencil, watercolour and body-colour [the basis for the finished watercolour II, A, 16, a], 13$\frac{1}{16}$ x 18$\frac{9}{16}$ in., (11), f. 12.
- ix. 'View of Fonthill Splendens from the West', pencil, 13¼ x 18⅜ in., (25), f. 13.
- x. 'Distant View of Fonthill Abbey, with an Aqueduct in the Fore-ground', pencil, 13$\frac{1}{16}$ x 18⅜ in., (6), f. 14.
- xi. 'View Across the Park at Fonthill' [from the perspective of the Abbey], pencil, 13 x 18⅜ in., (2), f. 15.
- xii. 'Fonthill Abbey Seen Between Trees', pencil and watercolour, 13 x 18⅜ in., (51), f. 16.
- xiii. 'Distant View of Fonthill Abbey from the South West; River,

with Bridge in Middle Distance', pencil with drops of blue, green, and orange colour [the basis for the finished watercolour II, B, 9], 11⅞ x 18⅜ in., (7), f. 17.

xiv. 'Fonthill Abbey Seen in the Distance Beyond Trees, the Ruins of Old Wardour Castle, and Farm Buildings in the Foreground', pencil, 12 x 18⅜ in., (9), f. 18.

xv. 'Distant View of Fonthill Abbey from the South, with the Ruins of Old Wardour Castle in the Right Foreground', pencil, 13¼ x 18⅜ in., (18), f. 19.

xvi. 'Distant View of Fonthill Abbey from the East, with the Lake in the Foreground and a Team of Oxen', pencil, watercolour and bodycolour, 13 x 18⅜ in., (46), f. 20.

xvii. 'Trees by the Lake in Old Fonthill Park, with a River God Seated Among Rushes', pencil with smears of blue, green, yellow and brown colour, 18⅜ x 13 in., (19), f. 21.

xviii. 'Distant View of Fonthill Abbey from the East', pencil [the basis for the finished watercolour II, A, 6, a)], 12⅜ x 18⅜ in., (8), f. 22.

xix. 'Fonthill Abbey Seen from the South through the Trees', pencil [the basis for the finished watercolour II, A, 9, a], 13⅛ x 18⅜ in., (13), f. 23.

xx. 'Near View of Fonthill Abbey with Bitham Lake in the Foreground', pencil, 18⅜ x 13 in., (4), f. 24.

xxi. 'Fonthill Abbey Seen from the South West', pencil [the basis for the finished watercolour II, A, 1, a], 13 x 18⅜ in., (12), f. 25.

xxii. 'Fonthill Abbey from the South West (?): Sunset', pencil and watercolour, 18⅜ x 13 in., (10), f. 26.

xxiii. 'Fonthill Abbey Seen from the South West, Beyond Trees', pencil, 13⅛ x 18½ in., (3), f. 27.

xxiv. 'Near View of the South Front of Fonthill Abbey from the Lawn', pencil, 18⅜ x 12⅞ in., (1), f. 28.

xxv. 'Near View of Fonthill Abbey from the South East', pencil, 13³⁄₁₆ x 18⅜ in., (5), f. 29.

b. J. M. W. Turner's 'Smaller Fonthill Sketchbook', Finberg inventory, T. B. XLVIII:

i. 'Distant View of Fonthill Abbey, with Unfinished Tower', pencil, 16¼ x 10½ in., f. 1.

c. J. M. W. Turner's 'Swans Sketchbook', c. 1798–9, Finberg's inventory, T. B. XLII:

i. 'View of Fonthill Abbey in a Hilly Landscape with the River Nadder', pencil with black and white chalk, 6⅞ x 4⅞ in., ff. 12–13.

   d. J. M. W. Turner's 'Dolbadarn Sketchbook', c. 1799–1800, Finberg
     Inventory, T. B. XLVI:

      i. 'Composition Study for a View of Fonthill from the South
        West', pencil, 3⅛ x 5¼ in., f. 106.
      ii. 'Rough Sketch of Fonthill Abbey Rising Above Woods', pencil,
        3⅛ x 5¼ in., f. 107.
      iii. 'Composition Study for a View of Fonthill from the West (?)',
        pencil on a pink ground, 3⅛ x 5¼ in., f. 111.
      iv. 'Rough Composition Study for a View of Fonthill from the
        North East', pencil on a pink ground, 3⅛ x 5¼ in., f. 113.

   e. 'View of Fonthill', c. 1799, pencil, watercolour and stopping-out, 41½
     x 28 in., Finberg inventory, T. B. LXX-P.

13 University of Kansas Museum of Art

   a. View of Fonthill Abbey [South-West], oil on panel by Robert Gibb
     (1801–37), 11¼ x 15¾ in., accession no. 54.335.

14 Victoria and Albert Museum

   a. Designs for Stained Glass Windows of Fonthill Abbey, thirty-two
     watercolour sketches on twenty-one sheets of paper by William
     Hamilton (1751–1801), 14⅛ x 4½ in. each, c. 1798, accession nos.
     7888. 1–32.
   b. 'Perspective View of Fonthill Abbey from the North West', water-
     colour by Charles Wild (1781–1835), 29.2 x 23.5 cm, c. 1799, acces-
     sion no. E84-1918. See II, B, 11 for larger version.

15 Yale Center for British Art, Paul Mellon Collection

   a. 'North-west View of a Building, Erecting at Fonthill at Wiltshire, the
     Seat of Wm Beckford Esq, in the Style of a Gothic Abbey', watercolour
     by James Wyatt (has been attributed to J. M. W. Turner), 67 x 105 cm,
     c. 1798, accession no. B1975.4.1800.
   b. 'Fonthill Abbey, Wiltshire', watercolour and graphite by Charles
     Hamilton Smith (1776–1859), 20.5 x 31 cm, bound in an album of
     drawings, vol. 1: 'Views: England & Wales', accession no.
     B1978.43.1816.

16 Whitworth Art Gallery, The University of Manchester

   a. 'North-east View of the Gothic Abbey (Sunset), now building at
     Fonthill, the seat of W. Beckford, Esq.', watercolour by J. M. W.
     Turner, 27 x 40½ in., 1799. Exhibited at the Royal Academy in 1800,
     no. 680, accession no. D. 1904.19.

b. 'East View of [Fonthill Abbey] (Noon)', amateur copy of watercolour by J. M. W. Turner at Brodick Castle, National Trust for Scotland, 22⅞ x 33⅛ in., accession no. D. 1949. 4

c. 'Autumn Morning, Near Fonthill, Wiltshire', watercolour by J. M. W. Turner, 321 x 465 mm., c. 1799, accession no. D. 1892.97

B *Private Collections*

1. 'East View of Fonthill Abbey Rising from the Woods', watercolour by W. H. Pyne (1769–1843), 5¼ x 9¼ in. Owner: Boyd Alexander Estate.

2. 'South View of Fonthill Abbey', watercolour by J. M. W. Turner, 31 x 45 cm, c. 1799. See no. 341, Andrew Wilton. *J. M. W. Turner: His Art and Life* (New York: Rizzoli, 1979), p. 339. Owner: Boyd Alexander Estate.

3. 'Fonthill Abbey from the South East, with Deer and Peacocks', watercolour by Thomas Higham (1795–1844), 31 x 44.5 cm, 24 July 1822 Owner: Neil Rimington.

4. 'Fonthill Abbey' [Moonlight View from South West without North Wing], pencil drawing by Harriet Carpendale (1750–1849), 20.5 x 26.5 cm, post 1812. Owner: Robert J. Gemmett.

5. 'Vue de Fonthill Abbey' [Distant South West], pencil drawing by E. Berg, 12 x 17 cm, c. 1823. Owner: Robert J. Gemmett.

6. 'Fonthill Abbey', fore-edge watercolour by George Elby (?), Norfolk, England, on *Montgomery's Poetical Works* (London: Longman, 1851), 8⅛ x 2⅛ in., 1920–60. Owner: Robert J. Gemmett.

7. 'Pictorial Relief of Fonthill Abbey from the South West', cardboard, glass with watercolour, artist unknown, 68.5 x 104 cm in a frame 93 x 129 cm, c. 1818. Owner: Neil Rimington.

8. Architectural Model of Fonthill Abbey, papier-mâché, attributed to James Wyatt, 82.5 length x 67.5 width x 65 height cm, c. 1806 with later modifications. Owner: Neil Rimington.

9. 'View of the Gothic Abbey (Afternoon), now Building at Fonthill, the seat of W. Beckford, Esq.', watercolour by J. M. W. Turner, 704 x 1053 mm, 1799. Exhibited at the Royal Academy in 1800, no. 328. Owner: Japanese collection.

10. 'Fonthill Abbey' [South West View], watercolour by Francis Danby (1793–1861), 9¼ x 12½ in., post 1813. Owner: British collection.

11. 'Perspective View of Fonthill Abbey from the North West', watercolour by Charles Wild, 54 x 39.4 cm, c. 1799. Owner: Unidentified. See II, A, 14, b for smaller version.

12. 'Fonthill' [Distant View from the South West], pencil drawing, artist unidentified, 18.3 x 26.7 cm, 6 August 1823. Owner: Unidentified.

See D1, *Souvenirs of Fonthill Abbey*. [Exhibition Catalogue] Bath, 1994.

13. 'Fonthill Abbey' [View from the South of the Eastern Transept and Rest of the Abbey in Ruins], pencil drawing, artist unidentified, 10.2 x 15.2 cm, May 29 1834, with inscription 'Miss J Pole with ?'s kind love'. Owner: Jon Millington.

14. 'Last Days of Fonthill' [View from the East of the Eastern Transept], pencil drawing, artist unidentified, 27.2 x 38 cm, Nov 2 [18]46. Owner: Unidentified. See D4, *Souvenirs of Fonthill Abbey*.

15. 'View of Fonthill Abbey from the South', watercolour over pencil, by George Cattermole (1800–68), 29 x 46.5 cm, [1823], sold at Sothebv's on 4 July 2002, lot 201. Owner: unidentified.

16. [Fonthill Abbey, Distant View from the South West with Grove of Trees in the Middle Distance, and a Solitary Figure Seated Under a Tree in the Foreground], pencil drawing on a stiff card, by J[ohn] B[ritton], 5¾ x 5 in., 1823. Owner: unidentified.

17. 'Fonthill Abbey' [Landscape View from Bitham Lake], sepia wash, artist unidentified, 22.2 x 32.4 cm, [1824?]. Owner: Robert J. Gemmett.

III BOOKS, GUIDE BOOKS, CATALOGUES

Alexander, Boyd, ed. *Life at Fonthill 1807–1822... From the Correspondence of William Beckford*. London: Rupert Hart-Davis, 1957.

Britton, John. *Graphical and Literary Illustrations of Fonthill Abbey, Wiltshire; with Heraldical and Genealogical Notices of the Beckford Family*. London, 1823.

Brockman, H. A. N. *The Caliph of Fonthill*. London: Werner Laurie, [1956].

A Catalogue Raisonné of the Collection of Paintings at Fonthill Abbey. London: J. Davy, 1823.

Christie Auction Catalogue. *A Capital and Truly Valuable Collection of Original High-Finished Drawings, the whole executed by that eminent artist the younger Cozens, during a Tour through the Tyrol and Italy, in company with an Amateur of distinguished taste, from whose cabinet they are now first brought forward to public inspection... to be sold by Mr. Christie... on Wednesday, April 10...* [London, 1805].

——. *A Most Superb, Capital and Valuable Collection of Italian, French, Flemish, and Dutch Pictures, the property of a Gentleman, highly distinguished for his fine taste in the Arts; the whole selected with unbounded liberality, and now brought from his Seat at Fonthill, in Wiltshire... to be sold by Mr. Christie... Feb. 27...* [London, 1802].

——. *A Small, Capital, Genuine, and Select Collection of Pictures, lately consigned from Paris... the property of a Gentleman, brought from his seat at Fonthill, Wilts., but which did not arrive in time for the former Sale...* to be sold by Mr. Christie... on Friday [26 March... London, 1802].

——. *The Magnificent Effects at Fonthill Abbey, Wilts. to be Sold by Mr. Christie, October 1822.* London, 1822.

Collection of Fonthill Prints and Drawings, Lewis Walpole Library, Yale University, Farmington, Connecticut.

Cundall, E. G. *Fonthill Abbey: A Descriptive Account of Five Water-Colour Drawings by J. M. W. Turner, R. A.* Haughton Hall Tarporley: Private Printing for Ralph Brocklebank, 1915.

Easton, James. *The Salisbury Guide, Giving an Account of the Antiquities of Old Sarum: the Ancient and Present State of New Sarum, or Salisbury, and the Cathedral. Comprising also a Brief Description of Fonthill Abbey; ... With the Distances of the Principal Towns and Villages... from Salisbury.* Salisbury, 1818 [other editions followed].

Evans Auction Catalogue. *Catalogue of a Collection of Curious, Rare and Valuable Books... the Whole are in Fine Condition, and Many from the Fonthill Collection, which will be sold by Auction, by Mr. Evans, at his house, No. 93, Pall Mall, on Monday, February 11, and three following days.* [London], 1828.

Gemmett, Robert J., 'William Beckford and the Picturesque: A Study of Fonthill'. Ph.D. diss., Syracuse University, 1967.

——., ed. *Sale Catalogues of Libraries of Eminent Persons*, Vol. 3, *William Beckford.* London: Mansell & Sotheby Parke-Bernet, 1972.

Gotlieb, Howard B. *Willliam Beckford of Fonthill, Writer, Traveller, Collector, Caliph 1760–1844: A Brief Narrative and Catalogue of an Exhibition to Mark the Two Hundredth Anniversary of Beckford's Death.* New Haven: Yale University Library, 1960.

Leigh, Sotheby Auction Catalogue. *A Catalogue of a Valuable and Elegant Collection of Books Selected with Superior Judgment and Taste... Being a Portion of the Library of a Very Distinguished Collector brought from his Seat in Wiltshire... Which will be Sold by Auction by Leigh and S. Sotheby ... Thursday, 9th June, 1808 and Two following days.* [London, 1808].

——. *A Catalogue of the Select and Valuable Library of Scarce and Curious Books of a Gentleman, lately deceased... Which will be Sold by Auction by Leigh, Sotheby, and Son... Thursday the 24th and Saturday the 26th Day of May, 1804.* [London, 1804].

Millington, Jon. *Souvenirs of Fonthill Abbey.* [Exhibition Catalogue] Bath: Bath Preservation Trust, 1994.

Neale, J. P. *Graphical Illustrations of Fonthill Abbey, the Seat of John Farquhar, Esq. with an historical description and notices of works of Art formerly preserved there.* London, 1824.

Nichols, John B. *Historical Notices of Fonthill Abbey, Wiltshire.* London, 1836.

Ostergard, Derek E. *William Beckford, 1760–1844: An Eye for the Magnificent.* [Exhibition Catalogue] New Haven and London: Yale University Press, 2001.

Phillips Auction Catalogue. *All of the magnificent Household Furniture [Glass, Statuary, Pictures, Drawings, China] ... and other valuable and splendid Effects, of Fonthill Mansion, near Salisbury, Wilts... to be sold by Mr. Phillips... on Monday, August 17, and 6 following days...* [London, 1807].

——. *Collection of Antient & Modern Prints & Drawings, Principally Formed by William Beckford, Esq. A Catalogue of the Collection of Rare and Estimable Original Drawings, Ancient & Modern Prints, and Books of Prints... Which will be Sold by Auction by Mr. Phillips... On Monday, 1st of March, 1824, & Three following Days.* [London, 1824].

——. *Part of the superlatively elegant and magnificent Household Furniture [Fittings, Organ by Crang, Marble busts, Bronzes, Pictures, Objets d'Art...] and a variety of rare, curious, and valuable Effects, the genuine property of William Beckford, Esq. of Fonthill, Wilts.... to be Sold by Mr. Phillips... on August 19 and 3 following days...* [London, 1801].

——. *The Unique and Splendid Effects of Fonthill Abbey. Catalogue of the Extensive Assemblage of Costly and Interesting Property Which Adorns this Magnificent Structure... Which will be Sold by Auction by Mr. Phillips, at the Abbey on Tuesday, the 23d of September, 1823, and Seven following Days and on Thursday, 16th October, and Four following Days.* [London, 1823].

——. *The Valuable Library of Books, in Fonthill Abbey... Which will be Sold by Auction by Mr. Phillips at the Abbey, on Tuesday, the 9th of September, 1823, and Nine following Days, on Friday, the 3d of October, & Four following Days, and on Thursday, 23d October, 1823, & Four following Days.* [London, 1823].

——. *The Whole of the Massive and Valuable Materials of that Noble Stone and Brick-Built Mansion called Fonthill, near Salisbury, Wilts; comprising many hundred tons of iron, lead, and stout copper covering, an immense quantity of hewn stone, in asherling, cornices, cills, porticos, columns, pilastres and frontispieces, 3 handsome geometrical stone-staircases, with ornamental and other railings; black and gold and veined marble and other paving, grating to area, kitchen range, grates, coppers, ovens, cisterns and reservoirs, a capital force pump, 11 water-closets, with mahogany fittings and apparatus, pannelled doors, with gilt metal fastenings, and their dressings, 130 mahogany and other sash frames, principally glazed with plate glass, with the shutters and dressings and brass and other fastenings, a large quantity of skirting, imposts, dadoes and wain-scoting; the bells and pulls, sundry large and convenient presses, cup-boards, dressers and shelves, and miscellaneous other articles suitable for building and repairing... .to be sold by Mr. H. Phillips... on Wednesday, Sept. 16, and following days... .*[London, 1807].

Rutter, John. *A Description of Fonthill Abbey and Desmesne, in the County of Wilts: Including a List of the Paintings, Cabinets, &c.* [six editions published for the year], Shaftesbury, 1822.

——. *A New Descriptive Guide to Fonthill Abbey and Demesne, for 1823, Including a List of its Paintings and Curiosities.* Shaftesbury, 1823.

——. *Delineations of Fonthill and its Abbey.* London, 1823.

Sotheby Auction Catalogue. *A Catalogue of a Portion of the Library of William Beckford, Esq. of Fonthill; Comprising Many Valuable Articles in Topography, History, and Antiquities...Which will be Sold by Auction by Mr. Sotheby... May 6, 1817, and Two following Days.* [London, 1817].

Storer, James. *A Description of Fonthill Abbey, Wiltshire.* London, 1812.

——. *A Description of Fonthill Abbey, Wiltshire.* London, 1822.

Summers, Peter, and Philippa Bishop. *William Beckford: Some Notes on his Life in Bath 1822–1844 and A Catalogue of the Exhibition in the Holburne of Menstrie Museum.* Privately Printed, 1966.

Thorpe, Thomas. *A Catalogue... Comprising Upwards of Thirty Thousand Volumes of Rare, Curious, and Useful Books... Selected from Fonthill and Other Sales... Now Selling by Thomas Thorpe, No. 38 Bedford Street, Covent Garden.* London [1824].

[Whittaker, G. and W. B.]. *A New Guide to Fonthill Abbey, Wiltshire, the Seat of William Beckford, Esq. Comprising a Description of the Park and Buildings; Together with Brief Notices of Most of the Remarkable Produc-tions of Nature and Art, Which are Now Deposited There, and Which are Exhibited and Offered for Sale by the Proprietor.* London, 1822.

William Beckford Exhibition 1976. The Victoria Gallery. [Bath, 1976].

Wischermann, Heinfried. *Fonthill Abbey Studien zur Profanen Neugotik Englands im 18. Jahrhundert.* Freiberg: Berichte, 1979.

IV ARTICLES ON FONTHILL

A Day at Fonthill Abbey', *The New Monthly Magazine and Literary Jour-nal*, VIII (1823), pp. 368–80.

An Architect [John Carter]. 'The Pursuits of Architectural Innovation', *The Gentleman's* Magazine, LXXXI, pt. 1 (May, 1801) pp. 417–18.

An Artist. 'Fonthill Abbey', *Morning Chronicle*, 2 September 1822, p. 3; 5 September 1822, p. 3.

A Passer By. [Fonthill Abbey], *The Gentleman's Magazine*, XCI, pt. 2 (December, 1821), pp. 495–6.

'A Visit to Fonthill Abbey', *The Weekly Entertainer and West of England Miscellany*, 9 September 1822, pp. 150–3; 16 September 1822, pp. 177–8; 23 September 1822, pp. 193–6.

'Account of the Christmas Activities at Fonthill', *The European Magazine and London Review*, XXXI (January, 1797), pp. 4–6.

'Account of the Works Now Executing at Fonthill', *The European Magazine and London Review*, XXXI (February, 1797), pp. 104–7.

A[dams], T[homas]. ['Abbey of Fonthill'], *The Gentleman's Magazine*, XCVI, pt. 1 (May, 1826), p. 424.

Aldrich, Megan. 'William Beckford's Abbey at Fonthill: From the Picturesque to the Sublime', in *William Beckford, 1760–1844: An Eye for the Magnificent*, ed. Derek Ostergood. New Haven and London: Yale University Press, 2001, pp. 117–35.

Alexander, Boyd. 'Fonthill, Wiltshire – II, The Abbey and Its Creator', *Country Life*, 1 December 1966, pp. 1430–4.

——. 'Fonthill, Wiltshire – III, William Beckford as Collector', *Country Life*, 8 December 1966, pp. 1572–6.

——. 'William Beckford Man of Taste', *History Today*, X (October, 1960), pp. 686–94.

——. 'William Beckford of Fonthill', *Yale University Library Gazette*, XXXV (April, 1961), pp. 161–9.

Alsop, Joseph. 'The Faker's Art', *New York Review of Books*, 23 October 1986, pp. 25–31.

'Anecdotes of Mr. Beckford', *Morning Post*, 20 September 20 1823, p. 3; 20 September 1823, p.2.

'Anecdotes of Mr. Beckford', *The Observer*, 21 September 1823, p. 2.

Ashworth, Katharine. 'Tisbury's Ancient Secrets', *Country Life*, 4 November 1954, pp. 1590–2.

Bath and Cheltenham Gazette, The, additional notices on Fonthill: 23 September 1823, p. 3; 30 September 1823, p. 3.; 28 October 1823, p. 3.

Bath Chronicle notices on Fonthill: 22 August 1822, p. 4; 29 August 1822, p. 3; 17 October 1822, p. 2.

Bath Journal and General Advertiser [from 1822 *Keene's Bath Journal*] notices on Fonthill: 19 August 1822, p.4; 14 October 1822, p. 4; 4 November 1822, p. 4; 25 August 1823, p. 4; 20 October 1823, p. 4.

Baylis, Sarah. 'Knights in Painted Glass', *Country Life*, 7 February 2002, pp. 64–7.

'Beckford and Fonthill', *Chambers's Edinburgh Journal*, II (17 August 1844), pp. 101–3.

'Biography of Eccentric Characters. William Beckford, Esq.', *The Ladies' Monthly Museum*, XIX (February, 1824), pp. 67–71.

Bishop, Philippa. 'Settees from Fonthill Splendens', *The Beckford Journal*, I (Spring, 1995), pp. 15–17.

Blunt, Anthony. 'Fonthill Abbey', *The Venture* (February, 1929), pp. 75–81.

Britton, John. 'Fonthill Abbey', in *The Beauties of Wiltshire*. London, 1825, III, pp. 328–31.

——. 'Fonthill', in *The Beauties of Wiltshire*. London, 1801, I, pp. 208–49.

[——]. 'Fonthill Abbey', *The Museum, or Record of Literature, Fine Arts, Science, Antiquities, the Drama &c.*, no. 17 (1822), pp. 264–5.

Brulé, André. 'Une visite à Fonthill en 1792', Revue Anglo-Americaine, X (1933), pp. 33–42.

Buckland, W[illia]m. ['The Topaz Cup'], *The Times* [London], 17 November 1823, p. 3.

Châtel, Laurent. 'The Mole, the Bat, and the Fairy or the Sublime Grottoes of "Fonthill Splendens"', *The Beckford Journal*, V (Spring, 1999), pp. 53–74.

Claésson, Dick. 'Staging and Adapting the Nelson Visit', in *The Narratives of the Biographical Legend: The Early Works of William Beckford*. Göteborgs Universitet: Dissertation Edition, 2001.

Clarke, Stephen. 'The Troubled Gestation of Britton's *Illustrations of Fonthill*', *The Beckford Journal*, VI (Spring, 2000), pp. 58–74.

[Clarke, William]. 'William Beckford Esq. Fonthill Abbey', in *Repertorium Bibliographicum; or, Some Account of the Most Celebrated British Libraries*. London, 1819, pp. 203–30.

Cooke, George A. *Cooke's Topographical Library, or, British Traveller's Pocket County Directory, Wiltshire*. London, [c. 1830], pp. 119–35.

Courier notices on Fonthill: 23 September 1822, p. 4; 9 October 1822, p. 4; 21 August 1823, p. 3; 11 September 1823, p. 2; 12 September 1823, p. 2; 17 September 1823, p. 3; 18 September 1823, p. 3; 20 September 1823, p. 3; 22 September 1823, p. 4; 29 September 1823, p. 4; 1 October 1823, p. 2; 2 October 1823, p. 2; 3 October 1823, p. 3; 4 October 1823, p. 4; 16 October 1823, p. 4; 18 October 1823, p. 4; 24 October 1823, p. 4; 28 October 1823, p. 2; 7 November 1823, p. 4.

Craft, Adrian. 'Subterranean Enlightenment at Fonthill', *The Beckford Journal*, III (Spring, 1997), pp. 30–3.

Crockery, Jr. 'The Fonthill Mania', *The Literary Chronicle and Weekly Review*, 20 September 1823, pp. 603–4.

Cundall, E. G. 'Turner Drawings of Fonthill Abbey', *The Burlington Magazine*, XXIX (1916), pp. 16–21.

Darton, Eric. 'Fonthill: John Farquhar and After', *Beckford Tower Trust Newsletter* (Spring, 1987), pp. 6–7.

Davies, Damian Walford and Laurent Châtel. '"A Mad Hornet": Beckford's Riposte to Hazlitt', *European Romantic Review*, X, XI (Fall, 1999; Winter, 2000), pp. 452-79; pp. 97-9.

Dillenberger, John. 'Paintings for William Beckford and Fonthill Abbey: 1795–1810', in *Benjamin West The Context of His Life's Work with Particular Attention to Paintings with Religious Subject Matter*. San Antonio: Trinity University Press, [1977], pp. 106–209.

E. M. S. [James Dallaway]. 'Progress, &c. of Stained Glass in England', *The Gentleman's Magazine*, LXXXVII, pt. 1 (April, 1817), pp. 309–15.

'Editor's Excursion to Fonthill Abbey, The', *New European Magazine*, I (October, 1822), pp. 364–70.

[Egan, Pierce]. *Real Life in London, or the Rambles and Adventures of Bob Tallyho, Esq. and His Cousin, the Hon. Tom Dashall, through the Metropolis*. London, 1824, II, pp. 640–8.

E[lderton ?], J[ohn]. 'Mr. Urban', *The Gentleman's Magazine*, XCII, pt.1 (April, 1822), pp. 325–7.

Elderton, John. 'Tour into the Lower Parts of Somersetshire', *The Gentleman's Magazine*, LXI, pt. 1 (February, 1791), pp. 229–31.

'Epitome of Public Affairs', *The Ladies' Monthly Museum*, XVI (November, 1822), pp. 284–5.

'Extracts from Curious Books in the Fonthill Library', *The Examiner*, 24 August 1823, p. 550; 31 August 1823, pp. 563–4.

'Fonthill', *The Adventurer of the Nineteenth Century*, 28 June 1823, pp. 177–81.

'Fonthill', *The Crypt, or Receptacle for Things Past*, 19 December 1827, p. 220.

'Fonthill', *The Gazette of Fashion and Magazine of Literature, the Fine Arts, and Belles Lettres*, 19 October 1822, pp. 181–2.

'Fonthill', *The Gentleman's Magazine*, LXXI, pt. 2 (September, 1801), pp. 853–4.

'Fonthill', *Handbook for Travellers in Wiltshire, Dorsetshire, and Somersetshire*. London: John Murray, 1869, pp. 151–3.

'Fonthill', *Morning Herald*, 11 September 1823, p. 3.

'Fonthill', *Morning Herald*, 12 September 1823, p. 3.

'Fonthill', *Morning Herald*, 24 September 1823, p. 2.

'Fonthill', *Morning Herald*, 27 September 1823, p. 3.

'Fonthill', *The New Times*, 10 October 1822, p. 4.

'Fonthill Abbey', *Apollo Magazine*, I (1823), pp. 203–6.

'Fonthill Abbey', *Dublin University Magazine*, LXXVI (August, 1870), pp. 196–9.

'Fonthill Abbey', *The Examiner*, 10 August 1823, p. 514.

'Fonthill Abbey', *The Gazette of Fashion and Magazine of Literature, the Fine Arts, and Belles Lettres*, 31 August 1822, pp. 65–7 .

[Fonthill Abbey], *The Gentleman's Magazine*, LXVI, pt. 2 (September, 1796), p. 784.

'Fonthill Abbey', *The Gentleman's Magazine*, XCIII, pt. 1 (January, 1823), p. 79.

'Fonthill Abbey', *The Gentleman's Magazine*, XCV, pt. 2 (December, 1825), p. 557.

'Fonthill Abbey', *The Gleaner, or, Weekly Historical Register*, 15 October 1823, pp. 385–7.

'Fonthill Abbey', *The Kaleidoscope, or, Literary and Scientific Mirror*, III (1822), p. 117.

'Fonthill Abbey', *The Mirror of Literature, Amusement, and Instruction*, 23 November 1822, pp. 49–52.

'Fonthill Abbey', *The Mirror of Literature, Amusement, and Instruction*, 28 January 1826, pp. 54–5.

'Fonthill Abbey', *Morning Chronicle*, 21 August 1823, p. 2.

'Fonthill Abbey', *Morning Chronicle*, 13 September 1823, p. 3.

'Fonthill Abbey', *Morning Chronicle*, 17 September 1823, p. 3.

'Fonthill Abbey', *Morning Chronicle*, 24 September 1823, p. 2.

'Fonthill Abbey', *Morning Chronicle*, 25 September 1823, p. 4.

'Fonthill Abbey', *Morning Chronicle*, 26 September 1823, p. 3.

'Fonthill Abbey', *Morning Chronicle*, 1 October 1823, p. 3.

'Fonthill Abbey', *Morning Chronicle*, 8 October 1823, p. 4.

'Fonthill Abbey', *Morning Herald*, 7 October 1822, pp. 2–3.

'Fonthill Abbey', *Morning Herald*, 8 October 1822, p. 3.

'Fonthill Abbey', *Morning Herald*, 16 October 1822, p. 3.

'Fonthill Abbey', *Morning Post*, 8 September 1823, p. 3.

'Fonthill Abbey', *Morning Post*, 10 September 1823, p. 3.

'Fonthill Abbey', *Morning Post*, 17 September 1823, p. 3.

'Fonthill Abbey', *Morning Post*, 24 September 1823, p. 3.

'Fonthill Abbey', *Morning Post*, 25 September 1823, p. 3.

'Fonthill Abbey', *Morning Post*, 27 September 1823, p. 3.

'Fonthill Abbey', *Morning Post*, 1 October 1823, p. 3.

'Fonthill Abbey', *The Museum, or Record of Literature, Fine Arts, Science, Antiquities, the Drama &c.*, no. 19 (1822), pp. 300–1.

'Fonthill Abbey', *The Observer*, 19 October 1823, p. 3.

'Fonthill Abbey', *Scientific American*, 29 July 1893, p. 75.

'Fonthill Abbey', *The Times* [London], 5 October 1822, p. 2.

'Fonthill Abbey', *The Times* [London], 15 August 1823, p. 3.

'Fonthill Abbey' [reprint of article in *Leeds Intelligencer*], *The Times* [London], 30 September 1823, p. 3.

'Fonthill Abbey, Description of This Wonderful Place, By a Gentleman in the Neighbourhood', *Morning Post*, 16 October 1823, p. 3.

'Fonthill Abbey, Further Particulars', *Morning Post*, 12 September 1823, p. 4.

'Fonthill Abbey – Mr. Beckford – and Vathek', *Sunday Times*, 28 September 1823, p. 4 and 5 October 1823, p. 1.

'Fonthill Abbey, Second Day's Sale', *Morning Post*, 12 September 1823, p. 3.

'Fonthill Abbey, South East View', *The Mirror of Literature, Amusement, and Instruction*, 8 July 1826, pp. 25–6.

'Fonthill Abbey, Wilts. The Seat of Sir Michael Shaw-Stewart, Bart.', *Country Life*, 28 December 1901, pp. 840–6.

'Fonthill and Its Late Owner', *The New Times*, 9 September 1823, p. 2.

'Fonthill Fete', *The Times* [London], 20 January 1797, p. 4.

'Fonthill Grand Disappointment', *Morning Post*, 8 October 1822, p. 3.

'Fonthill Property, The', *Morning Herald*, 1 October 1822, p. 1.

'Fonthill Property, The', *The Times* [London], 30 September 1822, p. 3; 1 October 1822, p. 2; 4 October 1822, p. 3; 7 October 1822, p. 3;

[Fonthill Sale], *The Literary Gazette and Journal of Belles Lettres*, 30 August 1823, p. 555.

'Fonthill Sale', *The Literary Gazette and Journal of Belles Lettres*, 20 September 1823, p. 602.

'Fonthill Sale', *The Literary Gazette and Journal of Belles Lettres*, 27 September 1823, pp. 617–18.

'Fonthill Sale', *The Times* [London], 23 September 1823, p. 3.

Frith, W. P. 'The Fonthill Story', in *My Autobiography and Reminiscences*. London, 1890, pp. 349–54.

G[arbett], W[illiam]. 'Candid Critique on the Architecture of Fonthill Abbey', *The Gentleman's Magazine*, XCII, pt. 2 (December, 1822), pp. 491–4.

Gardner, Albert Ten Eyck. 'Beckford's Gothic Wests', *Bulletin of the Metropolitan Museum of Art*, XIII (October, 1954), pp. 41–9.

Gatty, Richard. 'Fonthill', in *Portrait of a Merchant Prince: James Morrison 1789–1857*. Northallerton: Pepper Arden, [1976].

Gemmett, Robert J., 'Beckford's Fonthill: The Landscape as Art', *Gazette des Beaux-Arts*, LXXX (December, 1972), pp. 335–56.

——. 'The Critical Reception of William Beckford's Fonthill', *English Miscellany*, XIX (1968), pp. 133–51.

Goldsmith, Revd J. [Sir Richard R. Phillips]. 'Fonthill Abbey', in *The Natural and Artificial Wonders of the United Kingdom*. London, 1825, II, pp. 321–6.

'Gothic Revival's Grand Showman', *The Times* [London], 24 September 1960, p. 7.

Hall, Michael. 'Echoes of Fonthill', *Country Life*, 7 February 2002, pp. 68–71.

Hamilton-Phillips, Martha. 'Benjamin West and William Beckford: Some Projects for Fonthill', *Metropolitan Museum Journal*, XV (1981), pp. 157–74.

Harris, John. 'Fonthill, Wiltshire – I, Alderman Beckford's Houses', *Country Life*, 24 November 1966, pp. 1370–4.

Hauptman, William. 'Beckford, Brandoin, and the "Rajah" Aspects of an Eighteenth-Century Collection', *Apollo*, CXLIII (May, 1996), pp. 30–9.

Hayward, J. F. 'Royal Plate at Fonthill', *The Burlington Magazine*, CI (April, 1959), p. 145.

H[azlitt], W[illiam]. 'Fonthill Abbey', *The London Magazine*, VI (November, 1822), pp. 405–10.

[——]. 'The Main Chance', *The New Monthly Magazine*, XVII (February, 1828), p. 120.

[——]. 'Notices of Curious and Highly Finished Cabinet Pictures at Fonthill Abbey', *Morning Chronicle*, 20 August 1823, p. 3; 22 August 1823, p. 3; 25 August 1823, p. 3; 1 September 1823, p. 2.

[——]. 'Pictures at Wilton, Stourhead, &c.', *The London Magazine*, VIII (October, 1823), pp. 357– 60.

[——]. 'The Science of a Connoisseur', *Morning Chronicle*, 30 September 1823, p. 2.

Herrick, George H. 'Fabulous Fonthill', *College Art Journal*, XII (1953), pp. 128–31.

H[oare, Sir Richard Colt]. 'Fonthill Abbey in Ruins', *The Gentleman's Magazine*, XCVI, pt. 1 (February, 1826), p. 123.

'Illumination of the Abbey', *Morning Chronicle*, 24 October 1823, p. 4.

J. H.. 'The Topaz Cup;' *Morning Post*, 8 November 1823, p. 4.

'John Constable's Visit to Fonthill Abbey in 1823', *Beckford Tower Trust Newsletter* (Spring, 1983), pp. 8–9.

'John Farquhar, Esq.' [Obituary], *The Gentleman's Magazine*, XCVI, pt. 2 (September, 1826), pp. 278–80.

Jones, Stanley. 'The Fonthill Abbey Pictures: Two Additions to the Hazlitt Canon', *Journal of the Warburg and Courtauld Institutes*, XLI (1978), pp. 278–96.

Jourdain, Margaret. 'William Beckford of Fonthill', in *Memorials of Old Wiltshire*. Ed. Alice Dryden. London, 1906, pp. 116–27.

[Knight, Charles]. 'Fonthill Abbey', *The Guardian* [London], 25 August 1822, p. 269; 8 September 1822, p. 287; 15 September 1822, p. 294; 22 September 1822, p. 301; 29 September 1822, p. 309; 13 October 1822, p. 325.

Knight, Derrick. 'Xanadu of a Wiltshire Hilltop', in *Gentlemen of Fortune*. London: Frederick Muller, [1978], pp. 113–26.

Lacy, J. 'The Topaz Cup', *The Times* [London], 6 November 1823, p. 3.

L[ancaster Herald, George F. Beltz]. 'Armorial Decorations at Fonthill Abbey', *The Gentleman's Magazine*, XCII, pt. 2 (September, October, November, 1822), pp. 201–4; 317–20; 409–14.

Lane, Arthur. 'The Gaignières-Fonthill Vase; A Chinese Porcelain of about 1300', *The Burlington Magazine*, CIII (April, 1961), pp. 124–32.

Lawford, G[eorge]. 'Fonthill Sale', *The Times* [London], 26 September 1823, p. 3.

Lewis, Kensington. 'Fonthill Abbey: The Topaz Cup', *The Times* [London], 5 November 1823, p. 3.

Littlebury, Isaac [Thomas F. Dibdin]. 'Fonthill Campaign. A Slight Sketch', *The Literary Gazette and Journal of Belles Lettres*, 4 October 1823, pp. 634–5.

——— [Thomas F. Dibdin]. 'Fonthill', *Morning Chronicle*, 26 August 1823, p. 3; 30 August 1823, p. 3.

Longbourne, David. 'A Painting of Fonthill Abbey Discovered', *The Beckford Journal*, III (Spring, 1997), pp. 6–7.

Loudon, J. C. 'Notes on Gardens and Country Seats', *The Gardener's Magazine*, XI (September, 1835), pp. 441–9.

Luff, S. G. A. 'The Romantick Abbey: A Consideration of Beckford's Folly', *The Aylesford Review*, VI (Winter, 1963), pp. 26–32.

McGarvie, Michael. 'William Beckford, Gardener, at Witham and Fonthill', *Frome Society Yearbook*, VII (1997), pp. 112–21.

McLeod, Bet. 'Treasures of England's Wealthiest Son', *Country Life*, 7 February 2002, pp. 40–5.

[Macquin, Abbé Ange Denis] 'A Visit to Fonthill Abbey', *The Literary Gazette and Journal of Belles Lettres*, 17 August 1822, pp. 520–1; 24 August 1822, pp. 527–8; 31 August 1822, pp. 555–6; 14 September 1822, p. 585.

Marr, Alexander. 'William Beckford and the Landscape Garden', in *William Beckford, 1760–1844: An Eye for the Magnificent*, ed. Derek Ostergood. New Haven and London: Yale University Press, 2001, pp. 137–53.

Mayhew, Edgar. 'A View of Fonthill Abbey', *The Register of the Museum of Art, University of Kansas*, I (December, 1957), pp. 151–6.

Millington, Jon. 'A Reissue of Storer's Fonthill', *The Beckford Journal*, IV (Spring, 1998), pp. 71–5.

———. 'Engravings of Fonthill', *The Beckford Journal*, VII (Spring, 2001), pp. 47–59.

———. 'Fonthill After Beckford', *The Beckford Journal*, II (Spring, 1996), pp. 46–59.

———. 'Francis Danby', *Beckford Tower Trust Newsletter* (Spring, 1985), p. 3.

———. 'Nichols' *Historical Notices of Fonthill Abbey*', *The Beckford Journal*, VI (Spring, 2000), pp. 75–8.

——. 'Where Nelson Went in Fonthill Abbey', *The Beckford Journal*, VIII (Spring, 2002), pp. 43–9.

'Mr. Beckford', *Morning Herald*, 17 September 1823, p. 1.

'Mr. Beckford', *Morning Herald*, 6 October 1823, p. 4.

'Mr. Beckford', *Morning Herald*, 10 October 1823, p. 3.

'Mr. Beckford', *The Observer*, 21 September 1823, p. 4.

'Mr. Beckford and Fonthill', *Chambers Journal*, II (August, 1844) pp. 101–3.

'Mr. Beckford and the Fine Arts', *Morning Herald*, 27 September 1823, p. 3.

'Mr. Beckford. Fonthill Abbey', *The Gleaner, or, Weekly Historical Register*, 22 October 1823, pp. 407–9.

'Mr. Beckford's Critiques and Commentaries', *The Literary Chronicle and Weekly Review*, 20 September 1823, p. 602.

'Mr. Beckford – Several Anecdotes, Illustrative of This Gentleman's Character', *The Bath and Cheltenham Gazette*, 23 September 1823, p. 2.

'Mr. Farquhar and Fonthill', *The Times* [London], 11 October 1822, p. 3.

'Mr. Farquhar and Fonthill Abbey', *The Mirror of Literature, Amusement, and Instruction*, 16 November 1822, pp. 33–5.

'Mr. Farquhar and the Fonthill Estate', *The Observer*, 13 October 1822, p. 4.

M. J. 'Fonthill Abbey', *The Literary Chronicle and Weekly Review*, 19 October 1822, pp. 665–7.

Morning Chronicle additional notices on Fonthill: 20 September 1822, p. 4; 24 September 1822, p. 3; 10 October 1822, p. 3; 21 October 1822, p. 3; 1 November 1822, p.3; 4 November 1822, p. 4; 22 August 1823, p. 3; 11 September 1823, p. 3; 12 September 1823, p. 3; 18 September 1823, p. 2; 19 September 1823, p. 3; 20 September 1823, p. 2; 22 September 1823, p. 2; 27 September 1823, p. 2; 29 September 1823, p. 2; 2 October 1823, p. 4; 3 October 1823, p. 3; 4 October 1823, p. 3; 6 October 1823, p. 3; 9 October 1823, p. 4; 11 October 1823, p. 4; 13 October 1823, p. 4; 15 October 1823, p. 4; 16 October 1823, p. 4; 18 October 1823, p. 4; 20 October 1823, p. 4; 23 October 1823, p. 4; 25 October 1823, p. 1; 27 October 1823, p. 4; 11 November 1823, p. 4.

Morning Herald additional notices on Fonthill: 11 October 1822, p. 3; 8 September 1823, p. 3; 10 September 1823, p. 2; 13 September 1823, p. 3; 16 September 1823, p. 2; 17 September 1823, p. 2; 18 September 1823, p. 3; 20 September 1823, p. 2; 22 September 1823, p. 3; 26 September 1823, p. 3; 29 September 1823, p. 3; 1 October 1823, p. 3; 3 October 1823, p. 3; 15 October 1823, p. 3; 16 October 1823, p.3; 1 November 1823, p. 3.

Morning Post additional notices on Fonthill: 8 October 1822, p. 3; 8 August 1823, p. 3; 20 August 1823, p. 3; 22 August 1823, p. 3; 29 August 1823, p. 3; 2 September 1823, p. 3; 11 September 1823, p. 3; 13 September 1823, p. 3; 15 September 1823, p. 3; 18 September 1823, p. 3; 19 September 1823, p. 3; 20 September 1823, p. 3; 22 September 1823, p. 3; 26

September 1823, p. 3; 29 September 1823, p. 3; 2 October 1823, p. 3; 4 October 1823, pp. 3, 4; 9 October 1823, p. 3; 11 October 1823, p. 3; 13 October 1823, p. 3; 21 October 1823, p. 3; 24 October 1823, p. 3; 25 October 1823, p. 3; 28 October 1823, p. 2; 29 November 1823, p. 3.

Mowl, Tim. 'Inside Beckford's Landscape of the Mind', *Country Life*, 7 February 2002, pp. 60–3.

New Monthly Magazine and Literary Journal, The, additional notices on Fonthill: VI (October, 1822), pp. 479–80; XVIII (April, 1826), p. 169.

New Times, The, additional notices on Fonthill: 5 November 1822, p. 3; 27 August 1823, p. 4; 12 September 1823, pp. 3, 4; 13 September 1823, p. 4; 18 September 1823, p. 4.

Nightingale, James E. 'Some Account of the Objects of Interest in the Fonthill Excursion.' A paper read at the 17th annual meeting of the Wiltshire Archaeological and Natural History Society, at Wilton. Salisbury, 1870.

Observator. 'Letter to Mr. Urban', *The Gentleman's Magazine*, LXXVI, pt. 2 (December, 1806), pp. 1127–8.

Parkins, J. W. 'Mr. Farquhar', *Morning Chronicle*, 5 November 1822, p. 3.

[Patmore, Peter G.]. 'British Galleries of Art – No. IX Fonthill', *The New Monthly Magazine and Literary Journal*, VIII (1823), pp. 403–8.

Pearson, James. 'The Art of Staining Glass', *The Gentleman's Magazine*, LXXXV, pt. 2 (July, 1815), pp. 28–9.

Pendragon, Charles [Charles Knight]. 'An Episode of Vathek', *Knight's Quarterly Magazine*, I (July, 1823), pp. 309–14.

Pevsner, Nikolaus. 'Fonthill Abbey', in *The Buildings of England: Wiltshire*. London: Penguin Books, [1976], pp. 246–9.

Phillips, H[arry]. 'The Topaz Cup at Fonthill', *Morning Post*, 17 November 1823, p. 3.

Pressly, Nancy. *Revealed Religion: Benjamin West's Commissions for Windsor Castle and Fonthill Abbey*. San Antonio, 1983.

Reitlinger, Gerald. 'Further Adventures of the Gaignières-Fonthill Vase', *The Burlington Magazine*, CIV (1962), p. 34.

Roberts, Hugh. 'Beckford, Vuillamy and Old Japan', *Apollo*, CXXIV (1986), pp. 338–41.

Rogers, Millard F. 'Benjamin West and the Caliph: Two Paintings for Fonthill Abbey', *Apollo*, LXXXIII (June, 1966), pp. 420–5.

Ross, Marvin Chauncey. 'The Rubens Vase: Its History and Date', *The Journal of the Walters Art Gallery*, VI (1943), pp. 9–39.

Rushton, Andrée. 'The Fonthill Barrier', *The Beckford Journal*, IV (Spring, 1998), pp. 65–70.

'Sale at Fonthill', *The Gentleman's Magazine*, LXXVII, pt. 2 (September, 1807), p. 880.

'Sale at Fonthill Abbey', *The Museum, or Record of Literature, Fine Arts, Science, Antiquities, the Drama &c.*, no. 14 (1822), pp. 216–17.

'Sale of Effects at Fonthill Abbey', *The Observer*, 1 & 2 September 1822, pp. 3; 2.

'Sale of the Whole of the Fonthill Estate', *The Observer*, 13 October 1822, p. 4.

Salisbury and Winchester Journal notices on Fonthill: 26 August 1822, p. 4; 2 September 1822, p. 4; 9 September 1822, p. 4; 16 September 1822, p. 4; 23 September 1822, p. 4; 30 September 1822, p. 4; 14 October 1822, pp. 3, 4; 28 October 1822, p. 2; 4 August 1823, p. 4; 18 August 1823, p. 3; 25 August 1823, p. 4; 1 September 1823, p. 4; 8 September 1823, p. 4; 15 September 1823, p. 4; 22 September 1823, p. 4; 29 September 1823, p. 4; 6 October 1823, p. 4; 13 October 1823, p. 4; 20 October 1823, pp. 3, 4; 27 October 1823, p. 4; 3 November 1823, p. 2.

Scott, John. 'The Rise and Fall of Fonthill Abbey', *British History Illustrated*, II (August, 1975), pp. 3–11.

Scott, T. G. 'Fonthill Buildings', *Country Life*, 24 January 1957, p.157.

Skoggard, Carl. 'William Beckford, Fonthill Abbey', *Nest: A Magazine of Interiors*, no. 4 (Spring, 1999).

Smith, H. Clifford. 'The Van Diemen Box', *The Burlington Magazine*, XXIX (1916), pp. 299–303.

Snodin, Michael and Malcolm Baker. 'William Beckford's Silver: I', *The Burlington Magazine*, CXXII (November, 1980), pp. 735–48.

——. 'William Beckford's Silver: II', *The Burlington Magazine*, CXXII (December, 1980), pp. 820–34.

Stone, Richard E. 'A Noble Imposture: The Fonthill Ewer and Early-Nineteenth-Century Fakery', *Metropolitan Museum Journal*, XXXII (1997), pp.175–206.

——. 'The Fonthill Ewer Reconstructing the Renaissance', *Metropolitan Museum of Art Bulletin*, 55 (Winter, 1997), pp. 46–56.

Strong, Roy. 'The Fall of Fonthill', in *Lost Treasures of Britain*. London: Viking Penguin, [1990], pp. 188–201.

Templeton, A[rthur] M., Jr. 'A Second Visit to Fonthill Abbey', *New European Magazine*, III (August, 1823), pp. 135–42.

Thacker, Christopher. *Building Towers, Forming Gardens: Landscaping by Hamilton, Hoare and Beckford*. London: St Barnabas Press, [2002].

——. 'England's Kubla Khan', in *William Beckford Exhibition 1976*. [Bath, 1976], pp. 63–76.

——. 'Fonthill', in *The History of Gardens*. Berkeley: University of California Press, [1979], pp. 221–5.

——, Steven Ashley and Julian Berry. 'Twin Towers', *The Georgian Group Journal* (1995), pp. 115–18.

Times, The [London] additional notices on Fonthill: 20 May 1800, p. 3; 27 May 1800, p. 3; 24 December 1800, p. 3.; 21 August 1801, p. 2; 29 September 1807, p. 3; 14 September 1822, p. 2; 17 September 1822, p. 2; 20 September 1822, p. 2; 2 October 1822, p. 3; 3 October 1822, p. 2; 8 October 1822, p. 2; 9 October 1822, p. 2; 21 November 1822, p. 2; 15 August 1823, p. 3; 12 September 1823, p.2; 28 October 1823, p. 2; 30 October 1823, p. 2; 30 October 1829.

Tonstall, Cuthbert [Thomas F. Dibdin]. 'The Fonthill Fever', *The Museum, or Record of Literature, Fine Arts, Science, Antiquities, the Drama &c.*, 5 October 1822, pp. 379–80; 12 October 1822, pp. 393–5; 19 October 1822, pp. 410–12; 26 October 1822, pp. 428–30; 2 November 1822, pp. 441–2; 9 November 1822, pp. 455–6.

[Tresham, Henry]. 'Letter from a Gentleman, Present at the Festivities at Fonthill, to a Correspondent in Town', *The Gentleman's Magazine*, LXXXIX, pt. 1 (March, April, 1801), pp. 206–8; 297–8.

Viator [Sir Richard Colt Hoare]. 'Fonthill Abbey. On its Close', *The Gentleman's Magazine*, XCII, pt. 2 (October, 1822), pp. 291–2.

Wainwright, Clive. 'Fonthill Abbey', in *The Romantic Interior: The British Collector at Home 1750–1850*. New Haven: Yale University Press, 1989, pp. 109–46.

——. 'In Lucifer's Metropolis', *Country Life*, 1 October 1992, pp. 82–4.

——. 'William Beckford and His Collection', *Arte Illustrata*, IV (January–April, 1971), pp. 106–12.

——. 'William Beckford's Furniture', *Connoisseur*, CXCI (1976), pp. 290–6.

Watson, F. J. B. 'Beckford, Mme. de Pompadour, the duc de Bouillon and the Taste for Japanese Lacquer in Eighteenth Century France', *Gazette des Beaux-Arts*, LXI (1963), pp. 101–27.

Weeks, Donald. 'William Beckford and Fonthill Abbey', in *Pages: The World of Books, Writers, and Writing*, ed. Matthew Bruccoli. Detroit: Gale Research, [1976], pp. 58–61.

Whitehead, John. 'Some French Purchases by William Beckford', *The Beckford Journal*, II (Spring, 1996), pp. 39–44.

Wilkinson, Gerald. 'Fonthill', in *Turner's Early Sketchbooks*. New York: Watson-Guptill, [1972], pp. 100–4.

'William Bankes' Account of his Surreptitious Visit to Fonthill', *The Beckford Journal*, I (Spring, 1995), pp. 47–50.

Wilton-Ely, John. 'Beckford, Fonthill Abbey and the Picturesque', in *The Picturesque in Late Georgian England*, ed. Dana Arnold. London: The Georgian Group, [1995], pp. 35–44.

——. 'Beckford the Builder', in *William Beckford Exhibition 1976*. The Victoria Gallery. [Bath, 1976], pp. 35–62.

——. 'Beckford's Fonthill Abbey: a Theatre of the Arts', in *The Beckford Society Annual Lectures 1996–1999*, ed. Jon Millington. Bristol: The Beckford Society, 2000, pp. 3–22.

——. 'The Genesis and Evolution of Fonthill Abbey', *Architectural History*, 23 (1980), pp. 40–51.

——. 'A Model for Fonthill Abbey', in *The Country Seat: Studies in the History of the British Country House*, ed. Howard Colvin and John Harris. London: Penguin Press, [1970], pp. 199–204.

Woodward, Christopher. 'William Beckford and Fonthill Splendens: Early Works by Soane and Goodridge', *Apollo*, CXLVII (1998), pp. 31–40.

Wyatt, Benjamin. 'Fonthill Abbey', *Morning Post*, 1 November 1823, p. 2.

V POEMS ON FONTHILL

Bowles, William Lisle. 'Lines on a First View of Fonthill Abbey', *The Gentleman's Magazine*, XCII, pt. 2 (August, 1822), p. 102.

E. K. 'Fonthill Abbey, Wilts, Seat of W. Beckford, Esq. in July 1827', Jaulnah, Bombay, July 1856, from the Scrapbook of Ezra Hunt (1809–76), Bath Public Library.

'Fonthill', in *The Anniversary; or, Poetry and Prose for MDCCCXXIX*, ed. Allan Cunningham. London, 1829, pp. 214–16.

Jefferson, John. *Fonthill: A Poem*. Blandford, 1824.

[Lettice, John]. 'Written in an Arbour of the Alpine Garden Fronting the Lake', Fonthill 4 August 1800. MS. Beckford, Bodleian Library, c. 33, f. 73.

[——]. 'Written in the Grotto', 6 August 1800. MS. Beckford, Bodleian Library, c. 33, f. 72.

[Macquin, Abbé Ange Denis]. 'Fonthill Abbey', *The Literary Gazette and Journal of Belles Lettres*, 21 September 1822, pp. 602–3.

M. J. 'Fonthill: A Sonnet', *The Literary Chronicle and Weekly Review*, 24 August 1822, p. 540.

[Pickering, Henry]. 'On the Alienation of Fonthill Abbey', in *Ruins of Paestum: and Other Compositions in Verse*. Salem, Mass., 1822.

W[atts], A[laric] A. 'Fonthill Sale: A Parody', Broadside dated '19 Jan 1824', Beinecke Library, GEN MSS, 102, f. 100, Alaric Watts to John Britton.

VI SECONDARY SOURCES

Aldrich, Megan. *Gothic Revival*. London: Phaidon Press, 1994.

Alexander, Boyd, ed. *The Journal of William Beckford in Portugal, 1787–1788*. New York: John Day, 1955.

——. *England's Wealthiest Son: A Study of William Beckford*. [London]: Centaur Press, 1962.

——. 'Shades of Beckford', *Apollo*, CIV (August, 1976), pp.146–7.

Andersen, Jorgen. 'Giant Dreams: Piranesi's Influence in England', *English Miscellany*, II (1962), pp. 49–60.

Argenteries: Le Trésor du National Trust for Scotland. La Collection Beckford et Hamilton du Château de Brodick. National Trust for Scotland, 1992.

Bishop, Philippa. 'William Beckford 1760-1844: British Antiquarian and Connoisseur', *Encyclopedia of Interior Design*. Ed. Joanna Banham. London: Fitzroy Deaborn, [1997], I, 111–14.

Britton, John. *The Autobiography of John Britton*. 2 vols. London, 1850.

Chambers, William. *Dissertation on Oriental Gardening*. London, 1773.

Chapman, Guy. *Beckford*. London: Rupert Hart-Davis, 1952.

——., ed. *The Travel-Diaries of William Beckford of Fonthill*. 2 vols. Cambridge: Constable, 1928.

——., ed. *The Vision Liber Veritatis*. Cambridge: Constable, 1930.

Chase, Isabel. *Horace Walpole: Gardenist*. Princeton: Princeton University Press, 1943.

Clark, Kenneth. *The Gothic Revival: An Essay in the History of Taste*. London: Penguin Books, [1962].

Crowley, D. A. *A History of Wiltshire, XI, Downton Hundred, XIII, South-west Wiltshire*. Oxford: Oxford University Press, 1980.

Culme, John. 'Kensington Lewis, A Nineteenth-Century Businessman', *The Connoisseur*, CXC (1975), pp. 26–41.

Dale, Anthony. *James Wyatt, Architect: 1748–1813*. Oxford: Basil Blackwell, 1936.

Da Silva, José Cornélio and Gerald Luckhurst. *Sintra: A Landscape with Villas*. Ediçoes Inapa: The Genius of the Place Collection, [1989].

Eastlake, Charles L. *History of the Gothic Revival*. ed. J. M. Crook. Leicester: Leicester University Press, 1970.

Farington, Joseph. *The Diary of Joseph Farington*, ed. Kenneth Garlick, Angus Macintyre and Katherine Cave. 16 vols. New Haven: Yale University Press, 1978–84.

[Farquhar, John]. *Costly Furniture, Bronzes, Marbles... A Catalogue of the Superlatively Elegant Assemblage of Furniture... and Miscellaneous Objects, the Property of a Gentleman, Removed from His Mansion in the West of England*. Which will be Sold ... by Mr. Phillips... 22d day of June, 1825 and following days.

Fergusson, James. *History of the Modern Styles of Architecture*. London, 1873.

Finberg, A. J. *A Complete Inventory of the Drawings of the Turner Bequest*. 2 vols. London, 1909.

Fothergill, Brian. *Beckford of Fonthill*. London: Faber, [1979].

Frith, W. P. *My Autobiography and Reminiscences*. London, 1890.

Gauthier, Marie-Madeleine. *Émaux Méridionaux Catalogue International de L'oeuvre de Limoges*. Tome I, *L'Époque Romane*. Paris: Éditions du Centre National de la Recherche Scientifique, 1987.

Gemmett, Robert J., ed. *Biographical Memoirs of Extraordinary Painters*. Rutherford, N. J.: Fairleigh Dickinson University Press, 1969.

——, ed. *The Consummate Collector: William Beckford's Letters to His Bookseller*. Wilby, Norwich: Michael Russell, 2000.

——, ed. *Dreams, Waking Thoughts and Incidents*. Rutherford, N. J.: Fairleigh Dickinson University Press, 1971.

——. *William Beckford*. Boston: Twayne, [1977].

Gilpin, William. *The Essay on Prints* . London, 1768.

——. *Observations on the Western Parts of England, Relative Chiefly to Picturesque Beauty*. London, 1798.

——. *Three Essays on Picturesque Beauty: on Picturesque Travel; and on Sketching Landscape*. 3rd ed. London, 1808.

Gower, Lord Granville Leveson. *Lord Granville Leveson Gower, Private Correspondence, 1781–1821*, ed. Castalia Countess Granville. 2 vols. London, 1916.

Gregory, William. *The Beckford Family: Reminiscences of Fonthill Abbey and Lansdown Tower*. London, 1898.

H[arrison], W[illiam] H. 'Conversations of the Late W. Beckford, Esq.', *The New Monthly Magazine*, LXXII, no. vi (December, 1844), pp. 516–22.

Harris, John. 'C. R. Cockerell's "Ichnographica Domestica"', *Architectural History*, XIV (1971), pp. 5–29.

——. 'English Country House Guides, 1740–1840', in *Concerning Architecture*, ed. John Summerson. Baltimore: Penguin, [1968], pp. 58–74.

——. *Sir William Chambers, Knight of the Polar Star*. University Park: The Pennsylvania State University Press, [1970].

Haydon, F. W. *Benjamin Robert Haydon: Correspondence and Table Talk*. 2 vols. London, 1876.

H. 'Conversations with the Late W. Beckford, Esq.', *The New Monthly Magazine*, LXXII, nos. iii–v (September–November, 1844), pp. 18–24; 212–21; 418–27.

Herrmann, Frank. *The English Collectors: A Documentary Chrestomathy*. New York: W. W. Norton, 1972.

Hoare, Sir Richard Colt and James Everard, Baron Arundell. *The History of Modern Wiltshire*. Vol. 4, *Hundred of Dunworth and Vale of Noddre*. London, 1829.

Hodges, Alison. 'Painshill, Cobham, Surrey: The Grotto', *Garden History*, III (Autumn, 1974), pp. 23–8.

Hopkins, John H. *Essay on Gothic Architecture, with Various Plans and Drawings for Churches: Designed Chiefly for the Use of the Clergy.* Burlington, 1836.

Howe, P. P. *The Complete Works of William Hazlitt.* Vol. XIX. London: J. M. Dent, 1933.

Hussey, Christopher. *The Picturesque: Studies in a Point of View.* London: G. P. Putnam, 1927.

Jack, Malcolm. *William Beckford, An English Fidalgo.* New York: AMS Press, [1994].

Jerdan, William. *The Autobiography of William Jerdan.* 3 vols. London, 1853.

Jones, Barbara. *Follies & Grottoes.* London: Constable, [1953].

Knight, Charles. *Once Upon a Time.* London, 1865.

——. *Passages of a Working Life During Half a Century with a Prelude of Early Reminiscences.* 3 vols. London, 1864.

Knight, R. P. *The Landscape, A Didactic Poem in Three Books.* London, 1794.

Kuist, James M., ed. *The Nichols File of the Gentleman's Magazine.* Madison: University of Wisconsin, 1982.

Lansdown, Henry V. *Recollections of the Late William Beckford of Fonthill, Wilts.; and Lansdown, Bath.* Bath, 1893.

Lees-Milne, James. *William Beckford.* Tisbury: Compton Russell, [1976].

Leslie, C. R. *Memoirs of the Life of John Constable.* London: John Lehmann, 1949.

Macaulay, James. *The Gothic Revival 1745–1845.* London: Blackie, 1975.

Macaulay, Rose. *They Went to Portugal.* London: Jonathan Cape, [1946].

McCarthy, Michael. *The Origins of the Gothic Revival.* London: Paul Mellon Centre for Studies in British Art, 1987.

McLeod, Bet. 'Some Further Objects from William Beckford's Collection in the Victoria and Albert Museum', *The Burlington Magazine*, CXLIII (June, 2001), pp. 367–70.

Malins, Edward. *English Landscaping and Literature 1660–1840.* London: Oxford University Press, 1966.

Manwaring, Elizabeth. *Italian Landscape in Eighteenth-Century England.* New York: Oxford University Press, 1925.

Meister, J. Henri. *Letters Written During a Residence in England.* London, 1799.

Melville, Lewis. *The Life and Letters of William Beckford of Fonthill.* New York: Duffield, 1910.

'Memoirs of William Beckford, of Fonthill', *The Gentleman's Magazine*, CCVI (March, 1859), pp. 255–60.

Millington, Jon, ed. *Beckford and His Circle in the Gentleman's Magazine.* Bristol: Beckford Society, 2001.

Mitford, Mary Russell. *The Friendships of Mary Russell Mitford as Recorded in Letters from Her Literary Correspondents,* ed. Rev. A. G. L'Estrange. New York, 1882.

Moore, Thomas. *The Journal of Thomas Moore,* ed. Wilfred S. Dowden, Vols. 1–3. Newark: University of Delaware Press, [1984].

Morrison, Alfred. *Collection of Autograph Letters and Historical Documents.* (Second Series). Printed for private circulation, 1893.

——. *Collection of Autograph Letters and Historical Documents, The Hamilton and Nelson Papers* (Second Series). 2 vols. Printed for private circulation, 1893–4.

Mowl, Timothy. *William Beckford: Composing for Mozart.* London: John Murray, [1998].

Murphy, James Cavanah. *Plans, Elevations, Sections & Views of the Church of Batalha in the Province of Estremadura in Portugal.* London, 1836.

Neiman, Fraser. 'The Letters of William Gilpin to Samuel Henley', *Huntington Library Quarterly,* XXXV (February, 1972), pp. 159–69.

Newby, Evelyn. 'A Dutchman's Visit to Some English Gardens in 1791', *Journal of Garden History,* II (January–March, 1982), pp. 41–58.

Oliver, J. W. *The Life of William Beckford.* London: Oxford University Press, 1932.

Oppé, A. P. *Alexander and John Robert Cozens.* Cambridge: Harvard University Press, 1954.

Peniston, John. *The Letters of John Peniston, Salisbury Architect, Catholic, and Yeomanry Officer 1823–1830.* ed. Michael Cowan. Trowbridge: Wiltshire Record Society, 1996.

Pettigrew, T. J. *Memoirs of the Life of Vice-Admiral Lord Viscount Nelson, K. B.* 2 vols. London, 1849.

Pococke, Richard. *The Travels Through England.* ed. James J. Carwright. 2 vols. Westminster, 1889.

Powys, Mrs. Philip Lybbe. *Passages from the Diaries of Mrs. Philip Lybbe Powys.* ed. Emily J. Climenson. London: Longmans, 1899.

Price, Uvedale. *Essays on the Picturesque.* 2 vols. London, 1798.

Pückler-Muskau, Prince. *Tour in England, Ireland, and France, 1828-1829.* Philadelphia, 1833.

Quest-Ritson, Charles. *The English Garden Abroad.* London: Viking, [1992].

Redding, Cyrus. *Fifty Years' Recollections, Literary and Personal, with Observations on Men and Things.* 3 vols. London, 1858.

——. *Memoirs of William Beckford of Fonthill.* 2 vols. London, 1859.

——. *Past Celebrities Whom I Have Known.* 2 vols. London, 1866.

——. 'Recollections of the Author of *Vathek*', *The New Monthly Magazine*, LXXI (June, July, 1844), pp.143–58; 302–19.

Reynolds, Donald M. *et al. Fonthill Castle: Paradigm of Hudson-River Gothic*. Riverdale: College of Mount Saint Vincent-on-Hudson, 1976.

Robinson, John Martin. *The Wyatts: An Architectural Dynasty*. Oxford: Oxford University Press, 1979.

Rogers, Samuel. *Recollections of Samuel Rogers to Which is Added Porsoniana*. New York, 1856.

Shaffer, E. S. '"To remind us of China" – William Beckford, Mental Traveller on the Grand Tour: The Construction of Significance in Landscape', in *Transports: Travel, Pleasure, and Imaginative Geography, 1600–1830*, ed. Chloe Chard and Helen Langdon. New Haven: Yale University Press, [1996], pp. 207–42.

Sheard, Norah. *The History of Hindon*. Shaftesbury: The Shaston Printers, [1979].

Sherbo, Arthur. 'Isaac Reed and *The European Magazine*', *Studies in Bibliography*, XXXVII (1984), pp. 210–27

Simpson, Duncan. *Gothick 1720–1840* [Exhibition catalogue]. Brighton: Royal Pavilion, Art Gallery and Museums, [1975].

Sloan, Kim. *Alexander and Robert Cozens: The Poetry of Landscape*. New Haven: Yale University Press, 1986.

Smeeton, George. *The Unique*. London, 1824.

Steegman, John. *The Rule of Taste from George I to George IV*. London: Macmillan, 1936.

Sullivan, Alvin, ed. *British Literary Magazines: The Romantic Age, 1789–1836*. Westport, CT: Greenwood Press, 1983.

Summerson, John. *Architecture in Britain, 1530–1830*. London: Penguin Books, 1953.

'Thoughts on a Late Biography', *The Monthly Visitor*, II (October, 1797), p. 343.

Thrale, Hester Lynch. *Thraliana, The Diary of Mrs. Hester Lynch Thrale (Mrs. Piozzi), 1776–1809*, ed. Katherine Balderston. 2 vols. Oxford: Clarendon Press, 1951.

Tuohy, Thomas. 'William Beckford's Three Picture Collections: Idiosyncrasy and Innovation', *The British Art Journal*, II (Autumn, 2000), pp. 49–53.

Waagen, G. F. *Works of Art and Artists in England*. 3 vols. London, 1838.

Walpole, Horace. *Anecdotes of Painting in England*. ed. Ralph Wornum. 3 vols. London, 1849.

Ward, William S. *Literary Reviews in British Periodicals 1789–1797: A Bibliography*. New York: Garland Publishing, 1979.

Wardle, Ralph M. *Hazlitt*. Lincoln: University of Nebraska Press, [1971].

Warner, Richard. *Excursions from Bath*. Bath, 1801.

Watkin, David. *The English Vision: The Picturesque in Architecture, Landscape, and Garden Design*. New York: Harper & Row, 1982.

———. *Thomas Hope 1769–1831 and the Neo-Classical Idea*. [London]: John Murray, [1968].

Watts, Alaric Alfred. *Alaric Watts. A Narrative of His Life*. 2 vols. London, 1884.

Whibley, Charles. *The Pageantry of Life*. New York: Harper, 1900.

Wilton, Andrew. *J. M. W. Turner: His Life and Art*. New York: Rizzoli, 1979.

Index

[465]

Room, 37; enlarging the lake, 62; grottoes, 65–7, 216–17; hermitage and tunnel, 67–8, 190n; kitchen and flower garden, 64; pavilion, 129; stone quarry, 61, 64; tree planting, 62; Wyatt's landscape design, 62–3
Forrest, Edwin, 180
Foster, Mr (auctioneer), 135, 203n
Fownes, James, 124
Franchi, Gregorio, 89, 122, 124, 126, 136, 152, 166, 168

Gaignières vase, 110, 206n
Gainsborough, Thomas, 137
Garbett, Edward, 156
Garbett, William, 156–9, 205n, 293n
Gardener's Magazine, 140, 174
Garnett, Richard, 34
Garofalo, 318
Gastineau, Henry, 165
Gazette of Fashion, The, 108, 119, 122, 146
Gentleman's Magazine, The, 73, 84, 88, 123, 128, 140, 147, 161, 199n,
Gilpin, William, 52, 56, 61–3, 92
Gloucester, Duke of, 120
Gonzaga family, 135
Goodall, Mr, 130
Gower, Lord F. Leveson, 130
Grande Chartreuse, 31–3, 40
Gray, Thomas, 31, 36, 106
Green and Ward (goldsmiths), 112
Grosvenor, Earl, 122, 142

Hadlow Castle, 180
Hamilton, Alexander Douglas, 10th Duke of Hamilton, 89–90, 121

Hamilton, Lady Anne, 87–8, 103, 198n
Hamilton, Catherine, Lady, 43–4
Hamilton, Charles, 65, 69; Painshill, 65, 67, 190n
Hamilton, Emma, Lady, 84, 227, 282
Hamilton, Sir William, 43, 62, 84
Hamilton, William (artist), 77, 143
Harrison, William H., 163
Harvey, Daniel Whittle, 205n
Hawksmoor, Nicholas, 157, 291
Hawley, J. T. & C. (goldsmiths), 135, 203n
Haydon, Benjamin, 153
Hayter, George, 89–90
Hazlitt, William, 137, 148–55, 178, 300n, 321n
Heard, Sir Isaac, 79, 81, 84
Heber, Richard, 138
Heeley, Joseph, 52
Henley, Samuel, 63, 65
Henry VII, King, 112
Henry VII's Chapel, Westminster Abbey, 112
Henry VIII, King, 137
Hervey, Elizabeth, *Melissa and Marcia; or the Sisters*, 56–7, 66
Higham, Thomas, 165–6
Highcliffe Castle, 180
Hindon, 139, 373
Hoare, Sir Richard Colt, 128, 140, 146, 167–8, 196n
Holbein, Hans, 152; cabinet, 251–2, 279
Holy Trinity Church, Theale, 156
Houghton Hall, Norfolk, 59
Hughes, Thomas, 361n
Hughes, William, 169
Hume, Robert (cabinet-maker), 134
Humphrey, Ozias, 77

30 The Remains of Fonthill. Photograph by author.